I0794990

The *Journal* of JOSEPH

THE PROPHET
JOSEPH SMITH'S STORY
IN HIS OWN WORDS

The Journal of JOSEPH

JOSEPH SMITH JR.

COMPILED BY LEE NELSON

Council Press
An imprint of Cedar Fort, Inc.
Springville, Utah

ISBN 13: 978-1-4621-1513-6

Published by Council Press, an imprint of Cedar Fort, Inc.
2373 W. 700 S., Springville, UT 84663
Distributed by Cedar Fort, Inc., www.cedarfort.com

Library of Congress Control Number: 2014942602

Cover design by Shawnda T. Craig
Cover design © 2014 Lyle Mortimer
Typeset by Jessica B. Ellingson

Printed in the United States of America

10 9 8 7 6 5 4 3 2 1

Printed on acid-free paper

Contents

Introduction

This book is exactly what the title says it is—the personal journal and history of Joseph Smith Junior. It does not contain the usual interpretations and opinions of scholars, theologians, and historians. Instead, it contains Joseph's own account of his revelations, persecutions, disappointments, accomplishments, and day-to-day happenings.

Joseph dictated most of his journal entries to scribes, including his wife, Emma, Oliver Cowdery, Willard Richards, and others. The original documents are in the archives of the historical department of The Church of Jesus Christ of Latter-day Saints in Salt Lake City. These records were edited by Church historian B. H. Roberts and published in the seven-volume *History of the Church*, copyrighted by George Albert Smith for the Church in 1951. In reference to his editing, B. H. Roberts said, "Where grammatical accuracy was violated in the original record it has been corrected, so far as observed; but no historical or doctrinal statement has been changed."

This text assembles together in one volume the great majority of Joseph's first-person journal entries that are scattered throughout the seven-volume history among letters, revelations, footnotes, and numerous other documents. There has been no attempt to edit or condense any of Joseph's writings; although for the sake of brevity, some entries of little historical significance have been omitted. Nothing of doctrinal or controversial nature has been left out.

Chapter One

1805–1829

Owing to the many reports which have been put in circulation by evil-disposed and designing persons, in relation to the rise and progress of The Church of Jesus Christ of Latter-day Saints, all of which have been designed by the authors thereof to militate against its character as a Church and its progress in the world I have been induced to write this history, to disabuse the public mind, and put all inquirers after truth into possession of the facts, as they have transpired, in relation both to myself and the Church, so far as I have such facts in my possession. In this history I shall present the various events in relation to this Church, in truth and righteousness, as they have transpired, or as they at present exist, being now the eighth year since the organization of said Church.

I was born in the year of our Lord one thousand eight hundred and five, on the twenty-third day of December, in the town of Sharon, Windsor county, state of Vermont. My father, Joseph Smith, was born July 12th, 1771, in Topsfield, Essex county, Massachusetts; his father, Asael Smith, was born March 7th, 1744, in Topsfield, Massachusetts; his father, Samuel Smith, was born January 26th, 1714, in Topsfield, Massachusetts; his father, Samuel

Smith, was born January 26th, 1666, in Topsfield, Massachusetts; his father, Robert Smith, came from England. My father, Joseph Smith, Senior, left the state of Vermont, and moved to Palmyra, Ontario (now Wayne) county, in the state of New York, when I was in my tenth year, or thereabouts. In about four years after my father's arrival in Palmyra he moved with his family into Manchester, in the same county of Ontario—his family consisting of eleven souls, namely, my father, Joseph Smith; my mother, Lucy Smith (whose name, previous to her marriage, was Mack, daughter of Solomon Mack); my brothers, Alvin (who died November 19th, 1824, in the 27th year of his age), Hyrum, myself, Samuel Harrison, William, Don Carlos; and my sisters, Sophronia, Catherine, and Lucy.

Some time in the second year after our removal to Manchester, there was in the place where we lived an unusual excitement on the subject of religion. It commenced with the Methodists, but soon became general among all the sects in that region of country. Indeed, the whole district of country seemed affected by it, and great multitudes united themselves to the different religious parties, which created no small stir and division amongst the people, some crying, "Lo, here!" and others, "Lo, there!" Some were contending for the Methodist faith, some for the Presbyterian, and some for the Baptist. For, notwithstanding the great love which the converts to these different faiths expressed at the time of their conversion, and the great zeal manifested by the respective clergy, who were active in getting up and promoting this extraordinary scene of religious feeling, in order to have everybody converted, as they were pleased to call it, let them join what sect they pleased; yet when the converts began to file off, some to one party and some to another, it was seen that the seemingly good feelings of both the priests and the converts were more pretended than real; for a scene of great confusion and bad feeling ensued—priest contending against priest, and convert against convert; so that all their good feelings one for another, if they ever had any, were entirely lost in a strife of words and a contest of opinions.

I was at this time in my fifteenth year. My father's family was proselyted to the Presbyterian faith, and four of them joined that church, namely, my mother Lucy; my brothers Hyrum and Samuel Harrison; and my sister Sophronia. During this time of great excitement my mind was called up to serious reflection and great uneasiness; but though my feelings were deep and often poignant, still I kept myself aloof from all these parties, though I attended their several meetings as often as occasion would permit. In process of time my mind became somewhat partial to the Methodist sect, and I felt some desire to be united with them; but so great were the confusion and strife among the different denominations, that it was impossible for a person young as I was, and so unacquainted with men and things, to come to any certain conclusion who was right and who was wrong. My mind at times was greatly excited, the cry and tumult were so great and incessant. The Presbyterians were most decided against the Baptists and Methodists, and used all the powers of both reason and sophistry to prove their errors, or, at least, to make the people think they were in error. On the other hand, the Baptists and Methodists in their turn were equally zealous in endeavoring to establish their own tenets and disprove all others.

In the midst of this war of words and tumult of opinions, I often said to myself: What is to be done? Who of all these parties are right; or, are they all wrong together? If anyone of them be right, which is it, and how shall I know it? While I was laboring under the extreme difficulties caused by the contests of these parties of religionists, I was one day reading the Epistle of James, first chapter and fifth verse, which reads: "If any of you lack wisdom, let him ask of God, that giveth to all men liberally, and upbraideth not; and it shall be given him."

Never did any passage of scripture come with more power to the heart of man than this did at this time to mine. It seemed to enter with great force into every feeling of my heart. I reflected on it again and again, knowing that if any person needed wisdom

"IF ANY OF YOU
LACK WISDOM,
LET HIM ASK OF
GOD, THAT
GIVETH TO ALL
MEN LIBERALLY,
AND UPBRAIDETH
NOT; AND IT
SHALL BE
GIVEN HIM."

from God, I did; for how to act I did not know and unless I could get more wisdom than I then had, I would never know; for the teachers of religion of the different sects understood the same passage of scripture so differently as to destroy all confidence in settling the question by an appeal to the Bible. At length I came to the conclusion that I must either remain in darkness and confusion, or else I must do as James directs, that is, ask of God. I at length came to the determination to "ask of God," concluding that if He gave wisdom to them that lacked wisdom, and would give liberally, and not upbraid, I might venture. So, in accordance with this, my determination to ask God, I retired to the woods to make the attempt. It was on the morning of a beautiful, clear day, early in the spring of eighteen hundred and twenty. It was the first time in my life that I had made such an attempt, for amidst all my anxieties I had never as yet made the attempt to pray vocally.

After I had retired to the place where I had previously designed to go, having looked around me, and finding myself alone, I kneeled down and began to offer up the desires of my heart to God. I had scarcely done so, when immediately I was seized upon by some power which entirely overcame me, and had such an astonishing influence over me as to bind my tongue so that I could not speak. Thick darkness gathered around me, and it seemed to me for a time as if I were doomed to sudden destruction. But, exerting all my powers to call upon God to deliver me out of the power of this enemy which had seized upon me, and at the very moment when I was ready to sink into despair and abandon myself to destruction—not to an imaginary ruin, but to the power of some actual being from the unseen world, who had such marvelous power as I had never before felt in any being—just at this moment of great alarm, I saw a pillar of light exactly over my head, above the brightness of the sun, which descended gradually until it fell upon me.

It no sooner appeared than I found myself delivered from the enemy which held me bound. When the light rested upon me I saw two Personages, whose brightness and glory defy all description, standing above me in the air. One of them spake unto me, calling me by name, and said, pointing to the other—"This is My Beloved Son. Hear Him."

My object in going to inquire of the Lord was to know which of all the sects was right, that I might know which to join. No sooner, therefore, did I get possession of myself, so as to be able to speak, than I asked the Personages who stood above me in the light, which of all the sects was right—and which I should join. I was answered that I must join none of them, for they were all wrong; and the Personage who addressed me said that all their creeds were an abomination in His sight; that those professors were all corrupt; that "they draw near to me with their lips, but their hearts are far from me; they teach for doctrines the commandments of men: having a form of godliness, but they deny the power thereof." He again forbade me to join with any of them; and many other things did he say unto me, which I cannot write at this time. When I came to myself again, I found myself lying on my back, looking up into heaven. When the light had departed, I had no strength; but soon recovering in some degree, I went home. And as I leaned up to the fireplace, mother inquired what the matter was. I replied, "Never mind, all is well—I am well enough off." I then said to my mother, "I have learned for myself that Presbyterianism is not true."

It seems as though the adversary was aware, at a very early period of my life, that I was destined to prove a disturber and an annoyer of his kingdom; else why should the powers of darkness combine against me? Why the opposition and persecution that arose against me, almost in my infancy? Some few days after I had this vision, I happened to be in company with one of the Methodist preachers, who was very active in the before-mentioned religious excitement; and, conversing with him on the subject of religion, I took occasion to give him an account of the vision which I had had. I was greatly surprised at his behavior; he treated my communication not only lightly, but with great contempt, saying it was all of the devil, that there were no such things as visions or revelations in these days; that all such things had ceased with the Apostles, and that there would never be any more of them. I soon found, however, that my telling the story had excited a great deal of prejudice against me among professors of religion, and was the cause of great persecution, which continued to increase; and though I was an obscure boy, only between fourteen and fifteen years of age, and my circumstances in life such as to make a boy of no consequence in the world, yet men of high standing would take notice sufficient to excite the public mind against me, and create a bitter persecution; and this was common among all the sects—all united to persecute me.

It caused me serious reflection then, and often has since, how very strange it was that an obscure boy, of a little over fourteen years of age, and one, too, who was doomed to the necessity of obtaining a scanty maintenance by his daily labor, should be thought a character of sufficient importance to attract the attention of the great ones of the most popular sects of the day, and in a manner to create in them a spirit of the most bitter persecution and reviling. But strange or not, so it was, and it was often the cause of great sorrow to myself. However, it was nevertheless a fact that I had beheld a vision. I have thought since, that I felt much like Paul, when he made his defense before King Agrippa, and related the account of the vision he had when he saw a light, and heard a voice; but still there were but few who believed him. Some said he was dishonest, others said he was mad; and he was ridiculed and reviled. But all this did not destroy the reality of his vision. He had seen a vision, he knew he had, and all the persecution under heaven could not make it otherwise; and though they should persecute him unto death, yet he knew, and would know to the last breath that he had both seen a light, and heard a voice speaking unto him, and all the world could not make him think or believe otherwise. So it was with me. I had actually seen a light, and in the midst of that light I saw two Personages, and they did in reality speak to me;

and though I was hated and persecuted for saying that I had seen a vision, yet it was true; and while they were persecuting me, reviling me, and speaking all manner of evil against me falsely for so saying, I was led to say in my heart: Why persecute me for telling the truth? I have actually seen a vision; and who am I that I can withstand God, or why does the world think to make me deny what I have actually seen? For I had seen a vision; I knew it, and I knew that God knew it, and I could not deny it, neither dared I do it; at least I knew that by so doing I would offend God, and come under condemnation.

I had now got my mind satisfied so far as the sectarian world was concerned—that it was not my duty to join with any of them, but to continue as I was until further directed. I had found the testimony of James to be true—that a man who lacked wisdom might ask of God, and obtain, and not be upbraided.

I continued to pursue my common vocation in life until the twenty-first of September, one thousand eight hundred and twenty-three, all the time suffering severe persecution at the hands of all classes of men, both religious and irreligious, because I continued to affirm that I had seen a vision.

During the space of time which intervened between the time I had the vision and the year eighteen hundred and twenty-three—having been forbidden to join any of the religious sects of the day, and being of very tender years, and persecuted by those who ought to have been my friends and to have treated me kindly, and if they supposed me to be deluded to have endeavored in a proper and affectionate manner to have reclaimed me—I was left to all kinds of temptations; and, mingling with all kinds of society, I frequently fell into many foolish errors, and displayed the weakness of youth, and the foibles of human nature; which, I am sorry to say, led me into divers temptations, offensive in the sight of God. In making this confession, no one need suppose me guilty of any great or malignant sins. A disposition to commit such was never in my nature. But I was guilty of levity, and sometimes associated with jovial company, etc., not consistent with that character which ought to be maintained by one who was called of God as I had been. But this will not seem very strange to anyone who recollects my youth, and is acquainted with my native cheery temperament.

In consequence of these things, I often felt condemned for my weakness and imperfections; when, on the evening of the above-mentioned twenty-first of September, after I had retired to my bed for the night, I betook myself to prayer and supplication to Almighty God for forgiveness of all my sins and follies, and also for a manifestation to me, that I might know of my state and standing before Him; for I had full confidence in obtaining a divine manifestation, as I previously had done. While I was thus in the act of calling upon God, I discovered a light appearing in my room, which continued to increase until the room was lighter than at noonday, when immediately a personage appeared at my bedside, standing in the air, for his feet did not touch the floor. He had on a loose robe of most exquisite whiteness. It was a whiteness beyond anything earthly I had ever seen; nor do I believe that any earthly thing could be made to appear so exceedingly white and brilliant. His hands were naked and his arms also, a little above the wrist; so, also were his feet naked, as were his legs, a little above the ankles. His head and neck were also bare. I could discover that he had no other clothing on but this robe, as it was open, so that I could see into his bosom. Not only was his robe exceedingly white, but his whole person was glorious beyond description, and his countenance truly like lightning. The room was exceedingly light, but not so very bright as immediately around his person.

When first I looked upon him, I was afraid; but the fear soon left me. He called me by name, and said unto me that he was a messenger sent from the presence of God to me and that his name was Moroni; that God had a work for me to do; and that my name should be had for good and evil among all nations, kindreds, and tongues, or that it should be both good and evil spoken of among all people. He said there was a book deposited, written upon gold plates, giving an account of the former inhabitants of this continent, and the sources from whence they sprang. He also said that the fullness of the everlasting Gospel was contained in it, as delivered by the Savior to the ancient inhabitants; also, that there were two stones in silver bows—and these stones, fastened to a breastplate, constituted what is called the Urim and Thummim—deposited with the plates; and the possession and use of these stones were what constituted "seers" in ancient or former times; and that God had prepared them for the purpose of translating the book.

After telling me these things, he commenced quoting the prophecies of the Old Testament. He first quoted part of the third chapter of Malachi; and he quoted also the fourth or last chapter of the same prophecy, though with a little variation from the way it reads in our Bibles. Instead of quoting the first verse as it reads in our books, he quoted it thus:

> For behold the day cometh that shall burn as an oven, and all the proud, yea, and all that do wickedly shall burn as stubble; for they that come shall burn them, saith the Lord of Hosts, that it shall leave them neither root nor branch.

And again, he quoted the fifth verse thus:

> Behold I will reveal unto you the Priesthood, by the hand of Elijah the prophet, before the coming of the great and dreadful day of the Lord.

He also quoted the next verse differently:

> And he shall plant in the hearts of the children the promises made to the fathers, and the hearts of the children shall turn to their fathers. If it were not so, the whole earth would be utterly wasted at his coming.

In addition to these, he quoted the eleventh chapter of Isaiah, saying that it was about to be fulfilled. He quoted also the third chapter of Acts, twenty-second and twenty-third verses, precisely as they stand in our New Testament. He said that that prophet was Christ; but the day had not yet come when "they who would not hear his voice should be cut off from among the people," but soon would come. He also quoted the second chapter of Joel, from the twenty-eighth verse to the last. He also said that this was not yet fulfilled, but was soon to be. And he further stated that the fullness of the Gentiles was soon to come in. He quoted many other passages of scripture, and offered many explanations which cannot be mentioned here.

Again, he told me, that when I got those plates of which he had spoken—for the time that they should be obtained was not yet fulfilled—I should not show them to any person; neither the breastplate with the Urim and Thummim; only to those to whom I should be commanded to show them; if I did I should be destroyed. While he was conversing with me about the plates, the vision was opened to my mind that I could see the place where the plates were deposited, and that so clearly and distinctly that I knew the place again when I visited it.

After this communication, I saw the light in the room begin to gather immediately around the person of him who had been speaking to me, and it continued to do so until the room was again left dark, except just around me; when instantly I saw, as it were, a conduit open right up into heaven, and he ascended until he entirely disappeared, and the room was left as it had been before this heavenly light had made its appearance. I lay musing on the singularity of the scene and marveling greatly at what had been told to me by this extraordinary messenger; when, in the midst of my meditation, I suddenly discovered that my room was again beginning to get lighted, and in an instant, as it were, the same heavenly messenger was again by my bedside. He commenced, and again related the very same things which he had done at the first visit, without the least variation; which having done, he informed me of great judgments which were coming upon the earth, with great desolations by famine, sword, and pestilence; and that these grievous judgments would come on the earth in this generation. Having related these things, he again ascended as he had done before.

By this time, so deep were the impressions made on my mind, that sleep had fled from my eyes, and I lay overwhelmed in astonishment at what I had both seen and heard. But what was my surprise when again I beheld the same messenger at my bedside, and heard him rehearse or repeat over again to me the same things as before; and added a caution to me, telling me that Satan would try to tempt me (in consequence of the indigent circumstances of my father's family), to get the plates for the purpose of getting rich. This he forbade me, saying that I must have no other object in view in getting the plates but to glorify God, and must not be influenced by any other motive than that of building His kingdom; otherwise I could not get them. After this third visit, he again ascended into heaven as before, and I was again left to ponder on the strangeness of what I had just experienced; when almost immediately after the heavenly messenger had ascended from me the third time, the cock crowed, and I found that the day was approaching, so that our interviews must have occupied the whole of that night.

I shortly after arose from my bed, and, as usual, went to the necessary labors of the day; but, in attempting to work as at other times, I found my strength so exhausted as to render me entirely unable. My father, who was laboring along with me, discovered something to be wrong with me, and told me to go home. I started with the intention of going to the house; but, in attempting to cross the fence out of the field where we were, my strength entirely failed me, and I fell helpless on the ground, and for a time was quite unconscious of anything. The first thing that I can recollect was a voice speaking unto me, calling me by name. I looked up, and beheld the same messenger standing over my head, surrounded by light as before. He then again related unto me all that he had related to me the previous night, and commanded me to go to my father and tell him of the vision and commandments which I had received. I obeyed; I returned to my father in the field, and rehearsed the whole matter to him. He replied to me that it was of God, and told me to go and do as commanded by the messenger. I left the field, and went to the place where the messenger had told me the plates were deposited; and owing to the distinctness of the vision which I had had concerning it, I knew the place the instant that I arrived there.

Convenient to the village of Manchester, Ontario county, New York, stands a hill of considerable size, and the most elevated of any in the neighborhood. On the west side of this hill, not far from the top, under a stone of considerable size, lay the plates, deposited in a stone box. This stone was thick and rounding in the middle on the upper side, and thinner towards the edges, so that the middle part of it was visible above the ground, but the edge all around was covered with earth.

Having removed the earth, I obtained a lever, which I got fixed under the edge of the stone, and with a little exertion raised it up. I looked in, and there indeed did I behold the plates, the Urim and Thummim, and the breastplate, as stated by the messenger. The box in which they lay was formed by laying stones together in some kind of cement. In the bottom of the box were laid two stones crosswise of the box, and on these stones lay the plates and the other things with them.

I made an attempt to take them out, but was forbidden by the messenger, and was again informed that the time for bringing them forth had not yet arrived, neither would it, until four years from that time; but he told me that I should come to that place precisely in one year from that time, and that he would there meet with me, and that I should continue to do so until the time should come for obtaining the plates. Accordingly, as I had been commanded, I went at the end of each year, and at each time I found the same messenger there, and received instruction and intelligence from him at each of our interviews, respecting what the Lord was going to do, and how and in what manner His kingdom was to be conducted in the last days.

As my father's worldly circumstances were very limited, we were under the necessity of laboring with our hands, hiring out by day's work and otherwise, as we could get opportunity. Sometimes we were at home, and sometimes abroad, and by continued labor, were enabled to get a comfortable maintenance. In the year 1824 my father's family met with a great affliction by the death of my eldest brother, Alvin. In the month of October, 1825, I hired with an old gentleman by the name of Josiah Stoal, who lived in Chenango county, state of New York. He had heard something of a silver mine having been opened by the Spaniards in Harmony, Susquehanna county, state of Pennsylvania; and had, previous to my hiring to him, been digging, in order, if possible, to discover the mine. After I went to live with him, he took me, with the rest of his hands, to dig for the silver mine, at which I continued to work for nearly a month, without success in our undertaking, and finally I prevailed with the old gentleman to cease digging after it. Hence arose the very prevalent story of my having been a money-digger.

During the time that I was thus employed, I was put to board with a Mr. Isaac Hale, of that place; it was there I first saw my wife (his daughter), Emma Hale. On the 18th of January, 1827, we were married, while I was yet employed in the service of Mr. Stoal. Owing to my continuing to assert that I had seen a vision, persecution still followed me, and my wife's father's family were very much opposed to our being married. I was, therefore, under the necessity of taking her elsewhere; so we went and were married at the house of Squire Tarbill, in South Bainbridge, Chenango county, New York. Immediately after my marriage, I left Mr. Stoal's, and went to my father's, and farmed with him that season.

At length the time arrived for obtaining the plates, the Urim and Thummim, and the breastplate. On the twenty-second day of September, one thousand eight hundred and twenty-seven, having gone as usual at the end of another year to the place where they were deposited, the same heavenly messenger delivered them up to me with this charge: that I should be responsible for them; that if I should let them go carelessly, or through any neglect of mine, I should be cut off; but that if I would use all my endeavors to preserve them, until he, the messenger, should call for them, they should be protected.

I soon found out the reason why I had received such strict charges to keep them safe, and why it was that the messenger had said that when I had done what was required at my hand, he would call for them. For no sooner was it known that I had them, than the most strenuous exertions were used to get them from me. Every stratagem that could be invented was resorted to for that purpose. The persecution became more bitter and severe than before, and multitudes were on the alert continually to get them from me if possible. But by the wisdom of God, they remained safe in my hands, until I had accomplished by them what was required at my hand. When, according to arrangements, the messenger called for them, I delivered them up to him; and he has them in his charge until this day, being the second day of May, one thousand eight hundred and thirty-eight.

The excitement, however, still continued, and rumor with her thousand tongues was all the time employed in circulating falsehoods about my father's family, and about myself. If I were to relate a thousandth part of them, it would fill up volumes. The persecution, however, became so intolerable that I was under the necessity of leaving Manchester, and going with my wife to Susquehanna county, in the state of Pennsylvania.

While preparing to start—being very poor, and the persecution so heavy upon us that there was no probability that we would ever be otherwise—in the midst of our afflictions we found a friend in a gentleman by the name of Martin Harris, who came to us and gave me fifty dollars to assist us on our journey. Mr. Harris was a resident of Palmyra township, Wayne county, in the state of New York, and a farmer of respectability. By this timely aid was I enabled to reach the place of my destination in Pennsylvania; and immediately after my arrival there I commenced copying the characters off the plates. I copied a considerable number of them, and by means of the Urim and Thummim I translated some of them, which I did between the time I arrived at the house of my wife's father, in the month of December, and the February following.

Some time in this month of February, the aforementioned Mr. Martin Harris came to our place, got the characters which I had drawn off the plates, and started with them to the city of New York. For what took place relative to him and the characters, I refer to his own account of the circumstances, as he related them to me after his return, which was as follows:

> I went to the city of New York, and presented the characters which had been translated, with the translation thereof, to Professor Charles Anthon, a gentleman celebrated for his literary attainments. Professor Anthon stated that the translation was correct, more so than any he had before seen translated from the Egyptian. I then showed him those which were not yet translated, and he said that they were Egyptian, Chaldaic, Assyriac, and Arabic; and he said they were true characters. He gave me a certificate, certifying to the people of Palmyra that they were true characters, and that the translation of such of them as had been translated was also correct. I took the certificate and put it into my pocket, and was just leaving the house, when Mr. Anthon called me back, and asked me how the young man found out that there were gold plates in the place where he found them. I answered that an angel of God had revealed it unto him.
>
> He then said to me, "Let me see that certificate." I accordingly took it out of my pocket and gave it to him, when he took it and tore it to pieces, saying that there was no such thing now as ministering of angels, and that if I would bring the plates to him, he would translate them. I informed him that part of the plates were sealed, and that I was forbidden to bring them. He replied, "I cannot read a sealed book." I left him and went to Dr. Mitchell, who sanctioned what Professor Anthon had said respecting both the characters and the translation.

Mr. Harris, having returned from his tour, left me and went home to Palmyra, arranged his affairs, and returned again to my house about the 12th of April, 1828, and commenced writing for me while I translated from the plates, which we continued until the 14th of June following, by which time he had written one hundred and sixteen pages of manuscript on foolscap paper. Some time after Mr. Harris had begun to write for me, he began to importune me to give him liberty to carry the writings home and show them; and desired of me that I would inquire of the Lord, through the Urim and Thummim, if he might not do so. I did inquire, and the answer was that he must not. However, he was not satisfied with this answer, and desired that I should inquire again. I did so, and the answer was as before. Still he could not be contented, but insisted that I should inquire once more. After much solicitation I again inquired of the Lord, and permission was granted him to have the writings on certain conditions; which were that he show them only to his brother, Preserved Harris, his own wife, his father and his mother, and a Mrs. Cobb, a sister to his wife. In accordance with this last answer, I required of him that he should bind himself in a covenant to me in a most solemn manner that he would not do otherwise than had been directed. He did so. He bound himself as I required of him, took the writings, and went his way. Notwithstanding, however, the great restrictions which he had been laid under, and the solemnity of the covenant which he had made with me, he did show them to others, and by stratagem they got them away from him, and they never have been recovered unto this day.

In the meantime, while Martin Harris was gone with the writings, I went to visit my father's family at Manchester. I continued there for a short season, and then returned to my place in Pennsylvania. Immediately after my return home, I was walking out a little distance, when, behold, the former heavenly messenger appeared and handed to me the Urim and Thummim again—for it had been taken from me in consequence of my having wearied the Lord in asking for the privilege of letting Martin Harris take the writings, which he lost by transgression—and I inquired of the Lord through it, and obtained the following:

See Doctrine and Covenants 3.

After I had obtained the above revelation, both the plates and the Urim and Thummim were taken from me again; but in a few days they were returned to me, when I inquired of the Lord, and the Lord said thus unto me:

See Doctrine and Covenants 10.

I did not, however, go immediately to translating, but went to laboring with my hands upon a small farm which I had purchased of my wife's father, in order to provide for my family. In the month of February, 1829, my father came to visit us, at which time I received the following revelation for him:

See Doctrine and Covenants 4.

On the 5th day of April, 1829, Oliver Cowdery came to my house, until which time I had never seen him. He stated to me that having been teaching school in the neighborhood where my father resided, and my father being one of those who sent to the school, he went to board for a season at his house, and while there the family related to him the circumstance of my having received the plates, and accordingly he had come to make inquiries of me. Two days after the arrival of Mr. Cowdery (being the 7th of April) I commenced to translate the Book of Mormon, and he began to write for me, which having continued for some time, I inquired of the Lord through the Urim and Thummim, and obtained the following:

See Doctrine and Covenants 6.

After we had received this revelation, Oliver Cowdery stated to me that after he had gone to my father's to board, and after the family had communicated to him concerning my having obtained the plates, that one night after he had retired to bed he called upon the Lord to know if these things were so; and the Lord manifested to him that they were true, but he had kept the circumstance entirely secret, and had mentioned it to no one; so that after this revelation was given, he knew that the work was true, because no being living knew of the thing alluded to in the revelation, but God and himself.

During the month of April I continued to translate, and he to write, with little cessation, during which time we received several revelations. A difference of opinion arising between us about the account of John the Apostle, mentioned in the New Testament, as to whether he died or continued to live, we mutually agreed to settle it by the Urim and Thummim and the following is the word which we received:

See Doctrine and Covenants 7.

Whilst continuing the work of translation, during the month of April, Oliver Cowdery became exceedingly anxious to have the power to translate bestowed upon him, and in relation to this desire the following revelations were obtained:

See Doctrine and Covenants 8–9.

We still continued the work of translation, when in the ensuing month (May, 1829), we on a certain day went into the woods to pray and inquire of the Lord respecting baptism for the remission of sins, that we found mentioned in the translation of the plates. While we were thus employed, praying and calling upon the Lord, a messenger from heaven descended in a cloud of light, and having laid his hands upon us, he ordained us, saying:

See Doctrine and Covenants 13.

He said this Aaronic Priesthood had not the power of laying on hands for the gift of the Holy Ghost, but that this should be conferred on us hereafter; and he commanded us to go and be baptized, and gave us directions that I should baptize Oliver Cowdery, and afterwards that he should baptize me. Accordingly we went and were baptized. I baptized him first, and afterwards he baptized me—after which I laid my hands upon his head and ordained him to the Aaronic Priesthood, and afterwards he laid his hands on me and ordained me to the same Priesthood—for so we were commanded.

The messenger who visited us on this occasion and conferred this Priesthood upon us, said that his name was John, the same that is called John the Baptist in the New Testament, and that he acted under the direction of Peter, James and John, who held the keys of the Priesthood of Melchizedek, which Priesthood, he said, would in due time be conferred on us, and that I should be called the first Elder of the Church, and he (Oliver Cowdery) the second. It was on the 15th day of May, 1829, that we were ordained under the hand of this messenger, and baptized.

Immediately on our coming up out of the water after we had been baptized, we experienced great and glorious blessings from our Heavenly Father. No sooner had I baptized Oliver Cowdery, than the Holy Ghost fell upon him, and he stood up and prophesied many things which should shortly come to pass. And again, so soon as I had been baptized by him, I also had the spirit of prophecy, when, standing up, I prophesied concerning the rise of this Church, and many other things connected with the Church, and this generation of the children of men. We were filled with the Holy Ghost, and rejoiced in the God of our salvation.

Our minds being now enlightened, we began to have the scriptures laid open to our understandings, and the true meaning and intention of their more mysterious passages revealed unto us in a manner which we never could attain to previously, nor ever before had thought of. In the meantime we were forced to keep secret the circumstances of having received the Priesthood and our having been baptized, owing to a spirit of persecution which had already

"OUR MINDS BEING NOW ENLIGHTENED, WE BEGAN TO HAVE THE SCRIPTURES LAID OPEN TO OUR UNDERSTANDING . . ."

manifested itself in the neighborhood. We had been threatened with being mobbed from time to time and this, too, by professors of religion. And their intentions of mobbing us were only counteracted by the influence of my wife's father's family (under Divine Providence), who had become very friendly to me, and who were opposed to mobs, and were willing that I should be allowed to continue the work of translation without interruption; and therefore offered and promised us protection from all unlawful proceedings, as far as in them lay.

After a few days, however, feeling it to be our duty, we commenced to reason out of the scriptures with our acquaintances and friends, as we happened to meet with them. About this time my brother Samuel H. Smith came to visit us. We informed him of what the Lord was about to do for the children of men, and began to reason with him out of the Bible. We also showed him that part of the work which we had translated, and labored to persuade him concerning the gospel of Jesus Christ, which was now about to [be] revealed in its fulness. He was not, however, very easily persuaded of these things; but after much inquiry and explanation, he retired to the woods, in order that by secret and fervent prayer he might obtain of a merciful God wisdom to enable him to judge for himself. The result was that he obtained revelation for himself sufficient to convince him of the truth of our assertions to him; and on the twenty-fifth day of that same month in which we had been baptized and ordained, Oliver Cowdery baptized him; and he returned to his father's house, greatly glorifying and praising God, being filled with the Holy Spirit.

Not many days afterwards, my brother Hyrum Smith came to us to inquire concerning these things, when at his earnest request, I inquired of the Lord through the Urim and Thummim, and received for him the following:

See Doctrine and Covenants 11.

About the same time, an old gentleman came to visit us, of whose name I wish to make honorable mention—Mr. Joseph Knight, Sen., of Colesville, Broome county, New York, who, having heard of the manner in which we were occupying our time, very kindly and considerately brought us a quantity of provisions, in order that we might not be interrupted in the work of translation by the want of such necessaries of life; and I would just mention here, as in duty bound, that he several times brought us supplies, a distance of at least thirty miles, which enabled us to continue the work when otherwise we must have relinquished it for a season.

Being very anxious to know his duty as to this work, I inquired of the Lord for him, and obtained the following:

See Doctrine and Covenants 12.

Shortly after commencing to translate, I became acquainted with Mr. Peter Whitmer, of Fayette, Seneca county, New York, and also with some of his family. In the beginning of the month of June, his son, David Whitmer, came to the place where we were residing, and brought with him a two-horse wagon, for the purpose of having us accompany him to his father's place, and there remain until we should finish the work. It was arranged that we should have our board free of charge, and the assistance of one of his brothers to write for me, and also his own assistance when convenient. Having much need of such timely aid in an undertaking so arduous, and being informed that the people in the neighborhood of the Whitmers were anxiously awaiting the opportunity to inquire into these things, we accepted the invitation, and accompanied Mr. Whitmer to his father's house, and there resided until the translation was finished and the copyright secured. Upon our arrival, we found Mr. Whitmer's family very anxious concerning the work, and very friendly toward ourselves. They continued so, boarded and lodged us according to arrangements; and John Whitmer, in particular, assisted us very much in writing during the remainder of the work.

In the meantime, David, John and Peter Whitmer, Jun., became our zealous friends and assistants in the work; and being anxious to know their respective duties, and having desired with much earnestness that I should inquire of the Lord concerning them, I did so, through the means of the Urim and Thummim, and obtained for them in succession the following revelations:

See Doctrine and Covenants 14–16.

We found the people of Seneca county, in general, friendly, and disposed to inquire into the truth of these strange matters which now began to be noised abroad. Many opened their houses to us, in order that we might have an opportunity of meeting with our friends for the purpose of instruction and explanation. We met with many from time to time who were willing to hear us, and who desired to find out the truth as it is in Christ Jesus, and apparently willing to obey the gospel, when once fairly convinced and satisfied in their own minds; and in this same month of June, my brother Hyrum Smith, David Whitmer, and Peter Whitmer, Jun., were baptized in Seneca Lake, the two former by myself, the latter by Oliver Cowdery. From this time forth, many became believers, and some were baptized whilst we continued to instruct and persuade as many as applied for information.

In the course of the work of translation, we ascertained that three special witnesses were to be provided by the Lord, to whom He would grant that they should see the plates from which this work (the Book of Mormon) should be translated; and that these witnesses should bear record of the same, as will be found recorded, Book of Mormon; Book of Ether, chapter 5, verses 2, 3 and 4; also 2 Nephi, chapter 11, verse 3. Almost immediately after we had made this discovery, it occurred to Oliver Cowdery, David Whitmer and the aforementioned Martin Harris (who had come to inquire after our progress in the work) that they would have me inquire of the Lord to know if they might not obtain of

Him the privilege to be these three special witnesses; and finally they became so very solicitous, and urged me so much to inquire that at length I complied; and through the Urim and Thummim, I obtained of the Lord for them the following:

See Doctrine and Covenants 17.

Not many days after the above commandment was given, we four, viz., Martin Harris, David Whitmer, Oliver Cowdery and myself, agreed to retire into the woods, and try to obtain, by fervent and humble prayer, the fulfillment of the promises given in the above revelation—that they should have a view of the plates. We accordingly made choice of a piece of woods convenient to Mr. Whitmer's house, to which we retired; and, having knelt down, we began to pray in much faith to Almighty God to bestow upon us a realization of these promises.

According to previous arrangement, I commenced by vocal prayer to our Heavenly Father, and was followed by each of the others in succession. We did not at the first trial, however, obtain any answer or manifestation of divine favor in our behalf. We again observed the same order of prayer, each calling on and praying fervently to God in rotation, but with the same result as before.

Upon this, our second failure, Martin Harris proposed that he should withdraw himself from us, believing, as he expressed himself, that his presence was the cause of our not obtaining what we wished for. He accordingly withdrew from us, and we knelt down again, and had not been many minutes engaged in prayer, when presently we beheld a light above us in the air of exceeding brightness; and behold, an angel stood before us. In his hands he held the plates which we had been praying for these to have a view of. He turned over the leaves one by one, so that we could see them and discern the engravings thereon distinctly. He then addressed himself to David Whitmer, and said, "David, blessed is the Lord, and he that keeps His commandments;" when, immediately afterwards, we heard a voice from out of the bright light above us, saying, "These plates have been revealed by the power of God, and they have been translated by the power of God. The translation of them which you have seen is correct, and I command you to bear record of what you now see and hear."

I now left David and Oliver, and went in pursuit of Martin Harris, whom I found at a considerable distance, fervently engaged in prayer. He soon told me, however, that he had not yet prevailed with the Lord, and earnestly requested me to join him in prayer that he also might realize the same blessings which we had just received. We accordingly joined in prayer, and ultimately obtained our desires, for before we had yet finished, the same vision was opened to our view, at least it was again opened to me, and I once more beheld and heard the same things; whilst at the same moment, Martin Harris cried out, apparently in an ecstasy of joy, "'Tis enough; 'tis enough; mine eyes have beheld; mine eyes have beheld;" and jumping up, he shouted, "Hosanna," blessing God, and otherwise rejoiced exceedingly.

Having thus, through the mercy of God, obtained these glorious manifestations, it now remained for these three individuals to fulfill the commandment which they had received, viz., to bear record of these things; in order to accomplish which, they drew up and subscribed the following document:

See The Testimony of Three Witnesses in the Book of Mormon.

Meantime we continued to translate, at intervals, when not under the necessity of attending to the numerous inquirers who now began to visit us—some for the sake of finding the truth; others for the purpose of putting hard questions, and trying to confound us. Among the latter class were several learned priests, who generally came for the purpose of disputation. However, the Lord continued to pour out upon us His Holy Spirit, and as often as we had need, He gave us in that moment what to say; so that although unlearned and inexperienced in religious controversies, yet we were able to confound those learned priests of the day; whilst at the same time, we were enabled to convince the honest in heart that we had obtained, through the mercy of God, the true and everlasting gospel of Jesus Christ; and occasionally we administered the ordinance of baptism for the remission of sins to such as believed.

We now became anxious to have that promise realized to us, which the angel that conferred upon us the Aaronic Priesthood had given us, viz., that, provided we continued [to be] faithful, we should also have the Melchizedek Priesthood, which holds the authority of the laying on of hands for the gift of the Holy Ghost. We had for some time made this matter a subject of humble prayer, and at length we got together in the chamber of Mr. Whitmer's house in order more particularly to seek of the Lord what we now so earnestly desired; and here, to our unspeakable satisfaction, did we realize the truth of the Savior's promise—"Ask, and it shall be given you; seek, and ye shall find; knock, and it shall be opened unto you"—for we had not long been engaged in solemn and fervent prayer, when the word of the Lord came unto us in the chamber, commanding us that I should ordain Oliver Cowdery to be an Elder in the Church of Jesus Christ; and that he also should ordain me to the same office; and then to ordain others, as it should be made known unto us from time to time. We were, however, commanded to defer this, our ordination, until such times as it should be practicable to have our brethren, who had been and who should be baptized, assembled together; when we must have their sanction to our thus proceeding to ordain each other, and have them decide by vote whether they were willing to accept us as spiritual teachers or not; when also we were commanded to bless bread and break it with them, and to take wine, bless it, and drink it with them; afterward proceed to ordain each other according to commandment; then call out such men as the Spirit should dictate, and ordain them; and then attend to the laying on of hands for the gift of the Holy Ghost, upon all those whom we had previously baptized, doing all things in the name of the Lord. The following commandment will further illustrate the nature of our calling to this Priesthood, as well as that of others who were yet to be sought after:

See Doctrine and Covenants 18.

Chapter Two

1830

In this manner did the Lord continue to give us instructions from time to time, concerning the duties which now devolved upon us; and among many other things of the kind, we obtained of Him the following, by the spirit of prophecy and revelation; which not only gave us much information, but also pointed out to us the precise day upon which, according to His will and commandment, we should proceed to organize His Church once more here upon the earth:

See Doctrine and Covenants 20.

Meantime, our translation drawing to a close, we went to Palmyra, Wayne county, New York, secured the copyright, and agreed with Mr. Egbert B. Grandin to print five thousand copies for the sum of three thousand dollars.

I wish to mention here that the title page of the Book of Mormon is a literal translation, taken from the very last leaf, on the left-hand side of the collection or book of plates, which contained the record which has been translated, the language of the whole running the same as all Hebrew writing in general; and that said title page is not by any means a modern composition, either of mine or of any other man who has lived or does live in this generation. Therefore, in order to correct an error, which generally exists concerning it, I give below that part of the title page of the English version of the Book of Mormon, which is a genuine and literal translation of the title page of the original Book of Mormon as recorded on the plates:

See the title page to the Book of Mormon.

Whilst the Book of Mormon was in the hands of the printer, we still continued to bear testimony and give information, as far as we had opportunity; and also made known to our brethren that we had received a commandment to organize the Church; and accordingly, we met together for that purpose at the house of Mr. Peter Whitmer, Sen., (being six in number) on Tuesday, the sixth day of April, A.D., one thousand eight hundred and thirty. Having opened the meeting by solemn prayer to our Heavenly Father, we proceeded, according to previous commandment, to call on our brethren to know whether they accepted us as their teachers in the things of the kingdom of God, and whether they were satisfied that we should proceed and be organized as a church according to said commandment which we had received. To these several propositions, they consented by a unanimous vote. I then laid my hands upon Oliver Cowdery, and ordained him an Elder of the "Church of Jesus Christ of Latter-day Saints;" after which, he ordained me also to the office of an Elder of said Church. We then took bread, blessed it, and brake it with them; also wine, blessed it, and drank it with them. We then laid our hands on each individual member of the Church present, that they might receive the gift of the Holy Ghost, and be confirmed members of the Church of Christ. The Holy Ghost was poured out upon us to a very great degree—some prophesied, whilst we all praised the Lord, and rejoiced exceedingly. Whilst yet together, I received the following commandment:

See Doctrine and Covenants 21.

We now proceeded to call out and ordain some others of the brethren to different offices of the Priesthood, according as the Spirit manifested unto us; and after a happy time spent in witnessing and feeling for ourselves the powers and blessings of the Holy Ghost, through the grace of God bestowed upon us, we dismissed with the pleasing knowledge that we were now individually members of, and acknowledged of God, "The Church of Jesus Christ," organized in accordance with commandments and revelations given by Him to ourselves in these last days, as well as according to the order of the Church as recorded in the New Testament. Several persons who had attended the above meeting became convinced of the truth and came forward shortly after, and were received into the Church; among the rest, my own father and mother were baptized, to my great joy and consolation; and about the same time, Martin Harris and Orrin Porter Rockwell.

See Doctrine and Covenants 22.

The following persons being anxious to know of the Lord what might be their respective duties in relation to this work, I inquired of the Lord, and received for them the following:

See Doctrine and Covenants 23.

On Sunday, April 11th, 1830, Oliver Cowdery preached the first public discourse that was delivered by any of our number. Our meeting was held, by previous appointment, at the house of Mr. Peter Whitmer, Sen., Fayette. Large numbers of people attended, and the same day, the following were baptized, viz., Hiram Page, Katharine Page, Christian Whitmer, Anne Whitmer, Jacob Whitmer, Elizabeth Whitmer; and on the 18th day, Peter Whitmer, Sen., Mary Whitmer, William Jolly, Elizabeth Jolly, Vincent Jolly, Richard B. Peterson, and Elizabeth Anne Whitmer—all by Oliver Cowdery, in Seneca Lake.

During this month of April, I went on a visit to the residence of Mr. Joseph Knight, of Colesville, Broome county, New York, with whom and his family I had been for some time acquainted, and whose name I had previously mentioned as having been so kind and thoughtful towards us while translating the Book of Mormon. Mr. Knight and his family were Universalists, but were willing to reason with me upon my religious views, and were, as usual, friendly and hospitable. We held several meetings in the neighborhood; we had many friends, and some enemies. Our meetings were well attended, and many began to pray fervently to Almighty God, that He would give them wisdom to understand the truth.

Amongst those who attended our meetings regularly was Newel Knight, son of Joseph Knight. He and I had many serious conversations on the important subject of man's eternal salvation. We had got into the habit of praying much at our meetings, and Newel had said that he would try and take up his cross, and pray vocally during the meeting; but when we again met together, he rather excused himself. I tried to prevail upon him, making use of the figure, supposing that he should get into a mud hole, would he not try to help himself out? And I further said that we were willing now to help him out of the mud hole. He replied that, provided he had got into a mud hole through carelessness, he would rather wait and get out himself, than to have others help him; and so he would wait until he could get into the woods by himself, and there he would pray. Accordingly, he deferred praying until next morning when he retired into the woods; where, according to his own account afterwards, he made several attempts to pray, but could scarcely do so, feeling that he had not done his duty in refusing to pray in the presence of others. He began to feel uneasy, and continued to feel worse both in mind and body, until, upon reaching his own house, his appearance was such as to alarm his wife very much. He requested her to go and bring me to him. I went and found him suffering very much in his mind, and his body acted upon in a very strange manner; his visage and limbs distorted and twisted in every shape and appearance possible to imagine; and finally he was caught up off the floor of the apartment, and tossed about most fearfully.

His situation was soon made known to his neighbors and relatives, and in a short time, as many as eight or nine grown persons had got together to witness the scene. After he had thus suffered for a time, I succeeded in getting hold of him by the hand, when almost immediately he spoke to me, and with great earnestness requested me to cast the devil out of him, saying that he knew he was in him, and that he also knew that I could cast him out.

I replied, "If you know that I can, it shall be done;" and then almost unconsciously I rebuked the devil, and commanded him in the name of Jesus Christ to depart from him; when immediately Newel spoke out and said that he saw the devil leave him and vanish from his sight. This was the first miracle which was done in the Church, or by any member of it; and it was done not by man, nor by the power of man, but it was done by God, and by the power of godliness; therefore, let the honor and the praise, the dominion and the glory, be ascribed to the Father, Son, and Holy Spirit, for ever and ever. Amen.

This scene was now entirely changed, for as soon as the devil had departed from our friend, his countenance became natural, his distortions of body ceased, and almost immediately the Spirit of the Lord descended upon him, and the visions of eternity were opened to his view. So soon as consciousness returned, his bodily weakness was such that we were obliged to lay him upon his bed, and wait upon him for some time. He afterwards related his experience as follows:

> I now began to feel a most pleasing sensation resting on me, and immediately the visions of heaven were opened to my view. I felt myself attracted upward, and remained for some time enwrapt in contemplation, insomuch that I knew not what was going on in the room. By and by, I felt some weight pressing upon my shoulder and the side of my head, which served to recall me to a sense of

> my situation, and I found that the Spirit of the Lord had actually caught me up off the floor, and that my shoulder and head were pressing against the beams.

All this was witnessed by many, to their great astonishment and satisfaction, when they saw the devil thus cast out, and the power of God, and His Holy Spirit thus made manifest. As may be expected, such a scene as this contributed much to make believers of those who witnessed it, and finally, the greater part of them became members of the Church.

Soon after this occurrence, I returned to Fayette, Seneca county. The Book of Mormon (the stick of Joseph in the hands of Ephraim,) had now been published for some time, and as the ancient prophet had predicted of it, "it was accounted as a strange thing." No small stir was created by its appearance. Great opposition and much persecution followed the believers of its authenticity. But it had now come to pass that truth had sprung out of earth, and righteousness had looked down from heaven; so we feared not our opponents, knowing that we had both truth and righteousness on our side, that we had both the Father and the Son, because we had the doctrines of Christ, and abided in them; and therefore we continued to preach and to give information to all who were willing to hear.

During the last week in May, the above-mentioned Newel Knight came to visit us at Fayette, and was baptized by David Whitmer.

On the ninth day of June, 1830, we held our first conference as an organized church. Our numbers were about thirty, besides whom many assembled with us, who were either believers or anxious to learn. Having opened by singing and prayer, we partook together of the emblems of the body and blood of our Lord Jesus Christ. We then proceeded to confirm several who had lately been baptized, after which we called out and ordained several to the various offices of the Priesthood. Much exhortation and instruction was given, and the Holy Ghost was poured out upon us in a miraculous manner—many of our number prophesied, whilst others had the heavens opened to their view and were so overcome that we had to lay them on beds or other convenient places; among the rest was Brother Newel Knight, who had to be placed on a bed, being unable to help himself. By his own account of the transaction, he could not understand why we should lay him on the bed as he felt no sense of weakness. He felt his heart filled with love, with glory, and pleasure unspeakable, and could discern all that was going on in the room; when all of a sudden a vision of the future burst upon him. He saw there represented the great work which through my instrumentality was yet to be accomplished. He saw heaven opened, and beheld the Lord Jesus Christ seated at the right hand of the Majesty on high, and had it made plain to his understanding that the time would come when he would be admitted into His presence to enjoy His society for ever and ever. When their bodily strength was restored to these brethren, they shouted hosannas to God and the Lamb, and rehearsed the glorious things which they had seen and felt, whilst they were yet in the spirit.

Such scenes as these were calculated to inspire our hearts with joy unspeakable, and fill us with awe and reverence for that Almighty Being, by whose grace we had been called to be instrumental in bringing about, for the children of men, the enjoyment of such glorious blessings as were now at this time poured out upon us. To find ourselves engaged in the very same order of things as observed by the holy apostles of old; to realize the importance and solemnity of such proceedings; and to witness and feel with our own natural senses, the like glorious manifestations of the powers of the Priesthood, the gifts and blessings of the Holy Ghost, and the goodness and condescension of a merciful God unto such as obey the everlasting gospel of our Lord Jesus Christ, combined to create within us sensations of rapturous gratitude, and inspire us with fresh zeal and energy in the cause of truth.

Shortly after this conference, David Whitmer baptized the

"HE SAW HEAVEN
OPENED, AND
BEHELD
THE LORD
JESUS CHRIST
SEATED AT THE
RIGHT HAND OF
THE MAJESTY
ON HIGH."

following persons, in Seneca Lake, viz., John Poorman, John Jolly, Julia Anne Jolly, Harriet Jolly, Jerusha Smith, Katherine Smith, William Smith, Don C. Smith, Peter Rockwell, Caroline Rockwell, and Electa Rockwell.

Immediately after conference, I returned to my own house, and from thence, accompanied by my wife, Oliver Cowdery, John Whitmer and David Whitmer, went again on a visit to Mr. Knight, of Colesville, Broome county. We found a number in the neighborhood still believing, and now anxious to be baptized. We appointed a meeting for the Sabbath, and on the afternoon of Saturday we erected a dam across a stream of water, which was convenient, for the purpose of there attending to the ordinance of baptism; but during the night a mob collected and tore down our dam, which hindered us from attending to the baptism on the Sabbath. We afterward found out that this mob had been instigated to this act of molestation by certain sectarian priests of the neighborhood, who began to consider their craft in danger, and took this plan to stop the progress of the truth; and the sequel will show how determinedly they prosecuted their opposition, as well as to how little purpose in the end. The Sabbath arrived, and we held our meeting. Oliver Cowdery preached, and others of us bore testimony to the truth of the Book of Mormon, the doctrine of repentance, baptism for the remission of sins, and laying on of hands for the gift of the Holy Ghost, etc. Amongst our audience were those who had torn down our dam, and who seemed desirous to give us trouble, but did not until after the meeting was dismissed, when they immediately commenced talking to those whom they considered our friends, and tried to turn them against us and our doctrines.

Amongst the many present at this meeting was one Emily Coburn, sister to the wife of Newel Knight. The Rev. Mr. Shearer, a divine of the Presbyterian faith, who had considered himself her pastor, came to understand that she was likely to believe our doctrine, and had, a short time previous to this meeting, come to labor with her. But having spent some time with her without being able to persuade her against us, he endeavored to have her leave her sister's house and go with him to her father's, who lived at a distance. For this purpose, he had recourse to stratagem; he told her that one of her brothers was waiting at a certain place, desirous to have her go with him. He succeeded thus in getting her a little distance from the house, when, seeing that her brother was not in waiting for her, she refused to go any further with him; upon which he took hold of her by the arm to force her along. But her sister was soon with them, and as the two women were too many for him to cope with, he was forced to sneak off without accomplishing his errand, after all his labor and ingenuity. Nothing daunted, however, he went to her father, representing to him some thing or other, which induced the old gentleman to give him a power of attorney, which, as soon as our meeting was over, on the above-named Sunday evening, he immediately served upon her, and carried her off to her father's residence by open violence against her will. All his labor was in vain, however, for the said Emily Coburn in a short time afterwards was baptized and confirmed a member of the Church of Jesus Christ of Latter-day Saints.

Early on Monday morning we were on the alert, and before our enemies were aware of our proceedings, we had repaired the dam, and the following thirteen persons [were] baptized by Oliver Cowdery, viz., Emma Smith, Hezekiah Peck and wife, Joseph Knight, Sen., and wife, William Stringham and wife, Joseph Knight, Jun., Aaron Culver and wife, Levi Hale, Polly Knight, and Julia Stringham.

Before the baptizing was entirely finished, the mob began again to collect, and shortly after we had retired, they amounted to about fifty men. They surrounded the house of Mr. Knight—whither we had retired—raging with anger, and apparently determined to commit violence upon us. Some asked us questions, others threatened us, so that we thought it wisdom to leave and go to the house of Newel Knight. There also they followed us, and it was only by the exercise of great prudence on our part, and reliance in our Heavenly Father, that they were kept from laying violent hands upon us; and so long as they chose to stay, we were obliged to answer them various unprofitable questions, and bear with insults and threatenings without number.

We had appointed a meeting for this evening, for the purpose of attending to the confirmation of those who had been the same morning baptized. The time appointed had arrived and our friends had nearly all collected together, when to my surprise, I was visited by a constable, and arrested by him on a warrant, on the charge of being a disorderly person, of setting the country in an uproar by preaching the Book of Mormon, etc. The constable informed me, soon after I had been arrested, that the plan of those who had got out the warrant was to get me into the hands of the mob, who were now lying in ambush for me; but that he was determined to save me from them, as he had found me to be a different sort of person from what I had been represented to him. I soon found that he had told me the truth in this matter, for not far from Mr. Knight's house, the wagon in which we had set out was surrounded by a mob, who seemed only to await some signal from the constable; but to their great disappointment, he gave the horse the whip, and drove me out of their reach.

Whilst driving in great haste, one of the wagon wheels came off, which left us once more very nearly surrounded by them, as they had come on in close pursuit. However, we managed to replace the wheel and again left them behind us. He drove on to the town of South Bainbridge, Chenango county, where he lodged me for the time being in an upper room of a tavern; and in order that all might be right with himself and with me also, he slept during the night with his feet against the door and a loaded musket by his side, whilst I occupied a bed which was in the room, he having declared that if we were interrupted unlawfully, he would fight for me, and defend me as far as it was in his power.

On the day following, a court was convened for the purpose of investigating those charges which had been preferred against me.

A great excitement prevailed on account of the scandalous falsehoods which had been circulated, the nature of which will appear in the sequel. In the meantime, my friend, Joseph Knight, had repaired to two of his neighbors, viz., James Davidson and John Reid, Esqrs., respectable farmers, men renowned for their integrity, and well versed in the laws of their country; and retained them on my behalf during my trial.

At length the trial commenced amidst a multitude of spectators, who in general evinced a belief that I was guilty of all that had been reported concerning me, and of course were very zealous that I should be punished according to my crimes. Among many witnesses called up against me was Mr. Josiah Stoal—of whom I have made mention as having worked for him some time—and examined to the following effect:

"Did not the prisoner, Joseph Smith, have a horse of you?"

"Yes."

"Did not he go to you and tell you that an angel had appeared unto him and authorized him to get the horse from you?"

"No, he told me no such story."

"Well, how had he the horse of you?"

"He bought him of me as any other man would."

"Have you had your pay?"

"That is not your business."

The question being again put, the witness replied:

"I hold his note for the price of the horse, which I consider as good as the pay; for I am well acquainted with Joseph Smith, Jun., and know him to be an honest man; and if he wishes, I am ready to let him have another horse on the same terms."

Mr. Jonathan Thompson was next called up and examined:

"Has not the prisoner, Joseph Smith, Jun., had a yoke of oxen of you?"

"Yes."

"Did he not obtain them of you by telling you that he had a revelation to the effect that he was to have them?"

"No, he did not mention a word of the kind concerning the oxen; he purchased them the same as any other man would."

After a few more such attempts, the court was detained for a time in order that two young women, daughters of Mr. Stoal, with whom I had at times kept company, might be sent for, in order, if possible, to elicit something from them which might be made a pretext against me. The young ladies arrived, and were severally examined touching my character and conduct in general; but particularly as to my behavior towards them, both in public and private; when they both bore such testimony in my favor as left my enemies without a pretext on their account. Several other attempts were made to prove something against me, and even circumstances which were alleged to have taken place in Broome county were brought forward, but these my lawyers would not admit of as testimony against me; in consequence of which my persecutors managed to detain the court until they had succeeded in obtaining a warrant from Broome county, which warrant they served upon me at the very moment that I was acquitted by this court.

The constable who served this second warrant upon me had no sooner arrested me than he began to abuse and insult me; and so unfeeling was he with me that although I had been kept all the day in court without anything to eat since the morning, yet he hurried me off to Broome county, a distance of about fifteen miles, before he allowed me any kind of food whatever. He took me to a tavern, and gathered in a number of men, who used every means to abuse, ridicule and insult me. They spit upon me, pointed their fingers at me, saying, "Prophesy, prophesy!" and thus did they imitate those who crucified the Savior of mankind, not knowing what they did.

We were at this time not far distant from my own house. I wished to be allowed the privilege of spending the night with my wife at home, offering any wished for security for my appearance; but this was denied me. I applied for something to eat. The constable ordered me some crusts of bread and water, which was the only food I that night received. At length we retired to bed. The constable made me lie next to the wall. He then laid himself down by me and put his arm around me, and upon my moving in the least, would clench me fast, fearing that I intended to escape from him; and in this very disagreeable manner did we pass the night.

Next day I was brought before the magistrate's court at Colesville, Broome county, and put upon my trial. My former faithful friends and lawyers were again at my side; my former persecutors were arrayed against me. Many witnesses were again called forward and examined, some of whom swore to the most palpable falsehoods, and like the false witnesses which had appeared against me the day previous, they contradicted themselves so plainly that the court would not admit their testimony. Others were called, who showed by their zeal that they were willing enough to prove something against me, but all they could do was to tell something which somebody else had told them.

In this frivolous and vexatious manner did they proceed for a considerable time, when, finally, Newel Knight was called up and examined by Lawyer Seymour, who had been especially sent for on this occasion. One Lawyer Burch, also, was on the side of the prosecution; but Mr. Seymour seemed to be a more zealous Presbyterian, and appeared very anxious and determined that the people should not be deluded by anyone professing the power of godliness, and not "denying the power thereof."

Mr. Knight was sworn, and Mr. Seymour interrogated him as follows:

"Did the prisoner, Joseph Smith, Jun., cast the devil out of you?"

"No, sir."

"Why, have not you had the devil cast out of you?"

"Yes, sir."

"And had not Joe Smith some hand in its being done?"

"Yes, sir."

"And did not he cast him out of you?"

"No, sir; it was done by the power of God, and Joseph Smith

was the instrument in the hands of God, on the occasion. He commanded him to come out of me in the name of Jesus Christ."

"And are you sure that it was the devil?"

"Yes, sir."

"Did you see him after he was cast out of you?"

"Yes, sir! I saw him."

"Pray, what did he look like?"

(Here one of my lawyers informed the witness that he need not answer the question.) The witness replied:

"I believe I need not answer your last question, but I will do it, provided I be allowed to ask you one question first, and you answer me, viz., Do you, Mr. Seymour, understand the things of the spirit?"

"No," admitted Mr. Seymour, "I do not pretend to such big things."

"Well, then," replied Knight, "it would be of no use to tell you what the devil looked like, for it was a spiritual sight, and spiritually discerned; and of course you would not understand it were I to tell you of it."

The lawyer dropped his head, whilst the loud laugh of the audience proclaimed his discomfiture.

Mr. Seymour now addressed the court, and in a long and violent harangue endeavored to blacken my character and bring me in guilty of the charges which had been brought against me. Among other things, he brought up the story of my having been a money-digger, and in this manner proceeded, hoping evidently to influence the court and the people against me.

Mr. Davidson and Mr. Reid followed on my behalf. They held forth in true colors the nature of the prosecution, the malignancy of intention, and the apparent disposition to persecute their client, rather than to afford him justice. They took up the different arguments which had been brought by the lawyers for the prosecution; and having shown their utter futility and misapplication, then proceeded to scrutinize the evidence which had been adduced; and each, in his turn, thanked God that he had been engaged in so good a cause as that of defending a man whose character stood so well the test of such a strict investigation. In fact, these men, although not regular lawyers, were upon this occasion able to put to silence their opponents, and convince the court that I was innocent. They spoke like men inspired of God, whilst those who were arrayed against me trembled under the sound of their voices, and quailed before them like criminals before a bar of justice.

The majority of the assembled multitude had now begun to find that nothing could be sustained against me. Even the constable who arrested me, and treated me so badly, now came and apologized to me, and asked my forgiveness for his behavior towards me; and so far was he changed, that he informed me that the mob were determined, if the court acquitted me, that they would have me, and railride me, and tar and feather me; and further, that he was willing to favor me and lead me out in safety by a private way.

The court found the charges against me not sustained; I was accordingly acquitted, to the great satisfaction of my friends and vexation of my enemies, who were still determined upon molesting me. But through the instrumentality of my new friend the constable, I was enabled to escape them and make my way in safety to my wife's sister's house, where I found my wife awaiting with much anxiety the issue of those ungodly proceedings, and in company with her I arrived next day in safety at my own house.

After a few days I returned to Colesville, in company with Oliver Cowdery, for the purpose of confirming those whom we had been forced to leave for a time. We had scarcely arrived at Mr. Knight's when the mob was seen collecting together to oppose us, and we considered it wisdom to leave for home, which we did, without even waiting for any refreshments. Our enemies pursued us, and it was oftentimes as much as we could do to elude them. However, we managed to get home, after having traveled all night, except a short time, during which we were forced to rest ourselves under a large tree by the wayside, sleeping and watching alternately.

Thus were we persecuted on account of our religious faith—in a country the Constitution of which guarantees to every man the indefeasible right to worship God according to the dictates of his own conscience—and by men, too, who were professors of religion, and who were not backward to maintain the right of religious liberty for themselves, though they could thus wantonly deny it to us. For instance, Cyrus McMaster, a Presbyterian of high standing in his church, was one of the chief instigators of these persecutions; and he at one time told me personally that he considered me guilty without judge or jury. The celebrated Dr. Boyington, also a Presbyterian, was another instigator of these deeds of outrage; whilst a young man named Benton, of the same religious faith, swore out the first warrant against me. I could mention many others also, but for brevity's sake, will make these suffice for the present.

I will say, however, that amid all the trials and tribulations we had to wade through, the Lord, who well knew our infantile and delicate situation, vouchsafed for us a supply of strength, and granted us "line upon line of knowledge—here a little and there a little," of which the following was a precious morsel:

See the Pearl of Great Price and Moses 1.

Meantime, and notwithstanding all the rage of our enemies, we had much consolation, and many things occurred to strengthen our faith and cheer our hearts.

After our departure from Colesville, after the trial, the Church there were very anxious, as might be expected, concerning our again visiting them, during which time Sister Knight, wife of Newel Knight, had a dream, which enabled her to say that we would visit them that day, which really came to pass, for a few hours afterwards we arrived; and thus was our faith much strengthened concerning dreams and visions in the last days, foretold by the ancient Prophet Joel; and although we this time were forced to seek safety from our enemies by flight, yet did we feel confident that eventually we should come off victorious, if we only continued [to be] faithful to Him who had called us forth from darkness into the marvelous light of the everlasting gospel of our Lord Jesus Christ.

Shortly after our return home, we received the following commandments:

See Doctrine and Covenants 24–26.

Shortly after we had received the above revelations, Oliver Cowdery returned to Mr. Peter Whitmer's, Sen., and I began to arrange and copy the revelations, which we had received from time to time; in which I was assisted by John Whitmer, who now resided with me.

Whilst thus employed in the work appointed me by my Heavenly Father, I received a letter from Oliver Cowdery, the contents of which gave me both sorrow and uneasiness. Not having that letter now in my possession, I cannot of course give it here in full, but merely an extract of the most prominent parts, which I can yet, and expect long to, remember. He wrote to inform me that he had discovered an error in one of the commandments—Book of Doctrine and Covenants: "And truly manifest by their works that they have received of the Spirit of Christ unto a remission of their sins."

The above quotation, he said, was erroneous, and added: "I command you in the name of God to erase those words, that no priestcraft be amongst us!"

I immediately wrote to him in reply, in which I asked him by what authority he took upon him to command me to alter or erase, to add to or diminish from, a revelation or commandment from Almighty God.

A few days afterwards I visited him and Mr. Whitmer's family, when I found the family in general of his opinion concerning the words above quoted, and it was not without both labor and perseverance that I could prevail with any of them to reason calmly on the subject. However, Christian Whitmer at length became convinced that the sentence was reasonable, and according to scripture; and finally, with his assistance, I succeeded in bringing, not only the Whitmer family, but also Oliver Cowdery to acknowledge that they had been in error, and that the sentence in dispute was in accordance with the rest of the commandment. And thus was this error rooted out, which having its rise in presumption and rash judgment, was the more particularly calculated (when once fairly understood) to teach each and all of us the necessity of humility and meekness before the Lord, that He might teach us of His ways, that we might walk in His paths, and live by every word that proceedeth forth from His mouth.

Early in the month of August, Newel Knight and his wife paid us a visit at my place in Harmony, Pennsylvania; and as neither his wife nor mine had been as yet confirmed, it was proposed that we should confirm them, and partake together of the sacrament, before he and his wife should leave us. In order to prepare for this I set out to procure some wine for the occasion, but had gone only a short distance when I was met by a heavenly messenger, and received the following revelation, the first four paragraphs of which were written at this time, and the remainder in the September following:

See Doctrine and Covenants 27.

In obedience to the above commandment, we prepared some wine of our own making and held our meeting, consisting only of five, viz., Newel Knight and his wife, myself and my wife, and John Whitmer. We partook together of the sacrament, after which we confirmed these two sisters into the Church, and spent the evening in a glorious manner. The Spirit of the Lord was poured out upon us; we praised the Lord God, and rejoiced exceedingly.

About this time, a spirit of persecution began again to manifest itself against us in the neighborhood where I now resided, which was commenced by a man of the Methodist persuasion, who professed to be a minister of God. This man had learned that my father-in-law and his family had promised us protection, and were friendly, and inquiring into the work; and knowing that if he could get him turned against me, my friends in that place would be but few; he visited my father-in-law, and told him falsehoods concerning me of the most shameful nature, which turned the old gentleman and his family so much against us, that they would no longer promise us protection nor believe our doctrines.

Towards the latter end of August, in company with John and David Whitmer, and my brother Hyrum Smith, I visited the Church at Colesville, New York. Well knowing the determined hostility of our enemies in that quarter, and also knowing that it was our duty to visit the Church, we had called upon our Heavenly Father in mighty prayer, that He would grant us an opportunity of meeting with them, that He would blind the eyes of our enemies, so that they would not know us, and that we might on this occasion return unmolested. Our prayers were not in vain, for when within a little distance of Mr. Knight's place, we encountered a large company at work upon the public road, amongst whom were several of our most bitter enemies. They looked earnestly at us, but not knowing us, we passed on without interruption. That evening we assembled the Church, and confirmed them, partook of the sacrament, and held a happy meeting, having much reason to rejoice in the God of our salvation, and sing hosannas to His holy name. Next morning we set out on our return home; and although our enemies had offered a reward of five dollars to any one who would give them information of our arrival, yet did we get out of the neighborhood, without the least annoyance, and arrived home in safety. Some few days afterwards, however, Newel Knight came to my place, and from him we learned that, very shortly after our departure, the mob came to know of our having been there, when they immediately collected together, and threatened the brethren, and very much annoyed them during all that day.

Meantime, Brother Knight had come with his wagon, prepared to move my family to Fayette, New York. Mr. Whitmer, having heard of the persecutions against us at Harmony, Pennsylvania, had invited us to go and live with him; and during the last week in August we arrived at Fayette, amidst the congratulations of our brethren and friends.

To our great grief, however, we soon found that Satan had been lying in wait to deceive, and seeking whom he might devour. Brother Hiram Page had in his possession a certain stone, by which he had obtained certain "revelations" concerning the upbuilding of Zion, the order of the Church, etc., all of which were entirely at variance with the order of God's house, as laid down in the New Testament, as well as in our late revelations. As a conference meeting had been appointed for the 26th day of September, I thought it wisdom not to do much more than to converse with the brethren on the subject, until the conference should meet. Finding, however, that many, especially the Whitmer family and Oliver Cowdery, were believing much in the things set forth by this stone, we thought best to inquire of the Lord concerning so important a matter; and before conference convened, we received the following:

See Doctrine and Covenants 28–29.

At length, our conference assembled. The subject of the stone previously mentioned was discussed, and after considerable investigation, Brother Page, as well as the whole Church who were present, renounced the said stone, and all things connected therewith, much to our mutual satisfaction and happiness. We now partook of the sacrament, confirmed and ordained many, and attended to a great variety of Church business on the first and the two following days of the conference, during which time we had much of the power of God manifested amongst us; the Holy Ghost came upon us, and filled us with joy unspeakable; and peace, and faith, and hope, and charity abounded in our midst.

Before we separated we received the following:

See Doctrine and Covenants 30.

During this conference, which continued three days, the utmost harmony prevailed, and all things were settled satisfactorily to all present, and a desire was manifested by all the Saints to go forward and labor with all their powers to spread the great and glorious principles of truth, which had been revealed by our Heavenly Father. A number were baptized during the conference, and the word of the Lord spread and prevailed.

At this time a great desire was manifested by several of the elders respecting the remnants of the house of Joseph, the Lamanites, residing in the west—knowing that the purposes of God were great respecting that people, and hoping that the time had come when the promises of the Almighty in regard to them were about to be accomplished, and that they would receive the gospel, and enjoy its blessings. The desire being so great, it was agreed that we should inquire of the Lord respecting the propriety of sending some of the elders among them, which we accordingly did, and receiving the following:

See Doctrine and Covenants 32.

Immediately on receiving this revelation, preparations were made for the journey of the brethren therein designated to the borders of the Lamanites, and a copy of the revelation was given them. They bade adieu to their brethren and friends, and commenced their journey, preaching by the way, and leaving a sealing testimony behind them, lifting up their voice like a trump in the different villages through which they passed. They continued their journey until they came to Kirtland, Ohio, where they tarried some time, there being quite a number in that place and vicinity who believed their testimony, and came forward and obeyed the gospel. Among the number was Mr. Sidney Rigdon, and a large portion of the church over which he presided.

Previous to this, Elder Parley P. Pratt had been a preacher in the same church with Mr. Rigdon, and resided in the town of Amherst, Loraine county, in Ohio, and had been sent into the state of New York on a mission, where he became acquainted with the circumstances of the coming forth of the Book of Mormon, and was introduced to Joseph Smith, Jun., and other members of the Church. The belief that there were many in the church with which he had formerly been united who were honest seekers after truth induced Elder Pratt, while on his journey to the west, to call upon his friends, and make known the great things which the Lord had brought to pass.

The first house at which they called in the vicinity of Kirtland, was Mr. Rigdon's, and after the usual salutations, they presented him with the Book of Mormon, stating that it was a revelation from God. This being the first time he had ever heard of, or seen, the Book of Mormon, he felt very much surprised at the assertion, and replied that he had the Bible which he believed was a revelation from God, and with which he pretended to have some acquaintance; but with respect of the book they had presented him, he must say that he had considerable doubt. Upon this, they expressed a desire to investigate the subject, and argue the matter. But he replied, "No, young gentlemen, you must not argue with me on the subject; but I will read your book, and see what claims it has upon my faith, and will endeavor to ascertain whether it be a revelation from God or not."

After some further conversation, they expressed a desire to lay the subject before the people, and requested the privilege of preaching in Mr. Rigdon's chapel, to which he readily consented. The appointment was accordingly published, and a large and respectable congregation assembled. Oliver Cowdery and Parley P. Pratt severally addressed the meeting. At the conclusion, Mr. Rigdon arose, and stated to the congregation that the information they had that evening received was of an extraordinary character, and certainly demanded their most serious consideration; and as the

Apostle [Paul] advised his brethren to "prove all things, and hold fast that which is good," so he would exhort his brethren to do likewise, and give the matter a careful investigation, and not turn against it without being fully convinced of its being an imposition, lest they should, possibly, resist the truth.

A few miles from Mr. Rigdon's home in Mentor, at the town of Kirtland, lived a number of the members of his church. They lived together and had all things common—from which circumstance has risen the idea that this was the case with the Church of Jesus Christ. To that place the elders immediately repaired, and proclaimed the gospel unto them, with considerable success; for their testimony was received by many of the people, and seventeen came forward in obedience to the gospel.

While thus engaged, they visited Mr. Rigdon occasionally, and found him very earnestly reading the Book of Mormon, praying to the Lord for direction, and meditating on the things he heard and read; and after a fortnight from the time the book was put into his hands, he was fully convinced of the truth of the work, by a revelation from Jesus Christ, which was made known to him in a remarkable manner, so that he could exclaim, "Flesh and blood hath not revealed it unto me, but my Father which is in heaven." Accordingly, he and his wife were both baptized into the Church of Jesus Christ; and, together with those who had been previously admitted to baptism, made a little branch of the Church, in this section of Ohio, of about twenty members.

This much accomplished, the brethren bound for the borders of the Lamanites bade an affectionate farewell to the Saints in Kirtland and vicinity; and, after adding one of their new converts to their number—Dr. Frederick G. Williams—they went on their way rejoicing.

The Lord, who is ever ready to instruct such as diligently seek in faith, gave the following revelation at Fayette, New York:

See Doctrine and Covenants 33.

In the fore part of November, Orson Pratt, a young man nineteen years of age, who had been baptized at the first preaching of his brother, Parley P. Pratt, September 19th (his birthday), about six weeks previous, in Canaan, New York, came to inquire of the Lord what his duty was, and received the following answer:

See Doctrine and Covenants 34.

In December, Sidney Rigdon came to inquire of the Lord, and with him came Edward Partridge; the latter was a pattern of piety, and one of the Lord's great men. Shortly after the arrival of these two brethren, thus spake the Lord:

See Doctrine and Covenants 35.

It may be well to observe here that the Lord greatly encouraged and strengthened the faith of His little flock, which had embraced the fulness of the everlasting gospel, as revealed to them in the Book of Mormon, by giving some more extended information upon the scriptures, a translation of which had already commenced. Much conjecture and conversation frequently occurred among the Saints, concerning the books mentioned, and referred to, in various places in the Old and New Testaments, which were now nowhere to be found. The common remark was, "They are lost books;" but it seems the Apostolic Church had some of these writings, as Jude mentions or quotes the Prophecy of Enoch, the seventh from Adam. To the joy of the little flock, which in all, from Colesville to Canandaigua, New York, numbered about seventy members, did the Lord reveal the following doings of olden times, from the prophecy of Enoch:

See the Pearl of Great Price and Moses 7.

Soon after the words of Enoch were given, the Lord gave the following commandment:

See Doctrine and Covenants 37.

Chapter Three

1831

The year 1831 opened with a prospect great and glorious for the welfare of the kingdom; for on the 2nd of January, 1831, a conference was held in the town of Fayette, New York, at which the ordinary business of the Church was transacted; and in addition, the following revelation was received:

See Doctrine and Covenants 38.

Not long after this conference of the 2nd of January closed, there was a man came to me by the name of James Covill, who had been a Baptist minister for about forty years, and covenanted with the Lord that he would obey any command that the Lord would give to him through me, as His servant, and I received the following:

See Doctrine and Covenants 39.

As James Covill rejected the word of the Lord, and returned to his former principles and people, the Lord gave unto me and Sidney Rigdon the following revelation, explaining why he obeyed not the word:

See Doctrine and Covenants 40.

The latter part of January, in company with Brothers Sidney Rigdon and Edward Partridge, I started with my wife for Kirtland, Ohio, where we arrived about the first of February, and were kindly received and welcomed into the house of Brother Newel K. Whitney. My wife and I lived in [with] the family of Brother Whitney several weeks, and received every kindness and attention which could be expected, and especially from Sister Whitney.

The branch of the Church in this part of the Lord's vineyard, which had increased to nearly one hundred members, were striving to do the will of God, so far as they knew it, though some strange notions and false spirits had crept in among them. With a little caution and some wisdom, I soon assisted the brethren and sisters to overcome them. The plan of "common stock," which had existed in what was called "the family," whose members generally had embraced the everlasting gospel, was readily abandoned for the more perfect law of the Lord; and the false spirits were easily discerned and rejected by the light of revelation. The Lord gave unto the Church the following:

See Doctrine and Covenants 41.

On the 9th of February, 1831, at Kirtland, in the presence of twelve elders, and according to the promise heretofore made, the Lord gave the following revelation, embracing the law of the Church:

See Doctrine and Covenants 42.

Soon after the foregoing revelation was received, a woman came making great pretensions of revealing commandments, laws, and other curious matters; and as almost every person has advocates for both theory and practice, in the various notions and projects of the age, it became necessary to inquire of the Lord, when I received the following:

See Doctrine and Covenants 43.

The latter part of February I received the following revelation, which caused the Church to appoint a conference to be held early in the month of June ensuing:

See Doctrine and Covenants 44.

At this age of the Church (early in the spring of 1831) many false reports, lies, and foolish stories were published in the newspapers, and circulated in every direction, to prevent people from investigating the work, or embracing the faith. A great earthquake in China, which destroyed from one to two thousand inhabitants, was burlesqued in some papers as "'Mormonism' in China." But to the joy of the Saints, who had to struggle against everything that prejudice and wickedness could invent, I received the following:

See Doctrine and Covenants 45.

The next day, after the above was received, I also received the following revelation, relative to the gifts of the Holy Ghost:

See Doctrine and Covenants 46.

The same day that I received the foregoing revelation, I also received the following, setting apart John Whitmer as a historian, inasmuch as he is faithful:

See Doctrine and Covenants 47.

Upon inquiry how the brethren should act in regard to purchasing lands to settle upon, and where they should finally make a permanent location, I received the following:

See Doctrine and Covenants 48.

At about this time came Leman Copley, one of the sect called Shaking Quakers, and embraced the fulness of the everlasting gospel, apparently honest-hearted but still retaining the idea that the Shakers were right in some particulars of their faith. In order to have more perfect understanding on the subject, I inquired of the Lord, and received the following:

See Doctrine and Covenants 49.

During the month of April, I continued to translate the scriptures, as time would allow. In May, a number of elders being present, and not understanding the different spirits abroad in the earth, I inquired and received from the Lord the following:

See Doctrine and Covenants 50.

Not long after the foregoing was received, the Saints from the state of New York began to come on, and it seemed necessary to settle them; therefore, at the solicitation of Bishop Partridge, I inquired and received the following:

See Doctrine and Covenants 51.

On the 3rd of June, the elders from the various parts of the country where they were laboring, came in; and the conference before appointed, convened in Kirtland; and the Lord displayed His power to the most perfect satisfaction of the Saints. The man of sin was revealed, and the authority of the Melchizedek Priesthood was manifested and conferred for the first time upon several of the Elders. It was clearly evident that the Lord gave us power in proportion to the work to be done, and strength according to the race set before us, and grace and help as our needs required. Great harmony prevailed; several were ordained; faith was strengthened; and humility, so necessary for the blessing of God to follow prayer, characterized the Saints.

The next day, as a kind continuation of this great work of the last days, I received the following:

See Doctrine and Covenants 52.

Shortly after the foregoing was received, at the request of Algernon Sidney Gilbert I inquired, and obtained the following:

See Doctrine and Covenants 53.

The branch of the Church in Thompson, on account of breaking the covenant, and not knowing what to do, they sent in Newel Knight and other elders to ask me to inquire of the Lord for them; which I did, and received the following:

See Doctrine and Covenants 54.

Soon after I received the foregoing, Elder Thomas B. Marsh came to inquire what he should do; as Elder Ezra Thayre, his yoke-fellow in the ministry, could not get ready to start on his mission as soon as he (Marsh) would; and I inquired of the Lord, and received the following:

See Doctrine and Covenants 56.

On the 19th of June, in company with Sidney Rigdon, Martin Harris, Edward Partridge, William W. Phelps, Joseph Coe, Algernon S. Gilbert and his wife, I started from Kirtland, Ohio, for the land of Missouri, agreeable to the commandment before received, wherein it was promised that if we were faithful, the land of our inheritance, even the place for the city of the New Jerusalem, should be revealed. We went by wagon, canal boats, and stages to Cincinnati, where I had an interview with the Rev. Walter Scott, one of the founders of the Campbellites, or Newlight church. Before the close of our interview, he manifested one of the bitterest spirits against the doctrine of the New Testament (that "these signs shall follow them that believe," as recorded in Mark the 16th chapter) that I ever witnessed among men. We left Cincinnati in a steamer, and landed at Louisville, Kentucky, where we were detained three days in waiting for a steamer to convey us to St. Louis. At St. Louis, myself, Brothers Harris, Phelps, Partridge and Coe, went by land on foot to Independence, Jackson county, Missouri, where we arrived about the middle of July, and the rest of the company came by water a few days later.

Notwithstanding the corruptions and abominations of the times, and the evil spirit manifested towards us on account of our belief in the Book of Mormon, at many places and among various persons, yet the Lord continued His watchful care and loving kindness to us day by day; and we made it a rule, wherever there was an opportunity, to read a chapter in the Bible, and pray; and these seasons of worship gave us great consolation.

The meeting of our brethren, who had long awaited our arrival, was a glorious one, and moistened with many tears. It seemed good and pleasant for brethren to meet together in unity. But our reflections were many, coming as we had from a highly cultivated state of society in the east, and standing now upon the confines or western limits of the United States, and looking into the vast wilderness of those that sat in darkness; how natural it was to observe the degradation, leanness of intellect, ferocity, and jealousy of a people that were nearly a century behind the times, and to feel for those who roamed about without the benefit of civilization, refinement, or religion; yea, and exclaim in the language of the prophets: "When will the wilderness blossom as the rose? When will Zion be built up in her glory, and where will Thy temple stand, unto which all nations shall come in the last days?" Our anxiety was soon relieved by receiving the following:

See Doctrine and Covenants 57.

The first Sabbath after our arrival in Jackson county, Brother W. W. Phelps preached to a western audience over the boundary of the United States, wherein were present specimens of all the families of the earth: Shem, Ham, and Japheth; several of the Lamanites or Indians—representative of Shem; quite a respectable number of negroes—descendants of Ham; and the balance was made up of

"NOTWITHSTANDING THE CORRUPTIONS AND ABOMINATIONS OF THE TIMES, AND THE EVIL SPIRIT MANIFESTED TOWARDS US ON ACCOUNT OF OUR BELIEF . . . THE LORD CONTINUED HIS WATCHFUL CARE AND LOVING KINDNESS TO US DAY BY DAY."

citizens of the surrounding country, and fully represented themselves as pioneers of the West. At this meeting two were baptized, who had previously believed in the fulness of the gospel.

During this week the Colesville branch, referred to in the latter part of the last revelation, and Sidney Rigdon, Sidney Gilbert and wife, and Elders Morley and Booth arrived. I received the following:

See Doctrine and Covenants 58.

On the second day of August, I assisted the Colesville branch of the Church to lay the first log, for a house, as a foundation of Zion in Kaw township, twelve miles west of Independence. The log was carried and placed by twelve men, in honor of the twelve tribes of Israel. At the same time, through prayer, the land of Zion was consecrated and dedicated by Elder Sidney Rigdon for the gathering of the Saints. It was a season of joy to those present, and afforded a glimpse of the future, which time will yet unfold to the satisfaction of the faithful.

As we had received a commandment for Elder Rigdon to write a description of the land of Zion, we sought for all the information necessary to accomplish so desirable an object. The country is unlike the timbered states of the East. As far as the eye can reach the beautiful rolling prairies lie spread out like a sea of meadows; and are decorated with a growth of flowers so gorgeous and grand as to exceed description; and nothing is more fruitful, or a richer stockholder in the blooming prairie, than the honey bee. Only on the water courses is timber to be found. There in strips from one to three miles in width, and following faithfully the meanderings of the streams, it grows in luxuriant forests. The forests are a mixture of oak, hickory, black walnut, elm, ash, cherry, honey locust, mulberry, coffee bean, hackberry, boxelder, and bass wood; with the addition of cottonwood, butterwood, pecan, and soft and hard maple upon the bottoms. The shrubbery is beautiful and consists in part of plums, grapes, crab apple, and persimmons.

The soil is rich and fertile, from three to ten feet deep, and generally composed of a rich black mould, intermingled with clay and sand. It yields in abundance wheat, corn, sweet potatoes, cotton, and many other common agricultural products. Horses, cattle, and hogs—though of an inferior breed—are tolerably plentiful and seem nearly to raise themselves by grazing in the vast prairie range in summer, and feeding upon the bottoms in winter. The wild game is less plentiful of course where man has commenced the cultivation of the soil than in the wild prairies. Buffalo, elk, deer, bear, wolves, beaver, and many smaller animals here roam at pleasure. Turkeys, geese, swans, ducks, yea a variety of the feathered tribe, are among the rich abundance that grace the delightful regions of this goodly land—the heritage of the children of God.

The season is mild and delightful nearly three quarters of the year, and as the land of Zion, situated at about equal distances from the Atlantic and Pacific oceans, as well as from the Allegheny and Rocky mountains, in the thirty-ninth degree of north latitude, and between the sixteenth and seventeenth degrees of west longitude, it bids fair—when the curse is taken from the land—to become one of the most blessed places on the globe. The winters are milder than the Atlantic states of the same parallel of latitude, and the weather is more agreeable; so that were the virtues of the inhabitants only equal to the blessings of the Lord which He permits to crown the industry of those inhabitants, there would be a measure of the good things of life for the benefit of the Saints, full, pressed down, and running over, even an hundred-fold. The disadvantages here, as in all new countries, are self-evident: lack of mills and schools; together with the natural privations and inconveniences which the hand of industry, the refinement of society, and the polish of science, overcome.

But all these impediments vanish when it is recollected what the prophets have said concerning Zion in the last days; how the glory of Lebanon is to come upon her, the fir tree, the pine tree, and the box tree together, to beautify the place of His sanctuary, that He may make the place of His feet glorious. Where for brass, He will bring gold; and for the iron, He will bring silver; and for wood, brass; and for stones, iron; and where the feast of fat things will be given to the just; yea, when the splendor of the Lord is brought to our consideration for the good of His people, the calculations of men and the vain glory of the world vanish, and we exclaim, "Out of Zion the perfection of beauty, God hath shined."

On the third day of August, I proceeded to dedicate the spot for the temple, a little west of Independence, and there were also present Sidney Rigdon, Edward Partridge, W. W. Phelps, Oliver Cowdery, Martin Harris and Joseph Coe.

The scene was solemn and impressive.

On the 4th, I attended the first conference in the land of Zion. It was held at the house of Brother Joshua Lewis, in Kaw township, in the presence of the Colesville branch of the Church. The Spirit of the Lord was there.

On the 7th, I attended the funeral of Sister Polly Knight, the wife of Joseph Knight, Sen. This was the first death in the Church in this land, and I can say, a worthy member sleeps in Jesus till the resurrection.

I also received the following:

See Doctrine and Covenants 59–60.

On the 9th, in company with ten elders, I left Independence landing for Kirtland. We started down the river in canoes and went the first day as far as Fort Osage, where we had an excellent wild turkey for supper. Nothing very important occurred till the third day, when many of the dangers so common upon the western waters manifested themselves; and after we had encamped upon the bank of the river, at McIlwaine's Bend, Brother Phelps, in open vision by daylight, saw the destroyer in his most horrible power ride upon the face of the waters; others heard the noise, but saw not the vision.

The next morning after prayer, I received the following:

See Doctrine and Covenants 61.

On the 13th (August) I met several of the elders on their way to the land of Zion, and after the joyful salutations with which brethren meet each other, who are actually "contending for the faith once delivered to the Saints," I received the following:

See Doctrine and Covenants 62.

After this meeting with the elders, Sidney Rigdon, Oliver Cowdery, and myself continued our journey by land to St. Louis, where we overtook Brothers Phelps and Gilbert. From this place we took stage, and they went by water to Kirtland, where we arrived safe and well on the 27th (August). Many things transpired upon this journey to strengthen our faith, and which displayed the goodness of God in such a marvelous manner, that we could not help beholding the exertions of Satan to blind the eyes of the people, so as to hide the true light that lights every man that comes into the world.

In these infant days of the Church, there was a great anxiety to obtain the word of the Lord upon every subject that in any way concerned our salvation; and as the land of Zion was now the most important temporal object in view, I inquired of the Lord for further information upon the gathering of the Saints, and the purchase of the land, and other matters, and received the following:

See Doctrine and Covenants 63.

The early part of September was spent in making preparations to remove to the town of Hiram, and renew our work on the translation of the Bible. The brethren who were commanded to go up to Zion were earnestly engaged in getting ready to start in the coming October. On the 11th of September I received the following:

See Doctrine and Covenants 64.

On the 12th of September, I removed with my family to the township of Hiram, and commenced living with John Johnson. Hiram was in Portage county, and about thirty miles southeasterly from Kirtland. From this time until the forepart of October, I did little more than prepare to re-commence the translation of the Bible.

About this time Ezra Booth came out as an apostate. He came into the Church upon seeing a person healed of an infirmity of many years standing. He had been a Methodist priest for some time previous to his embracing the fulness of the gospel, as developed in the Book of Mormon; and upon his admission into the Church he was ordained an Elder. As will be seen by the foregoing revelations, he went up to Missouri as a companion of Elder Morley; but when he actually learned that faith, humility, patience, and tribulation go before blessing, and that God brings low before He exalts; that instead of the "Savior's granting him power to smite men and make them believe," (as he said he wanted God to do in his own case)—when he found he must become all things to all men, that he might peradventure save some; and that, too, by all diligence, by perils by sea and land, as was the case in the days of Jesus—then he was disappointed. In the 6th chapter of St. John's Gospel, 26th verse, it is written: "Verily, verily, I say unto you, Ye seek me, not because ye saw the miracles, but because ye did eat of the loaves, and were filled." So it was with Booth; and when he was disappointed by his own evil heart, he turned away, and, as said before, became an apostate, and wrote a series of letters, which, by their coloring, falsity, and vain calculations to overthrow the work of the Lord, exposed his weakness, wickedness, and folly, and left him a monument of his own shame, for the world to wonder at.

My time was occupied closely in reviewing the commandments and sitting in conference, for nearly two weeks; for from the first to the twelfth of November we held four special conferences. In the last which was held at Brother Johnson's, in Hiram, after deliberate consideration, in consequence of the book of revelations, now to be printed, being the foundation of the Church in these last days, and a benefit to the world, showing that the keys of the mysteries of the kingdom of our Savior are again entrusted to man; and the riches of eternity within the compass of those who are willing to live by every word that proceedeth out of the mouth of God—therefore the conference voted that they prize the revelations to be worth to the Church the riches of the whole earth, speaking temporally. The great benefits to the world which result from the Book of Mormon and the revelations which the Lord has seen fit in His infinite wisdom to grant unto us for our salvation, and for the salvation of all that will believe, were duly appreciated; and in answer to an inquiry, I received the following:

See Doctrine and Covenants 70.

After Oliver Cowdery and John Whitmer had departed for Jackson county, Missouri, I resumed the translation of the scriptures, and continued to labor in this branch of my calling with Elder Sidney Rigdon as my scribe, until I received the following:

See Doctrine and Covenants 71.

Knowing now the mind of the Lord, that the time had come that the gospel should be proclaimed in power and demonstration to the world, from the scriptures, reasoning with men as in days of old, I took a journey to Kirtland, in company with Elder Sidney Rigdon on the 3rd day of December, to fulfill the above revelation. On the 4th, several of the elders and members assembled together to learn their duty, and for edification, and after some time had been spent in conversing about our temporal and spiritual welfare, I received the following:

See Doctrine and Covenants 72.

Chapter Four

1832

From this time until the 8th or 10th of January, 1832, myself and Elder Rigdon continued to preach in Shalersville, Ravenna, and other places, setting forth the truth: vindicating the cause of our Redeemer; showing that the day of vengeance was coming upon this generation like a thief in the night; that prejudice, blindness and darkness filled the minds of many, and caused them to persecute the true Church, and reject the true light; by which means we did much towards allaying the excited feelings which were growing out of the scandalous letters then being published in the *Ohio Star*, at Ravenna, by the before-mentioned apostate, Ezra Booth. On the 10th of January, I received the following revelation making known the will of the Lord concerning the elders of the Church until the convening of the next conference.

See Doctrine and Covenants 73.

Upon the reception of the foregoing word of the Lord, I recommenced the translation of the scriptures, and labored diligently until just before the conference, which was to convene on the 25th of January. During this period, I also received the following, as an explanation of the First Epistle to the Corinthians, 7th chapter, 14th verse:

See Doctrine and Covenants 74.

A few days before the conference was to commence in Amherst, Lorain county, I started with the elders that lived in my own vicinity, and arrived in good time. At this conference much harmony prevailed, and considerable business was done to advance the kingdom, and promulgate the gospel to the inhabitants of the surrounding country. The elders seemed anxious for me to inquire of the Lord that they might know His will, or learn what would be most pleasing to Him for them to do, in order to bring men to a sense of their condition; for, as it was written, all men have gone out of the way, so that none doeth good, no, not one. I inquired and received the following:

See Doctrine and Covenants 75.

Upon my return from Amherst conference, I resumed the translation of the scriptures. From sundry revelations which had been received, it was apparent that many important points touching the salvation of man had been taken from the Bible, or lost before it was compiled. It appeared self-evident, from what truths were left, that if God rewarded every one according to the deeds done in the body, the term "Heaven," as intended for the Saints' eternal home, must include more kingdoms than one. Accordingly, on the 16th of February, 1832, while translating St. John's Gospel, myself and Elder Rigdon saw the following vision:

See Doctrine and Covenants 76.

Nothing could be more pleasing to the Saints upon the order of the kingdom of the Lord than the light which burst upon the world through the foregoing vision. Every law, every commandment, every promise, every truth, and every point touching the destiny of man, from Genesis to Revelation, where the purity of the scriptures remains unsullied by the folly of men, go to show the perfection of the theory (of different degrees of glory in the future life) and witnesses the fact that that document is a transcript from the records of the eternal world. The sublimity of the ideas; the purity of the language; the scope for action; the continued duration for completion, in order that the heirs of salvation may confess the Lord and bow the knee; the rewards for faithfulness, and the punishments for sins, are so much beyond the narrow-mindedness of men that every honest man is constrained to exclaim: "It came from God."

I received a letter from the brethren who went up to the land of Zion, stating that they had arrived at Independence, Missouri, in good health and spirits, with a printing press and a store of goods. Agreeable to the instructions of the fall conference, they also sent me the prospectus of a monthly paper, *The Evening and Morning Star.*

According to previous intentions, we now began to make preparations to visit the brethren who had removed to the land of Missouri. Before going to Hiram to live with Father Johnson, my wife had taken two children (twins), of John Murdock's, to rear. She received them when only nine days old; they were now nearly eleven months. I would remark that nothing important had occurred since I came to reside in Father Johnson's house in Hiram, except that I had held meetings on the Sabbaths and evenings, and baptized a number.

Father Johnson's son, Olmsted Johnson, about this time came home on a visit, during which I told him if he did not obey the gospel, the spirit he was of would lead him to destruction, and when he went away, he would never return or see his father again. He went to the Southern States and Mexico; on his return he took sick and died in Virginia.

In addition to the apostate Ezra Booth, Simonds Ryder, Eli Johnson, Edward Johnson and John Johnson, Jun., had apostatized.

On the 24th of March, the twins before mentioned, which had been sick of the measles for some time, caused us to be broken of our rest in taking care of them, especially my wife. In the evening I told her she had better retire to rest with one of the children, and I would watch with the sicker child. In the night she told me I had better lie down on the trundle bed, and I did so, and was soon after awakened by her screaming murder, when I found myself going out of the door, in the hands of about a dozen men; some of whose hands were in my hair, and some had hold of my shirt, drawers and limbs. The foot of the trundle bed was towards the door, leaving only room enough for the door to swing open. My wife heard a gentle tapping on the windows which she then took no particular notice of (but which was unquestionably designed for ascertaining whether or not we were all asleep), and soon after the mob burst open the door and surrounded the bed in an instant, and, as I said, the first I knew I was going out of the door in the hands of an infuriated mob. I made a desperate struggle, as I was forced out, to extricate myself, but only cleared one leg, with which I made a pass at one man, and he fell on the door steps. I was immediately overpowered again; and they swore by G——, they would kill me if I did not be still, which quieted me. As they passed around the house with me, the fellow that I kicked came to me and thrust his hand, all covered with blood, into my face and with an exulting hoarse laugh, muttered: "Ge, gee, G——d—— ye, I'll fix ye."

They then seized me by the throat and held on till I lost my breath. After I came to, as they passed along with me, about thirty rods from the house, I saw Elder Rigdon stretched out on the ground, whither they had dragged him by his heels. I supposed he was dead. I began to plead with them, saying, "You will have mercy and spare my life, I hope." To which they replied, "G——d—— ye, call on yer God for help, we'll show ye no mercy;" and the people began to show themselves in every direction; one coming from the orchard had a plank; and I expected they would kill me, and carry me off on the plank. They then turned to the right, and went on about thirty rods further; about sixty rods from the house, and thirty from where I saw Elder Rigdon, into the meadow, where they stopped, and one said, "Simonds, Simonds," (meaning, I supposed, Simonds Ryder,) "pull up his drawers, pull up his drawers, he will take cold." Another replied: "Ain't ye going to kill 'im? Ain't ye going to kill 'im?" when a group of mobbers collected a little way off, and said: "Simonds, Simonds, come here;" and "Simonds" charged those who had hold of me to keep me from touching the ground (as they had done all the time), lest I should get a spring upon them. They held a council, and as I could occasionally overhear a word, I supposed it was to know whether or not it was best to kill me. They returned after a while, when I learned that they had concluded not to kill me, but to beat and scratch me well, tear off my shirt and drawers, and leave me naked. One cried, "Simonds, Simonds, where's the tar bucket?" "I don't know," answered one, "where 'tis, Eli's left it." They ran back and fetched the bucket of tar, when one exclaimed, with an oath, "Let us tar up his mouth;" and they tried to force the tar paddle into my mouth; I twisted my head around, so that they could not; and they cried out, "G——d—— ye, hold up yer head and let us give ye some tar." They then tried to force a vial into my mouth, and broke it in my teeth. All my clothes were torn off me except my shirt collar; and one man fell on me and scratched my body with his nails like a mad cat, and then muttered out: "G——d—— ye, that's the way the Holy Ghost falls on folks!"

They then left me, and I attempted to rise, but fell again; I pulled the tar away from my lips, so that I could breathe more freely, and after a while I began to recover, and raised myself up, whereupon I saw two lights. I made my way towards one of them, and found it was Father Johnson's. When I came to the door I was naked, and the tar made me look as if I were covered with blood, and when my wife saw me she thought I was all crushed to pieces, and fainted. During the affray abroad, the sisters of the neighborhood had collected at my room. I called for a blanket, they threw me one and shut the door; I wrapped it around me and went in.

In the meantime, Brother John Poorman heard an outcry across the corn field, and running that way met Father Johnson, who had been fastened in his house at the commencement of the assault by having his door barred by the mob, but on calling to his wife to bring his gun, saying he would blow a hole through the door, the mob fled, and Father Johnson, seizing a club, ran after the party that had Elder Rigdon, and knocked down one man, and raised his club to level another, exclaiming, "What are you doing here?" when they left Elder Rigdon and turned upon Father Johnson, who, turning to run toward his own house, met Brother Poorman coming out of the corn field; each supposing the other to be a mobber, an encounter ensued, and Poorman gave Johnson a severe blow on the left shoulder with a stick or stone, which brought him to the ground. Poorman ran immediately towards Father Johnson's, and arriving while I was waiting for the blanket, exclaimed, "I'm afraid I've killed him." "Killed who?" asked one; when Poorman hastily related the circumstances of the encounter near the corn field, and went into the shed and hid himself. Father Johnson soon recovered so as to come to the house, when the whole mystery was quickly solved concerning the difficulty between him and Poorman, who, on learning the facts, joyfully came from his hiding place.

My friends spent the night in scraping and removing the tar, and washing and cleansing my body, so that by morning I was ready to be clothed again. This being the Sabbath morning, the people assembled for meeting at the usual hour of worship, and among them came also the mobbers, viz., Simonds Ryder; a Campbellite preacher and leader of the mob; one McClentic, who had his hands in my hair; one Streeter, son of a Campbellite minister; and Felatiah Allen, Esq., who gave the mob a barrel of whiskey to raise their spirits. Besides these named, there were many others in the mob. With my flesh all scarified and defaced, I preached to the congregation as usual, and in the afternoon of the same day baptized three individuals.

The next morning I went to see Elder Rigdon, and found him crazy, and his head highly inflamed, for they had dragged him by his heels, and those, too, so high from the ground that he could not raise his head from the rough, frozen surface, which lacerated it exceedingly; and when he saw me he called to his wife to bring him his razor. She asked him what he wanted of it; and he replied, to kill me. Sister Rigdon left the room, and he asked me to bring his razor; I asked him what he wanted of it, and he replied he wanted to kill his wife; and he continued delirious some days. The feathers which were used with the tar on this occasion, the mob took out of Elder Rigdon's house. After they had seized him, and dragged him out, one of the banditti returned to get some pillows, when the women shut him in and kept him a prisoner some time.

During the mobbing, one of the twins contracted a severe cold, continued to grow worse until Friday, and then died. The mobbers were composed of various religious parties, but mostly Campbellites, Methodists, and Baptists, who continued to molest and menace Father Johnson's house for a long time. Elder Rigdon removed to Kirtland with his family—then sick with the measles—the following Wednesday; and, on account of the mob, he went to Chardon on Saturday, March 31st.

April first, I started for Missouri, in company with Newel K. Whitney, Peter Whitmer, and Jesse Gause, to fulfill the revelation. Not wishing to go by Kirtland, as another mob existed in that neighborhood (and indeed, the spirit of mobocracy was very prevalent through that whole region of country at the time), brother George Pitkin took us in his wagon by the most expeditious route to Warren, where we arrived the same day and were there joined by Elder Rigdon, who left Chardon in the morning; and proceeding onward, we arrived at Wellsville the next day, and the day following at Steubenville, where we left the wagon; and on Wednesday, the 4th of April, we took passage on board a steam packet for Wheeling, Virginia, where we purchased a lot of paper for the press in Zion, then in care of W. W. Phelps.

After we left Hiram, fearing for the safety of my family, on account of the mob, I wrote to my wife (in connection with Bishop Whitney) suggesting that she go to Kirtland and tarry with Brother Whitney's family until our return. From Wheeling we took passage on board the steamer *Trenton*. While at the dock, during the night, the boat was twice on fire burning the whole width of the boat through into the cabin, but with so little damage that the boat went on in the morning; and when we arrived at Cincinnati, some of the mob which had followed us, left us, and we arrived at Louisville the same night. Captain Brittle offered us protection on board of his boat, and gave us supper and breakfast gratuitously. At Louisville we were joined by Elder Titus Billings, who was journeying with a company of Saints from Kirtland to Zion, and we took passage on the steamer *Charleston* for St. Louis, where we parted from Brother Billings and company, and by stage arrived at Independence, Missouri, on the twenty-fourth of April, having traveled a distance of about three hundred miles from St. Louis. We found the brethren in Zion, generally enjoying health and faith; and they were extremely glad to welcome us among them.

On the 26th, I called a general council of the Church, and was acknowledged as the president of the high priesthood, according to a previous ordination at a conference of high priests, elders, and members, held at Amherst, Ohio, on the 25th of January, 1832. The right hand of fellowship was given to me by the bishop, Edward Partridge, in behalf of the Church. The scene was solemn, impressive, and delightful. During the intermission, a difficulty or hardness which had existed between Bishop Partridge and Elder Rigdon, was amicably settled, and when we came together in the afternoon, all hearts seemed to rejoice and I received the following:

See Doctrine and Covenants 82.

On the 27th, we transacted considerable business for the salvation of the Saints, who were settling among a ferocious set of mobbers, like lambs among wolves. It was my endeavor to so organize the Church that the brethren might eventually be independent of every incumbrance beneath the celestial kingdom, by bonds and covenants of mutual friendship, and mutual love.

On the 28th and 29th, I visited the brethren above Big Blue river, in Kaw township, a few miles west of Independence, and received a welcome only known by brethren and sisters united as one in the same faith, and by the same baptism, and supported by the same Lord. The Colesville branch, in particular, rejoiced as the ancient Saints did with Paul. It is good to rejoice with the people of God. On the 30th, I returned to Independence, and again sat in council with the brethren, and received the following:

See Doctrine and Covenants 83.

Our council was continued on the 1st of May, when it was ordered that three thousand copies of the Book of Commandments be printed in the first edition; that William W. Phelps, Oliver Cowdery, and John Whitmer be appointed to review and prepare such revelations for the press as shall be deemed proper for publication, and print them as soon as possible at Independence, Missouri; the announcement to be made that they are "Published by W. W. Phelps & Co." It was also ordered that W. W. Phelps correct and print the hymns which had been selected by Emma Smith in fulfillment of the revelation.

Arrangements were also made for supplying the Saints with stores in Missouri and Ohio, which action, with a few exceptions, was hailed with joy by the brethren. Before we left Independence, Elder Rigdon preached two powerful discourses, which, so far as outward appearance was concerned, gave great satisfaction to the people.

On the 6th day of May, I gave the parting hand to the brethren in Independence, and, in company with Brothers Rigdon and Whitney, commenced a return to Kirtland, by stage to St. Louis,

"HE LAID HIS
HANDS ON ME
AND
ADMINISTERED
TO ME IN THE NAME
OF THE LORD,
AND I WAS
HEALED
IN AN INSTANT."

from thence to Vincennes, Indiana; and from thence to New Albany, near the falls of the Ohio river. Before we arrived at the latter place, the horses became frightened, and while going at full speed, Bishop Whitney attempted to jump out of the coach, but having his coat fast, caught his foot in the wheel, and had his leg and foot broken in several places; at the same time I jumped out unhurt. We put up at Mr. Porter's public house, in Greenville, for four weeks, while Elder Rigdon went directly forward to Kirtland. During all this time, Brother Whitney lost not a meal of victuals or a night's sleep, and Dr. Porter, our landlord's brother, who attended him, said it was a pity we had not got some "Mormon" there, as they could set broken bones or do anything else. I tarried with Brother Whitney and administered to him till he was able to be moved. While at this place, I frequently walked out in the woods, where I saw several fresh graves; and one day when I rose from the dinner table, I walked directly to the door and commenced vomiting most profusely. I raised large quantities of blood and poisonous matter, and so great were the muscular contortions of my system, that my jaw in a few moments was dislocated. This I succeeded in replacing with my own hands, and made my way to Brother Whitney (who was on the bed), as speedily as possible; he laid his hands on me and administered to me in the name of the Lord, and I was healed in an instant, although the effect of the poison was so powerful, as to cause much of the hair to become loosened from my head. Thanks be to my Heavenly Father for His interference in my behalf at this critical moment, in the name of Jesus Christ. Amen.

Brother Whitney had not had his foot moved from the bed for nearly four weeks, when I went into his room, after a walk in the grove, and told him if he would agree to start for home in the morning, we would take a wagon to the river, about four miles, and there would be a ferry boat in waiting which would take us quickly across, where we would find a hack which would take us directly to the landing, where we should find a boat, in waiting, and we would be going up the river before ten o'clock, and have a prosperous journey home. He took courage and told me he would go. We started next morning, and found everything as I had told him, for we were passing rapidly up the river before ten o'clock, and, landing at Wellsville, took stage coach to Chardon, from thence in a wagon to Kirtland, where we arrived some time in June.

As soon as I could arrange my affairs, I recommenced the translation of the scriptures, and thus I spent most of the summer. In July, we received the first number of *The Evening and Morning Star*, which was a joyous treat to the Saints. Delightful, indeed, was it to contemplate that the little band of brethren had become so large, and grown so strong, in so short a time as to be able to issue a paper of their own, which contained not only some of the revelations, but other information also, which would gratify and enlighten the humble inquirer after truth.

So embittered was the public mind against the truth that the press universally had been arrayed against us; and although many newspapers published the prospectus of our paper, yet it appeared to have been done more to calumniate the editor than give publicity to the forthcoming periodical. Editors thought to do us harm, while the Saints rejoiced that they could do nothing against the truth but for it.

The elders during the month of September began to return from their missions to the Eastern States, and present the histories of their several stewardships in the Lord's vineyard; and while together in these seasons of joy, I inquired of the Lord, and received on the 22nd and 23rd of September, the following revelation on Priesthood:

See Doctrine and Covenants 84.

I continued the translation of the Bible and ministering to the Church through the fall, excepting a hurried journey to Albany, New York, and Boston, in company with Bishop Whitney, from which I returned on the 6th of November; immediately after the birth of my son Joseph Smith, the third.

About the 8th of November I received a visit from Elders Joseph Young, Brigham Young, and Heber C. Kimball of Mendon, Monroe county, New York. They spent four or five days at Kirtland, during which we had many interesting moments. At one of our interviews, Brothers Brigham Young and John P. Greene spoke in tongues, which was the first time I had heard this gift among the brethren; others also spoke, and I received the gift myself.

Appearances of troubles among the nations became more visible this season than they had previously been since the Church began her journey out of the wilderness. The ravages of the cholera were frightful in almost all the large cities on the globe. The plague broke out in India, while the United States, amid all her pomp and greatness, was threatened with immediate dissolution. The people of South Carolina, in convention assembled (in November), passed ordinances, declaring their state a free and independent nation; and appointed Thursday, the 31st day of January, 1833, as a day of humiliation and prayer, to implore Almighty God to vouchsafe His blessings, and restore liberty and happiness within their borders. President Jackson issued his proclamation against this rebellion, called out a force sufficient to quell it, and implored the blessings of God to assist the nation to extricate itself from the horrors of the approaching and solemn crisis.

On Christmas day (1832), I received the following revelation and prophecy on war.

See Doctrine and Covenants 87.

Two days after the preceding prophecy, on the 27th of December, I received the following:

See Doctrine and Covenants 88.

Chapter Five

1833

This winter (1832–33) was spent in translating the scriptures; in the School of the Prophets; and sitting in conferences. I had many glorious seasons of refreshing. The gifts which follow them that believe and obey the gospel, as tokens that the Lord is ever the same in His dealings with the humble lovers and followers of truth, began to be poured out among us as in ancient days—for as we were assembled in conference, on the 22nd day of January, I spoke to the conference in another tongue, and was followed in the same gift by Brother Zebedee Coltrin, and he by Brother William Smith, after which the Lord poured out His Spirit in a miraculous manner, until all the elders spake in tongues, and several members, both male and female, exercised the same gift. Great and glorious were the divine manifestations of the Holy Spirit. Praises were sung to God and the Lamb; speaking and praying, all in tongues, occupied the conference until a late hour at night, so rejoiced were we at the return of these long absent blessings.

On the 23rd of January, we again assembled in conference; when, after much speaking, singing, praying, and praising God, all in tongues, we proceeded to the washing of feet (according to the practice recorded in the 13th chapter of John's Gospel), as commanded of the Lord. Each Elder washed his own feet first, after which I girded myself with a towel and washed the feet of all of them, wiping them with the towel with which I was girded. Among the number, my father presented himself, but before I washed his feet, I asked of him a father's blessing, which he granted by laying his hands upon my head, in the name of Jesus Christ, and declaring that I should continue in the Priest's office until Christ comes. At the close of the scene, Brother Frederick G. Williams, being moved upon by the Holy Ghost, washed my feet in token of his fixed determination to be with me in suffering, or in journeying, in life or in death, and to be continually on my right hand; in which I accepted him in the name of the Lord.

I then said to the elders, "As I have done so do ye; wash ye, therefore, one another's feet;" and by the power of the Holy Ghost I pronounced them all clean from the blood of this generation; but if any of them should sin wilfully after they were thus cleansed, and sealed up unto eternal life, they should be given over unto the buffetings of Satan until the day of redemption. Having continued all day in fasting, and prayer, and ordinances, we closed by partaking of the Lord's Supper. I blessed the bread and wine in the name of the Lord, when we all ate and drank, and were filled; then we sang a hymn, and the meeting adjourned.

I completed the translation and review of the New Testament, on the 2nd of February, 1833, and sealed it up, no more to be opened till it arrived in Zion.

In the month of April, the first regular mob rushed together, in Independence, to consult upon a plan for the removal, or immediate destruction, of the Church in Jackson county. The number of the mob was about three hundred. A few of the first elders met in secret, and prayed to Him who said to the wind, "Be still," to frustrate them in their wicked designs. The mob, therefore, after spending the day in a fruitless endeavor to unite upon a general scheme for "moving the Mormons out of their diggings" (as they asserted), became a little the worse for liquor and broke up in a regular Missouri "row," showing a determined resolution that every man would "carry his own head."

May 25—My uncle John Smith and family arrived in Kirtland, from Potsdam, New York, my uncle being an Elder in the Church; and his wife and eldest son, George Albert Smith, a lad of fifteen, were members. They were the first of my father's relatives who obeyed the gospel.

June 1—Great preparations were making to commence a house of the Lord; and notwithstanding the Church was poor, yet our unity, harmony, and charity abounded to strengthen us to do the commandments of God. The building of the house of the Lord in Kirtland was a matter that continued to increase in its interest in the hearts of the brethren.

June 5—George A. Smith hauled the first load of stone for the temple, and Hyrum Smith and Reynolds Cahoon commenced digging the trench for the walls of the Lord's house, and finished the same with their own hands.

July, which once dawned upon the virtue and independence of the United States, now dawned upon the savage barbarity and mobocracy of Missouri. Most of the clergy acting as missionaries to the Indians, or to the frontier inhabitants, were among the most prominent characters that rose up and rushed on to destroy the rights of the Church, as well as the lives of her members. One Reverend Pixley, who had been sent by the Missionary Society to civilize and Christianize the heathen of the West, was a black rod in the hands of Satan, as well as a poisoned shaft in the hands of our other foes. He wrote horrible falsehoods about the Saints which he sent to the religious papers in the East, from time to time, in order to sour the public mind against them; and used his influence among both Indians and whites to overthrow the Church in Jackson county. On the first of July, he wrote a slanderous tract entitled, "Beware of False Prophets," which he carried from house to house, to incense the inhabitants against the Church, to mob them, and drive them away. The July number of *The Evening and Morning Star*, pursued a mild and pacific course; the first article therein, entitled, "Beware of False Prophets," was calculated to disabuse the honest public mind from Pixley's falsehoods; and the caution against "Free People of Color," settling in Missouri, was sufficient to silence the fears of every sober mind, yet, it was all in vain; the hour of trial must come; notwithstanding the constitution of Missouri.

On the 20th of July, the mob collected and demanded the discontinuance of the Church printing establishment in Jackson county, the closing of the store, and the cessation of all mechanical labors. The brethren refused compliance, and the consequence was that the house of W. W. Phelps, which contained the printing establishment, was thrown down, the materials taken possession of by the mob, many papers destroyed, and the family and furniture thrown out of doors.

The mob then proceeded to violence towards Edward Partridge, the bishop of the Church.

Charles Allen was next stripped and tarred and feathered, because he would not agree to leave the country, or deny the Book of Mormon. Others were brought up to be served likewise or whipped.

But from some cause the mob ceased operations, and adjourned until Tuesday, the 23rd. Elder Sidney Gilbert, the keeper of the store, agreed to close it; and that may have been one reason why the work of destruction was suddenly stopped for two days.

In the course of this day's wicked, outrageous, and unlawful proceedings, many solemn realities of human degradation, as well as thrilling incidents, were presented to the Saints. An armed and well organized mob, in a government professing to be governed by law, with the Lieutenant Governor (Lilburn W. Boggs), the second officer in the state, calmly looking on, and secretly aiding every movement, saying to the Saints, "You now know what our Jackson boys can do, and you must leave the country;" and all the justices, judges, constables, sheriffs, and military officers, headed by such western missionaries and clergymen as the Reverends McCoy, Kavanaugh, Hunter, Fitzhugh, Pixley, Likens, and Lovelady, consisting of Methodists, Baptists, Presbyterians, and all the different sects of religionists that inhabited that country, with that great moral reformer, and register of the land office at Lexington, forty miles east, known as the head and father of the Cumberland Presbyterians, even the Reverend Finis Ewing, publicly publishing that "Mormons were the common enemies of mankind, and ought to be destroyed"—all these solemn realities were enough to melt the heart of a savage; while there was not a solitary offense on record, or proof, that a Saint had broken the law of the land.

When Bishop Partridge, who was without guile, and Elder Charles Allen, walked off, coated like some unnamed, unknown bipeds, one of the sisters cried aloud: "While you, who have done this wicked deed, must suffer the vengeance of God, they, having endured persecution, can rejoice, for henceforth for them, is laid up a crown eternal in the heavens."

Surely this was a time for awful reflection; man, unrestrained, like the brute beast, may torment the body; but God will punish the soul!

After the mob had retired, and while evening was spreading her dark mantle over the scene, as if to hide it from the gaze of day, men, women, and children, who had been driven or frightened from their homes, by yells and threats, began to return from their hiding places in thickets, corn fields, woods, and groves, and view with heavy hearts the scene of desolation and wo; and while they mourned over fallen man, they rejoiced with joy unspeakable that they were accounted worthy to suffer in the glorious cause of their Divine Master. There lay the printing office a heap of ruins; Elder Phelps' furniture strewed over the garden as common plunder; the revelations, book works, papers, and press in the hands of the mob, as the booty of highway robbers; there was Bishop Partridge, in the midst of his family, with a few friends, endeavoring to scrape off the tar which, from its eating his flesh, seemed to have been prepared with lime, pearl-ash, acid, or some flesh-eating substance, to destroy him; and there was Charles Allen in the same awful condition. The heart sickens at the recital, how much more at the picture! More than once, those people, in this boasted land of liberty, were brought into jeopardy, and threatened with expulsion or death, because they desired to worship God according to the revelations of heaven, the constitution of their country, and the dictates of their own consciences. Oh, liberty, how art thou fallen! Alas, clergymen, where is your charity!

Early in the morning of the 23rd of July, the mob again assembled, armed with weapons of war, and bearing a red flag; whereupon the elders, led by the Spirit of God, and in order to save time, and stop the effusion of blood, entered into a treaty with the mob, to leave the county within a certain time.

The declaration of the mob, by which they pledged to each other their lives, their bodily powers, fortunes, and sacred honors to remove the Church from Jackson county, is a very good climax for all the arguments used, falsehoods set forth, and even a full interpretation of the sublime admission that "vengeance belongs to God alone." The events that followed from this time till November explain the modus operandi much more clearly than the publication in the *Monitor*, or other papers that generally were so willing to give the western missionaries, the doctors, lawyers, judges, justices, sheriffs, constables, military officers and other distinguished personages a fair chance against the Mormons.

On the same day (July 23rd), while the brethren in Missouri were preparing to leave the county, through the violence of the mob, the corner stones of the Lord's house were laid in Kirtland, after the order of the Holy Priesthood.

October 5—I started on a journey to the east, and to Canada, in company with Elders Rigdon and Freeman Nickerson, and arrived the same day at Lamb's tavern, in Ashtabula; and the day following, the Sabbath, we arrived in Springfield, whilst the brethren

"THE MOB AGAIN ASSEMBLED, ARMED WITH WEAPONS OF WAR, AND BEARING A RED FLAG."

were in meeting, and Elder Rigdon spoke to the congregation. A large and attentive congregation assembled at Brother Rudd's in the evening, to whom we bore our testimony. We continued at Springfield until the 8th of October, when we removed to Brother Roundy's at Elk creek; and continuing our journey on the evening of the 9th, we arrived at a tavern, and on the 10th, at Brother Job Lewis' in Westfield, where we met the brethren according to previous appointment, and spoke to them as the Spirit gave utterance, greatly to their gratification.

At this time the evil and designing circulated a report that Zion was to be extended as far east as Ohio, which in some degree tended to distract the minds of the Saints, and produced a momentary indecision about removing thither, according to the commandments; but the report was soon corrected, and the brethren continued to remove to Zion and Kirtland.

On the 11th of October, we left Westfield, and continuing our journey, stayed that night with a man named Nash, an infidel, with whom we reasoned, but to no purpose. On the 12th, we arrived at Father Nickerson's, at Perrysburg, New York, where I received the following revelation:

See Doctrine and Covenants 100.

On the day following (October 13th), Elder Rigdon preached to a large congregation, at Freeman Nickerson's, and I bore record while the Lord gave His Spirit in a remarkable manner.

Monday, 14—Continued our journey towards Canada, and arrived at Lodi, where we had an appointment, and preached in the evening to a small assembly, and made an appointment for Tuesday, the 15th, at 10 o'clock a.m., to be in the Presbyterian meeting house. When the hour arrived, the keeper of the house refused to open the doors, and the meeting was thus prevented. We came immediately away, leaving the people in great confusion, and continued our journey till Friday, the 18th, when we arrived at the house of Freeman A. Nickerson, in Upper Canada, having passed through a fine and well-cultivated country, after entering the province, and having had many peculiar feelings in relation to both the country and people. We were kindly received by Freeman A. Nickerson, who lived at Mount Pleasant, which was near Brantford, the county seat of Brant county.

Sunday, 20—At 10 o'clock we met an attentive congregation at Brantford; and the same evening a large assembly at Mount Pleasant, at Mr. Nickerson's. The people gave good heed to the things spoken.

Tuesday, 22—We went to the village of Colburn; and although it snowed severely, we held a meeting by candlelight on Wednesday evening, and were publicly opposed by a Wesleyan Methodist. He was very tumultuous, but exhibited a great lack of reason, knowledge, and wisdom, and gave us no opportunity to reply.

Thursday, 24—At the house of Mr. Beman, in Colburn, whence we left for Waterford, where we spoke to a small congregation; thence to Mount Pleasant, and preached to a large congregation the same evening, when Freeman A. Nickerson and his wife declared their belief in the work, and offered themselves for baptism. Great excitement prevailed in every place we visited.

Saturday, 26—Preached at Mount Pleasant; the people were very tender and inquiring.

Sunday, 27—Preached to a large congregation at Mount Pleasant, after which I baptized twelve, and others were deeply impressed, and desired another meeting, which I appointed for the day following.

Monday, 28—In the evening, we broke bread, and laid on hands for the gift of the Holy Ghost, and for confirmation, having baptized two more. The Spirit was given in great power to some, and peace to others.

Tuesday, 29—After preaching at 10 o'clock a.m., I baptized two, and confirmed them at the water's side. Last evening we ordained F. A. Nickerson an Elder; and one of the sisters received the gift of tongues, which made the Saints rejoice exceedingly. Tuesday, the

29th of October, also we took our departure from Mount Pleasant, on our return to Kirtland, and arrived at Buffalo, New York, on the 31st.

Friday, November 1—I left Buffalo, New York, at 8 o'clock a.m., and arrived at my house in Kirtland on Monday, the 4th, 10 a.m. and found my family well, according to the promise of the Lord in the revelation of October 12th, for which I felt to thank my Heavenly Father.

Thursday night, the 31st of October, gave the Saints in Zion abundant proof that no pledge on the part of their enemies, written or verbal, was longer to be regarded; for on that night, between forty and fifty persons in number, many of whom were armed with guns, proceeded against a branch of the Church, west of the Big Blue, and unroofed and partly demolished ten dwelling houses; and amid the shrieks and screams of the women and children, whipped and beat in a savage and brutal manner several of the men, while their horrid threats frightened women and children into the wilderness. Such of the men as could escape fled for their lives, for very few of them had arms, neither were they organized; and they were threatened with death if they made any resistance; such therefore as could not escape by flight received a pelting with stones and a beating with guns and whips. On Friday, the first of November, women and children sallied forth from their gloomy retreats, to contemplate with heartrending anguish the ravages of a ruthless mob, in the lacerated and bruised bodies of their husbands, and in the destruction of their houses and their furniture. Houseless and unprotected by the arm of the civil law in Jackson county, the dreary month of November staring them in the face and loudly proclaiming an inclement season at hand; the continual threats of the mob that they would drive every "Mormon" from the county; and the inability of many to move, because of their poverty, caused an anguish of heart indescribable.

On Friday night, the 1st of November, a party of the mob proceeded to attack a branch of the Church settled on the prairie, about twelve or fourteen miles from the town of Independence. Two of their number were sent in advance, as spies, viz., Robert Johnson, and —— Harris, armed with two guns and three pistols. They were discovered by some of the Saints, and without the least injury being done to them, said mobber Robert Johnson struck Parley P. Pratt over the head with the breech of his gun, after which they were taken and detained till morning, which action, it was believed, prevented a general attack of the mob that night. In the morning the two prisoners, notwithstanding their attack upon Parley P. Pratt the evening previous, were liberated without receiving the least injury.

The same night (Friday), another party in Independence commenced stoning houses, breaking down doors and windows, and destroying furniture. This night the brick part attached to the dwelling house of A. S. Gilbert was partly pulled down, and the windows of his dwelling broken in with brickbats and rocks, while a gentleman, a stranger, lay sick with fever in his house. The same night three doors of the store of Messrs. Gilbert & Whitney were split open, and after midnight the goods, such as calicos, handkerchiefs, shawls, cambrics, lay scattered in the streets. An express came from Independence after midnight to a party of the brethren who had organized about half a mile from the town for the safety of their lives, and brought the information that the mob were tearing down houses, and scattering goods of the store in the streets. Upon receiving this information, the company of brethren referred to marched into Independence, but the main body of the mob fled at their approach. One Richard McCarty, however, was caught in the act of throwing rocks and brickbats into the doors, while the goods lay scattered around him in the streets. He was immediately taken before Samuel Weston, Esq., justice of the peace, and complaint was then made to said Weston, and a warrant requested, that McCarty might be secured; but Weston refused to do anything in the case at that time, and McCarty was liberated.

The same night some of the houses of the Saints in Independence had long poles thrust through the shutters and sash into the rooms of defenseless women and children, from whence their husbands and fathers had been driven by the dastardly attacks of the mob, which were made by ten, fifteen, or twenty men upon a house at a time. Saturday, the 2nd of November, all the families of the Saints in Independence moved with their goods about half a mile out of town and organized to the number of thirty, for the preservation of life and personal effects. The same night a party from Independence met a party from west of the Blue, and made an attack upon a branch of the Church located at the Blue, about six miles from the village of Independence. Here they tore the roof from one dwelling and broke open another house; they found the owner, David Bennett, sick in bed, and beat him most inhumanly, swearing they would blowout his brains. They discharged a pistol at him, and the ball cut a deep gash across the top of his head. In this skirmish, a young man of the mob was shot in the thigh; but by which party the shot was fired is not known.

The next day, Sunday, November 3rd, four of the brethren, viz., Joshua Lewis, Hiram Page, and two others, were dispatched for Lexington to see the circuit judge, and obtain a peace warrant. Two other brethren called on Esquire Silvers, in Independence, and asked him for a peace warrant, but he refused to issue one on account, as he afterwards declared, of his fears of the mob. This day many of the citizens, professing friendship, advised the Saints to leave the county as speedily as possible; for the Saturday night affray had enraged the whole county, and the people were determined to come out on Monday and massacre indiscriminately; and, in short, it was commonly declared among the mob, that "Monday would be a bloody day."

Monday came, and a large party of the mob gathered at the Blue, took the ferry boat belonging to the Church, threatened lives, etc. But they soon abandoned the ferry, and went to Wilson's store, about one mile west of the Blue. Word had been previously sent to a branch of the Church, several miles west of the Blue, that the mob were destroying property on the east side of the river, and the sufferers there wanted help to preserve lives and property. Nineteen men volunteered, and started to their assistance; but discovering that fifty or sixty of the mob had gathered at said Wilson's they turned back. At this time two small boys passed on their way to Wilson's who gave information to the mob that the "Mormons" were on the road west of them. Between forty and fifty of the mob, armed with guns, immediately started on horseback and on foot in pursuit; after riding about two or two and a half miles, they discovered them, when the said company of nineteen brethren immediately dispersed, and fled in different directions. The mob hunted them, turning their horses meantime into a corn field belonging to the Saints. Corn fields and houses were searched, the mob at the same time threatening women and children that they would pull down their houses and kill them if they did not tell where the men had fled. Thus they were employed in hunting the men and threatening the women, when a company of thirty of the brethren from the prairie, armed with seventeen guns, made their appearance.

The former company of nineteen had dispersed, and fled, and but one or two of them returned in time to take part in the subsequent battle. On the approach of the latter company of thirty men, some of the mob cried, "Fire, G——d—— ye, fire." Two or three guns were then fired by the mob, which fire was returned by the other party without loss of time. This company is the same that is represented by the mob as having gone forth in the evening of the above incident bearing the olive branch of peace. The mob retreated immediately after the first fire, leaving some of their horses in Whitmer's corn field, and two of their number, Hugh L. Brazeale and Thomas Linvill dead on the ground. Thus fell Hugh L. Brazeale, who had been heard to say, "With ten fellows, I will wade to my knees in blood, but that I will drive the 'Mormons' from Jackson county." The next morning the corpse of Brazeale was discovered on the battle ground with a gun by his side. Several were wounded on both sides, but none mortally among the brethren except Andrew Barber, who expired the next day. This attack of the mob was made about sunset, Monday, November the 4th; and the same night, runners were dispatched in every direction under pretense of calling out the militia; spreading every rumor calculated to alarm and excite the uninformed as they went; such as that the "Mormons" had taken Independence, and that the Indians had surrounded it, the "Mormons" and Indians being colleagued together.

The same evening, November 4th—not being satisfied with breaking open the store of Gilbert & Whitney, and demolishing a part of the dwelling house of said Gilbert the Friday night previous—the mob permitted the said McCarty, who was detected on Friday night as one of the breakers of the store doors, to take out a warrant, and arrest the said Gilbert and others of the Church, for a pretended assault, and false imprisonment of said McCarty. Late in the evening, while the court was proceeding with their trial in the court house, a gentleman unconnected with the court, as was believed, perceiving the prisoners to be without counsel and in imminent danger, advised Brother Gilbert and his brethren to go to jail as the only alternative to save life; for the north door of the court house was already barred, and an infuriated mob thronged the house with a determination to beat and kill; but through the interposition of this gentleman (Samuel C. Owens, clerk of the county court, so it was afterwards learned), said Gilbert and four of his brethren were committed to the county jail of Jackson county, the dungeon of which must have been a palace compared with a court room where dignity and mercy were strangers, and naught but the wrath of man as manifested in horrid threats shocked the ears of the prisoners.

The same night, the prisoners, Gilbert, Morley, and Corrill, were liberated from the jail that they might have an interview with their brethren, and try to negotiate some measures for peace; and on their return to jail about 2 o'clock, Tuesday morning, in the custody of the deputy sheriff, an armed force of six or seven men stood near the jail and hailed them. They were answered by the sheriff, who gave his name and the names of the prisoners, crying, "Don't fire, don't fire, the prisoners are in my charge." They, however, fired one or two guns, when Morley and Corrill retreated; but Gilbert stood, firmly held by the sheriff, while several guns were presented at him. Two, more desperate than the rest, attempted to shoot, but one of their guns flashed, and the other missed fire. Gilbert was then knocked down by Thomas Wilson, who was a grocer living at Independence. About this time a few of the inhabitants of the town arrived, and Gilbert again entered the jail, from which he, with three of his brethren, were liberated about sunrise, without further prosecution of the trial. William E. M'Lellin was one of the prisoners.

On the morning of the 5th of November, Independence began to be crowded with individuals from different parts of the county armed with guns and other weapons; and report said the militia had been called out under the sanction or at the instigation of Lieutenant Governor Boggs; and that one Colonel Pitcher had the command. Among this militia (so-called) were included the most conspicuous characters of the mob; and it may truly be said that the appearance of the ranks of this body was well calculated to excite suspicion of their horrible designs.

Very early on the same morning, several branches of the Church received intelligence that a number of their brethren were in prison, and the determination of the mob was to kill them; and that the branch of the Church near the town of Independence was in imminent danger, as the main body of the mob was gathered at that place. In this critical situation, about one hundred of the Saints, from different branches, volunteered for the protection of their brethren near Independence, and proceeded on the road towards Independence, and halted about one mile west of the town, where they awaited further information concerning the movements of the mob. They soon learned that the prisoners were not massacred, and that the mob had not fallen upon the branch

"THE SAINTS WOULD
HAVE CHEERFULLY
SHED THEIR
BLOOD IN
DEFENSE OF
THEIR RIGHTS,
THE LIBERTIES OF
THEIR COUNTRY
AND OF THEIR
WIVES AND
CHILDREN."

of the Church near Independence, as had been reported. They were also informed that the militia had been called out for their protection; but in this they placed little confidence, for the body congregated had every appearance of a mob; and subsequent events fully verified their suspicions.

On application to Colonel Pitcher, it was found that there was no alternative but for the Church to leave the county forthwith, and deliver into his hands certain men to be tried for murder, said to have been committed by them in the battle, as he called it, of the previous evening. The arms of the Saints were also demanded by Colonel Pitcher. Among the committee appointed to receive the arms of the brethren were several of the most unrelenting of the old July mob committee, who had directed in the demolishing of the printing office, and the personal injuries inflicted on brethren that day, viz., Henry Chiles, Abner Staples, and Lewis Franklin, who had not ceased to pursue the Saints, from the first to the last, with feelings the most hostile.

These unexpected requisitions of the Colonel, made him appear like one standing at the head of both civil and military law, stretching his authority beyond the constitutional limits that regulate both civil and military power in our Republic. Rather than to have submitted to these unreasonable requirements, the Saints would have cheerfully shed their blood in defense of their rights, the liberties of their country and of their wives and children; but the fear of violating law, in resisting this pretended militia, and the flattering assurance of protection and honorable usage promised by Lieutenant Governor Boggs, in whom, up to this time, they had reposed confidence, induced the Saints to submit, believing that he did not tolerate so gross a violation of all law as had been practiced in Jackson county. But as so glaringly exposed in the sequel, it was the design and craft of this man to rob an innocent people of their arms by stratagem, and leave more than one thousand defenseless men, women and children to be driven from their homes among strangers in a strange land to seek shelter from the stormy blast of winter. All earth and hell cannot deny that a baser knave, a greater traitor, and a more wholesale butcher, or murderer of mankind ever went untried, unpunished, and unhung—since hanging is the popular method of execution among the Gentiles in all countries professing Christianity, instead of blood for blood, according to the law of heaven. The conduct of Colonels Lucas and Pitcher had long proven them to be open and avowed enemies of the Saints. Both of these men had their names attached to the mob circular, as early as the July previous, the object of which was to drive the Saints from Jackson county. But with assurances from the Lieutenant Governor and others that the object was to disarm the combatants on both sides, and that peace would be the result, the brethren surrendered their arms to the number of fifty or upwards.

The men present, who were accused of being in the battle the evening before, also gave themselves up for trial; but after detaining them one day and a night on a pretended trial for murder, in which time they were threatened and brick-batted, Colonel Pitcher, after receiving a watch of one of the prisoners to satisfy "costs of court," took them into a corn field, and said to them, "Clear!" (Meaning, of course, clear out, leave.)

After the Saints had surrendered their arms, which had been used only in self-defense, the tribes of Indians in time of war let loose upon women and children could not have appeared more hideous and terrific than did the companies of ruffians who went in various directions, well-armed, on foot and on horseback, bursting into houses without fear—knowing the arms were secured—frightening distracted women with what they would do to their husbands if they could catch them, warning women and children to flee immediately or they would tear their houses down over their heads and massacre them before night. At the head of these companies appeared the Reverend Isaac McCoy, with a gun upon his shoulder, ordering the Saints to leave the country forthwith, and surrender what arms they had. Other pretended preachers of the gospel took a conspicious part in the persecution, calling the

"Mormons" the "common enemy of mankind," and exulting in their afflictions.

On Tuesday and Wednesday nights, the 5th and 6th of November, women and children fled in every direction before the merciless mob. One party of about one hundred and fifty women and children fled to the prairie, where they wandered for several days with only about six men to protect them. Other parties fled to the Missouri river, and took lodging for the night where they could find it. One Mr. Barnet opened his house for a night's shelter to a wandering company of distressed women and children, who were fleeing to the river. During this dispersion of the women and children, parties of the mob were hunting the men, firing upon some, tying up and whipping others, and pursuing others with horses for several miles.

Thursday, November 7th, the shores of the Missouri river began to be lined on both sides of the ferry, with men, women, and children; goods, wagons, boxes, chests, and provisions; while the ferrymen were busily employed in crossing them over. When night again closed upon the Saints, the wilderness had much the appearance of a camp meeting. Hundreds of people were seen in every direction, some in tents, and some in the open air around their fires, while the rain descended in torrents. Husbands were inquiring for their wives, and women for their husbands; parents for children, and children for parents. Some had the good fortune to escape with their families, household goods, and some provisions; while others knew not the fate of their friends, and had lost all their effects. The scene was indescribable, and would have melted the hearts of any people upon earth, except the blind oppressor, and the prejudiced and ignorant bigot. Next day the company increased, and they were chiefly engaged in felling small cottonwood trees, and erecting them into temporary cabins, so that when night came on, they had the appearance of a village of wigwams, and the night being clear, the occupants began to enjoy some degree of comfort.

Lieutenant Governor Boggs has been represented as merely a curious and disinterested observer of these events; yet he was evidently the head and front of the mob; for as may easily be seen by what follows, no important move was made without his sanction. He certainly was the secret mover in the affairs of the 20th and 23rd of July; and, as will appear in the sequel, by his authority the mob was converted into militia, to effect by stratagem what he knew, as well as his hellish host, could not be done by legal force. As Lieutenant Governor, he had only to wink, and the mob went from maltreatment to murder. The horrible calculations of this second Nero were often developed in a way that could not be mistaken. Early on the morning of the 5th, say at 1 o'clock a.m., he came to Phelps, Gilbert, and Partridge, and told them to flee for their lives. Now, unless he had given the order to murder, no one would have attempted it, after the Church had agreed to go away. His conscience, however, seemed to vacillate at its moorings, and led him to give the secret alarm to these men.

The Saints who fled from Jackson county, took refuge in the neighboring counties, chiefly in Clay county, the inhabitants of which received them with some degree of kindness. Those who fled to the county of Van Buren were again driven and compelled to flee, and these who fled to Lafayette county were soon expelled, or the most of them, and had to move wherever they could find protection.

November 13—About 4 o'clock a.m. I was awakened by Brother Davis knocking at my door, and calling on me to arise and behold the signs in the heavens. I arose, and to my great joy, beheld the stars fall from heaven like a shower of hailstones; a literal fulfillment of the word of God, as recorded in the holy scriptures, and a sure sign that the coming of Christ is close at hand. In the midst of this shower of fire, I was led to exclaim, "How marvelous are Thy works, O Lord! I thank Thee for Thy mercy unto Thy servant; save me in Thy kingdom for Christ's sake. Amen."

The appearance of these signs varied in different sections of the country: in Zion, all heaven seemed enwrapped in splendid fireworks, as if every star in the broad expanse had been suddenly hurled from its course, and sent lawless through the wilds of ether. Some at times appeared like bright shooting meteors, with long trains of light following in their course, and in numbers resembled large drops of rain in sunshine. These seemed to vanish when they fell behind the trees, or came near the ground. Some of the long trains of light following the meteoric stars were visible for some seconds; these streaks would curl and twist up like serpents writhing. The appearance was beautiful, grand, and sublime beyond description; and it seemed as if the artillery and fireworks of eternity were set in motion to enchant and entertain the Saints, and terrify and awe the sinners of the earth. Beautiful and terrific as was the scenery, it will not fully compare with the time when the sun shall become black like sack-cloth of hair, the moon like blood, and the stars fall to the earth. —Rev. 6:13.

Nothing of note occurred from the falling of the stars on the 13th, to this date, November 19th, when my heart is somewhat sorrowful, but I feel to trust in the Lord, the God of Jacob. I have learned in my travels that man is treacherous and selfish, but few excepted.

Brother Sidney is a man whom I love, but he is not capable of that pure and steadfast love for those who are his benefactors that should characterize a president of the Church of Christ. This, with some other little things, such as selfishness and independence of mind, which too often manifested destroy the confidence of those who would lay down their lives for him—these are his faults. But notwithstanding these things, he is a very great and good man; a man of great power of words, and can gain the friendship of his hearers very quickly. He is a man whom God will uphold, if he will continue faithful to his calling. O God, grant that he may, for the Lord's sake. Amen.

And again, blessed be Brother Sidney: notwithstanding he shall be high and lifted up, yet he shall bow down under the yoke like unto an ass that croucheth beneath his burthen, that learneth his master's will by the stroke of the rod; thus saith the Lord: yet, the Lord will have mercy on him, and he shall bring forth much fruit, even as the vine of the choice grape, when her clusters are ripe, before the time of the gleaning of the vintage; and the Lord shall make his heart merry as with sweet wine, because of Him who putteth forth His hand, and lifteth him up out of deep mire, and pointeth him out the way, and guideth his feet when he stumbles, and humbleth him in his pride. Blessed are his generations; nevertheless one shall hunt after them as a man hunteth after an ass that has strayed in the wilderness, and straightway findeth him and bringeth him into the fold. Thus shall the Lord watch over his generation, that they may be saved. Even so, Amen.

The man who willeth to do well, we should extol his virtues, and speak not of his faults behind his back. A man who willfully turneth away from his friend without a cause, is not easily forgiven. The kindness of a man should never be forgotten. That person who never forsaketh his trust should ever have the highest place of regard in our hearts, and our love should never fail, but increase more and more, and this is my disposition and these my sentiments.

Brother Frederick G. Williams is one of those men in whom I place the greatest confidence and trust, for I have found him ever full of love and brotherly kindness. He is not a man of many words, but is ever winning, because of his constant mind. He shall ever have place in my heart, and is ever entitled to my confidence. He is perfectly honest and upright, and seeks with all his heart to magnify his presidency in the Church of Christ, but fails in many instances, in consequence of a want of confidence in himself. God grant that he may overcome all evil. Blessed be Brother Frederick, for he shall never want a friend, and his generation after him shall flourish. The Lord hath appointed him an inheritance upon the land of Zion: yea, and his head shall blossom, and he shall be as an olive branch that is bowed down with fruit. Even so. Amen.

Those who were threatened by the mob on Sunday, the 24th, fled into Clay county, and encamped on the banks of the Missouri river. A number of the families went into Van Buren county; their whole number of men, women, and children, being upwards of one hundred and fifty.

About the 1st of December, Elder Cowdery and Bishop Whitney arrived at Kirtland with a new press and type, and on the 4th commenced distributing the type.

December 12—An express arrived at Liberty, from Van Buren county, with information that those families, which had fled from Jackson county and located there, were about to be driven from that county, after building their houses and carting their winter's store of provisions, grain, etc., forty or fifty miles. Several families are already fleeing from thence. The contaminating influence of the Jackson county mob is predominant in this new county of Van Buren, the whole population of which is estimated at about thirty or forty families. The destruction of crops, household furniture, and clothing is very great, and much of their stock is lost. The main body of the Church is now in Clay county, where the people are as kind and accommodating as could reasonably be expected. The continued threats of deaths to individuals of the Church, if they make their appearance in Jackson county, prevent the most of them, even at this day, from returning to that county, to secure personal property, which they were obliged to leave in their flight.

December 18—The elders assembled in the printing office, and bowed down before the Lord, and I dedicated the printing press, and all that pertained thereunto, to God, which dedication was confirmed by Elder Rigdon, and my brother, Hyrum Smith. We then proceeded to take the first proof sheet of the reprinted Star, edited by Elder Oliver Cowdery.

Blessed of the Lord is Brother Oliver, nevertheless there are two evils in him that he must needs forsake, or he cannot altogether escape the buffetings of the adversary. If he forsake these evils he shall be forgiven, and shall be made like unto the bow which the Lord hath set in the heavens; he shall be a sign and an ensign unto the nations. Behold, he is blessed of the Lord for his constancy and steadfastness in the work of the Lord; wherefore, he shall be blessed in his generation, and they shall never be cut off, and he shall be helped out of many troubles; and if he keep the commandments, and hearken unto the counsel of the Lord, his rest shall be glorious.

And again, blessed of the Lord is my father, and also my mother, and my brothers and my sisters; for they shall yet find redemption in the house of the Lord, and their offspring shall be a blessing, a joy, and a comfort unto them.

Blessed is my mother, for her soul is ever filled with benevolence and philanthropy; and notwithstanding her age, yet she shall receive strength, and shall be comforted in the midst of her house, and she shall have eternal life.

And blessed is my father, for the hand of the Lord shall be over him, for he shall see the affliction of his children pass away; and when his head is fully ripe, he shall behold himself as an olive tree, whose branches are bowed down with much fruit; he shall also possess a mansion on high.

Blessed of the Lord is my brother Hyrum, for the integrity of his heart; he shall be girt about with truth, and faithfulness shall be the strength of his loins: from generation to generation he shall be a shaft in the hands of his God to execute judgment upon his enemies; and he shall be hid by the hand of the Lord, that none of his secret parts shall be discovered unto his hurt; his name shall be accounted a blessing among men; and when he is in trouble, and great tribulation hath come upon him, he shall remember the God of Jacob; and He will shield him from the power of Satan; and he shall receive counsel in the house of the Most High, that he may be strengthened in hope, that the goings of his feet may be established for ever.

Blessed of the Lord is my brother Samuel, because the Lord shall say unto him, Samuel, Samuel; therefore he shall be made a teacher in the house of the Lord, and the Lord shall mature his mind in judgment, and thereby he shall obtain the esteem and fellowship of his brethren, and his soul shall be established and he shall benefit the house of the Lord, because he shall obtain answer to prayer in his faithfulness.

Brother William is as the fierce lion, which divideth not the spoil because of his strength; and in the pride of his heart he will neglect the more weighty matters until his soul is bowed down in sorrow; and then he shall return and call on the name of his God, and shall find forgiveness, and shall wax valiant, therefore, he shall be saved unto the uttermost; and as the roaring lion of the forest in the midst of his prey, so shall the hand of his generation be lifted up against those who are set on high, that fight against the God of Israel; fearless and undaunted shall they be in battle, in avenging the wrongs of the innocent, and relieving the oppressed; therefore, the blessings of the God of Jacob shall be in the midst of his house, notwithstanding his rebellious heart.

And now, O God, let the residue of my father's house ever come up in remembrance before Thee, that Thou mayest save them from the hand of the oppressor, and establish their feet upon the rock of ages, that they may have place in Thy house, and be saved in Thy kingdom; and let all things be even as I have said, for Christ's sake. Amen.

Monday night, the 24th of December, four aged families, living near the town of Independence, whose penury and infirmities, incidents to old age, forbade a speedy removal, were driven from their homes by a party of the mob, who tore down their chimneys, broke in their doors and windows, and hurled large stones into their houses, by which the life of old Mr. Miller, in particular, was greatly endangered. Mr. Miller is aged sixty-five years, and the youngest man in the four families. Some of these men have toiled and bled in the defense of their country; and old Mr. Jones, one of the sufferers, served as life guard to General George Washington, in the Revolution. Well may the soldier of "Seventy-six" contemplate with horror the scenes which surround him at this day in Jackson county, where liberty, law, and equal rights are trodden under foot. It is now apparent that no man embracing the faith of the Latter-day Saints, whatever be his age or former standing in society, may hope to escape the wrath of the Jackson county mob whenever it is in their power to inflict abuse.

A court of inquiry was held at Liberty, Clay county, Missouri, the latter part of this month, to inquire into the conduct of Colonel Pitcher, for driving the Saints, or "Mormons," from Jackson county, which resulted in his arrest for further trial by a court-martial.

The mob in Jackson county sold the materials, or rather gave Messrs. Davis and Kelly leave to take *The Evening and Morning Star* establishment to Liberty, Clay county, where they commenced the publication of *The Missouri Enquirer*, a weekly paper.

Chapter Six

1834

Monday, March 31—This day, Ira J. Willis, a young man who had been in the Church for some time, and who was driven from Jackson county into Clay county, returned thither to look for a stray cow, and while at the house of Esquire Manship, a justice of the peace (where he had called with Brother John Follet, to prove his title to the cow), was caught by that unhung land pirate and inhuman monster, Moses Wilson, and whipped in a most cruel and savage manner, while surrounded by some half dozen of the old mobbers. This was an unpardonable act; all that know Mr. Willis can bear testimony that he is a young man, honest, peaceable and unoffending, working righteousness, and molesting no one. May God reward Moses Wilson according to his works.

Thursday, April 17—I attended a meeting agreeable to appointment, at which time the important subjects of the deliverance of Zion and the building of the Lord's house in Kirtland were discussed by Elder Rigdon. After the lecture, I requested the brethren and sisters to contribute all the money they could for the deliverance of Zion; and received twenty-nine dollars and sixty-eight cents.

About the last of April I received, by letters from friends in the East, and of brethren in Kirtland, the sum of two hundred and fifty-one dollars and sixty cents, towards the deliverance of Zion.

May 1—More than twenty of the brethren left Kirtland for Missouri, according to previous appointment, accompanied by four baggage wagons. They traveled to New Portage, and there tarried with the church until the remainder of the Kirtland company, who were not in readiness to start with them, arrived.

May 5—Having gathered and prepared clothing and other necessaries to carry to our brethren and sisters, who had been robbed and plundered of nearly all their effects; and having provided for ourselves horses, and wagons, and firearms, and all sorts of munitions of war of the most portable kind for self-defense—as our enemies are thick on every hand—I started with the remainder of the company from Kirtland for Missouri. This day we went as far as the town of Streetsborough, twenty-seven miles from Kirtland. We stayed in Mr. Ford's barn, where Uncle John Smith and Brigham Young had been preaching three months before. This day Brothers Brigham and Joseph Young went to Israel Barlow's, about three-quarters of a mile, and tarried over night. Brother Barlow returned with them in the morning and joined the camp. Brother Brigham Young had taken the families of Solomon Angel and Lorenzo Booth into his house, that they might accompany us to Missouri.

On the 6th we arrived at New Portage, about fifty miles distance from Kirtland, and joined our brethren who had gone before.

My company from Kirtland consisted of about one hundred men, mostly young men, and nearly all elders, priests, teachers or deacons. As our wagons were nearly filled with baggage, we had mostly to travel on foot.

On the 7th we made preparations for traveling, gathered all the moneys of every individual of the company, and appointed Frederick G. Williams paymaster to disburse the funds thus collected; and Zerubbabel Snow was chosen commissary general. The whole company now consisted of more than one hundred and thirty men, accompanied by twenty baggage wagons. We left but few men in Kirtland, viz., Elders Sidney Rigdon, Oliver Cowdery, a few working on the temple, and the aged.

Through the remainder of this day I continued to organize the company, appoint such other officers as were required, and gave such instructions as were necessary for the discipline, order, comfort and safety of all concerned. I also divided the whole band into companies of twelve, leaving each company to elect its own captain, who assigned each man in his respective company his post and duty, generally in the following order: two cooks, two firemen, two tent men, two watermen, one runner, two wagoners and horsemen, and one commissary. We purchased flour and meal, baked our own bread, and cooked our own food, generally, which was good, though sometimes scanty; and sometimes we had johnny-cake, or corndodger, instead of flour bread. Every night before retiring to rest, at the sound of the trumpet, we bowed before the Lord in the several tents, and presented our thank-offerings with prayer and supplication; and at the sound of the morning trumpet, about four o'clock, every man was again on his knees before the Lord, imploring His blessing for the day.

On the 8th we recommenced our march towards Zion, and pitched our tents for the night in a beautiful grove at Chippeway, twelve miles from New Portage.

On the morning of the 9th we completed our organization by companies and proceeded onward, and encamped near Wooster; and on Saturday the 10th, passing through Mansfield, encamped for the Sabbath in Richfield township. About one hour after we had encamped, Elders Lyman E. Johnson, Willard Snow and a number of others joined the camp from the north part of Vermont.

Sunday 11—Elder Sylvester Smith preached, and the company received the sacrament of bread and wine.

Here we were increased in number by eight brethren, in company of Elder Elias Benner, from Richland and Stark counties, most of whom were Germans.

Monday, May 12—We left Richfield, traveled about thirty-five miles, passed the Bucyrus, and encamped on the Sandusky plains, at a short distance from the place where the Indians roasted General Crawford, and near the Indian settlements.

On the 13th we passed through a long range of beech woods, where the roads were very bad. In many instances we had to fasten ropes to the wagons to haul them out of the sloughs and mud holes. Brother Parley P. Pratt broke his harness; the brethren fastened their ropes to his wagon, and drew it about three miles to the place of encampment on the Scioto river, while he rode singing and whistling.

Wednesday, May 14—We passed on to Belle Fontaine, where we discovered refractory feelings in Sylvester Smith, who expressed great dissatisfaction because we were short of bread, although we had used all diligence to procure a supply, and Captain Brigham Young had previously sent two men ahead to provide supplies for his company.

Thursday, May 15—We forded Mad river, and passing through a beautiful country, encamped a little west of Springfield. This night Moses Martin fell asleep on sentry duty, and I went and took his sword, and left him asleep.

Friday, May 16—About nine o'clock, while I was riding in a wagon with Brother Hyrum, Ezra Thayer and George A. Smith, we came into a piece of thick woods of recent growth, where I told them that I felt much depressed in spirit and lonesome, and that there had been a great deal of bloodshed in that place, remarking that whenever a man of God is in a place where many have been killed, he will feel lonesome and unpleasant, and his spirits will sink.

In about forty rods from where I made this observation we came through the woods, and saw a large farm, and there near the road on our left, was a mound sixty feet high, containing human bones. This mound was covered with apple trees, and surrounded with oat fields, the ground being level for some distance around.

At dinner time some of the brethren expressed considerable fear on account of milk sickness, with which the people were troubled along our route. Many were afraid to use milk or butter, and appealed to me to know if it was not dangerous. I told them to use all they could get, unless they were told it was "sick." Some expressed fears that it might be sold to us by our enemies for the purpose of doing us injury. I told them not to fear; that if they would follow my counsel, and use all they could get from friend or enemy, it should do them good, and none be sick in consequence of it; and although we passed through neighborhoods where many of the people and cattle were infected with the sickness, yet my words were fulfilled.

While passing through Dayton, Ohio, great curiosity was manifested, various reports of our numbers and designs having gone before us. Some of the inhabitants inquired of the company where they were from, when Captain Young replied: "From every place but this, and we will soon be from this." "Where are you going?" "To the West."

Some ten or a dozen gentlemen came over from Dayton to ascertain our numbers, which they reported to be at least six hundred. These gentlemen also inquired of almost every man in the camp where he was from and where he was going, and what was his business. They returned to Dayton and reported that every man in the company was a gentleman and gave a respectful answer to every question asked, but they could not ascertain where we were going, or what was our business.

This evening a court martial was held in the camp for the trial of Moses Martin for falling asleep while on picket duty. Brother Martin pleaded his own case, saying that he was overcome with fatigue and so overpowered that he could not keep awake, etc. I decided that he should be acquitted with a warning never to go to sleep again on watch, which was sanctioned by the court, and I took occasion from this circumstance to give the brethren much useful instruction.

We forded the Miami river with our baggage wagons, most of the men wading through the water. On the 17th of May we crossed the state line of Ohio, and encamped for the Sabbath just within the limits of Indiana, having traveled about forty miles that day. Our feet were very sore and blistered, our stockings wet with blood, the weather being very warm. At night a spy attempted to get into our camp, but was prevented by our guard. We had our sentinels posted every night, on account of spies who were continually striving to harass us, steal our horses, etc.

This evening there was a difficulty between some of the brethren and Sylvester Smith, on occasion of which I was called to decide in the matter. Finding a rebellious spirit in Sylvester Smith, and to some extent in others, I told them they would meet with misfortunes, difficulties, and hinderances, and said, "and you will know it before you leave this place," exhorting them to humble themselves before the Lord and become united, that they might not be scourged. A very singular occurrence took place that night and the next day, concerning our teams. On Sunday morning, when we arose, we found almost every horse in the camp so badly foundered that we could scarcely lead them a few rods to the water. The brethren then deeply realized the effects of discord. When I learned the fact, I exclaimed to the brethren that for a witness that God overruled and had His eye upon them, all those who would humble themselves before the Lord should know that the hand of God was in this misfortune, and their horses should be restored to health immediately; and by twelve o'clock the same day the horses were as nimble as ever, with the exception of one of Sylvester Smith's, which soon afterwards died.

Sunday, May 15—We had preaching as usual, and the administration of the sacrament.

About this time the Saints in Clay county, Missouri, established an armory, where they commenced manufacturing swords, dirks, pistols, stocking rifles, and repairing arms in general for their own defense against mob violence; many arms were purchased; for the leading men in Clay county rendered every facility in their power, in order, as they said, "to help the 'Mormons' settle their own difficulties, and pay the Jackson mob in their own way."

Monday, May, 19—We traveled thirty-one miles and encamped in Franklin township, Henry county, in the beech woods.

Tuesday, May 20—We encamped near Greenfield, having traveled about twenty-five miles, some part of the way being so bad I walked over the tops of my boots in mud, helping to pull through the wagons with ropes.

While we were eating dinner three gentlemen came riding up on very fine looking horses and commenced their inquiries of various ones concerning our traveling in so large a body, asking where we were from, and where we were going. The reply was as usual—some from the state of Maine; another would say, "I am from York state;" some from Massachusetts; some from Ohio; and some replied, "We are from the East, and as soon as we have done eating dinner we shall be going to the West again." They then addressed themselves to Dr. Frederick G. Williams to see if they could find out who the leader of the camp was. The doctor replied, "We have no one in particular." They asked if we had not a general to take the lead of the company. The reply was, "No one in particular." "But," said they, "is there not some one among you whom you call your captain, or leader, or who is superior to the rest?" He answered, "Sometimes one and sometimes another takes charge of the company, so as not to throw the burden upon anyone in particular." These spies, who had come from the west, passed us several times that same day and the next.

Although threatened by our enemies that we should not pass through Indianapolis, we passed through that city on the 21st unmolested. All the inhabitants were quiet. At night we encamped a few miles west of Indianapolis. There had previously been so many reports that we should never be permitted to pass through this place, and that the governor would have us dispersed, that some of the brethren were afraid that we might have difficulty there. But I had told them, in the name of the Lord, we should not be disturbed and that we would pass through Indianapolis without the people knowing it. When near the place, many got into the wagons, and, separating some little distance, passed through the city, while others walked down different streets, leaving the inhabitants wondering "when that big company would come along."

Since the 18th we had followed the national road where it was passable, but frequently we had to take by-roads, which were miry and led through thick woods.

Thursday, May 22—We encamped on a small stream of water in a grove near Belleville.

Friday, May 23—We encamped about four miles from Greencastle, after a hard drive.

Saturday, May 24—We crossed the Wabash river at Clinton in ferry boats, in quick time, and pushed on to the state line, where we arrived late in the evening, and encamped in an oak opening in Edgar county, Illinois.

Sunday, May 25—We had no meeting, but attended to washing, baking, and preparing to resume our journey. A man in disguise, having on an old sealskin cap, came into our camp. He swore we were going up to Jackson county, and that we would never get over the Mississippi river alive. It was evident he was a spy, and I recollected having seen him in Jackson county, Missouri.

Monday, May 26—A very hot day. We traveled through Paris and across a sixteen-mile prairie; at noon we stopped to bait at a slough, about six miles from the timber, having no water to drink but such as was filled with living animals commonly called wigglers, and as we did not like to swallow them, we strained the water before using it. This was the first prairie of any extent that we had come to on our journey, and was a great curiosity to many of the brethren. It was so very level that the deer miles off appeared but a short distance away; some of the brethren started out in pursuit before they were apprised of their mistake as to the distance. We continued our march, pulling our wagons through a small creek with ropes,

"WE FOUND A WELL OF WATER, WHICH WAS ONE OF THE GREATEST COMFORTS WE COULD HAVE RECEIVED, AS WE WERE ALMOST FAMISHED."

and came to the house of Mr. Wayne, the only settler in the vicinity, where we found a well of water, which was one of the greatest comforts we could have received, as we were almost famished, and it was a long time before we could, or dared to satisfy our thirst. We crossed the Embarras river and encamped on a small branch of the same about one mile west. In pitching my tent we found three massasaugas or prairie rattlesnakes, which the brethren were about to kill, but I said, "Let them alone—don't hurt them! How will the serpent ever lose his venom, while the servants of God possess the same disposition and continue to make war upon it? Men must become harmless, before the brute creation; and when men lose their vicious dispositions and cease to destroy the animal race, the lion and the lamb can dwell together, and the sucking child can play with the serpent in safety." The brethren took the serpents carefully on sticks and carried them across the creek. I exhorted the brethren not to kill a serpent, bird, or an animal of any kind during our journey unless it became necessary in order to preserve ourselves from hunger.

I had frequently spoken on this subject, when on a certain occasion I came up to the brethren who were watching a squirrel on a tree, and to prove them and to know if they would heed my counsel, I took one of their guns, shot the squirrel and passed on, leaving the squirrel on the ground. Brother Orson Hyde, who was just behind, picked up the squirrel, and said, "We will cook this, that nothing may be lost." I perceived that the brethren understood what I did it for, and in their practice gave more heed to my precept than to my example, which was right.

This evening Brother Parley P. Pratt and Amasa Lyman returned from the Eugene branch, Indiana (where I had sent them), with a company of about a dozen men.

The reports of mobs which were continually saluting our ears caused the brethren to be constantly alive to the subject, and about eleven o'clock this evening our picket guards reported that they saw the fires of the mob on the southeast of us. I instantly arose and discovered the mistake; but wishing the brethren to enjoy the scene as well as myself, immediately discharged my gun, which was a signal to call all men to arms. When the companies were all paraded and ready for battle, I pointed them to the reflection of the rising moon resting on points of timber in the east, which gave the appearance of the reflection of the light of a number of camp fires. The scenery was most delightful, and was well worth the trouble of any man rising from his couch to witness, who had never seen the like on the broad prairie before. This circumstance proved that nearly every man in the camp was ready for battle, except Dean Gould, who was not baptized, and Captain Jazeniah B. Smith, who was suddenly taken with the colic, and did not leave his tent. The whole incident was very amusing.

Tuesday, May 27—Notwithstanding our enemies were continually breathing threats of violence, we did not fear, neither did we hesitate to prosecute our journey, for God was with us, and His angels went before us, and the faith of our little band was unwavering. We know that angels were our companions, for we saw them.

We arrived at the Okaw branch of the Kaskaskia, where we found log canoes, which we lashed together, and ferried our baggage across the stream. We then swam our horses and wagons, and when we arrived at the opposite shore, the brethren fastened ropes to the wagon tongues and helped the teams out of the water and up the steep, miry banks. Some of the brethren felled a tall tree across the river, on which they passed over, and carried some of their baggage on their backs. While we were passing over, George A. Smith discovered a spring that with a little digging furnished us with an abundant supply of excellent water, which afterwards received the name of "the Mormon Spring." This afternoon, Elder Solomon Humphreys, an aged brother of the camp, having become exceedingly weary, lay down on the prairie to rest himself and fell asleep. When he awoke he saw, coiled up within one foot of his head, a rattlesnake lying between him and his hat, which he had in his hand when he fell asleep. The brethren gathered around him, saying, "It is a rattlesnake, let us kill it;" but Brother Humphreys said, "No, I'll protect him; you shan't hurt him, for he and I had a good nap together."

Wednesday, May 28—We passed on as usual, except suffering much from want of water and provisions, and arrived at Decatur township. We encamped on a small stream of water, and here one of Brother Tanner's horses died.

Thursday, May 29—Having to buy a horse, we were detained until near noon.

There was some murmuring among the brethren, many wishing to go on and not tarry with the rest of the company for the day, and some were already started. I sent for them to return and collected the whole company together, and instructed them not to scatter. I told them if they went ahead of the camp in a scattered condition they would become weary, lie down on the ground when their blood was heated, and they would be liable to take diseases, such as fever and ague, which are prevalent in this climate. They would also be in danger of being killed by an enemy, and none of us be the wiser for it.

I then proposed for a diversion that we divide the camp into three parts and have a sham battle, which was agreed to. Brother Roger Orton led one division, Frederick G. Williams another division, while I retired in the camp with the third division. They retired to the woods with their divisions, and soon attacked the camp, which we defended by various maneuvers for some time. Many of our captains showed considerable tact and more acquaintance with military matters than I had expected. Everything passed off with good feelings, although Captain Heber C. Kimball, in receiving a charge, grasped Captain Lewis Zobriski's sword, and in endeavoring to take it from him, had the skin cut from the palm of his hand. After the sham battle was over, I called the camp together and cautioned the men to be careful in the future and control their spirits in such circumstances so as never to injure each other.

We traveled across the prairie and encamped in a strip of timber. When we stopped to dine, I wrote a letter to the brethren in Missouri, dated "Camp of Israel," requesting some of them to meet us as soon as possible and give me information of the state of things in Upper Missouri, and sent the letter to Springfield post office by Dr. Frederick G. Williams.

At this place I discovered that a part of my company had been served with sour bread, while I had received good, sweet bread from the same cook. I reproved Brother Zebedee Coltrin for this partiality, for I wanted my brethren to fare as well as I did.

Friday, May 30—Frederick G. Williams and Almon W. Babbitt went ahead of the camp into Springfield in disguise, to learn the feeling of the people and procure some powder. We passed through Springfield; our appearance excited considerable curiosity, and a great many questions were asked. The spies who had followed us so long pursued us very closely, changing their dress and horses several times a day.

Brother Eleazer Miller with others joined the company with three horses about noon, a little east of Rochester. This reinforcement was very seasonable, as many of our horses were afflicted as they very frequently are in changing country, climate, and food. Many of the horses after eating the dry corn and prairie grass would be seized with colic and bloat very badly. Brother Ezra Thayre administered medicine mixed in a quart stone bottle, prepared as follows: A three penny paper of tobacco, half an ounce of copperas and two table spoons full of cayenne pepper, and the bottle filled with water when he could not procure whisky. One-half of a bottle constituted a dose, and would almost invariably cure a sick horse in a few minutes, and is worthy of remembrance. Brother Thayre called his medicine "18 by 24."

We encamped about three miles from Springfield on Spring creek. Frederick G. Williams and Almon W. Babbitt returned to the camp with two kegs of powder, and reported that the people were somewhat excited, more however from a curiosity to know where we were going than from a desire to hinder us. A brother came to see us with the news that my brother Hyrum had passed on west the day before with a company, about fifty miles north of us, saying, "He has a fine company, and they all look mighty pert." I asked him to accompany us to Missouri, but he replied, "I cannot." He went and stayed at a tavern over night with the spies, who said they followed us three hundred miles on purpose to take some advantage of us.

Saturday, May 31—In the morning this brother came to me and said: "I would be mighty glad to go with you, but my business is such I cannot. Will a hundred dollars do you any good?" I replied, "Yes, it will, for we are short of money." He immediately remounted his horse and rode to Springfield, and within an hour after the camp had started he returned and said to me: "I am mighty sorry I cannot go with you. Here is a hundred dollars, and if I had had a few days' notice I could have got more."

At noon we halted for dinner. A man, apparently drunk, came to the camp and said he had a large farm and forty cows a little way ahead, and if we would go there, he would give us all we wanted to eat and drink, feed our horses, etc. But I soon discovered that he was more sober than drunk, and that he was probably a spy.

Near night we arrived at a small stream of water about one mile from Jacksonville, where we found a pawpaw bush in the road, which had been dropped by Dr. Frederick G. Williams as a signal for us to camp. I had sent Dr. Williams forward in the morning on horseback to select a camp ground and watch the movements of our enemies. We pitched our tents in the place he had selected.

Agreeable to my instructions, about sunset Brother Roger Orton proclaimed aloud that there would be preaching under the trees within the camp at half-past ten o'clock on the morrow. There was only one stranger in the camp to hear the appointment. Dr. Williams had gone on to Jacksonville with his pill bags to spend the night.

Sunday, June 1—We had preaching, and many of the inhabitants of the town came to hear. Elder John Carter, who had formerly been a Baptist preacher, spoke in the morning, and was followed by four other elders in the course of the day, all of whom had formerly been preachers for different denominations. When the inhabitants heard these elders they appeared much interested, and were very desirous to know who we were, and we told them one had been a Baptist preacher, and one a Campbellite; one a Reformed Methodist, and another a Restorationer. During the day many questions were asked, but none could learn our names, professions, business, or destination; and, although they suspected we were "Mormons," they were very civil.

Our enemies had threatened that we should not cross the Illinois river, but on Monday the 2nd we were ferried over without any difficulty. The ferryman counted, and declared there were five hundred of us, yet our true number was only about one hundred and fifty. Our company had been increased since our departure from Kirtland by volunteers from different branches of the Church through which we had passed. We encamped on the bank of the river until Tuesday the 3rd.

During our travels we visited several of the mounds which had been thrown up by the ancient inhabitants of this country—Nephites, Lamanites, etc.—and this morning I went up on a high mound, near the river, accompanied by the brethren. From this mound we could overlook the tops of the trees and view the prairie on each side of the river as far as our vision could extend, and the scenery was truly delightful.

On the top of the mound were stones which presented the appearance of three altars having been erected one above the other, according to the ancient order; and the remains of bones were strewn over the surface of the ground. The brethren procured a shovel and a hoe, and removing the earth to the depth of about one foot, discovered the skeleton of a man, almost entire, and between his ribs the stone point of a Lamanitish arrow, which evidently produced his death. Elder Burr Riggs retained the arrow. The contemplation of the scenery around us produced peculiar sensations in our bosoms; and subsequently the visions of the past being opened to my understanding by the Spirit of the Almighty,

I discovered that the person whose skeleton was before us was a white Lamanite, a large, thick-set man, and a man of God. His name was Zelph. He was a warrior and chieftain under the great prophet Onandagus, who was known from the Hill Cumorah, or eastern sea to the Rocky mountains. The curse was taken from Zelph, or, at least, in part—one of his thigh bones was broken by a stone flung from a sling, while in battle, years before his death. He was killed in battle by the arrow found among his ribs, during the last great struggle of the Lamanites and Nephites.

While we were refreshing ourselves and teams about the middle of the day (June 3rd), I got up on a wagon wheel, called the people together, and said that I would deliver a prophecy. After giving the brethren much good advice, exhorting them to faithfulness and humility, I said the Lord had revealed to me that a scourge would come upon the camp in consequence of the fractious and unruly spirits that appeared among them, and they should die like sheep with the rot; still, if they would repent and humble themselves before the Lord, the scourge, in a great measure, might be turned away; but, as the Lord lives, the members of this camp will suffer for giving way to their unruly temper.

When we arrived at Atlas, I had a conversation with Colonel Ross, a wealthy gentleman of the neighborhood, who gave us a flattering account of the country, and wished to employ one hundred men, for which he proposed to make ready payment. He wanted brick makers, builders, etc.

Here our commissary purchased twenty-five gallons of honey at twenty-five cents per gallon, and a dozen Missouri cured hams, which proved to have been a little injured on the outside. There not being enough to supply one for every company, my company agreed to do without. Our supper consisted of mush and honey, as we had been unable to procure flour on account of the scarcity of mills. After the fatigues of the day it hardly satisfied hunger; but when we had finished, some six of the hams were brought to our tent door and thrown down in anger, the remark being, "We don't

"I DISCOVERED
THAT THE
PERSON WHOSE
SKELETON
WAS BEFORE US WAS
A WHITE
LAMANITE,
A LARGE,
THICK-SET MAN,
AND A
MAN OF GOD."

eat stinking meat." I called on Brother Zebedee Coltrin, our cook, and told him to be quick and fry some ham, as I had not had my hunger fairly allayed for forty-eight hours. He immediately commenced cooking the ham, and for once my company feasted to their full satisfaction.

We had just retired to rest when the picket guard announced Luke S. Johnson.

He came into our camp and made his report. He had visited a number of influential men, among the rest a Baptist minister, who expressed great anxiety that our company should be stopped, and went to a magistrate to inquire if there was not some law or pretext for stopping us. He, the priest, said to the magistrate, "That company march and have guns like an army. They pitch their tents by the side of the road; they set out guards, and let nobody pass into their camp in the night; and they are Mormons, and I believe they are going to kill the people up in Jackson county, Missouri, and retake their lands." The magistrate replied, "If you were traveling, and did not wish to put up at public houses, or there were none in the country, would you not camp by the road side in a tent? And if you were afraid that your horses and property would be stolen in a strange country, would you not watch and keep guards?" "Why, yes," said the priest; "but they are Mormons!" "Well, I can't hear but they mind their own business, and if you and this stranger (meaning Luke S. Johnson) will mind your own business, everything will be right." This Baptist priest treated Brother Luke S. Johnson with great politeness. He gave him his dinner, his wife washed his stockings; he gave him letters of introduction to men in Jackson county, and delivered to his charge some letters which he had received from Jackson county, which Brother Luke brought into the camp. He also stated that he had seen a man that morning who informed him that four hundred men were in readiness on the Missouri side, with ten hours' notice, to use up all the camp, and he was on his way to give them the notice.

A little before midnight we heard several guns fired to the west of us, which appeared to be answered by one directly east. There was no settlement west of us nearer than the state of Missouri. This appearing so much like a signal, in addition to the many threats of our being attacked on crossing the Mississippi, I considered sufficient cause of alarm to put out a double picket guard and put the camp in a state of defense, so that every man might be ready at a moment's notice. It however proved to be a false alarm.

Continuing our journey on the 4th, we encamped on the banks of the Mississippi river. At this place we were somewhat afflicted, and our enemies strongly threatened that we should not cross over into Missouri. The river being a mile and a half wide, and having but one ferry boat, it took two days for us to pass over. While some were ferrying, others were engaged in hunting, fishing, etc. As we arrived, we encamped on the bank, within the limits of Missouri.

While at this place, Sylvester Smith rebelled against the order of the company, and gave vent to his feelings against myself in particular. This was the first outbreak of importance which had occurred to mar our peace since we commenced our journey.

June 6—We resumed our journey, and on the evening of the 7th encamped in a piece of woods, near a spring of water, at Salt River. Here was a branch of the Church.

Sunday, June 8—We had preaching, and in the course of the day were joined by Brothers Hyrum Smith and Lyman Wight, with a company of volunteers which they had gathered in Michigan. The whole company now consisted of two hundred and five men, and twenty-five baggage wagons with two or three horses each. We remained at Salt River until the 12th, refreshing and reorganizing the camp, which reorganizing was done by electing Lyman Wight general of the camp. I chose twenty men for my life guards, of whom my Brother Hyrum was chosen captain, and George A. Smith was my armor bearer. The remainder of the company was organized according to the pattern at New Portage. While at Salt River, General Wight marched the camp on the prairie, inspected our firelocks, ordered a discharge of the same at targets by platoons, drilled us half a day, and returned to camp.

About this time I dispatched Elders Orson Hyde and Parley P. Pratt to Jefferson City with a message to Governor Dunklin, to ascertain if he was ready to fulfill the proposition which he had previously made to the brethren to reinstate them on their lands in Jackson county, and leave them there to defend themselves.

June 12—We left Salt River and traveled about fourteen miles. The inhabitants of Salt River manifested a great respect for us, and many of them accompanied us some distance on our journey. I instructed the camp in the morning that if a gun was fired it would be considered an alarm; but in the course of the day, while I was a little ahead, I shot a squirrel for Brother Foster, when several of the brethren came running up to see what was the matter. I told them Brother Foster was sick; "I want you to pray for him."

Friday, June 13—Elder Kimball's horses, through the negligence of the guards, got loose and went back ten miles with others. He pursued them and returned with them to camp. Frederick G. Williams and Roger Orton received a very severe chastisement for neglect of orders in not taking care of the teams when in charge of the guard. The reproof given to Roger Orton was more particularly for suffering Elder Kimball to go back after the horses, and he was one of my life guards, and it belonged to Orton to see that the team was attended to. But as the team was Kimball's, and he had taken the care of it all through, Orton still threw the care on him. The Silver Grey company, numbering fourteen, were attached to my mess, making it twenty-eight in number.

Saturday, June 14—Brother Joseph Hancock and another of the brethren were chased a considerable portion of the day by four suspicious fellows on horseback, armed with guns, whom they eluded by traveling in the brush and thickets where horsemen could not ride. It was late when they returned to the camp.

At night we encamped in an unsafe and unpleasant situation in a ravine, the only place we could get water for some miles. The country was a wild and uncultivated region.

Sunday, June 15—Traveled twelve miles. While on the way Orson Hyde and Parley P. Pratt returned to us from Jefferson City, and reported that Governor Dunklin refused to fulfill his promise to reinstate the brethren on their lands in Jackson county on the ground of impracticability.

We crossed the Chariton river at its mouth and encamped on the west bank.

Bishop Partridge came into the camp from Clay county. We received much information from him concerning the hostile feelings and prejudices that existed against us in Missouri in all quarters, but it gave us great satisfaction to receive intelligence from him of the union and good feeling that prevailed among the brethren. We were in perils and threatened all the while, we were much troubled to get provisions, and had to live principally on corn meal, and were glad to get that. Here Dean Gould was baptized by Lyman Wight.

Monday, June 16—Traveled to Grand river, ferried over it, and encamped on its bank. The ferryman intended charging seventeen dollars; the brethren said they would not pay it, but would sooner make a raft and ferry themselves over. He then agreed to take them over for twelve dollars which offer we accepted. This morning was excessively hot, no air stirring, and traveling in the thick woods, a thunder shower coming on, the brethren caught all the water they could on the brims of their hats, and not catching enough to satisfy their thirst, they drank out of the horse tracks.

Martin Harris having boasted to the brethren that he could handle snakes with perfect safety, while fooling with a black snake with his bare feet, he received a bite on his left foot. The fact was communicated to me, and I took occasion to reprove him, and exhort the brethren never to trifle with the promises of God. I told them it was presumption for anyone to provoke a serpent to bite him, but if a man of God was accidentally bitten by a poisonous serpent, he might have faith, or his brethren might have faith for him, so that the Lord would hear his prayer and he might be healed; but when a man designedly provokes a serpent to bite him, the principle is the same as when a man drinks deadly poison knowing it to be such. In that case no man has any claim on the promises of God to be healed.

On this day, June 16th, the citizens of Clay county, to the number of eight hundred or a thousand, among whom were the brethren, assembled at the court house in Liberty, in accordance with the request of Judge Ryland.

Samuel C. Owens made a flaming war-speech, and General Doniphan replied on the side of peace.

The Rev. Mr. Riley, a Baptist priest, made a hot speech against the "Mormons," and said, "The Mormons have lived long enough in Clay county; and they must either clear out or be cleared out."

Mr. Turnham, the moderator of the meeting, answered in a masterly manner; saying, "Let us be republicans; let us honor our country, and not disgrace it like Jackson county. For God's sake don't disfranchise or drive away the Mormons. They are better citizens than many of the old inhabitants."

General Doniphan exclaimed, "That's a fact, and as the Mormons have armed themselves, if they don't fight they are cowards. I love to hear that they have brethren coming to their assistance. Greater love can no man show, than he who lays down his life for his brethren."

At this critical instant, the cocking of pistols, and the unsheathing of other implements of death, denoted desperation. One moved "adjournment," another cried "go on," and in the midst of this awful crisis a person bawled in at the door, "a man stabbed!" The mass instantly rushed out to the spot, in hopes, as some said, that "a Mormon had got killed," but as good luck would have it, only one Missourian had dirked another (one Calbert, a blacksmith, had stabbed one Males, who had previously whipped one Mormon nearly to death, and boasted of having whipped many more). The wound was dangerous, but the incident appeared providential as it seemed as though the occurrence was necessary to break up the meeting without further bloodshed, and give the Saints a chance to consult what would be the most advisable thing to do in such a critical instant.

It may be thought, at first view, that the mob committee made a fair proposition to the Saints, in offering to buy their lands at a price fixed by disinterested arbitrators and one hundred per centum added thereto, payment to be made in thirty days, and offering theirs on the same terms; but when it is understood that the mob held possession of a much larger quantity of land than the Saints, and that they only offered thirty days for the payment, having previously robbed the Saints of nearly everything, it will be readily seen that they were only making a sham to cover their previous unlawful conduct.

The tempest of an immediate conflict seemed to be checked, and the Jackson mob to the number of about fifteen, with Samuel C. Owens and James Campbell at their head, started for Independence, Jackson county, to raise an army sufficient to meet me, before I could get into Clay county. Campbell swore, as he adjusted his pistols in his holsters, "The eagles and turkey buzzards shall eat my flesh if I do not fix Joe Smith and his army so that their skins will not hold shucks, before two days are passed." They went to the ferry and undertook to cross the Missouri river after dusk, and the angel of God saw fit to sink the boat about the middle of the river, and seven out of twelve that attempted to cross, were drowned. Thus, suddenly and justly, went they to their own place. Campbell was among the missing. He floated down the river some four or five miles, and lodged upon a pile of drift wood, where the eagles, buzzards, ravens, crows, and wild animals ate his flesh from his bones, to fulfill his own words, and left him a horrible example of God's vengeance. He was discovered about three weeks after by one Mr. Purtle. Owens saved his life only, after floating four miles down the stream, where he lodged upon an island, "swam off naked about day light, borrowed a mantle to hide his shame, and slipped home rather shy of the vengeance of God."

Tuesday, June 17—At noon we crossed the Wakenda; it being high, we had to be ferried over. We were informed here that a party of men were gathered together on the Missouri river with the intention of attacking us that night. The prairie ahead of us was twenty-three miles long without any timber or palatable, healthy water. Some of the brethren wished to stop near the timber, and were about making arrangements to pitch their tents. We had but little provisions. I proposed to get some wood and water to carry with us, and go on into the prairie eight or ten miles. My brother Hyrum said he knew, in the name of the Lord, that it was best to go on to the prairie; and as he was my elder brother, I thought best to heed his counsel, though some were murmuring in the camp. We accordingly started. When Lyman Wight crossed the river he disapproved of our moving on to the prairie, upon which Sylvester Smith placed himself in the road, turned back all that he could by saying, "Are you following your general, or some other man?" and twenty stayed behind with Lyman Wight. We drove about eight miles on the prairie and encamped out of sight of timber. The sun apparently went down, and rose again next morning in the grass. Our company had filled a couple of empty powder kegs with water; it tasted so bad we could not drink it, and all the water that we had was out of a slough filled with red living animals, and was putrid. About eleven o'clock Lyman Wight arrived with the company that had remained with him. I called them together and reproved them for tarrying behind, and not obeying my counsel, and told Lyman Wight never to do so again. He promised that he would stand by me forever, and never forsake me again, let the consequence be what it would; but Sylvester Smith manifested very refractory feelings.

Wednesday, June 18—As Hyrum Stratton and his companion were taking up their blankets this morning, they discovered two prairie rattlesnakes quietly sleeping under them, which they carefully carried out of the camp. This day my health was so poor I left the affairs of the camp to the management of General Wight. Having no provisions, we traveled seventeen miles before breakfast, and I rode in Elder Kimball's wagon. We crossed a slough half a mile wide through which most of the brethren were obliged to wade waist deep in mud and water. General Lyman Wight, who had traveled from Kirtland without a stocking on his foot, carried Brother Joseph Young through on his back. Our breakfast consisted entirely of corn meal mush, or hasty pudding. We had not meal enough in our company to make the mush of the consistence of good starch.

After our ten o'clock breakfast we passed on to within one mile of Richmond.

We encamped in a very small prairie surrounded by a thicket of hazel brush. When I arrived where the camp had pitched their tents, and viewed our unsafe location, considering the danger of an attack from our enemies, I almost forgot my sickness, went some distance in the brush, bowed down and prayed my Heavenly Father to suffer no evil to come upon us, but keep us safe through the night. I obtained an assurance that we should be safe until morning, notwithstanding about fifty of the Jackson county mob crossed the Lexington Ferry that evening for the purpose of joining the Ray county mob and of making an attack upon us. All was quiet in the camp through the night. While the brethren were making their bed in Captain Brigham Young's tent, one of them discovered a very musical rattlesnake which they were about to kill. Captain Young told them not to hurt him but carry him out of the tent, whereupon Brother Carpenter took him in his hands, carried him beyond all danger, and left him to enjoy his liberty, telling him not to return.

Thursday, June 19—At daybreak, feeling that we were in a very unsafe situation, I counseled the camp to move forward without delay, and continued a lively march for about nine miles, when we stopped for breakfast. While passing through Richmond, Brother

Luke Johnson observed a black woman in a gentleman's garden near the road. She beckoned to him and said, "Come here, Massa." She was evidently much agitated in her feelings. He went up to the fence, and she said to him, "There is a company of men lying in wait here, who are calculating to kill you this morning as you pass through." We halted for breakfast on an eminence near a farm house. The owner furnished us with a large quantity of milk, which gave a great relish to our bacon and corn dodger, which our commissary had procured that morning. When we asked the price of his milk he replied: "He is a mean man that will sell milk; I could have let you have more, if I had known you had been coming." He further said: "You have many enemies about here, and you may meet with some trouble; and it is a damned shame that every man can't come up and enjoy his religion, and everything else without being molested." It was near noon when we finished our breakfast, and we passed on in fine spirits, determined to go through and meet the brethren in Clay county. We traveled but a short distance when one wagon broke down, and the wheels ran off from others; and there seemed to be many things to hinder our progress, although we strove with all diligence to speed our way forward. This night we camped on an elevated piece of land between Little Fishing and Big Fishing rivers, which streams were formed by seven small streams or branches.

As we halted and were making preparations for the night, five men armed with guns rode into our camp, and told us we should "see hell before morning;" and their accompanying oaths partook of all the malice of demons. They told us that sixty men were coming from Richmond, Ray county, and seventy more from Clay county, to join the Jackson county mob, who had sworn our utter destruction.

During this day, the Jackson county mob, to the number of about two hundred, made arrangements to cross the Missouri river, above the mouth of Fishing river, at Williams' ferry, into Clay county, and be ready to meet the Richmond mob near Fishing

"VERY LITTLE HAIL FELL IN OUR CAMP, BUT . . . AROUND, THE STONES . . . CUT DOWN THE CROPS OF CORN AND VEGETATION GENERALLY, EVEN CUTTING LIMBS FROM TREES, WHILE THE TREES THEMSELVES WERE TWISTED INTO WITHES BY THE WIND."

river ford, for our utter destruction; but after the first scow load of about forty men had been set over the river, the scow in returning was met by a squall, and had great difficulty in reaching the Jackson side by dark.

When these five men were in our camp, swearing vengeance, the wind, thunder, and rising clouds indicated an approaching storm, and in a short time after they left the rain and hail began to fall. The storm was tremendous; wind and rain, hail and thunder met them in great wrath, and soon softened their direful courage, and frustrated all their designs to "kill Joe Smith and his army." Instead of continuing a cannonading which they commenced when the sun was about one hour high, they crawled under wagons, into hollow trees, and filled one old shanty, till the storm was over, when their ammunition was soaked, and the forty in Clay county were extremely anxious in the morning to return to Jackson, having experienced the pitiless pelting of the storm all night; and as soon as arrangements could be made, this "forlorn hope" took the "back track" for Independence, to join the main body of the mob, fully satisfied, as were those survivors of the company who were drowned, that when Jehovah fights they would rather be absent. The gratification is too terrible.

Very little hail fell in our camp, but from half a mile to a mile around, the stones or lumps of ice cut down the crops of corn and vegetation generally, even cutting limbs from trees, while the trees themselves were twisted into withes by the wind. The lightning flashed incessantly, which caused it to be so light in our camp through the night, that we could discern the most minute objects; and the roaring of the thunder was tremendous. The earth trembled and quaked, the rain fell in torrents, and, united, it seemed as if the mandate of vengeance had gone forth from the God of battles, to protect His servants from the destruction of their enemies, for the hail fell on them and not on us, and we suffered no harm, except the blowing down of some of our tents, and getting wet; while our enemies had holes made in their hats, and otherwise received damage, even the breaking of their rifle stocks, and the fleeing of their horses through fear and pain.

Many of my little band sheltered in an old meetinghouse through this night, and in the morning the water in Big Fishing river was about forty feet deep, where, the previous evening, it was no more than to our ankles, and our enemies swore that the water rose thirty feet in thirty minutes in the Little Fishing river. They reported that one of their men was killed by lightning, and that another had his hand torn off by his horse drawing his hand between the logs of a corn crib while he was holding him on the inside. They declared that if that was the way God fought for the Mormons, they might as well go about their business.

Friday, June 20—This morning I counseled the brethren to discharge all their firearms, when it was found that we had nearly six hundred shots, very few of which missed fire, which shows how very careful the brethren had been in taking care of their arms during the storm.

We drove five miles on to the prairie where we could procure food for ourselves and horses, and defend ourselves from the rage of our enemies. While camped here on Saturday the 21st, Colonel Sconce, with two other leading men from Ray county, came to see us, desiring to know what our intentions were; "for," said he, "I see that there is an Almighty power that protects this people, for I started from Richmond, Ray county, with a company of armed men, having a fixed determination to destroy you, but was kept back by the storm, and was not able to reach you." When he entered our camp he was seized with such a trembling that he was obliged to sit down to compose himself; and when he had made known the object of their visit, I arose, and, addressing them, gave a relation of the sufferings of the Saints in Jackson county, and also our persecutions generally, and what we had suffered by our enemies for our religion; and that we had come one thousand miles to assist our brethren, to bring them clothing, etc., and to reinstate them upon their own lands; and that we had no intention to molest or injure any people, but only to administer to the wants of our afflicted friends; and that the evil reports circulated about us were false, and got up by our enemies to procure our destruction. When I had closed a lengthy speech, the spirit of which melted them into compassion, they arose and offered me their hands, and said they would use their influence to allay the excitement which everywhere prevailed against us; and they wept when they heard of our afflictions and persecutions, and learned that our intentions were good. Accordingly they went forth among the people, and made unwearied exertions to allay the excitement.

Brother Ezra Thayre and Joseph Hancock are sick with the cholera. Thomas Heyes was taken today. Previous to crossing the Mississippi river I had called the camp together and told them that in consequence of the disobedience of some who had been unwilling to listen to my words, but had rebelled, God had decreed that sickness should come upon the camp, and if they did not repent and humble themselves before God they should die like sheep with the rot; that I was sorry, but could not help it. The scourge must come; repentance and humility may mitigate the chastisement, but cannot altogether avert it. But there were some who would not give heed to my words.

June 22—Brother Lyman Smith received a wound from the accidental discharge of a horse-pistol, from which he recovered in about three days.

Cornelius Gillium, the sheriff of Clay county, came to our camp to hold consultation with us. I marched my company into a grove near by, and formed in a circle, with Gillium in the centre. Gillium commenced by saying that he had heard that Joseph Smith was in the camp, and if so he would like to see him. I arose and replied, "I am the man." This was the first time that I had been discovered or made known to my enemies since I left Kirtland. Gillium then gave us instruction concerning the manners, customs, and dispositions of the people, and what course we ought to pursue to secure their favor and protection, making certain inquiries, to which we replied, which were afterwards published, and will appear under date of publication.

I received the following:

See Doctrine and Covenants 105.

June 23—We resumed our march for Liberty, Clay county, taking a circuitous course around the heads of Fishing river, to avoid the deep water. When within five or six miles of Liberty, we were met by General Atchison and other gentlemen, who desired us not to go to Liberty because the feelings of the people were so much enraged against us. At their solicitation we turned our course, wheeling to the left, and crossing the prairie and woodland, came to Brother Algernon Sidney Gilbert's residence, and encamped on the bank of Rush creek, in Brother Burket's field.

A council of high priests assembled in fulfillment of the revelation given the day previous, and the following individuals were called and chosen, as they were made manifest unto me by the voice of the Spirit and revelation, to receive their endowments:

Edward Partridge was called and chosen, to go to Kirtland and receive his endowment with power from on high, and also, to stand in his office as bishop to purchase lands in the state of Missouri.

William W. Phelps was called and chosen, and it was appointed unto him to receive his endowment with power from on high, and help to carry on the printing establishment in Kirtland, until Zion is redeemed.

Isaac Morley and John Corrill were called and chosen, and it was appointed unto them to receive their endowment with power from on high in Kirtland, and assist in gathering up the strength of the Lord's house, and preach the gospel.

John Whitmer and David Whitmer were called and chosen, and appointed to receive their endowment in Kirtland, and continue in their offices.

Algernon Sidney Gibert was called and chosen, and appointed

to receive his endowment in Kirtland, and to assist in gathering up the strength of the Lord's house, and to proclaim the everlasting gospel until Zion is redeemed. But he said he "could not do it."

Peter Whitmer, Jun., Simeon Carter, Newel Knight, Parley P. Pratt, Christian Whitmer and Solomon Hancock were called and chosen, and it was appointed unto them to receive their endowment in Kirtland, with power from on high, to assist in gathering up the strength of the Lord's house, and to preach the everlasting gospel.

Thomas B. Marsh was called and chosen, and it was appointed unto him to receive his endowment in Kirtland, his office to be made known hereafter.

Lyman Wight was called and chosen, and it was appointed unto him to receive his endowment in Kirtland, with power from on high, and return to Zion and have his office appointed unto him hereafter.

June 24—This night the cholera burst forth among us, and about midnight it was manifested in its most virulent form. Our ears were saluted with cries, and moanings, and lamentations on every hand; even those on guard fell to the earth with their guns in their hands, so sudden and powerful was the attack of this terrible disease. At the commencement, I attempted to lay on hands for their recovery, but I quickly learned by painful experience, that when the great Jehovah decrees destruction upon any people, and makes known His determination, man must not attempt to stay His hand. The moment I attempted to rebuke the disease I was attacked, and had I not desisted in my attempt to save the life of a brother, I would have sacrificed my own. The disease seized upon me like the talons of a hawk, and I said to the brethren: "If my work were done, you would have to put me in the ground without a coffin."

Early on the morning of the 25th, the camp was separated into small bands, and dispersed among the brethren living in the vicinity.

I left Rush creek the same day in company with David Whitmer and two other brethren, for the western part of Clay county. While traveling, we called at the house of a Mr. Moss for a drink of water. The woman of the house shouted from the door that they had "no water for Mormons," that they were "afraid of the cholera," etc., at the same time throwing out her arms as if defending herself from the cholera in the form of a personage. We turned and departed, according to the commandment, and before a week had passed, the cholera entered that house, and that woman and three others of the family were dead.

When the cholera made its appearance, Elder John S. Carter was the first man who stepped forward to rebuke it, and upon this, was instantly seized, and became the first victim in the camp. He died about six o'clock in the afternoon; and Seth Hitchcock died in about thirty minutes afterwards. Erastus Rudd died about the same moment, although a half a mile distant. He was buried by Jesse Smith, George A. Smith and two or three others, and while burying him, Jesse Smith was attacked with the cholera. As it was impossible to obtain coffins, the brethren rolled the corpses in blankets, carried them on a horse-sled about half a mile, buried them on the bank of a small stream, which empties into Rush creek, all of which was accomplished by dark. When they had returned from the burial, the brethren unitedly covenanted and prayed, hoping the disease would be stayed; but in vain, for while thus covenanting, Eber Wilcox died; and while some were digging the grave, others stood sentry with their fire arms, watching their enemies.

The cholera continued its ravages for about four days, when a remedy for the purging, vomiting, and cramping, was discovered, viz., dipping the persons afflicted in cold water, or pouring it upon them, and giving them whisky thickened with flour to the consistency of starch. Whisky was the only kind of spirits that could be procured at this place. About sixty-eight of the Saints suffered from this disease, of which number fourteen died, viz., John S. Carter, Eber Wilcox, Seth Hitchcock, Erastus Rudd, Algernon Sidney Gilbert, Alfred Fisk, Edward Ives, Noah Johnson, Jesse B. Lawson,

Robert McCord, Elial Strong, Jesse J. Smith, Warren Ingalls and Betsy Parrish.

Among the most active of those who were engaged in taking care of the sick at the camp, burying the dead, etc., were John D. Parker, John Tanner, Nathan Tanner, Joseph B. Noble, Brigham Young, Joseph Young, Heber C. Kimball, Luke S. Johnson and Eleazar Miller.

I sent Hiram Page with instructions to bring Jesse J. Smith and George A. Smith to me at all hazards to the west part of the county, having had intimations that they were sick. He found that Jesse had been severely racked with the cholera all day. George A. Smith had taken care of him for upwards of thirty hours. Dr. Frederick G. Williams decided that the cholera had left him, and he would recover if not moved. On the morning of the 28th, George A. Smith was attacked and was immediately mounted on a hard-riding horse, rode fifteen miles, and came to me.

The last days of June I spent with my old Jackson county friends, in the western part of Clay county.

On the 1st of July Jesse J. Smith died. I crossed the Missouri river, in company with a few friends, into Jackson county, to set my feet once more on the "goodly land;" and on the 2nd I went down near Liberty, and visited the brethren. A considerable number of the Camp met me at Lyman Wight's. I told them if they would humble themselves before the Lord and covenant to keep His commandments and obey my counsel, the plague should be stayed from that hour, and there should not be another case of the cholera among them. The brethren covenanted to that effect with uplifted hands, and the plague was stayed.

The excitement of the people began to subside and the Saints, both in Missouri and Ohio, began to enjoy a little peace. The elders began to go forth, two and two, preaching the word to all that would hear, and many were added to the Church daily.

September 1—I continued to preside over the Church, and in forwarding the building of the house of the Lord in Kirtland. I acted as foreman in the Temple stone quarry, and when other duties would permit, labored with my own hands.

October 1–15—Great exertions were made to expedite the work of the Lord's house, and notwithstanding it was commenced almost with nothing, as to means, yet the way opened as we proceeded, and the Saints rejoiced.

Having accomplished all that could be done at present, on the 16th of the month, in company with my brother Hyrum Smith, and Elders David Whitmer, Frederick G. Williams, Oliver Cowdery, and Roger Orton, left Kirtland for the purpose of visiting some Saints in the state of Michigan, where, after a tolerably pleasant journey, we arrived at Pontiac on the 20th.

While on our way up the lake on board the steamer *Monroe*, Elder Cowdery had a short discussion with a man calling his name Ellmer. He said that he was "personally acquainted with Joe Smith, had heard him preach his lies, and now, since he was dead, he was glad! He had heard Joe Smith preach in Bainbridge, Chenango county, New York, five years since; he knew it to be him, that he (Joseph Smith) was a dark complexioned man," etc. Ellmer appeared to exult most in that "Joe" was dead, and made his observations in my presence. I concluded that he learned it from the popular priests of the day, who, through fear that their craft will be injured, if their systems are compared with the truth, seek to ridicule those who teach the truth, and thus I am suffering under the tongue of slander for Christ's sake, unceasingly. God have mercy on such, if they will quit their lying. I need not state my complexion to those that have seen me, and those who have read my history thus far, will recollect that five years ago I was not a preacher, as Ellmer represented; neither did I ever preach in Bainbridge.

After preaching, and teaching the Saints in Michigan as long as our time would allow, we returned to Kirtland, greatly refreshed from our journey, and much pleased with our friends in that section of the Lord's vineyard.

It now being the last of the month, and the elders beginning to come in, it was necessary to make preparations for the school for the elders, wherein they might be more perfectly instructed in the great things of God, during the coming winter. A building for a printing office was nearly finished, and the lower story of this building was set apart for that purpose, (the school) when it was completed. So the Lord opened the way according to our faith and works, and blessed be His name.

No month ever found me more busily engaged than November; but as my life consisted of activity and unyielding exertions, I made this my rule: When the Lord commands, do it.

I continued my labors daily, preparing for the school, and received the following:

See Doctrine and Covenants 106.

November 30—While reflecting on the goodness and mercy of God this evening, a prophecy was put into our hearts, that in a short time the Lord would arrange His providences in a merciful manner and send us assistance to deliver us from debt and bondage.

December 1—Our school for the elders was now well attended, and with the lectures on theology, which were regularly delivered, absorbed for the time being everything else of a temporal nature. The classes, being mostly elders, gave the most studious attention to the all-important object of qualifying themselves as messengers of Jesus Christ, to be ready to do His will in carrying glad tidings to all that would open their eyes, ears and hearts.

Chapter Seven

1835

January—During the month of January, I was engaged in the school of the elders, and in preparing the lectures on theology for publication in the book of Doctrine and Covenants, which the committee appointed last September were now compiling.

Certain brethren from Bolton, New York, came for counsel, relative to their proceeding to the West; and the High Council assembled on the 18th. After a long investigation I decided that Elder Tanner assist with his might to build up the cause by tarrying in Kirtland; which decision received the unanimous vote of the council.

The school of the elders will continue, and arrangements were also made, according to the revelation of June, 1829, for choosing "the Twelve Apostles" to be especial messengers to bear the gospel among the nations.

On the Sabbath previous to the 14th of February, (February 8th) Brothers Joseph and Brigham Young came to my house after meeting, and sung for me; the Spirit of the Lord was poured out upon us, and I told them I wanted to see those brethren together, who went up to Zion in the camp, the previous summer, for I had a blessing for them; and a meeting was appointed.

The school in Kirtland closed the last week in March, to give the elders an opportunity to go forth and proclaim the gospel, preparatory to the endowment.

Sunday, March 29—I preached about three hours, at Huntsburgh—where William E. M'Lellin had been holding a public discussion, on a challenge from J. M. Tracy, a Campbellite preacher, the two days previous, on the divinity of the Book of Mormon—at the close of which two were baptized; and, on Monday, four more came forward for baptism.

The presidency, bishop, and high council of Zion, having removed to Kirtland, or gone forth in the vineyard, I caused it to be published in the June number of the *Messenger and Advocate*, that according to the order of the kingdom begun in the last days, to prepare men for the rest of the Lord, the elders in Zion or in her immediate region, have no authority or right to meddle with her spiritual affairs, to regulate her concerns; or hold councils for the expulsion of members, in her unorganized condition. The high council has been expressly organized to administer in all her spiritual affairs; and the bishop and his council are set over her temporal matters; so that the elders' acts are null and void. Now, the Lord wants the wheat and tares to grow together; for Zion must be redeemed with judgment, and her converts with righteousness. Every elder that can, after providing for his family (if he has any) and paying his debts, must go forth and clear his skirts from the blood of this generation. While they are in that region, (Missouri) instead of trying members for transgression, or offenses, let every one labor to prepare himself for the vineyard, sparing a little time to comfort the mourners, to bind up the broken-hearted, to reclaim the backslider, to bring back the wanderer, to re-invite into the kingdom such as have been cut off, by encouraging them to lay to while the day lasts, and work righteousness, and, with one heart and one mind, prepare to help to redeem Zion, that goodly land of promise, where the willing and obedient shall be blessed.

June 18—Nine hundred and fifty dollars were subscribed for the temple, by the Saints in Kirtland. Great anxiety was manifested to roll on the work.

The twenty-first, being Sunday, I preached in Kirtland on the Evangelical Order.

Thursday, June 25—There was a meeting in Kirtland to subscribe for the building of the Temple; and $6,232.50 was added to the list. Joseph Smith subscribed $500; Oliver Cowdery, $750; W. W. Phelps, $500; John Whitmer, $500; and Frederick G. Williams, $500; of the above, all of which they paid within one hour, and the people were astonished.

On the 3rd of July, Michael H. Chandler came to Kirtland to exhibit some Egyptian mummies. There were four human figures, together with some two or more rolls of papyrus covered with hieroglypic figures and devices. As Mr. Chandler had been told I could translate them, he brought me some of the characters, and I gave him the interpretation.

Sunday, July 5—I preached in the afternoon. Michael H. Barton tried to get into the Church, but he was not willing to confess and forsake all his sins—and he was rejected.

Soon after this, some of the Saints at Kirtland purchased the mummies and papyrus, a description of which will appear hereafter, and with W. W. Phelps and Oliver Cowdery as scribes, I commenced the translation of some of the characters or hieroglyphics, and much to our joy found that one of the rolls contained the writings of Abraham, another the writings of Joseph of Egypt, etc., a more full account of which will appear in its place, as I proceed to examine or unfold them. Truly we can say, the Lord is beginning to reveal the abundance of peace and truth.

The remainder of this month, I was continually engaged in translating an alphabet to the Book of Abraham, and arranging a grammar of the Egyptian language as practiced by the ancients.

August 2nd, being the Sabbath, I preached a part of the day.

September 16—I labored in obtaining blessings, which were written by Oliver Cowdery. We were thronged with company, so that our labor in this thing was hindered; but we obtained many precious things, and our souls were blessed. O Lord, may Thy Holy Spirit be with Thy servants forever. Amen.

September 23—I was at home writing blessings for my most beloved brethren, but was hindered by a multitude of visitors. The Lord has blessed our souls this day, and may God grant to continue His mercies unto my house this night, for Christ's sake. This day my soul has desired the salvation of Brother Ezra Thayre. Also Brother Noah Packard came to my house and loaned the committee one thousand dollars to assist building the house of the Lord. Oh! may God bless him a hundred fold, even of the things of the earth, for this righteous act. My heart is full of desire today, to be blessed of the God of Abraham with prosperity, until I shall be able to pay all my debts, for it is the delight of my soul to be honest. O Lord, that Thou knowest right well. Help me, and I will give to the poor.

Brothers William, John, and Joseph Tippits started for Missouri, the place designated for Zion, or the Saints' gathering place. They came to bid us farewell. The brethren came in to pray with them, and Brother David Whitmer acted as spokesman. He prayed in the spirit, and a glorious time succeeded his prayer; joy filled our hearts and we blessed them and bid them God speed, and promised them a safe journey, and took them by the hand and bid them farewell for a season. May God grant them long life and good days. These blessings I ask upon them for Christ's sake. Amen.

The high council met at my house on the 24th to take into consideration the redemption of Zion. And it was the voice of the Spirit of the Lord that we petition the governor, that is, those who have been driven out, shall petition to be set back on their own lands next spring, and that we go next season, to live or die on our own lands, which we have purchased in Jackson county, Missouri.

We truly had a good time, and covenanted to struggle for this thing, until death shall dissolve the union; and if one falls, that the remainder be not discouraged, but pursue this object until it be accomplished; which may God grant unto us in the name of Jesus Christ our Lord. Also, this day drew up a subscription for enrolling the names of those who are willing to go up to Missouri next spring and settle; and I ask God in the name of Jesus that we may obtain eight hundred or one thousand emigrants.

I spent the 25th of September at home.

Sunday, September 27—I attended meeting. Elders Thomas B. Marsh, David W. Patten, Brigham Young and Heber C. Kimball preached and broke bread. The Lord poured out His Spirit and my soul was edified.

October 1—This afternoon I labored on the Egyptian alphabet, in company with Brothers Oliver Cowdery and W. W. Phelps, and during the research, the principles of astronomy as understood by Father Abraham and the ancients unfolded to our understanding, the particulars of which will appear hereafter.

Sunday, 4—I started early in the morning, with Brother John Corrill, to hold a meeting in Perry. When about a mile from home we discovered two deer playing in the field, which diverted our minds by giving an impetus to our thoughts upon the subject of the creation of God. We conversed on many topics. The day passed off very agreeably, and the Lord blessed our souls. When we arrived at Perry, we were disappointed of a meeting, through mis-arrangement, but conversed freely with Brother Corrill's relatives, which allayed much prejudice. May the Lord have mercy on their souls.

Monday, 5—I returned home, being much fatigued from riding in the rain.

Spent the remainder of the day in reading and meditation, and in the evening attended a council of the Twelve Apostles; had a glorious time, and gave them much instruction concerning their duties for time to come; told them that it was the will of God they should take their families to Missouri next season; also this fall to attend the solemn assembly of the first elders, for the organization of the School of the Prophets; and attend to the ordinance of the washing of feet; and to prepare their hearts in all humility for an endowment with power from on high; to which they all agreed with one accord, and seemed to be greatly rejoiced. May God spare the lives of the Twelve to a good old age, for Christ the Redeemer's sake. Amen.

Thursday, 8—At home. I attended on my father with great anxiety.

Friday, 9—At home. Waited on my father.

Saturday, 10—At home, and visited the house of my father, found him failing very fast.

Sunday, 11—Waited on my father again, who was very sick. In secret prayer in the morning, the Lord said, "My servant, thy father shall live." I waited on him all this day with my heart raised to God in the name of Jesus Christ, that He would restore him to health, that I might be blessed with his company and advice, esteeming it one of the greatest earthly blessings to be blessed with the society of parents, whose mature years and experience render them capable of administering the most wholesome advice. At evening Brother David Whitmer came in. We called on the Lord in mighty prayer in the name of Jesus Christ, and laid our hands on him, and rebuked the disease. And God heard and answered our prayers—to the great joy and satisfaction of our souls. Our aged father arose and dressed himself, shouted, and praised the Lord. Called Brother William Smith, who had retired to rest, that he might praise the Lord with us, by joining in songs of praise to the Most High.

Monday, October 12—Rode to Willoughby, in company with my wife, to purchase some goods at William Lyon's store. On our return we found a Mr. Bradley lying across the road. He had been thrown from his wagon, and was much injured by the fall.

Tuesday, October 13—Visited my father, who was very much recovered from his sickness, indeed, which caused us to marvel at the might, power, and condescension of our Heavenly Father, in answering our prayers in his behalf.

"IN SECRET PRAYER IN THE MORNING, THE LORD SAID, 'MY SERVANT, THY FATHER SHALL LIVE.'"

Wednesday, October 14—At home.

Thursday, October 15—Labored in father's orchard, gathering apples.

Friday, October 23—At home. At four o'clock, afternoon, Oliver Cowdery, David Whitmer, Hyrum Smith, John Whitmer, Sidney Rigdon, Samuel H. Smith, Frederick G. Williams and W. W. Phelps assembled, and we united in prayer, with one voice, before the Lord, for the following blessings: that the Lord would give us means sufficient to deliver us from all our afflictions and difficulties wherein we are placed by reason of our debts; that He would open the way and deliver Zion in the appointed time, and that without the shedding of blood; that He would hold our lives precious, and grant that we may live to the common age of man, and never fall into the hands nor power of the mob in Missouri, nor in any other place; that He would also preserve our posterity, that none of them fall, even unto the end of time; that He would give us blessings of the earth sufficient to carry us to Zion, and that we may purchase inheritances in that land, even enough to carry on and accomplish the work unto which He has appointed us; and also that He would assist all others who desire, according to His commandments, to go up and purchase inheritances, and all this easily and without perplexity and trouble; and finally, that in the end He would save us in His celestial kingdom. Amen.

Saturday, October 24—Mr. Goodrich and wife called to see the ancient (Egyptian) records, and also Dr. Frederick G. Williams to see the mummies. Brothers Hawkes and Carpenter, from Michigan, visited us and tarried over night.

Sunday, October 25—Attended meeting with Brothers Hawkes and Carpenter.

President Rigdon preached in the forenoon, Elder Lyman E. Johnson in the afternoon, after which Elder Seymour Brunson joined Brother William Perry and Sister Eliza Brown in matrimony, and I blessed them with long life and prosperity in the name of Jesus Christ.

In the evening I attended prayer meeting, opened it, and exhorted the brethren and sisters about one hour. The Lord poured out His Spirit, and some glorious things were spoken in the gift of tongues and interpreted concerning the redemption of Zion.

Friday, November 13—Attended school during school hours: after school, returned home. Mr. Messenger, a Universalist minister, of Bainbridge, Chenango county, New York, came in to make some inquiries about Hezekiah Peck's family. We entered into conversation upon religious subjects, and went to President Rigdon's and spent the evening in conversation. We preached the gospel to him, and bore testimony of what we had seen and heard.

He attempted to raise some objections, but the force of truth bore him down, and he was silent, although unbelieving.

I returned home and retired to rest.

Monday, November 16—In the evening, Bishop Whitney, his wife, father, mother, and sister-in-law came and invited me and my wife to go with them and visit Father Smith and family. My wife was unwell, and could not go, but my scribe and I went.

When we arrived, some of the young elders were about engaging in a debate on the subject of miracles. The question—"Was it, or was it not, the design of Christ to establish His gospel by miracles?" After an interesting debate of three hours or more, during which time much talent was displayed, it was decided, by the president of the debate, in the negative, which was a righteous decision.

I discovered in this debate, much warmth displayed, too much zeal for mastery, too much of that enthusiasm that characterizes a lawyer at the bar, who is determined to defend his cause, right or wrong. I therefore availed myself of this favorable opportunity to drop a few words upon this subject, by way of advice, that they might improve their minds and cultivate their powers of intellect in a proper manner, that they might not incur the displeasure of heaven; that they should handle sacred things very sacredly, and with due deference to the opinions of others, and with an eye single to the glory of God.

Thursday, November 19—Went, in company with Dr. Williams and my scribe, to see how the workmen prospered in finishing the house of the Lord. The masons in the inside had commenced putting on the finishing coat of plaster. On my return, I met Lloyd and Lorenzo Lewis, and conversed with them upon the subject of their being disaffected. I found that they were not so, as touching the faith of the Church, but were displeased with some of the members. I returned home and spent the day in translating the Egyptian records. A warm and pleasant day.

Friday, November 20—At home in the morning. Weather warm and rainy. We spent the day in translating, and made rapid progress.

In the evening, President Cowdery returned from New York, bringing with him a quantity of Hebrew books, for the benefit of the school. He presented me with a Hebrew Bible, Lexicon, and Grammar, also a Greek Lexicon, and Webster's English Dictionary. President Cowdery had a prosperous journey, according to the prayers of the Saints in Kirtland.

Saturday, November 21—Spent the day at home, in examining my books, and studying the Hebrew alphabet.

At evening, met with our Hebrew class, to make some arrangements about a teacher. It was decided, by the voice of the school, to send to New York, for a Jew to teach us the language, if we could get released from the engagements we had made with Dr. Piexotto to teach us, having ascertained that he was not qualified to give us the knowledge we wished to acquire of the Hebrew.

Tuesday, November 24—At home. Spent the forenoon instructing those that called to inquire concerning the things of God in the last days.

In the afternoon we translated some of the Egyptian records.

I had an invitation to attend a wedding at Brother Hyrum Smith's in the evening; also to solemnize the matrimonial ceremony between Newel Knight and Lydia Goldthwaite. My wife accompanied me. On our arrival a considerable company had collected. The bridegroom and bride came in, and took their seats, which gave me to understand that they were ready. After prayers, I requested them to rise, and join hands. I then remarked that marriage was an institution of heaven, instituted in the Garden of Eden; that it was necessary it should be solemnized by the authority of the everlasting priesthood. The ceremony was original with me, and in substance as follows—You covenant to be each other's companions through life, and discharge the duties of husband and wife in every respect; to which they assented. I then pronounced them husband and wife in the name of God, and also pronounced upon them the blessings that the Lord conferred upon Adam and Eve in the garden of Eden, that is, to multiply and replenish the earth, with the addition of long life and prosperity. Dismissed them and returned home. Freezing cold, some snow on the ground.

Wednesday, November 25—Spent the day in translating. Harvey Redfield and Jesse Hithcock arrived from Missouri. The latter says that he has no doubt but a dose of poison was administered to him, in a bowl of milk, but God delivered him.

Thursday, November 26—Spent the day in translating Egyptian characters from the papyrus, though severely afflicted with a cold. Robert Rathbone and George Morey arrived from Zion.

Friday, November 27—Much afflicted with my cold, yet I am determined to overcome in the name of the Lord Jesus Christ. Spent the day at home, reading Hebrew. Brother Parrish, my scribe, being afflicted with a cold, asked me to lay my hands on him in the name of the Lord. I did so, and in return I asked him to lay his hands on me. We were both relieved.

Saturday, November 28—Spent the morning in comparing our *Journal*. Elder Josiah Clark, from the state of Kentucky, called on me. Considerably recovered from my cold. Cold and stormy, snow falling, and winter seems fast to be closing in, all nature shrinks before the chilling blasts of rigid winter. Elder Clark, above mentioned, whose residence is about three miles from Cincinnati, was bitten by a mad dog some three or four years since: has doctored much, and received some benefit, but is much afflicted notwithstanding. He came here that he might be benefitted by the prayers of the Church. Accordingly we prayed for him and laid hands on him in the name of the Lord Jesus Christ, and anointed him with oil, and rebuked his afflictions, praying our Heavenly Father to hear and answer our prayers, according to our faith. Cold and snowy.

Sunday, November 29—Went to meeting at the usual hour. Elder Morley preached; and in the afternoon, Bishop Partridge. These discourses were well adapted to the times in which we live, and the circumstances under which we are placed. Their words were words of wisdom, like apples of gold in pictures of silver, spoken in the simple accents of a child, yet sublime as the voice of an angel. The Saints appeared to be much pleased with the beautiful discourses of these two fathers in Israel. After these services closed, three of the Zion brethren came forward and received their blessings, and Solon Foster was ordained an elder. The Lord's supper was administered. Spent the evening at home. Snow fell about one foot deep. Very cold.

Monday, November 30—The snow continues to fall—an uncommon storm for this country and this season of the year. Spent the day in reviewing and copying the letter I dictated on the 16th, concerning the gathering, for the *Messenger and Advocate.* Henry Capron, an old acquaintance from Manchester, New York, called on me. I showed him the Egyptian records.

December 1—At home. Spent the day in writing for the *Messenger and Advocate.* Fine sleighing, and the snow yet falling.

Wednesday, December 2—A fine morning. I started to ride to Painesville with my family and scribe. When we were passing through Mentor Street, we overtook a team, with two men in the sleigh; I politely asked them to let me pass. They granted my request, and as we passed them they bawled out, "Do you get any revelations lately?" with an addition of blackguard language that I did not understand. This is a fair sample of the character of Mentor Street inhabitants, who are ready to abuse and scandalize men who never laid a straw in their way; and, in fact, those whose faces they never saw, and (whom they) cannot bring an accusation against, either of a temporal or spiritual nature, except their firm belief in the fullness of the gospel. I was led to marvel at the longsuffering and condescension of our Heavenly Father in permitting these ungodly wretches to possess this goodly land, which is indeed as beautifully situated, and its soil is as fertile, as any in this region of country, and its inhabitants are wealthy even blessed above measure in temporal things; and fain would God bless them with spiritual blessings, even eternal life, were it not for their evil hearts of unbelief. And we are led to mingle our prayers with those of the Saints that have suffered the like treatment before us, whose souls are under the altar, crying to the Lord for vengeance upon those that dwell upon the earth. And we rejoice that the time is at hand, when the wicked who will not repent will be swept from the earth as with a besom of destruction, and the earth become an inheritance of the poor and the meek.

When we arrived at Painesville, we called at Sister Harriet Howe's, and left my wife and family to visit her, while we rode into town to do some business. Called and visited H. Kingsbury. Dined with Sister Howe and returned home. Had a fine ride sleighing good, weather pleasant.

Saturday, December 5—Weather cold and freezing, with a moderate fall of snow. In the forenoon studying Hebrew with Dr. Frederick G. Williams and President Cowdery. I am laboring under some indisposition of health. Slept awhile, and arose feeling tolerably well, through the mercy of God. I received a letter from Reuben McBride, Vilanovia, New York; also another from Parley P. Pratt's mother-in-law, Herkimer county, New York, of no consequence as to what it contained, but it cost me twenty-five cents for postage. I mention this, as it is a common occurrence, and I am subjected to a great deal of expense by those whom I know nothing about, only that they are destitute of good manners; for if people wish to be benefitted with information from me, common respect and good breeding would dictate them to pay the postage on their letters.

Wednesday, December 9—At home. Wind south, strong, and chilly. Elder Packard came in this morning, and made me a present of twelve dollars, which he held in a note against me. May God bless him for his liberality. Also, James Aldrich sent me my note by the hand of Jesse Hitchcock, on which there were twelve dollars due. And may God bless him for his kindness to me.

My heart swells with gratitude inexpressible when I realize the great condescension of my Heavenly Father, in opening the hearts of these my beloved brethren to administer so liberally to my wants. And I ask God, in the name of Jesus Christ, to multiply blessings without number upon their heads, and bless me with much wisdom and understanding, and dispose of me to the best advantage for my brethren, and the advancement of His cause and kingdom. And whether my days are many or few, whether in life or in death, I say in my heart, O Lord, let me enjoy the society of such brethren.

Elder Tanner brought me half of a fatted hog for the benefit of my family. A few days since, Elder Shadrach Roundy brought me a quarter of beef. And may all the blessings named above be poured upon their heads, for their kindness towards me.

Thursday, December 10—This morning a number of brethren called to see the records, (Egyptian) which I exhibited to their satisfaction. This day my brethren met according to previous arrangement to chop and haul wood for me. Beautiful morning, indeed, and fine sleighing.

This afternoon I was called, in company with President David Whitmer, to visit Angeline Works. We found her very sick, and so much deranged that she did not recognize her friends and intimate acquaintances. We prayed for her and laid hands on her in the name of Jesus Christ, and commanded her in His name to receive her senses, which were immediately restored. We also prayed that she might be restored to health; and she said she was better.

"MY HEART SWELLS WITH GRATITUDE INEXPRESSIBLE WHEN I REALIZE THE GREAT CONDESCENSION OF MY HEAVENLY FATHER."

The board kiln had taken fire, and on our return we found the brethren engaged in extinguishing the flames. After laboring about one hour against this destructive element, we succeeded in conquering it, and probably saved about one-fourth part of the lumber. I do not know the amount of loss the committee have sustained, but it must have been considerable, as there was much lumber in the kiln. There were about two hundred brethren engaged on this occasion; they displayed much activity and interest, and deserve much credit. The brethren have also been very industrious, and supplied me with my winter's wood, for which I am sincerely grateful to each and every one of them, and shall remember, with warm emotions, this expression of their goodness to me. And in the name of Jesus Christ I invoke the rich benediction of heaven to rest upon them and their families; and I ask my Heavenly Father to preserve their health, and that of their wives and children, that they may have strength of body to perform their labors in their several occupations in life, and the use and activity of their limbs, also powers of intellect and understanding hearts, that they may treasure up wisdom, understanding and intelligence above measure, and be preserved from plagues, pestilence, and famine, and from the power of the adversary, and the hands of evil-designing men, and have power over all their enemies, and the way be prepared for them that they may journey to the land of Zion, and be established on their inheritances, to enjoy undisturbed peace and happiness forever, and ultimately be crowned with everlasting life in the celestial kingdom of God, which blessing I ask in the name of Jesus of Nazareth. Amen.

I would remember Elder Leonard Rich, who was the first one that proposed to the brethren to assist me in obtaining wood for the use of my family, for which I pray my Heavenly Father to bless him with all the blessings named above. And I shall ever remember him with much gratitude, for this testimony of benevolence and respect, and thank the Great I Am for putting into his heart to do me this kindness. And I say in my heart, I will trust in Thy goodness and mercy forever, O Lord, for Thy wisdom and benevolence, are unbounded, and beyond the comprehension of men, and all of Thy ways cannot be found out.

Saturday, December 12—Spent the forenoon in reading. About twelve o'clock a number of young persons called to see the Egyptian records. My scribe exhibited them. One of the young ladies who had been examining them, was asked if they had the appearance of antiquity. She observed, with an air of contempt, that they had not. On hearing this, I was surprised at the ignorance she displayed, and I observed to her, that she was an anomaly in creation, for all the wise and learned that had examined them, without hesitation pronounced them ancient. I further remarked, that it was downright wickedness, ignorance, bigotry and superstition had caused her to make the remark; and that I would put it on record. And I have done so, because it is a fair sample of the prevailing spirit of the times, showing that the victims of priestcraft and superstition would not believe though one should rise from the dead.

Monday, December 14—A number of brethren from New York called to visit me and see the Egyptian records. Also Elder Harris returned from Palmyra, New York, and Brother Francis Eaton of the same place, and Sister Harriet Howe called to visit us.

After dinner, attended the funeral of Sylvester Smith's youngest child. And in the evening met, according to previous notice, to make arrangements to guard against fire, and organize a company for this purpose; also counseled on other affairs of a temporal nature. Samuel Barnum came to my house, much afflicted with a swollen arm. As he had not sufficient faith to be healed, my wife applied a poultice of herbs, and he tarried over night. I spent the day at home reading Hebrew, and visiting with friends who called to see me.

Sunday, December 20—At home all day. Took solid comfort with my family. Had many serious reflections. Brothers Palmer and Taylor called to see me. I showed them the sacred records to their joy and satisfaction. O! may God have mercy upon these men, and keep them in the way of everlasting life, in the name of Jesus. Amen.

Tuesday, December 22—At home. Continued my studies. O may God give me learning, even language; and endue me with qualifications to magnify His name while I live.

I also delivered an address to the Church, this evening. The Lord blessed my soul. My scribe is unwell. O may God heal him. And for his kindness to me, O my soul, be thou grateful to him, and bless him. And he shall be blessed of God for ever, for I believe him to be a faithful friend to me, therefore my soul delighteth in him. Amen.

Thursday, December 31—The public mind has been excited of late, by reports which have been circulated concerning certain Egyptian mummies and ancient records, which were purchased by certain gentlemen of Kirtland, last July. It has been said that the purchasers of these antiquities pretend they have the bodies of Abraham, Abimelech, (the king of the Philistines,) Joseph, who was sold into Egypt, & c., & c., for the purpose of attracting the attention of the multitude, and gulling the unwary; which is utterly false. Who these ancient inhabitants of Egypt were, I do not at present say. Abraham was buried on his own possession "in the cave of Machpelah, in the field of Ephron, the son of Zohah, the Hittite, which is before Mamre," which he purchased of the sons of Heth. Abimelech lived in the same country, and for aught we know, died there; and the children of Israel carried Joseph's bones from Egypt, when they went out under Moses; consequently, these could not have been found in Egypt, in the nineteenth century. The record of Abraham and Joseph, found with the mummies, is beautifully written on papyrus, with black, and a small part red, ink or paint, in perfect preservation. The characters are such as you find upon the coffins of mummies—hieroglyphics, etc.; with many characters of letters like the present (though probably not quite so square) form of the Hebrew without points. The records were obtained from one of the catacombs in Egypt, near the place where once stood the renowned city of Thebes, by the celebrated

French traveler, Antonio Sebolo, in the year 1831. He procured license from Mehemet Ali, then Viceroy of Egypt, under the protection of Chevalier Drovetti, the French Consul, in the year 1828, and employed four hundred and thirty-three men, four months and two days (if I understand correctly)—Egyptian or Turkish soldiers, at from four to six cents per diem, each man. He entered the catacomb June 7, 1831, and obtained eleven mummies. There were several hundred mummies in the same catacomb; about one hundred embalmed after the first order, and placed in niches, and two or three hundred after the second and third orders, and laid upon the floor or bottom of the grand cavity. The two last orders of embalmed were so decayed, that they could not be removed, and only eleven of the first, found in the niches. On his way from Alexandria to Paris, he put in at Trieste, and, after ten days' illness, expired. This was in the year 1832. Previous to his decease, he made a will of the whole, to Mr. Michael H. Chandler, (then in Philadelphia, Pa.) his nephew, whom he supposed to be in Ireland. Accordingly, the whole were sent to Dublin, and Mr. Chandler's friends ordered them to New York, where they were received at the custom house, in the winter or spring of 1833. In April, of the same year, Mr. Chandler paid the duties and took possession of his mummies. Up to this time, they had not been taken out of the coffins, nor the coffins opened. On opening the coffins, he discovered that in connection with two of the bodies, was something rolled up with the same kind of linen, saturated with the same bitumen, which, when examined, proved to be two rolls of papyrus, previously mentioned. Two or three other small pieces of papyrus, with astronomical calculations, epitaphs, &c., were found with others of the mummies. When Mr. Chandler discovered that there was something with the mummies, he supposed or hoped it might be some diamonds or valuable metal, and was no little chagrined when he saw his disappointment. "He was immediately told, while yet in the custom house, that there was no man in that city who could translate his roll: but was referred, by the same gentleman, (a stranger) to Mr. Joseph Smith, Jun., who, continued he, possesses some kind of power or gifts, by which he had previously translated similar characters." I was then unknown to Mr. Chandler, neither did he know that such a book or work as the record of the Nephites, had been brought before the public. From New York, he took his collection on to Philadelphia, where he obtained the certificate of the learned, and from thence came on to Kirtland, as before related, in July. Thus I have given a brief history of the manner in which the writings of the fathers, Abraham and Joseph, have been preserved, and how I came in possession of the same—a correct translation of which I shall give in its proper place.

Chapter Eight

1836

Friday Morning, January 1, 1836—This being the beginning of a new year, my heart is filled with gratitude to God that He has preserved my life, and the lives of my family, while another year has passed away. We have been sustained and upheld in the midst of a wicked and perverse generation, although exposed to all the afflictions, temptations, and misery that are incident to human life; for this I feel to humble myself in dust and ashes, as it were, before the Lord. But notwithstanding the gratitude that fills my heart on retrospecting the past year, and the multiplied blessings that have crowned our heads, my heart is pained within me, because of the difficulty that exists in my father's family. The devil has made a violent attack on my brother William and Calvin Stoddard, and the powers of darkness seem to lower over their minds, and not only over theirs, but they also cast a gloomy shade over the minds of my brethren and sisters, which prevents them from seeing things as they really are; and the powers of earth and hell seem combined to overthrow us and the Church, by causing a division in the family; and indeed the adversary is bringing into requisition all his subtlety to prevent the Saints from being endowed, by causing a division among the Twelve, also among the Seventy, and bickering and jealousies among the elders and the official members of the Church; and so the leaven of iniquity ferments and spreads among the members of the Church. But I am determined that nothing on my part shall be lacking to adjust and amicably dispose of and settle all family difficulties on this day, that the ensuing year and years, be they few or many, may be spent in righteousness before God. And I know that the cloud will burst, and Satan's kingdom be laid in ruins, with all his black designs; and that the Saints will come forth like gold seven times tried in the fire, being made perfect through sufferings and temptations, and that the blessings of heaven and earth will be multiplied upon their heads; which may God grant for Christ's sake. Amen.

Brothers William and Hyrum, and Uncle John Smith, came to my house, and we went into a room by ourselves, in company with father and Elder Martin Harris. Father Smith then opened our interview by prayer, after which he expressed himself on the occasion in a very feeling and pathetic manner, even with all the sympathy of a father, whose feelings were deeply wounded on account of the difficulty that was existing in the family; and while he addressed us, the Spirit of God rested down upon us in mighty power, and our hearts were melted. Brother William made a humble confession and asked my forgiveness for the abuse he had offered me. And wherein I had been out of the way, I asked his forgiveness. And the spirit of confession and forgiveness was mutual among us all, and we covenanted with each other, in the sight of God, and the holy angels, and the brethren, to strive thenceforward to build each other up in righteousness in all things, and not listen to evil reports concerning each other; but, like brothers indeed, go to each other, with our grievances, in the spirit of meekness, and be reconciled, and thereby promote our happiness, and the happiness of the family, and, in short, the happiness and well-being of all. My wife and mother and my scribe were then called in, and we repeated the covenant to them that we had entered into; and while gratitude swelled our bosoms, tears flowed from our eyes. I was then requested to close our interview, which I did, with prayer; and it was truly a jubilee and time of rejoicing; after which we all unitedly administered, by laying on of hands, to my cousin George A. Smith, who was immediately healed of a severe rheumatic affection all over the body, which caused excruciating pain.

Monday, January 4—Met and organized our Hebrew school according to the arrangements that were made on Saturday last. We had engaged Doctor Piexotto to teach us in the Hebrew language, when we had our room prepared. We informed him that we were ready and our room was prepared. And he agreed to wait on us this day, and deliver his introductory lecture. Yesterday he sent us word that he could not come until Wednesday next. A vote was then called to know whether we would submit to such treatment or not; and carried in the negative; and Elder Sylvester Smith was appointed clerk to write him on the subject, and inform him that his services were not wanted; and Elders William E. M'Lellin and Orson Hyde despatched to Hudson Seminary to hire a teacher. They were appointed by the voice of the school to act in their behalf. However, we concluded to go on with our school and do the best we could until we obtained a teacher; and by the voice of the school I consented to render them all the assistance I was able to for the time being.

We are occupying the translating room for the use of the school, until another room can be prepared. It is the west room in the upper part of the temple, and was consecrated this morning by prayer, offered up by Father Smith. This is the first day we have occupied it. This is a rainy time, and the roads are extremely muddy.

Met this evening at the temple, to make arrangements for a singing school.

After some discussion, a judicious arrangement was made, a committee of six was chosen to take charge of the singing department.

Tuesday, January 5—Attended the Hebrew school, divided it into classes. Had some debate with Elder Orson Pratt concerning the pronunciation of a Hebrew letter. He manifested a stubborn spirit, at which I was much grieved.

Wednesday, January 6—Attended school and spent most of the forenoon in settling the unpleasant feelings that existed in the breast of Elder Orson Pratt. After much controversy, he confessed his fault for entering into any controversy concerning so small a matter as the sound of a Hebrew letter, and asked the forgiveness of the whole school, and was cheerfully forgiven by all.

Elder M'Lellin returned from Hudson, and reported to the school that he had hired a teacher to teach us the term of seven weeks, for three hundred and twenty dollars; that is, forty scholars for that amount; to commence in about fifteen days. He is highly celebrated as a Hebrew scholar, and proposes to give us sufficient knowledge during the above term to start us in reading and translating the language.

Much has been said and done of late by the general government in relation to the Indians (Lamanites) within the territorial limits of the United States. One of the most important points in the faith of the Church of the Latter-day Saints, through the fullness of the everlasting gospel, is the gathering of Israel (of whom the Lamanites constitute a part)—that happy time when Jacob shall go up to the house of the Lord, to worship Him in spirit and in truth, to live in holiness; when the Lord will restore His judges as at the first, and His counselors as at the beginning; when every man may sit under his own vine and fig tree, and there will be none to molest or make afraid; when He will turn to them a pure language, and the earth will be filled with sacred knowledge, as the waters cover the great deep; when it shall no longer be said, the Lord lives that brought up the children of Israel out of the land of Egypt, but the Lord lives that brought up the children of Israel from the land of the north, and from all the lands whither

He has driven them. That day is one, all important to all men.

In view of its importance, together with all that the prophets have said about it before us, we feel like dropping a few ideas in connection with the official statements from the government concerning the Indians. In speaking of the gathering, we mean to be understood as speaking of it according to scripture, the gathering of the elect of the Lord out of every nation on earth, and bringing them to the place of the Lord of hosts, when the city of righteousness shall be built, and where the people shall be of one heart and one mind, when the Savior comes; yea, where the people shall walk with God like Enoch, and be free from sin. The word of the Lord is precious; and when we read that the vail spread over all nations will be destroyed, and the pure in heart see God, and reign with Him a thousand years on earth, we want all honest men to have a chance to gather and build up a city of righteousness, where even upon the bells of the horses shall be written Holiness to the Lord.

The joy that we shall feel, in common with every honest American, and the joy that will eventually fill their bosoms on account of nationalizing the Indians, will be reward enough when it is shown that gathering them to themselves, and for themselves, to be associated with themselves, is a wise measure, and it reflects the highest honor upon our government. May they all be gathered in peace, and form a happy union among themselves, to which thousands may shout, ústo perpetua.

Thursday, January 7—Attended a sumptuous feast at Bishop Newel K. Whitney's. This feast was after the order of the Son of God—the lame, the halt, and the blind were invited, according to the instructions of the Savior. Our meeting was opened by singing, and prayer by Father Smith; after which Bishop Whitney's father and mother, and a number of others, were blessed with a patriarchal blessing. We then received a bountiful refreshment, furnished by the liberality of the bishop. The company was large, and before we partook we had some of the songs of Zion sung; and our hearts were made glad by a foretaste of those joys that will be poured upon the heads of the Saints when they are gathered together on Mount Zion, to enjoy one another's society for evermore, even all the blessings of heaven, when there will be none to molest or make us afraid. Returned home, and spent the evening.

Friday, January 8—Spent the day in the Hebrew school, and made rapid progress in our studies. The plastering and hard-finishing on the outside of the Lord's house was commenced on the 2nd of November, 1835, and finished this day. The job was let to Artemas Millet and Lorenzo Young, at one thousand dollars. Jacob Bump took the job of plastering the inside of the house throughout, at fifteen hundred dollars, and commenced the same on the 9th of November last. He is still continuing the work, notwithstanding the inclemency of the weather.

Thursday, January 14—Nine o'clock. Met the Hebrew class at the school room in the temple, and made some arrangements about our anticipated teacher, Mr. Joshua Seixas, of Hudson, Ohio.

Returned home and spent the afternoon. Towards evening President Cowdery returned from Columbus, the capital of the state. I could spend but little time with him, being under obligation to attend at Mrs. Wilcox's, to join Mr. John Webb and Mrs. Catherine Wilcox in matrimony; also Mr. Thomas Carrico and Miss Elizabeth Baker, at the same place; all of which I performed in the customary manner in the midst of a large assembly. We then partook of some refreshments, and our hearts were made glad with the fruit of the vine. This is according to the pattern set by our Savior Himself, and we feel disposed to patronize all the institutions of heaven.

Friday, January 15—At nine a.m., met in council agreeable to adjournment, at the council room in the temple, and seated the authorities of the Church agreeable to their respective offices. I then made some observations respecting the order of the day, and the great responsibility we were under to transact all our business in righteousness before God, inasmuch as our decisions will have a bearing upon all mankind, and upon all generations to come.

Sunday, January 17—Attended meeting at the school house at the usual hour; a large congregation assembled. I proceeded to arrange the several quorums present, first the Presidency, then the Twelve, and the Seventy who were present, also the councilors of Kirtland and Zion.

President Rigdon then arose and observed that instead of preaching the time would be occupied by the Presidency and Twelve, in speaking each in his turn until they had all spoken. The Lord poured out His Spirit upon us, and the brethren began to confess their faults one to the other, and the congregation was soon overwhelmed in tears, and some of our hearts were too big for utterance. The gift of tongues came on us also, like the rushing of a mighty wind, and my soul was filled with the glory of God.

In the afternoon I joined three couples in matrimony, in the public congregation, viz., William F. Cahoon and Maranda Gibbs, Harvey Stanley and Larona Cahoon, Tunis Rapley and Louisa Cutler. We then administered the sacrament and dismissed the congregation, which was so large that it was very unpleasant for all. We were then invited to a feast at Elder Cahoon's which was prepared for the occasion, and had a good time while partaking of the rich repast; and I verily realized that it was good for brethren to dwell together in unity, like the dew upon the mountains of Israel, where the Lord commanded blessings, even life forevermore. Spent the evening at home.

Monday, January 18—Attended the Hebrew school. This day the elders' school was removed into the temple, in the room adjoining the Hebrew school.

Tuesday, January 19—Spent the day at school. The Lord blessed us in our studies. This day we commenced reading in our Hebrew Bibles with much success. It seems as if the Lord opens our minds in a marvelous manner, to understand His word in the original language; and my prayer is that God will speedily endow us with a knowledge of all languages and tongues, that His servants may go forth for the last time the better prepared to bind up the law, and seal up the testimony.

Thursday, January 21—This morning, a minister from Connecticut, by the name of John W. Olived, called at my house and inquired of my father: "Does the Prophet live here?" My father replied he did not understand him. Mr. Olived asked the same question again and again, and received the same answer. He finally asked:

"Does Mr. Smith live here?" Father replied: "O yes, sir, I understand you now." Father then stepped into my room and informed me that a gentleman had called to see me. I went into the room where he was, and the first question he asked me, after passing a compliment was: "How many members have you in your Church?" I replied that we had between fifteen hundred and two thousand in this branch. He then asked: "Wherein do you differ from other Christian denominations?" I replied, that we believe the Bible, and they do not. However, he affirmed that he believed the Bible. I told him then to be baptized. He replied that he did not realize it to be his duty. But when I laid before him the principles of the gospel, viz., faith and repentance; baptism, for the remission of sins; and the laying on of hands, for the reception of the Holy Ghost, he manifested much surprise. I observed that the hour for school had arrived, and I must attend. The man appeared astonished at our doctrine, but by no means hostile.

About three o'clock, p.m., I dismissed the school, and the Presidency retired to the attic story of the printing office, where we attended the ordinance of washing our bodies in pure water. We also perfumed our bodies and our heads, in the name of the Lord.

At early candle-light I met with the Presidency at the west school room, in the temple, to attend to the ordinance of anointing our heads with holy oil; also the councils of Kirtland and Zion met in the two adjoining rooms, and waited in prayer while we attended to the ordinance. I took the oil in my left hand, Father Smith being seated before me, and the remainder of the Presidency

"THE HEAVENS WERE OPENED UPON US, AND I BEHELD THE CELESTIAL KINGDOM OF GOD."

encircled him round about. We then stretched our right hands towards heaven, and blessed the oil, and consecrated it in the name of Jesus Christ.

We then laid our hands upon our aged Father Smith, and invoked the blessings of heaven. I then anointed his head with the consecrated oil, and sealed many blessings upon him. The Presidency then in turn laid their hands upon his head, beginning at the oldest, until they had all laid their hands upon him, and pronounced such blessings upon his head, as the Lord put into their hearts, all blessing him to be our patriarch, to anoint our heads, and attend to all duties that pertain to that office. The Presidency then took the seat in their turn, according to their age, beginning at the oldest, and received their anointing and blessing under the hands of Father Smith. And in my turn, my father anointed my head, and sealed upon me the blessings of Moses, to lead Israel in the latter days, even as Moses led him in days of old; also the blessings of Abraham, Isaac and Jacob. All of the Presidency laid their hands upon me, and pronounced upon my head many prophecies and blessings, many of which I shall not notice at this time. But as Paul said, so say I, let us come to visions and revelations.

The heavens were opened upon us, and I beheld the celestial kingdom of God, and the glory thereof, whether in the body or out I cannot tell. I saw the transcendent beauty of the gate through which the heirs of that kingdom will enter, which was like unto circling flames of fire; also the blazing throne of God, whereon was seated the Father and the Son. I saw the beautiful streets of that kingdom, which had the appearance of being paved with gold. I saw Fathers Adam and Abraham, and my father and mother, my brother, Alvin, that has long since slept, and marvelled how it was that he had obtained an inheritance in that kingdom, seeing that he had departed this life before the Lord had set His hand to gather Israel the second time, and had not been baptized for the remission of sins.

And I also beheld that all children who die before they arrive at the years of accountability, are saved in the celestial kingdom of heaven. I saw the Twelve Apostles of the Lamb, who are now upon the earth, who hold the keys of this last ministry, in foreign lands, standing together in a circle, much fatigued, with their clothes tattered and feet swollen, with their eyes cast downward, and Jesus standing in their midst, and they did not behold Him. The Savior looked upon them and wept.

I also beheld Elder McLellin in the south, standing upon a hill, surrounded by a vast multitude, preaching to them, and a lame man standing before him supported by his crutches; he threw them down at his word and leaped as a hart, by the mighty power of God. Also, I saw Elder Brigham Young standing in a strange land, in the far south and west, in a desert place, upon a rock in the midst of about a dozen men of color, who appeared hostile. He was preaching to them in their own tongue, and the angel of God standing above his head, with a drawn sword in his hand, protecting him, but he did not see it. And I finally saw the Twelve in the celestial kingdom of God. I also beheld the redemption of Zion, and many things which the tongue of man cannot describe in full.

Many of my brethren who received the ordinance with me saw glorious visions also. Angels ministered unto them as well as to myself, and the power of the Highest rested upon us, the house was filled with the glory of God, and we shouted hosanna to God and the Lamb. My scribe also received his anointing with us, and saw, in a vision, the armies of heaven protecting the Saints in their return to Zion, and many things which I saw.

The bishop of Kirtland with his counselors, and the bishop of Zion with his counselors, were present with us, and received their anointings under the hands of Father Smith, and this was confirmed by the Presidency, and the glories of heaven were unfolded to them also.

We then invited the high councilors of Kirtland and Zion into our room, and President Hyrum Smith anointed the head of the president of the councilors in Kirtland, and President David Whitmer the head of the president of the councilors of Zion.

The president of each quorum then anointed the heads of his colleagues, each in his turn, beginning at the oldest.

The visions of heaven were opened to them also. Some of them saw the face of the Savior, and others were ministered unto by holy angels, and the spirit of prophecy and revelation was poured out in mighty power; and loud hosannas, and glory to God in the highest, saluted the heavens, for we all communed with the heavenly host. And I saw in my vision all of the Presidency in the celestial kingdom of God, and many others that were present. Our meeting was opened by singing, and prayer was offered up by the head of each quorum; and closed by singing, and invoking the benediction of heaven, with uplifted hands. Retired between one and two o'clock in the morning.

Friday, January 22—Attended at the school room at the usual hour, but instead of pursuing our studies, we spent the time in rehearsing to each other the glorious scenes that occurred on the preceding evening, while attending to the ordinance of holy anointing.

In the evening we met at the same place, with the Council of the Twelve, and the Presidency of the Seventy, who were to receive this ordinance (of anointing and blessing). The high councils of Kirtland and Zion were present also.

After calling to order and organizing, the Presidency proceeded to consecrate the oil.

We then laid our hands upon Elder Thomas B. Marsh, who is President of the Twelve, and ordained him to the authority of anointing his brethren. I then poured the consecrated oil upon his head, in the name of Jesus Christ, and sealed such blessings upon him as the Lord put into my heart. The rest of the Presidency then laid their hands upon him and blessed him, each in his turn, beginning at the oldest. He then anointed and blessed his brethren from the oldest to the youngest. I also laid my hands upon them, and pronounced many great and glorious things upon their heads. The heavens were opened, and angels ministered unto us.

The Twelve then proceeded to anoint and bless the Presidency of the Seventy, and seal upon their heads power and authority to anoint their brethren.

The heavens were opened unto Elder Sylvester Smith, and he, leaping up, exclaimed: "The horsemen of Israel and the chariots thereof."

Brother Don C. Smith was also anointed and blessed to preside over the high priests' quorum.

President Rigdon arose to conclude the services of the evening by invoking the blessing of heaven upon the Lord's anointed, which he did in an eloquent manner; the congregation shouted a long hosanna: the gift of tongues fell upon us in mighty power, angels mingled their voices with ours, while their presence was in our midst, and unceasing praises swelled our bosoms for the space of half an hour.

I then observed to the brethren, that it was time to retire. We accordingly closed our interview and returned home at about two o'clock in the morning, and the Spirit and visions of God attended me through the night.

Tuesday, January 26—Mr. Seixas arrived from Hudson, to teach the Hebrew language, and I attended upon the organizing of the class, for the purpose of receiving lectures upon Hebrew grammar. His hours of instruction are from ten to eleven, a.m.; and from two to three, p.m. His instruction pleased me much. I think he will be a help to the class in learning Hebrew.

Wednesday, January 27—Attended school as usual, and also attended to other matters which came before me.

Thursday, January 28—Attended school at the usual hour.

In the evening met the quorum of high priests, in the west room of the upper loft of the Lord's house, and, in company with my counselors, consecrated and anointed the counselors of the presidents of the high priests' quorum, and, having instructed them and set the quorum in order, I left them to perform the holy anointing, and went to the quorum of elders at the other end of the room. I assisted in anointing the counselors of the president of the elders, and gave the instruction necessary for the occasion, and left the president and his counselors to anoint the elders, while I should go to the adjoining room, and attend to organizing and instructing the Quorum of the Seventy.

I found the Twelve Apostles assembled with this quorum, and I proceeded, with the quorum of "the Presidency, to instruct them, and also the seven Presidents of the Seventy elders, to call upon God with up-lifted hands, to seal the blessings which had been promised to them by the holy anointing. As I organized this quorum, with the Presidency in this room, President Sylvester Smith saw a pillar of fire rest down and abide upon the heads of the quorum, as we stood in the midst of the Twelve.

When the Twelve and the seven presidents were through with their sealing prayer, I called upon President Sidney Rigdon to seal them with up-lifted hands; and when he had done this, and cried hosanna, that all the congregation should join him, and shout hosanna to God and the Lamb, and glory to God in the highest. It was done so, and Elder Roger Orton saw a mighty angel riding upon a horse of fire, with a flaming sword in his hand, followed by five others, encircle the house, and protect the Saints, even the Lord's anointed, from the power of Satan and a host of evil spirits, which were striving to disturb the Saints.

President William Smith, one of the Twelve, saw the heavens opened, and the Lord's host protecting the Lord's anointed.

President Zebedee Coltrin, one of the seven Presidents of the Seventy, saw the Savior extended before him, as upon the cross, and a little after, crowned with glory upon his head above the brightness of the sun.

After these things were over, and a glorious vision, which I saw, had passed, I instructed the seven presidents to proceed and anoint the Seventy, and returned to the room of the high priests and elders, and attended to the sealing of what they had done, with up-lifted hands.

The Lord assisted my brother, Don Carlos, the president of the high priests, to go forward with the anointing of the high priests, so that he had performed it to the acceptance of the Lord, notwithstanding he was very young and inexperienced in such duties; and I felt to praise God with a loud hosanna, for His goodness to me and my father's family, and to all the children of men. Praise the Lord, all ye, His Saints, praise His holy name.

After these quorums were dismissed, I retired to my home, filled with the Spirit, and my soul cried hosanna to God and the Lamb, through the silent watches of the night; and while my eyes were closed in sleep, the visions of the Lord were sweet unto me, and his glory was round about me. Praise the Lord.

Friday, January 29—Attended school and read Hebrew. I received a line from the presidency of the elders' quorum, they wishing to know whom they should receive into their quorum, I answered verbally.

Afternoon, I called in all my father's family and made a feast, and related my feelings towards them. My father pronounced patriarchal blessings on the heads of Henry Gannet, Charles H. Smith, Marietta Carter, Angeline Carter, Johanna Carter, and Nancy Carter. This was a good time to me, and all the family rejoiced together. We continued the meeting till about eight o'clock in the evening, and related the goodness of God to us, in opening our eyes to see the visions of heaven, and in sending His holy angels to minister unto us the word of life. We sang the praise of God in animated strains, and the power of union and love was felt and enjoyed.

Saturday, January 30—Attended school, as usual, and waited upon several visitors, and showed them the record of Abraham. Mr. Seixas, our Hebrew teacher, examined it with deep interest, and pronounced it to be original beyond all doubt. He is a man of excellent understanding, and has a knowledge of many languages which were spoken by the ancients, and he is an honorable man, so far as I can judge yet.

In the evening, went to the upper rooms of the Lord's house, and set the different quorums in order. Instructed the presidents of the Seventy concerning the order of their anointing, and requested them to proceed and anoint the Seventy. Having set all the quorums in order, I returned to my house, being weary with continual anxiety and labor, in putting all the authorities in order, and in striving to purify them for the solemn assembly, according to the commandment of the Lord.

Sunday, January 31—Attended divine service in the school house, arranged the several quorums of the authorities of the Church, appointed doorkeepers to keep order about the door, because of the crowd, and to prevent the house from being excessively crowded. The high council of Zion occupied the first part of the day, in speaking as they were led, and relating experiences, trials, etc.

Afternoon. House came to order, as usual, and President Sidney Rigdon delivered a short discourse, and we attended to the breaking of bread.

In the evening, my father attended to the blessing of three brethren, at President Oliver Cowdery's. Spent the evening at home.

Thursday, February 4—Attended school, and assisted in forming a class of twenty-two members to read at three o'clock, p.m. The other twenty-three read at eleven o'clock. The first class recites at a quarter before ten, a.m., and the second a quarter before two, p.m. We have a great want of books, but are determined to do the best we can. May the Lord help us to obtain this language, that we may read the scriptures in the language in which they were given.

Saturday, February 6—President William Smith, one of the Twelve, saw a vision of the Twelve, and Seven in council together, in old England, and prophesied that a great work would be done by them in the old countries, and God was already beginning to work in the hearts of the people.

President Zebedee Coltrin, one of the Seven, saw a vision of the Lord's host.

And others were filled with the Spirit, and spake with tongues and prophesied. This was a time of rejoicing long to be remembered. Praise the Lord.

Wednesday, February 10—At ten o'clock, met at the school room to read Hebrew.

Afternoon, read in the upper room of the printing office.

At four o'clock, called at the school room in the temple to make some arrangements concerning the classes. On my return, I was informed that Brother Hyrum Smith had cut himself. I immediately repaired to his house, and found him badly wounded in his left arm, he had fallen on his ax, which caused a wound about four or five inches in length. Doctor Williams sewed it up and dressed it, and I feel to thank God that it is no worse, and I ask my Heavenly Father in the name of Jesus Christ to heal my brother Hyrum, and bless my father's family, one and all, with peace and plenty, and eternal life.

Thursday, February 11—Attended school, and read Hebrew with the morning class.

Spent the afternoon in reading, and in exhibiting the Egyptian records to those who called to see me, and heaven's blessings have attended me.

Saturday, February 13—Spent the day in reading Hebrew.

At noon I prepared a horse and sleigh for Professor Seixas to go to Hudson and see his family.

Monday, February 15—Attended school at the usual hours.

Spent the afternoon in reading Hebrew and in receiving and waiting on visitors.

On this day we commenced translating the Hebrew language, under the instruction of Professor Seixas, and he stated that we were the most forward of any class he ever instructed for the same length of time.

Wednesday, February 17—Attended the school and read and translated with my class as usual. My soul delights in reading the word of the Lord in the original, and I am determined to pursue the study of the languages, until I shall become master of them, if I am permitted to live long enough. At any rate, so long as I do live, I am determined to make this my object; and with the blessing of God, I shall succeed to my satisfaction.

Elder Coe called to make some arrangements about the Egyptian mummies and records. He proposes to hire a room at John Johnson's Inn, and exhibit them there from day to day, at certain hours, that some benefit may be derived from them. I complied with his request, and only observed that they must be managed with prudence and care, especially the manuscripts.

Sunday, February 21—Spent the day at home in reading, meditation and prayer.

I reviewed my lesson in Hebrew. Some three or four persons were baptized, and the powers of darkness seem to be giving way on all sides. Many who have been enemies to the work of the Lord are beginning to enquire into the faith of the Latter-day Saints, and are friendly.

Monday, February 22—The lower room of the temple is now prepared for painting. Elder Brigham Young was obliged to leave the Hebrew class and superintend the painting of the lower room until finished.

This afternoon the sisters met to make the veil of the temple. Father Smith presided over them, and gave them much good instruction. Closed by singing and prayer, which is customary at the commencement and close of all councils and meetings of the Church of Latter-day Saints, although not always mentioned in this record.

Thursday, February 25—Attended to my studies as usual, and made some advancement.

In the afternoon I was called upon by Elder Rigdon to go and see his wife, who was very sick. I did so in company with my scribe. We prayed for her and anointed her in the name of the Lord, and she began to recover from that very hour. Returned home and spent the evening there.

Monday, February 29—Spent the day in studying as usual. A man called to see the house of the Lord, in company with another gentleman. On entering the door they were politely invited, by the gentleman who had charge of the house, to take off their hats. One of them replied with the request unhesitatingly, while the other observed that he would not take off his hat nor bow to "Jo Smith," but that he had made "Jo" bow to him at a certain time. He was immediately informed by Elder Morey, the keeper of the house, that his first business was to leave, for when a man insulted Joseph Smith he, Brother Morey, was himself insulted. The man manifested much anger, but left the house. For this independence and resolution of Elder Morey, I respect him, and for the love he manifested towards me; and may Israel's God bless him, and give him an ascendency over all his enemies.

Sunday, March 27—The congregation began to assemble at the temple, at about seven o'clock, an hour earlier than the doors were to be opened. Many brethren had come in from the regions round about, to witness the dedication of the Lord's House and share in His blessings; and such was the anxiety on this occasion that some hundreds (probably five or six) assembled before the doors were opened. The presidents entered with the doorkeepers, and stationed the latter at the inner and outer doors; also placed our stewards to receive donations from those who should feel "disposed to contribute something to defray the expense of building the house of the Lord. We also dedicated the pulpits, and consecrated them to the Lord.

The doors were then opened. Presidents Rigdon, Cowdery and myself seated the congregation as they came in, and, according to the best calculation we could make, we received between nine and ten hundred, which were as many as could be comfortably seated. We then informed the doorkeepers that we could receive no more, and a multitude were deprived of the benefits of the meeting on account of the house not being sufficiently capacious to receive them; and I felt to regret that any of my brethren and sisters should be deprived of the meeting, and I recommended them to repair to the schoolhouse and hold a meeting, which they did, and filled that house also, and yet many were left out.

Received by contribution—nine hundred and sixty-three dollars.

At nine o'clock a.m. President Sidney Rigdon commenced the services of the day by reading the 96th and 24th Psalms. He spoke two hours and a half in his usual logical manner. His prayer and address were very forcible and sublime, and well adapted to the occasion. At one time, in the course of his remarks, he was rather pathetic, and drew tears from many eyes. He was then taking a retrospective view of the toils, privations, and anxieties of those who had labored upon the walls of the house to erect them; and added, there were those who had wet them with their tears, in the silent shades of night, while they were praying to the God of heaven to protect them, and stay the unhallowed hands of ruthless spoilers, who had uttered a prophecy, when the foundation was laid, that the walls would never be reared.

After closing his discourse he called upon the several quorums, commencing with the Presidency, to manifest, by rising, their willingness to acknowledge me as a prophet and seer, and uphold me as such, by their prayers of faith. All the quorums, in turn, cheerfully complied with this request. He then called upon all the congregation of Saints, also, to give their assent by rising on their feet, which they did unanimously.

I then made a short address, and called upon the several quorums, and all the congregation of Saints, to acknowledge the Presidency as prophets and seers, and uphold them by their prayers. They all covenanted to do so, by rising.

The vote was unanimous in every instance, and I prophesied to all, that inasmuch as they would uphold these men in their several stations (alluding to the different quorums in the Church), the Lord would bless them; yea, in the name of Christ, the blessings of heaven should be theirs; and when the Lord's anointed go forth to proclaim the word, bearing testimony to this generation, if they receive it they shall be blessed; but if not, the judgments of God will follow close upon them, until that city or that house which rejects them, shall be left desolate.

The dedicatory prayer was then offered:

See Doctrine and Covenants 109.

The choir then sang: *The Spirit of God.*

I then asked the several quorums separately, and then the congregation, if they accepted the dedication prayer, and acknowledged the house dedicated. The vote was unanimous in the affirmative, in every instance.

The Lord's supper was then administered; President Don Carlos Smith blessed the bread and the wine, which was distributed by several elders to the Church; after which I bore record of my mission and of the ministration of angels.

President Don Carlos Smith also bore testimony of the truth of the work of the Lord in which we were engaged.

President Oliver Cowdery testified of the truth of the Book of Mormon, and of the work of the Lord in these last days.

President Frederick G. Williams arose and testified that while President Rigdon was making his first prayer, an angel entered the window and took his seat between Father Smith and himself, and remained there during the prayer.

President David Whitmer also saw angels in the house.

President Hyrum Smith made some appropriate remarks congratulating those who had endured so many toils and privations to build the house.

President Rigdon then made a few appropriate closing remarks, and a short prayer, at the close of which we sealed the proceedings of the day by shouting hosanna, hosanna, hosanna to God and the Lamb, three times, sealing it each time with amen, amen, and amen.

President Brigham Young gave a short address in tongues, and David W. Patten interpreted, and gave a short exhortation in tongues himself, after which I blessed the congregation in the name of the Lord, and the assembly dispersed a little past four o'clock, having manifested the most quiet demeanor during the whole exercise.

I met the quorums in the evening and instructed them respecting the ordinance of washing of feet, which they were to attend to on Wednesday following; and gave them instructions in relation to the spirit of prophecy, and called upon the congregation to speak, and not to fear to prophesy good concerning the Saints, for if you prophesy the falling of these hills and the rising of the valleys, the downfall of the enemies of Zion and the rising of the kingdom of God, it shall come to pass. Do not quench the Spirit, for the first one that opens his mouth shall receive the spirit of prophecy.

Brother George A. Smith arose and began to prophesy, when a noise was heard like the sound of a rushing mighty wind, which filled the temple, and all the congregation simultaneously arose, being moved upon by an invisible power; many began to speak in tongues and prophesy; others saw glorious visions; and I beheld the temple was filled with angels, which fact I declared to the congregation. The people of the neighborhood came running together (hearing an unusual sound within, and seeing a bright light like a pillar of fire resting upon the temple), and were astonished at what was taking place. This continued until the meeting closed at eleven p.m.

The number of official members present on this occasion was four hundred and sixteen, being a greater number than ever assembled on any former occasion.

Monday, March 28—Attended school. Very warm, like spring.

Tuesday, March 29—Attended school, which was the last day of our course of lectures in Hebrew, by Professor Seixas.

At eleven o'clock, a.m., Presidents Joseph Smith, Jun., Frederick G. Williams, Sidney Rigdon, Hyrum Smith, and Oliver

Cowdery met in the most holy place in the Lord's house, and sought for a revelation from Him concerning the authorities of the Church going to Zion, and other important matters. After uniting in prayer, the voice of the Spirit was that we should come into this place three times, and also call the other presidents, the two bishops and their counselors, each to stand in his place, and fast through the day and also the night, and that during this, if we would humble ourselves, we should receive further communications from Him. After this word was received we immediately sent for the other brethren, who came.

The Presidency proceeded to ordain George Boosinger to the high priesthood, and anoint him. This was in consequence of his having administered unto us in temporal things in our distress, and also because he left the place just previous to the dedication of the Lord's house, to bring us the temporal means, previously named. Soon after this, the word of the Lord came, through President Joseph Smith, Jun., that those who had entered the holy place, must not leave the house until morning, but send for such things as were necessary, and, also, during our stay, we must cleanse our feet and partake of the sacrament that we might be made holy before Him, and thereby be qualified to officiate in our calling, upon the morrow, in washing the feet of the elders.

Accordingly we proceeded to cleanse our faces and our feet, and then proceeded to wash one another's feet. President Sidney Rigdon first washed President Joseph Smith, Junior's feet, and then, in turn, was washed by him; after which President Rigdon washed President Joseph Smith, Sen., and Hyrum Smith. President Joseph Smith, Jun., washed President Frederick G. Williams, and then President Hyrum Smith washed President David Whitmer's and President Oliver Cowdery's feet. Then President David Whitmer washed President William W. Phelps' feet, and in turn President Phelps washed President John Whitmer's feet. The bishops and their counselors were then washed, after which we partook of the bread and wine. The Holy Spirit rested down upon us, and we continued in the Lord's house all night, prophesying and giving glory to God.

Wednesday, March 30—At eight o'clock, according to appointment, the Presidency, the Twelve, the Seventies, the high council, the bishops and their entire quorums, the elders and all the official members in this stake of Zion, amounting to about three hundred, met in the Temple of the Lord to attend to the ordinance of washing of feet. I ascended the pulpit, and remarked to the congregation that we had passed through many trials and afflictions since the organization of the Church, and that this is a year of jubilee to us, and a time of rejoicing, and that is was expedient for us to prepare bread and wine sufficient to make our hearts glad, as we should not, probably, leave this house until morning; to this end we should call on the brethren to make a contribution. The stewards passed round and took up a liberal contribution, and messengers were dispatched for bread and wine.

Tubs, water, and towels were prepared, and I called the house to order, and the Presidency proceeded to wash the feet of the Twelve, pronouncing many prophecies and blessings upon them in the name of the Lord Jesus; and then the Twelve proceeded to wash the feet of the presidents of the several quorums. The brethren began to prophesy upon each other's heads, and upon the enemies of Christ, who inhabited Jackson county, Missouri; and continued prophesying, and blessing, and sealing them with hosanna and amen, until nearly seven o'clock in the evening.

The bread and wine were then brought in, and I observed that we had fasted all the day, and lest we faint, as the Savior did so shall we do on this occasion; we shall bless the bread, and give it to the Twelve, and they to the multitude. While waiting, I made the following remarks: that the time that we were required to tarry in Kirtland to be endowed, would be fulfilled in a few days, and then the elders would go forth, and each must stand for himself, as it was not necessary for them to be sent out, two by two, as in former times, but to go in all meekness, in sobriety, and preach

Jesus Christ and Him crucified; not to contend with others on account of their faith, or systems of religion, but pursue a steady course. This I delivered by way of commandment; and all who observe it not, will pull down persecution upon their heads, while those who do, shall always be filled with the Holy Ghost; this I pronounced as a prophecy, and sealed with hosanna and amen. Also that the Seventies are not called to serve tables, or preside over churches, to settle difficulties, but are to preach the gospel and build them up, and set others, who do not belong to these quorums, to preside over them, who are high priests. The Twelve also are not to serve tables, but to bear the keys of the kingdom to all nations, and unlock the door of the gospel to them, and call upon the Seventies to follow after them, and assist them. The Twelve are at liberty to go wheresoever they will, and if anyone will say, I wish to go to such a place, let all the rest say amen.

The Seventies are at liberty to go to Zion if they please, or go wheresoever they will, and preach the gospel; and let the redemption of Zion be our object, and strive to effect it by sending up all the strength of the Lord's house, wherever we find them; and I want to enter into the following covenant, that if any more of our brethren are slain or driven from their lands in Missouri, by the mob, we will give ourselves no rest, until we are avenged of our enemies to the uttermost. This covenant was sealed unanimously, with a hosanna and an amen.

I then observed to the quorums, that I had now completed the organization of the Church, and we had passed through all the necessary ceremonies, that I had given them all the instruction they needed, and that they now were at liberty, after obtaining their licenses, to go forth and build up the kingdom of God, and that it was expedient for me and the Presidency to retire, having spent the night previously in waiting upon the Lord in His temple, and having to attend another dedication on the morrow, or conclude the one commenced on the last Sabbath, for the benefit of those of my brethren and sisters who could not get into the house on the former occasion, but that it was expedient for the brethren to tarry all night and worship before the Lord in His house.

I left the meeting in the charge of the Twelve, and retired about nine o'clock in the evening. The brethren continued exhorting, prophesying, and speaking in tongues until five o'clock in the morning. The Savior made His appearance to some, while angels ministered to others, and it was a Pentacost and an endowment indeed, long to be remembered, for the sound shall go forth from this place into all the world, and the occurrences of this day shall be handed down upon the pages of sacred history, to all generations; as the day of Pentacost, so shall this day be numbered and celebrated as a year of jubilee, and time of rejoicing to the Saints of the Most High God.

Thursday, March 31—This day being set apart to perform again the ceremonies of the dedication, for the benefit of those who could not get into the house on the preceding Sabbath, I repaired to the temple at eight, a.m., in company with the Presidency, and arranged our door keepers and stewards as on the former occasion. We then opened the doors, and a large congregation entered the house, and were comfortably seated. The authorities of the Church were seated in their respective places, and the services of the day were commenced, prosecuted and terminated in the same manner as at the former dedication, and the Spirit of God rested upon the congregation, and great solemnity prevailed.

Sunday, April 3—Attended meeting in the Lord's house, and assisted the other presidents of the Church in seating the congregation, and then became an attentive listener to the preaching from the stand. Thomas B. Marsh and David W. Patten spoke in the forenoon to an attentive audience of about one thousand persons. In the afternoon, I assisted the other presidents in distributing the Lord's supper to the Church, receiving it from the Twelve, whose privilege it was to officiate at the sacred desk this day. After having performed this service to my brethren, I retired to the pulpit, the veils being dropped,

"THE SAVIOR
MADE HIS
APPEARANCE
TO SOME, WHILE
ANGELS
MINISTERED
TO OTHERS."

and bowed myself, with Oliver Cowdery, in solemn and silent prayer. After rising from prayer, the following vision was opened to both of us:

See Doctrine and Covenants 110.

Monday, April 4—The elders began to spread abroad in all parts of the land, preaching the word.

Saturday, April 9—Myself and the principal heads of the Church accompanied the wise men of Zion, namely, Bishop Partridge and his counselors, Isaac Morley and John Corrill, and President W. W. Phelps, on their way home, as far as Chardon; and after staying with them all night, blessed them in the morning, and returned to Kirtland.

May 16—President Oliver Cowdery having preferred, to the high council, a charge of unchristianlike conduct against Wilkins J. Salisbury, the council assembled in the Lord's house, when it was proved that he had so conducted himself as to bring unnecessary persecution on me; that he had neglected his family, leaving them without wood, without provisions, or telling them where he was going, or when he would return; that he used strong drink and had been intimate with other women.

Elder Salisbury confessed his propensity for tale-bearing, and drinking strong liquor, but denied the other charges. The council decided that he could no longer be an elder or member in the Church until there was a thorough reformation.

Charges of unchristianlike conduct were also preferred against Sisters Hannah Brown, and L. Elliot. They confessed they had been guilty of telling falsehoods.

The council reproved them, but permitted them to retain their standing in the Church.

May 17—I went in company with my brother Hyrum, in a carriage to Fairport, and brought home my grandmother, Mary Smith, aged ninety-three years. She had not been baptized, on account of the opposition of Jesse Smith, her eldest son, who has always been an enemy to the work. She had come five hundred miles to see her children, and knew all of us she had ever seen.

She was much pleased at being introduced to her great grand-children, and expressed much pleasure and gratification on seeing me.

My grandfather, Asael Smith, long ago predicted that there would be a prophet raised up in his family, and my grandmother was fully satisfied that is was fulfilled in me. My grandfather Asael died in East Stockholm, St. Lawrence county, New York, after having received the Book of Mormon, and read it nearly through; and he declared that I was the very prophet that he had long known would come in his family.

On the 18th, my uncle Silas Smith and family arrived from the east. My father, three of his brothers, and their mother met the first time for many years. It was a happy day, for we had long prayed to see our grandmother and uncles in the Church.

On May 27, after a few days' visit with her children, which she enjoyed extremely well, my grandmother fell asleep without sickness, pain or regret. She breathed her last about sunset, and was buried in the burial ground near the temple, after a funeral address had been delivered by Sidney Rigdon. She had buried one daughter, Sarah; two sons, Stephen and Samuel; and her husband, who died October 30, 1830, and left five sons and three daughters still living.

On the 31st of December, at the setting of the sun, Dr. Willard Richards was baptized at Kirtland, under the hands of President Brigham Young, in the presence of Heber C. Kimball and others, who had spent the afternoon in cutting the ice to prepare for the baptism.

Chapter Nine

1837

June 11—In this state of things, and but a few weeks before the Twelve were expecting to meet in full quorum (some of them having been absent for some time), God revealed to me that something new must be done for the salvation of His Church. And on or about the first of June, 1837, Heber C. Kimball, one of the Twelve, was set apart by the spirit of prophesy and revelation, prayer and laying on of hands, of the First Presidency, to preside over a mission to England, to be the first foreign mission of the Church of Christ in the last days. While we were about ordaining him, Orson Hyde, another of the Twelve, came in, and upon listening to what was passing, his heart melted within him (for he had begun to drink of the cup filled with the overflowings of speculation), he acknowledged all his faults, asked forgiveness, and offered to accompany President Kimball on his mission to England. His offer was accepted and he was set apart for that purpose.

The same evening, (11th of June) while I was engaged in giving some special instructions to Elders Kimball and Hyde, and Priest Joseph Fielding, concerning their mission to England, President Brigham Young came into my house, where we were sitting, accompanied by Dr. Willard Richards, who had just returned from a special business mission to New York, Boston, and other eastern cities, on which he started with President Young on the 14th of March—Dr. Richards having been previously ordained an elder, viz., on the 6th of March, and President Young having returned from the mission a few days previous. My instructions to the brethren were, when they arrived in England, to adhere closely to the first principles of the gospel, and remain silent concerning the gathering, the vision, and the Book of Doctrine and Covenants, until such time as the work was fully established, and it should be clearly made manifest by the Spirit to do otherwise.

Monday, June 12—I was taken sick, and kept my room, unable to attend to business.

Wednesday, June 14—I continued to grow worse and worse until my sufferings were excruciating, and although in the midst of it all I felt to rejoice in the salvation of Israel's God, yet I found it expedient to call to my assistance those means which a kind Providence had provided for the restoration of the sick, in connection with the ordinances; and Dr. Levi Richards, at my request, administered to me herbs and mild food, and nursed me with all tenderness and attention; and my Heavenly Father blessed his administrations to the easing and comforting of my system, for I began to amend in a short time, and in a few days I was able to resume my usual labors.

This is one of the many instances in which I have suddenly been brought from a state of health, to the borders of the grave, and as suddenly restored, for which my heart swells with gratitude to my Heavenly Father, and I feel renewedly to dedicate myself and all my powers to His service.

While I was thus afflicted, the enemy of all righteousness was suggesting, apostates reporting, and the doubtful believing that my afflictions were sent upon me, because I was in transgression and had taught the Church things contrary to godliness; but of this the Lord judge between me and them, while I pray my Father to forgive them the wrong they do.

Some time previous to this I resigned my office in the "Kirtland Safety Society," disposed of my interest therein, and withdrew from the institution; being fully aware, after so long an experiment, that no institution of the kind, established upon just and righteous principles for a blessing not only to the Church but the whole nation, would be suffered to continue its operations in such an age of darkness, speculation and wickedness. Almost all banks throughout the country, one after the other, have suspended specie payment, and gold and silver have risen in value in direct ratio with the depreciation of paper currency. The great pressure of the money market is felt in England as well as America, and bread stuffs are everywhere high. The season has been cool, wet and backward.

Mexico, unwilling to acknowledge the independence of Texas, considers her inhabitants as rebellious subjects. Spain is divided against herself, wasting her blood and treasure in her own destruction. Portugal is rapidly exhausting her resources in princely luxuries. Poland has lost her rank among the nations to gratify the ambition of Nicholas, the Russian autocrat. The government of Buenos Ayres has declared war against Peru, and nearly all the republics of South America are mingled in the strife, while the Indians continue their depredations on the inhabitants of Florida. Trouble and distress are the grand topics of conversation amongst politicians, merchants, mechanics and demagogues; and crimes, misdemeanors, and casualties, occupy a large space in the public journals.

Chapter Ten

1838

January, 1838—A new year dawned upon the Church in Kirtland in all the bitterness of the spirit of apostate mobocracy; which continued to rage and grow hotter and hotter, until Elder Rigdon and myself were obliged to flee from its deadly influence, as did the apostles and prophets of old, and as Jesus said, "when they persecute you in one city, flee to another." On the evening of the 12th of January, about ten o'clock, we left Kirtland, on horseback, to escape mob violence, which was about to burst upon us under the color of legal process to cover the hellish designs of our enemies, and to save themselves from the just judgment of the law.

We continued our travels during the night, and at eight o'clock on the morning of the 13th, arrived among the brethren in Norton township, Medina county, Ohio, a distance of sixty miles from Kirtland. Here we tarried about thirty-six hours, when our families arrived; and on the 16th we pursued our journey with our families, in covered wagons towards the city of Far West, in Missouri. We passed through Dayton and Eaton, in Ohio, and Dublin, Indiana; in the latter place we tarried nine days, and refreshed ourselves.

About January 16, 1838, being destitute of money to pursue

my journey, I said to Brother Brigham Young: "You are one of the Twelve who have charge of the kingdom in all the world; I believe I shall throw myself upon you, and look to you for counsel in this case." Brother Young thought I was not earnest, but I told him I was. Brother Brigham then said, "If you will take my counsel it will be that you rest yourself, and be assured you shall have money in plenty to pursue your journey."

There was a brother living in the place who had tried for some time to sell his farm but could not; he asked counsel of Brother Young concerning his property; Brother Young told him that if he would do right, and obey counsel, he should have an opportunity to sell. In about three days Brother Tomlinson came to Brother Brigham and said he had an offer for his place; Brother Brigham told him that this was the manifestation of the hand of the Lord to deliver Brother Joseph Smith from his present necessities. Brother Brigham's promise was soon verified, and I got three hundred dollars from Brother Tomlinson, which enabled me to pursue my journey.

The weather was extremely cold. We were obliged to secrete ourselves in our wagons, sometimes, to elude the grasp of our pursuers, who continued their pursuit of us more than two hundred miles from Kirtland, armed with pistols and guns, seeking our lives. They frequently crossed our track, twice they were in the houses where we stopped, once we tarried all night in the same house with them, with only a partition between us and them; and heard their oaths and imprecations, and threats concerning us, if they could catch us; and late in the evening they came in to our room and examined us, but decided we were not the men. At other times we passed them in the streets, and gazed upon them, and they on us, but they knew us not. One Lyons was one of our pursuers.

I parted with Brother Rigdon at Dublin, and traveling different routes we met at Terre Haute, where, after resting, we separated again, and I pursued my journey, crossing the Mississippi river at Quincy, Illinois.

When I had arrived within one hundred and twenty miles of Far West, the brethren met me with teams and money to help me forward; and when eight miles from the city, we were met by an escort, viz., Thomas B. Marsh and others, who received us with open arms; and on the 13th of March, with my family and some others I put up at Brother Barnard's for the night. Here we were met by another escort of the brethren from the town, who came to make us welcome to their little Zion.

On the 14th of March, as we were about entering Far West, many of the brethren came out to meet us, who also with open arms welcomed us to their bosoms. We were immediately received under the hospitable roof of Brother George W. Harris, who treated us with all possible kindness, and we refreshed ourselves with much satisfaction, after our long and tedious journey, the brethren bringing in such things as we had need of for our comfort and convenience.

After being here two or three days, my brother Samuel arrived with his family. President Rigdon arrived at Far West with his family, Wednesday, April 4th, having had a tedious journey, and his family having suffered many afflictions.

April 27—This day I chiefly spent in writing a history of the Church from the earliest period of its existence, up to this date.

Saturday, May 5—The Presidency wrote for the *Elders' Journal*; also received intelligence from Canada by Brother Bailey, that two hundred wagons, with families, would probably be here in three weeks; also listened to an address on political matters delivered by General Wilson, Federal candidate for Congress.

Sunday, May 6—I preached to the Saints, setting forth the evils that existed, and that would exist, by reason of hasty judgment, or decisions upon any subject given by any people, or in judging before they had heard both sides of a question. I also cautioned the Saints against men who came amongst them whining and growling about their money, because they had kept the Saints, and borne some of the burden with others, and thus thinking that others, who are still poorer, and have borne greater burdens than they themselves, ought to make up their losses. I cautioned the Saints to beware of such, for they were throwing out insinuations here and there, to level a dart at the best interests of the Church, and if possible destroy the character of its Presidency. I also gave some instructions in the mysteries of the kingdom of God; such as the history of the planets, Abraham's writings upon the planetary systems, etc.

In the afternoon I spoke again on different subjects: the principle of wisdom, and the Word of Wisdom.

Saturday, May 12—President Rigdon and myself attended the high council for the purpose of presenting for their consideration some business relating to our pecuniary concerns.

We stated to the council our situation, as to maintaining our families, and the relation we now stand in to the Church, spending as we have for eight years, our time, talents, and property, in the service of the Church: and being reduced as it were to beggary, and being still detained in the business and service of the Church, it appears necessary that something should be done for the support of our families by the Church, or else we must do it by our own labors; and if the Church say to us, "Help yourselves," we will thank them and immediately do so; but if the Church say, "Serve us," some provision must be made for our sustenance.

The council investigated the matter, and instructed the bishop to make over to President Joseph Smith, Jun., and Sidney Rigdon, each an eighty-acre lot of land from the property of the Church, situated adjacent to the city corporation; also appointed three of their number, viz., George W. Harris, Elias Higbee and Simeon Carter, a committee to confer with said Presidency, and satisfy them for their services the present year; not for preaching, or for receiving the word of God by revelation, neither for instructing the Saints in righteousness, but for services rendered in the printing establishment, in translating the ancient records, etc., etc. Said committee agreed that Presidents Smith and Rigdon should receive $1,100 each as a just remuneration for their services this year.

Sunday, May 13—Elder Reynolds Cahoon preached in the forenoon. In the afternoon President Rigdon preached a funeral sermon on the death of Swain Williams, son of Frederick G. Williams.

Monday, May 14—I spent in plowing my garden, while Elder Rigdon was preparing and correcting some matter for the press.

Friday, May 18—I left Far West, in company with Sidney Rigdon, Thomas B. Marsh, David W. Patten, Bishop Partridge, Elias Higbee, Simeon Carter, Alanson Ripley, and many others, for the purpose of visiting the north country, and laying of a stake of Zion; making locations, and laying claim to lands to facilitate the gathering of the Saints, and for the benefit of the poor, in upholding the Church of God. We traveled to the mouth of Honey creek, which is a tributary of Grand River, where we camped for the night. We passed through a beautiful country, the greater part of which is prairie, and thickly covered with grass and weeds, among which is plenty of game, such as deer, turkey, and prairie hen. We discovered a large, black wolf, and my dog gave him chase, but he outran us. We have nothing to fear in camping out, except the rattlesnake, which is native to this country, though not very numerous. We turned our horses loose, and let them feed on the prairie.

Saturday, May 19—This morning we struck our tents and formed a line of march, crossing Grand River at the mouth of Honey creek and Nelson's ferry.

Grand River is a large, beautiful, deep and rapid stream, during the high waters of spring, and will undoubtedly admit of navigation by steamboat and other water craft. At the mouth of Honey creek is a good landing. We pursued our course up the river, mostly through timber, for about eighteen miles, when we arrived at Colonel Lyman Wight's home. He lives at the foot of Tower Hill (a name I gave the place in consequence of the remains of an old Nephite altar or tower that stood there), where we camped for the Sabbath.

In the afternoon I went up the river about half a mile to Wight's ferry, accompanied by President Rigdon, and my clerk, George W. Robinson, for the purpose of selecting and laying claim to a city plat near said ferry in Daviess county, township 60, ranges 27 and 28, and sections 25, 36, 31, and 30, which the brethren called "Spring Hill," but by the mouth of the Lord it was named Adam-ondi-Ahman, because, said He, it is the place where Adam shall come to visit his people, or the Ancient of Days shall sit, as spoken of by Daniel the Prophet.

Tuesday, May 22—President Rigdon went east with a company, and selected some of the best locations in the county, and returned with a good report of that vicinity, and with information of valuable locations which might be secured. Following awhile the course of the company, I returned to camp in Robinson's Grove, and thence went west to obtain some game to supply our necessities. We discovered some antiquities about one mile west of the camp, consisting of stone mounds, apparently erected in square piles, though somewhat decayed and obliterated by the weather of many years. These mounds were probably erected by the aborigines of the land, to secrete treasures. We returned without game.

Wednesday, May 23—We all traveled east, locating lands, to secure a claim, on Grove creek, and near the city of Adam-ondi-Ahman. Towards evening I accompanied Elder Rigdon to Colonel Wight's, and the remainder of the company returned to their tents.

Thursday, May 24—This morning the company returned to Grove creek to finish the survey, accompanied by President Rigdon and Colonel Wight, and I returned to Far West.

June 16—My uncle, John Smith, and family, with six other families, arrived in Far West, all in good health and spirits. I counseled them to settle at Adam-ondi-Ahman.

July 4—The day was spent in celebrating the Declaration of Independence of the United States of America, and also by the Saints making a "Declaration of Independence" from all mobs and persecutions which have been inflicted upon them, time after time, until they could bear it no longer; having been driven by ruthless mobs and enemies of truth from their homes, and having had their property confiscated, their lives exposed, and their all jeopardized by such barbarous conduct. The corner stones of the houses of the Lord, agreeable to the commandments of the Lord unto us, given April 26, 1838, were laid.

Joseph Smith, Jun., was president of the day; Hyrum Smith, vice-president; Sidney Rigdon, orator; Reynolds Cahoon, chief marshal; George M. Hinckle and J. Hunt, assistant marshals; and George W. Robinson, clerk.

The order of the day was splendid. The procession commenced forming at 10 o'clock a.m., in the following order: first, the infantry (militia); second, the patriarchs of the Church; the president, vice-president, and orator; the Twelve Apostles, presidents of the stakes, and high council; bishop and counselors, architects, ladies and gentlemen. The cavalry brought up the rear of the large procession, which marched to music, and formed a circle, with the ladies in front, round the excavation. The southeast corner stone of the Lord's house in Far West, Missouri, was then laid by the presidents of the stake, assisted by twelve men. The southwest corner, by the presidents of the elders, assisted by twelve men. The northwest corner by the bishop, assisted by twelve men. The northeast corner by the president of the teachers, assisted by twelve men. This house is to be one hundred and ten feet long, and eighty feet broad.

The oration was delivered by President Rigdon, at the close of which was a shout of hosanna, and a song, composed for the occasion by Levi W. Hancock, was sung by Solomon Hancock. The most perfect order prevailed throughout the day.

July 6—The three revelations which I received January 12, 1838, the day I left Kirtland, were read in the public congregation at Far West; and the same day I inquired of the Lord, "O Lord! Show unto thy servant how much thou requirest of the properties of thy people for a tithing," and received the following answer, which was also read in public:

See Doctrine and Covenants 119.

Also I received the following:

See Doctrine and Covenants 120.

Monday, August 6—Some two weeks previous to this, Judge Morin, who lived at Mill Port, informed John D. Lee and Levi Stewart, that it was determined by the mob to prevent the "Mormons" from voting at the election on the sixth day of August, and thereby elect Colonel William P. Peniston, who led the mob in Clay county. He also advised them to go prepared for an attack, to stand their ground, and have their rights.

The brethren, hoping better things, gave little heed to Judge Morin's friendly counsel, and repaired to the polls at Gallatin, the shire town of Daviess county, without weapons.

About eleven o'clock a.m., William P. Peniston mounted a barrel, and harangued the electors for the purpose of exciting them against the "Mormons," saying, "The Mormon leaders are a set of horse thieves, liars, counterfeiters, and you know they profess to heal the sick, and cast out devils, and you all know that is a lie." He further said that the members of the Church were dupes, and not too good to take a false oath on any common occasion; that they would steal, and he did not consider property safe where they were; that he was opposed to their settling in Daviess county; and if they suffered the "Mormons" to vote, the people would soon lose their suffrage; "and," said he, addressing the Saints, "I headed a mob to drive you out of Clay county, and would not prevent your being mobbed now."

Richard (called Dick) Welding, the mob bully, just drunk enough for the occasion, began a discussion with Brother Samuel Brown, by saying, "The Mormons were not allowed to vote in Clay county no more than the negroes," and attempted to strike Brown, who gradually retreated, parrying the blow with his umbrella, while Welding continued to press upon him, calling him a liar, etc., and meanwhile trying to repeat the blow on Brown. Perry Durphy sought to suppress the difficulty by holding Welding's arm, when five or six of the mobbers seized Durphy and commenced beating him with clubs, boards, and crying, "Kill him, kill him," when a general scuffle commenced with fists and clubs, the mobbers being about ten to one of the brethren. Abraham Nelson was knocked down, and had his clothes torn off, and while trying to get up was attacked again, when his brother, Hyrum Nelson, ran in amongst them, and knocked the mobbers down with the butt of his whip. Riley Stewart struck Welding on the head, which brought him to the ground. The mob cried out, "Dick Weldin's dead; who killed Dick?" And they fell upon Riley, knocked him down, kicked him, crying, "Kill him, kill him; shoot him," and they would have killed him, had not John L. Butler sprung in amongst them and knocked them down. During about five minutes it was one succession of knock downs, when the mob dispersed to get fire arms.

Very few of the brethren voted. Riley, escaping across the river, had his wounds dressed, and returned home.

John L. Butler called the brethren together and made a speech, saying, "We are American citizens; our fathers fought for their liberty, and we will maintain the same principles." The authorities of the county finally came to the brethren, and requested them to withdraw, stating that it was a premeditated thing to prevent the "Mormons" from voting.

The brethren held a council about one-fourth of a mile out of town, where they saw mob recruits coming in, in small parties, from five and ten, to twenty-five in number, cursing and swearing, and armed with clubs, pistols, dirks, and some guns. The brethren not having arms, thought it wisdom to return to their farms, collect their families, and hide them in a thicket of hazel bush, which they did, and stood guard around them through the night, while the women and children lay on the ground in the rain.

Tuesday, August 7—A report came to Far West this morning, by way of those not belonging to the Church, to the effect that at the election at Gallatin, yesterday, two or three of our brethren were killed by the Missourians, and left upon the ground, and not suffered to be interred; that the brethren were prevented from voting, and a majority of the inhabitants of Daviess county were determined to drive the Saints from that county.

On hearing this report, I started for Gallatin, to assist the brethren, accompanied by President Rigdon, Brother Hyrum Smith, and fifteen or twenty others, who were armed for their own protection; and the command of the company was given to George W. Robinson.

On our way we were joined by the brethren from different parts of the county, some of whom were attacked by the mob, but we all reached Colonel Wight's that night in safety, where we found some of the brethren who had been mobbed at Gallatin, with others, waiting for our counsel. Here we received the cheering intelligence that none of the brethren were killed, although several were badly wounded.

From the best information, about one hundred and fifty Missourians warred against from six to twelve of our brethren, who fought like lions. Several Missourians had their skulls cracked. Blessed be the memory of those few brethren who contended so strenuously for their constitutional rights and religious freedom, against such an overwhelming force of desperadoes!

Wednesday, August 8—After spending the night in counsel at Colonel Wight's, I rode out with some of the brethren to view the situation of affairs in that region, and among others, called on Adam Black, justice of the peace, and judge elect for Daviess county, who had some time previous sold his farm to Brother Vinson Knight, and received part pay according to agreement, and afterwards united himself with a band of mobbers to drive the Saints from, and prevent their settling in, Daviess county. On interrogation, he confessed what he had done, and in consequence of this violation of his oath as magistrate, we asked him to give us some satisfaction so that we might know whether he was our friend or enemy, whether or not he would administer the law in justice; and politely requested him to sign an agreement of peace, but being jealous, he would not sign it, but said he would write one himself to our satisfaction, and sign it.

Hoping he would abide his own decision, and support the law, we left him in peace, and returned to Colonel Wight's at Adam-ondi-Ahman.

In the evening some of the citizens from Mill Port called on us, and we agreed to meet some of the principal men of the county in council, at Adam-ondi-Ahman the next day at twelve o'clock, noon.

Thursday, August 9—The committee assembled at Adam-ondi-Ahman at twelve, according to previous appointment, viz., on the part of Mill Port citizens: Joseph Morin, senator elect; John Williams, representative elect; James B. Turner, clerk of the circuit court, and others; on the part of the Saints: Lyman Wight, Vinson Knight, John Smith, Reynolds Cahoon, and others. At this meeting both parties entered into a covenant of peace, to preserve each other's rights, and stand in each other's defense; that if men did wrong, neither party would uphold them or endeavor to screen them from justice, but deliver up all offenders to be dealt with according to law and justice. The assembly dispersed on these friendly terms, myself and friends returning to Far West, where we arrived about midnight and found all quiet.

At this time some of the brethren had removed with their families from the vicinity of Gallatin, to Diahman and Far West, for safety.

Saturday, August 11—This morning I left Far West, with my council and Elder Almon W. Babbitt, to visit the brethren on the forks of Grand River, who had come from Canada with Elder Babbitt, and settled at that place contrary to counsel.

Sunday, August 12—I continued with the brethren at the forks of Grand River, offering such counsel as their situation required.

Monday, August 13—I returned with my council to Far West. We were chased ten or twelve miles, by some evil designing men, but we eluded their pursuit. When within about eight miles of home, we met some brethren who had come to inform us that a writ had been issued by Judge King, for my arrest, and that of Lyman Wight, for attempting to defend our rights against the mob.

Tuesday and Wednesday, August 14 and 15—I spent principally at home, engaged in domestic affairs.

Thursday, August 16—I spent principally at home.

The sheriff of Daviess county, accompanied by Judge Morin, called and notified me, that he had a writ to take me to Daviess county, for trial, for visiting that county on the seventh instant.

It had been currently reported that I would not be apprehended by legal process, and that I would not submit to the laws of the land; but I told the sheriff that I intended always to submit to the laws of our country, but I wished to be tried in my own county, as the citizens of Daviess county were highly exasperated at me, and that the laws of the country gave me this privilege. Upon hearing this, the sheriff declined serving me the writ, and said he would go to Richmond, and see Judge King on the subject. I told him I would remain at home until his return.

The sheriff returned from Richmond, and found me at home (where I had remained during his absence), and informed me very gravely, that I was out of his jurisdiction, and that he could not act in Caldwell county, and retired.

August 20—Nothing peculiar transpired at Far West, from the sixteenth to this day, when the inhabitants of the different parts of the county met to organize themselves into agricultural companies. I was present and took part in their deliberations. One company was formed, called the "Western Agricultural Company," which voted to enclose one field for grain containing twelve sections, seven thousand six hundred and eighty acres of land. Another company was also organized, called the "Eastern Agricultural Company," the extent of the field not decided.

Tuesday, August 21—Another company was formed, called the "Southern Agricultural Company," the field to be as large as the first mentioned.

Wednesday, August 22—I spent part of the day in counseling with several brethren upon different subjects.

The brethren continued to gather to Zion daily.

Some time this month the Saints were warned by the mob to leave De Witt, Carroll county.

Thursday, August 30—I spent considerable time today in conversation with Brother John Corrill, in consequence of some expressions made by him, in presence of several brethren who had not been long in the place. Brother Corrill's conduct for some time had been very unbecoming, especially in a man in whom so much confidence had been placed. He said he would not yield his judgment to anything proposed by the Church, or any individuals of the Church, or even the Great I Am, given through the appointed organ, as revelation, but would always act upon his own judgment, let him believe in whatever religion he might. He stated he would always say what he pleased, for he was a Republican, and as such would do, say, act, and believe what he pleased.

Mark such republicanism as this! A man to oppose his own judgment to the judgment of God, and at the same time to profess to believe in that same God, who has said: "The foolishness of God is wiser than man; and the weakness of God is stronger than man."

President Rigdon also made some observations to Brother Corrill, which he afterwards acknowledged were correct, and that he understood things different after the interview from what he did before.

Saturday, September 1—There is great excitement at present among the Missourians, who are seeking if possible an occasion against us. They are continually chafing us, and provoking us to anger if possible, one sign of threatening after another, but we do not fear them, for the Lord God, the Eternal Father is our God, and Jesus the Mediator is our Savior, and in the Great I Am is our strength and confidence.

We have been driven time after time, and that without cause; and smitten again and again, and that without provocation; until we have proved the world with kindness, and the world has proved us, that we have no designs against any man or set of men, that we injure no man, that we are peaceable with all men, minding our own business, and our business only. We have suffered our rights and our liberties to be taken from us; we have not avenged ourselves of those wrongs; we have appealed to magistrates, to sheriffs, to judges, to government and to the President of the United States, all in vain; yet we have yielded peaceably to all these things. We have not complained at the great God, we murmured not, but peaceably left all; and retired into the back country, in the broad and wild prairies, in the barren and desolate plains, and there commenced anew; we made the desolate places to bud and blossom as the rose; and now the fiend-like race is disposed to give us no rest. Their father the devil, is hourly calling upon them to be up and doing, and they, like willing and obedient children, need not the second admonition; but in the name of Jesus Christ, the Son of the living God, we will endure it no longer, if the great God will arm us with courage, with strength and with power, to resist them in their persecutions. We will not act on the offensive, but always on the defensive; our rights and our liberties shall not be taken from us, and we peaceably submit to it, as we have done heretofore, but we will avenge ourselves of our enemies, inasmuch as they will not let us alone.

But to return again to our subject. We found the place for the city, and the brethren were instructed to gather immediately into it, and soon they should be organized according to the laws of God. A more particular history of this city may be expected hereafter, perhaps at its organization and dedication. We found a new route home, saving, I should think, three or four miles. We arrived at Far West about the close of the day.

"WE HAVE BEEN DRIVEN TIME AFTER TIME, AND THAT WITHOUT CAUSE; AND SMITTEN AGAIN AND AGAIN, AND THAT WITHOUT PROVOCATION; UNTIL WE HAVE PROVED THE WORLD WITH KINDNESS."

The high priests met at Brother Pea's at Far West, and received Levi Richards into their quorum.

Monday, September 3—Nothing of importance occurred today. Reports come in concerning the collection of a mob in Daviess county, which has been collecting ever since the election in Daviess county, on the sixth of August last. I was at home most of the day.

This evening General Atchison arrived in Far West.

Tuesday, September 4—This day I spent in council with General Atchison. He says he will do all in his power to disperse the mob. We employed him and Alexander Doniphan (his partner) as our counsel in law. They are considered the first lawyers in upper Missouri.

President Rigdon and myself commenced this day the study of law, under the instruction of Generals Atchison and Doniphan. They think, by diligent application, we can be admitted to the bar in twelve months.

The result of our consultation with our lawyers was that myself and Colonel Wight volunteer to be tried by Judge King in Daviess county. Colonel Wight was present, having been previously notified to attend the consultation. Accordingly, Thursday next, was appointed for the trial, and word to that effect was sent to Judge King (who had previously agreed to try the case). All are to meet at Brother Littlefield's, near the county line in the southern part of Daviess county. I was at home in the evening after six o'clock.

Wednesday, September 5—Judge King arrived at Far West, on his way to Daviess to meet the proposed trial. General Atchison had gone before Judge King arrived, and the judge tarried all night. I was at home after six o'clock in the evening.

Thursday, September 6—At half-past seven this morning, I started on horseback, accompanied by several brethren, among whom were my brother Hyrum and Judge Elias Higbee, to attend my trial at Brother Littlefield's. I thought it not wisdom to make my appearance before the public at the county seat of Daviess county, in consequence of the many threats made against me, and the high state of excitement. The trial could not proceed, on account of the absence of the plaintiff, and lack of testimony, and the court adjourned until tomorrow at ten o'clock in the morning, at a Mr. Raglin's, some six or eight miles further south, and within half a mile of the line of Caldwell. Raglin is a regular mob character. We all returned to Far West, where we arrived before dark.

Friday, September 7—About sunrise I started with my friends, and arrived at Mr. Raglin's at the appointed hour. We did not know but there would be a disturbance among the mob characters today; we accordingly had a company of men placed at the county line, so as to be ready at a minute's warning, if there should be any difficulty at the trial.

The trial commenced; William P. Peniston, who was the prosecutor, had no witnesses but Adam Black, but he contrived to swear to a great many things that never had an existence, and I presume never entered into the heart of any other man, and in fine, I think he swore by the job, and that he was employed so to do by Peniston.

The witnesses on the part of the defense were Dimick B. Huntington, Gideon Carter, Adam Lightner, and George W. Robinson.

The judge bound Colonel Wight and myself over to court in a five-hundred-dollar bond. There was no proof against us to criminate us, but it is supposed he did it to pacify, as much as possible, the feelings of the mobbers. The judge stated afterwards, in the presence of George W. Robinson, that there was nothing proven against us worthy of bonds, but we submitted without murmuring a word, gave the bonds, with sufficient securities, and all returned home the same evening.

I found two persons in Daviess county at the trial, who were sent from Chariton county as a committee, to inquire into all this matter, as the mobbers had sent to that place for assistance, they said, to take Smith and Wight; but their real object was to drive the brethren from the county of Daviess, as had been done in Jackson county. They said the people in Chariton county did not see proper to send help without knowing for what purpose they were doing it, and this they said was their errand. They accompanied us to Far West, to hold a council with us, in order to learn the facts of this great excitement, which is, as it were, turning the world upside down. We arrived home in the evening.

The Presidency met in council with the committee from Chariton county, together with General Atchison, where a relation was given of our affairs in general, the present state of excitement, and the cause of all this confusion. The gentlemen from Chariton expressed their fullest satisfaction upon the subject, and considered they had been outrageously imposed upon in this matter. They left this afternoon apparently perfectly satisfied with the interview.

News came this evening that the mobs were to attack Adam-ondi-Ahman, and a few of the brethren from Far West started to assist the brethren to defend themselves.

Sunday, September 9—This morning a company in addition to that which went last evening went to Adam-ondi-Ahman to assist the brethren there in their defense against the mob.

Captain William Allred took a company of ten mounted men and went to intercept a team with guns and ammunition, sent from Richmond to the mob in Daviess county. They found the wagon broken down, and the boxes of guns drawn into the high grass near by the wagon; there was no one present that could be discovered. In a short time two men on horseback came from towards the camp of the mob, and immediately behind them was a man with a wagon; they all came up and were taken by virtue of a writ on the supposition that they were abetting the mob, by carrying guns and ammunition to them. The men were taken together with the guns to Far West; the guns were distributed among the brethren, for their defense, and the prisoners were held in custody. This was a glorious day indeed, the plans of the mob were frustrated in losing their guns, and all their efforts appeared to be blasted. Captain Allred acted under the civil authorities in Caldwell, who issued the writ for securing the arms and arresting the carriers. The prisoners were brought to Far West for trial.

The mob continue to take prisoners at their pleasure; some they keep, and some they let go. They try all in their power to make us commit the first act of violence. They frequently send in word that they are torturing the prisoners to death, in the most cruel manner, but we understand all their ways, and their cunning and wisdom are not past finding out.

Monday, September 10—This day the prisoners taken by Captain Allred on Sunday, viz., John B. Comer, William L. McHoney, and Allen Miller, were brought before Albert Petty, justice of the peace, for examination. The prisoners asked for bail, to allow time to get counsel. The law allowed no bail, but the court adjourned till Wednesday to give time to the prisoners to get counsel.

After the arrest the facts were communicated to Judge King by letter, under date of Richmond, September 10th, asking his advice how to dispose of the guns and prisoners.

Judge King advised by letter to turn the prisoners loose, and let them receive kind treatment; that the guns were government property, in the care of Captain Pollard of his vicinity, but whether they went by his authority or permission he could not say, he was at a loss to give any advice about them; but said that they should not, through any agency of his, be taken from us to be converted and used for illegal purposes. The letter was signed by A.A. King (directed to Messrs. Smith and Rigdon).

Under the same date Judge King advised General Atchison "to send two hundred or more men, and dispel the forces in Daviess county and all the assembled armed forces in Caldwell, and cause those 'Mormons' who refuse to give up, to surrender, and be recognized, for it will not do to compromise the law with them." What compromise need there be, Judge King, for no "Mormons" had refused to surrender to the requisitions of the law? It is mob violence, alone, that the "Mormons" are contending against.

A petition was this day made out by the citizens of Ray county, directed to General Atchison, asking him to call out the militia to suppress the insurrection in Caldwell and Daviess counties, and save the effusion of blood, which must speedily take place unless prevented. Signed by Jesse Coates and twenty-eight others.

Wednesday, September 12—This day the prisoners, (Allred's) John B. Corner and his comrades, were put upon trial. It was proven to the court that the guns were taken by one of the prisoners and that he with the others were taking them to Daviess county to arm the mob. It was also proved that the mob was collecting for the purpose of driving the Saints from their homes. The prisoners were held to bail for their appearance at the circuit court, Comer as principal, the others were merely in his service.

This day also a communication was sent to Governor Boggs, dated Daviess county, containing all the falsehoods and lies that the evil genius of mobocrats, villians, and murderers could invent, charging the "Mormons" with every crime they themselves had been guilty of, and calling the "Mormons" imposters, rebels, Canadian refugees, emissaries of the prince of darkness, and signed, "The Citizens of Daviess and Livingston Counties."

Under this date, General Atchison informed the governor, by letter from headquarters at Richmond, that on the solicitation of the citizens and the advice of the judge of the circuit, he had ordered out four companies of fifty men each from the militia of Clay county, and a like number from Ray; also four hundred men to hold themselves in readiness if required, all mounted riflemen, except one company of infantry. The troops were to proceed immediately to the scene of excitement and insurrection.

About this time (September 12) sixty or more mobbers entered De Witt and warned the brethren to leave that place.

Monday, October 1—I returned home about five o'clock where I tarried the remainder of the evening. The mob having left Daviess county (after they were organized into a militia by Atchison, Doniphan, and Parks and disbanded) went to Carroll county and gathered at De Witt, threatening vengeance to the Saints without regard to age, sex or condition; but Daviess county was for a season freed from those peace disturbers.

Tuesday, October 2—The mob pressed harder upon De Witt and fired upon the Saints.

The Kirtland camp arrived in Far West from Kirtland. I went in company with Sidney Rigdon, Hyrum Smith, Isaac Morley and George W. Robinson, and met them some miles out, and escorted them into the city, where they encamped on the public square directly south, and close by the excavation for the Lord's house. Here friends greeted friends in the name of the Lord. Isaac Morley, patriarch at Far West, furnished a beef for the camp. President Rigdon provided a supper for the sick, and the brethren provided for them like men of God, for they were hungry, having eaten but little for several days, and having traveled eleven miles this day; eight hundred and sixty miles from Kirtland, the way the camp traveled.

This day also (October 5) General Atchison wrote the governor from Boonville, that in Carroll county the citizens were in arms for the purpose of driving the "Mormons" from that county.

About this time I took a journey in company with some others, to the lower part of the county of Caldwell, for the purpose of selecting a location for a town. While on my journey, I was met by one of the brethren from De Witt, in Carroll county, who stated that our people who had settled in that place were and had been some time, surrounded by a mob, who had threatened their lives, and had shot at them several times; and that he was on his way to Far West, to inform the brethren there of the facts.

I was surprised on receiving this intelligence, although there had, previous to this time, been some manifestations of mobs, but I had hoped that the good sense of the majority of the people, and their respect for the Constitution, would have put down any spirit of persecution which might have been manifested in that neighborhood.

Immediately on receiving this intelligence I made preparations to go to that place, and endeavor, if possible, to allay the feelings of the citizens, and save the lives of my brethren who were thus exposed to their wrath.

Saturday, October 6—I arrived at De Witt, and found that the accounts of the situation of that place were correct; for it was with much difficulty, and by traveling unfrequented roads, that I was able to get there, all the principal roads being strongly guarded by the mob, who refused all ingress as well as egress. I found my brethren, who were only a handful in comparison to the mob by which they were surrounded, in this situation, and their provisions nearly exhausted, and no prospect of obtaining any more. We thought it necessary to send immediately to the governor, to inform him of the circumstances, hoping to receive from the executive the protection which we needed; and which was guaranteed to us in common with other citizens. Several gentlemen of standing and respectability, who lived in the immediate vicinity who were not in any way connected with the Church of Latter-day Saints, who had witnessed the proceedings of our enemies, came forward and made affidavits to the treatment we had received, and concerning our perilous situation; and offered their services to go and present the case to the governor themselves.

Under the same date, (October 6th) from the mob camp near De Witt, eleven blood-thirsty fellows, viz., Congrave Jackson, Larkin H. Woods, Thomas Jackson, Rolla M. Daviess, James Jackson, Jun., Johnson Jackson, John L. Tomlin, Sidney S. Woods, Geo. Crigler, William L. Banks, and Whitfield Dicken, wrote a most inflammatory, lying and murderous communication to the citizens of Howard county, calling upon them as friends and fellow citizens to come to their immediate rescue, as the "Mormons" were then firing upon them and they would have to act on the defensive until they could procure more assistance.

A. C. Woods, a citizen of Howard county, made a certificate to the same lies, which he gathered in the mob camp; he did not go into De Witt, or take any trouble to learn the truth of what he certified. While the people will lie and the authorities will uphold them, what justice can honest men expect?

Tuesday, October 9—General Clark wrote the governor from Boonville, that the names subscribed to the paper named above, are worthy, prudent and patriotic citizens of Howard county, yet these men would leave their families and everything dear, and go to a neighboring county to seek the blood of innocent men, women and children! If this constitutes "worth, prudence and patriotism," let me be worthless, imprudent and unpatriotic.

The messenger, Mr. Caldwell, who had been dispatched to the governor for assistance, returned, but instead of receiving any aid or even sympathy from his Excellency, we were told that "the quarrel was between the Mormons and the mob," and that "we might fight it out."

About this time a mob, commanded by Hyrum Standly, took Smith Humphrey's goods out of his house, and said Standly set fire to Humphrey's house and burned it before his eyes, and ordered him to leave the place forthwith, which he did by fleeing from De Witt to Caldwell county. The mob had sent to Jackson county and got a cannon, powder and balls, and bodies of armed men had gathered in, to aid them, from Ray, Saline, Howard, Livingston, Clinton, Clay, Platte counties and other parts of the state, and a man by the name of Jackson, from Howard county, was appointed their leader.

The Saints were forbidden to go out of the town under pain of death, and were shot at when they attempted to go out to get food, of which they were destitute. As fast as their cattle or horses got where the mob could get hold of them, they were taken as spoil, as also other kinds of property. By these outrages the brethren were obliged, most of them, to live in wagons or tents.

Application had been made to the judge of the circuit court for protection, and he ordered out two companies of militia, one commanded by Captain Samuel Bogart, a Methodist minister, and one of the worst of the mobocrats. The whole force was placed under the command of General Parks, another mobber, if his letter speaks his feelings, and his actions do not belie him, for he never made the first attempt to disperse the mob, and when asked the reason of his conduct, he always replied that Bogart and his company were mutinous and mobocratic, that he dare not attempt a dispersion of the mob. Two other principal men of the mob were Major Ashly, member of the Legislature, and Sashiel Woods, a Presbyterian clergyman.

General Parks informed us that a greater part of his men under Captain Bogart had mutinied, and that he would be obliged to draw them off from the place, for fear they would join the mob; consequently he could offer us no assistance.

We had now no hopes whatever of successfully resisting the mob, who kept constantly increasing; our provisions were entirely exhausted, and we were worn out by continually standing on guard, and watching the movements of our enemies, who, during the time I was there, fired at us a great many times. Some of the brethren perished from starvation; and for once in my life, I had the pain of beholding some of my fellow creatures fall victims to the spirit of persecution, which did then, and has since, prevailed to such an extent in Upper Missouri. They were men, too, who were virtuous and against whom no legal process could for one moment be sustained, but who, in consequence of their love of God, attachment to His cause, and their determination to keep the faith, were thus brought to an untimely grave.

In the meantime Henry Root and David Thomas, who had been the soul cause of the settlement of our people in De Witt, solicited the Saints to leave the place. Thomas said he had assurances from the mob, that if they would leave the place they would not be hurt, and that they would be paid for all losses which they had sustained, and that they had come as mediators to accomplish this object, and that persons should be appointed to set a value on the property which they had to leave, and that they should be paid for it. The Saints finally, through necessity, had to comply, and leave the place. Accordingly the committee was appointed—Judge

Erickson was one of the committee, and Major Florey, of Rutsville, another, the names of others are not remembered. They appraised the real estate, that was all.

When the people came to start, many of their horses, oxen and cows were gone, and could not be found. It was known at the time, and the mob boasted of it, that they had killed the oxen and lived on them. Many houses belonging to my brethren were burned, their cattle driven away, and a great quantity of their property was destroyed by the mob. The people of De Witt utterly failed to fulfill their pledge to pay the Saints for the losses they sustained. The governor having turned a deaf ear to our entreaties, the militia having mutinied, the greater part of them being ready to join the mob, the brethren, seeing no prospect of relief, came to the conclusion to leave that place, and seek a shelter elsewhere. Gathering up as many wagons as could be got ready, which was about seventy, with a remnant of the property they had been able to save from their ruthless foes, they left De Witt and started for Caldwell county on the afternoon of Thursday, October 11, 1838. They traveled that day about twelve miles, and encamped in a grove of timber near the road.

That evening a woman, of the name of Jensen, who had some short time before given birth to a child, died in consequence of the exposure occasioned by the operations of the mob, and having to move before her strength would properly admit of it. She was buried in the grove, without a coffin.

During our journey we were continually harassed and threatened by the mob, who shot at us several times, whilst several of our brethren died from the fatigue and privation which they had to endure, and we had to inter them by the wayside, without a coffin, and under circumstances the most distressing. We arrived in Caldwell on the twelfth of October.

No sooner had the brethren left De Witt than Sashiel Woods called the mob together, and made a speech to them to the effect that they must hasten to assist their friends in Daviess county. The land sales, he said, were coming on, and if they could get the

"Mormons" driven out, they could get all the lands entitled to preemptions, and that they must hasten to Daviess county in order to accomplish their object; that if they would join and drive out the Saints, the old settlers could get all the lands back again, as well as all the pay they had received for them. He assured the mob that they had nothing to fear from the state authorities in so doing, for they had now full proof that those authorities would not assist the "Mormons," and that they (the mob) might as well take their property from them as not. His proposition was agreed to, and accordingly the whole banditti started for Daviess county, taking with them their cannon.

In the meantime, Cornelius Gilliam was busily engaged in raising a mob in Platte and Clinton counties, to aid Woods in his effort to drive peaceable citizens from their homes and take their property.

On my arrival in Caldwell, I was informed by General Doniphan, of Clay county, that a company of mobbers, eight hundred strong, were marching toward a settlement of our people in Daviess county. He ordered out one of the officers to raise a force and march immediately to what he called Wight's Town (Adam-ondi-Ahman), and defend our people from the attacks of the mob, until he should raise the militia in his (Clay) and the adjoining counties to put them down. A small company of militia, who were on their way to Daviess county, and who had passed through Far West, he ordered back again, stating that they were not to be depended upon, as many of them were disposed to join the mob, and to use his own expression, were "damned rotten hearted."

Sunday, October 14—I preached to the brethren at Far West from the saying of the Savior: "Greater love hath no man than this, that he lay down his life for his brethren." At the close I called upon all that would stand by me to meet me on the public square the next day.

There were seven cut off from the Church in Preston, England, this day. It was a general time of pruning in England. The powers of darkness raged, and it seemed as though Satan was fully determined to make an end of the work in that kingdom. Elders Joseph Fielding and Willard Richards had as much as they could do for some time, to see to the branches already planted, without planting new ones.

Monday, October 15—The brethren assembled on the public square of Far West and formed a company of about one-hundred, who took up a line of march for Adam-ondi-Ahman. Here let it be distinctly understood that this company were militia of the county of Caldwell, acting under Lieutenant-Colonel George M. Hinkle, agreeable to the order of General Doniphan, and the brethren were very careful in all their movements to act in strict accordance with the constitutional laws of the land.

The special object of this march was to protect Adam-ondi-Ahman, and repel the attacks of the mob in Daviess county. Having some property in that county, and having a house building there, I went up at the same time. While I was there a number of houses belonging to our people were burned by the mob, who committed many other depredations, such as driving off horses, sheep, cattle, hogs, etc. A number of those whose houses were burned down, as well as those who lived in scattered and lonely situations, fled into the town for safety, and for shelter from the inclemency of the weather, as a considerable snowstorm took place on the 17th and 18th. Women and children, some in the most delicate condition, were thus obliged to leave their homes and travel several miles in order to effect their escape. My feelings were such as I cannot describe when I saw them flock into the village, almost entirely destitute of clothes, and only escaping with their lives.

During this state of affairs, General Parks arrived in Daviess county, and was at the house of Colonel Lyman Wight on the 18th, when the intelligence was brought that the mob were burning houses; and also when women and children were fleeing for safety, among whom was Agnes M. Smith, wife of my brother, Don Carlos Smith, who was absent on a mission in Tennessee. Her house had been plundered and burned by the mob, and she had traveled nearly three miles, carrying her two helpless babes, and had to wade Grand River.

Colonel Wight, who held a commission in the 59th regiment under his (General Parks') command, asked what was to be done. Parks told him that he must immediately call out his men and go and put the mob down. Accordingly a force was immediately raised for the purpose of quelling the mob, and in a short time was on its march, with a determination to disperse the mob, or die in the attempt; as the people could bear such treatment as was being inflicted upon them no longer.

The mob, having learned the orders of General Parks, and likewise being aware of the determination of the oppressed, broke up their encampment and fled. The mob seeing that they could not succeed by force, now resorted to strategem; and after removing their property out of their houses, which were nothing but log cabins, they fired them, and then reported to the authorities of the state that the "Mormons" were burning and destroying all before them.

About this time William Morgan, sheriff of Daviess county, Samuel Bogart, Colonel William P. Peniston, Doctor Samuel Venable, Jonathan J. Dryden, James Stone, and Thomas J. Martin made communications or affidavits of the most inflammatory kind, charging upon the "Mormons" those depredations which had been committed by the mob, endeavoring thereby to raise the anger of those in authority, rallying a sufficient force around their standard, and produce a total overthrow, massacre, or banishment of the "Mormons" from the state. These and their associates were the ones who fired their own houses and then fled the country crying "fire and murder."

It was reported in Far West today (October 19th) that Orson Hyde had left that place, the night previous, leaving a letter for one of the brethren, which would develop the secret.

Monday, October 22—On the retreat of the mob from Daviess county, I returned to Caldwell, with a company of the brethren, and arrived at Far West about seven in the evening, where I had hoped to enjoy some respite from our enemies, at least for a short time; but upon my arrival there, I was informed that a mob had commenced hostilities on the borders of Caldwell county, adjoining Ray county, and that they had taken some of our brethren prisoners, burned some houses, and had committed depredations on the peaceable inhabitants.

Tuesday, October 23—News came to Far West, this morning, that the brethren had found the cannon, which the mob brought from Independence, buried in the earth, and had secured it by order of General Parks. The word of the Lord was given several months since, for the Saints to gather into the cities, but they have been slow to obey until the judgments were upon them, and now they are gathering by flight and haste, leaving all their effects, and are glad to get off at that. The city of Far West is literally crowded, and the brethren are gathering from all quarters.

Fourteen citizens of Ray county, one of whom was a Mr. Hudgins, a postmaster, wrote the governor an inflammatory epistle. Thomas C. Burch, of Richmond, wrote a similar communication. Also the citizens of Ray county, in public meeting, appealed to the governor of the state, to give the people of Upper Missouri protection from the fearful body of "thieves and robbers;" while the fact is the Saints were minding their own business, only as they were driven from it by those who were crying thieves and robbers.

The mail came in this evening, but not a single letter to anybody, from which it is evident there is no deposit sacred to those marauders who are infesting the country and trying to destroy the Saints.

Wednesday, October 24—Austin A. King and Adam Black renewed their inflammatory communications to the governor, as did other citizens of Richmond, viz., C. R. Morehead, William Thornton, and Jacob Gudgel, who scrupled at no falsehood or exaggeration, to raise the governor's anger against us.

Thomas B. Marsh, formerly president of the Twelve, having apostatized, repaired to Richmond and made affidavit before

Henry Jacobs, justice of the peace, to all the vilest slanders, aspersions, lies and calumnies towards myself and the Church, that his wicked heart could invent. He had been lifted up in pride by his exaltation to office and the revelations of heaven concerning him, until he was ready to be overthrown by the first adverse wind that should cross his track, and now he has fallen, lied and sworn falsely, and is ready to take the lives of his best friends. Let all men take warning by him, and learn that he who exalteth himself, God will abase. Orson Hyde was also at Richmond and testified to most of Marsh's statements.

This day about noon, Captain Bogart, with some thirty or forty men called on Brother Thoret Parsons, at the head of the east branch of Log creek, where he was living, and warned him to be gone before next day at ten in the morning, declaring also that he would give Far West thunder and lightning before next day at noon, if he had good luck in meeting Neil Gillum, (Cornelius Gilliam) who would camp about six miles west of Far West that night, and that he should camp on Crooked creek. He then departed towards Crooked creek.

Brother Parsons dispatched a messenger with this news to Far West, and followed after Bogart to watch his movements. Brothers Joseph Holbrook and David Juda, who went out this morning to watch the movements of the enemy, saw eight armed mobbers call at the house of Brother Pinkham, where they took three prisoners, Nathan Pinkham, Brothers William Seely and Addison Green, and four horses, arms, etc. When departing they threatened Father Pinkham that if he did not leave the state immediately they "would have his damned old scalp." Having learned of Bogart's movements the brethren returned to Far West near midnight, and reported their proceedings and those of the mob.

On hearing the report, Judge Elias Higbee, the first judge of the county, ordered Lieutenant-Colonel Hinkle, the highest officer in command in Far West, to send out a company to disperse the mob and retake their prisoners, whom, it was reported, they intended

"HE HAD BEEN **LIFTED** UP IN **PRIDE** BY HIS **EXALTATION** TO OFFICE AND THE REVELATIONS OF **HEAVEN** CONCERNING HIM, UNTIL HE WAS READY TO BE **OVERTHROWN** BY THE FIRST **ADVERSE** WIND THAT SHOULD CROSS HIS TRACKS."

to murder that night. The trumpet sounded, and the brethren were assembled on the public square about midnight, when the facts were stated, and about seventy-five volunteered to obey the judge's order, under command of Captain David W. Patten, who immediately commenced their march on horseback, hoping without the loss of blood to surprise and scatter the camp, retake the prisoners and prevent the attack threatening Far West.

Thursday, October 25—Fifteen of the company were detached from the main body while sixty continued their march till they arrived near the ford of Crooked river, (or creek) where they dismounted, tied their horses, and leaving four or five men to guard them, proceeded towards the ford, not knowing the location of the encampment. It was just at the dawning of light in the east, when they were marching quietly along the road, and near the top of the hill which descends to the river that the report of a gun was heard, and young Patrick O'Banion reeled out of the ranks and fell mortally wounded. Thus the work of death commenced, when Captain Patten ordered a charge and rushed down the hill on a fast trot, and when within about fifty yards of the camp formed a line. The mob formed a line under the bank of the river, below their tents. It was yet so dark that little could be seen by looking at the west; while the mob looking towards the dawning light, could see Patten and his men, when they fired a broadside, and three or four of the brethren fell. Captain Patten ordered the fire returned, which was instantly obeyed, to great disadvantage in the darkness which yet continued. The fire was repeated by the mob, and returned by Captain Patten's company, who gave the watchword "God and Liberty." Captain Patten then ordered a charge, which was instantly obeyed. The parties immediately came in contact, with their swords, and the mob were soon put to flight, crossing the river at the ford and such places as they could get a chance. In the pursuit, one of the mob fled from behind a tree, wheeled, and shot Captain Patten, who instantly fell, mortally wounded, having received a large ball in his bowels.

The ground was soon cleared, and the brethren gathered up a wagon or two, and making beds therein of tents, etc, took their wounded and retreated towards Far West. Three brethren were wounded in the bowels, one in the neck, one in the shoulder, one through the hips, one through both thighs, one in the arms, all by musket shot. One had his arm broken by a sword. Brother Gideon Carter was shot in the head, and left dead on the ground so defaced that the brethren did not know him. Bogart reported that he had lost one man. The three prisoners were released and returned with the brethren to Far West. Captain Patten was carried some of the way in a litter, but it caused so much distress that he begged to be left by the way side. He was carried into Brother Winchester's, three miles from the city of Far West, where he died that night. Patrick O'Banion died soon after, and Brother Carter's body was also brought from Crooked river, when it was discovered who he was.

I went with my brother Hyrum and Lyman Wight to meet the brethren on their return, near Log creek, where I saw Captain Patten in a most distressing condition. His wound was incurable.

Brother David Patten was a very worthy man, beloved by all good men who knew him. He was one of the Twelve Apostles, and died as he had lived, a man of God, and strong in the faith of a glorious resurrection, in a world where mobs will have no power or place. One of his last expressions to his wife was, "Whatever you do else, O! do not deny the faith."

Saturday, October 27—Brother Patten was buried this day at Far West, and before the funeral, I called at Brother Patten's house, and while meditating on the scene before me in presence of his friends, I could not help pointing to his lifeless body and testifying, "There lies a man that has done just as he said he would—he has laid down his life for his friends."

Great excitement now prevailed, and mobs were heard of in every direction, who seemed determined on our destruction. They burned the houses in the country, and took off all the cattle they could find. They destroyed corn fields, took many prisoners, and threatened death to all the Mormons.

Lilburn W. Boggs had become so hardened by mobbing the Saints in Jackson county, and his conscience so "seared as with a hot iron," that he was considered a fit subject for the gubernatorial chair; and it was probably his hatred to truth and the "Mormons," and his blood-thirsty, murderous disposition, that raised him to the station he occupied. His exterminating order of the twenty-seventh aroused every spirit in the state, of the like stamp of his own; and the Missouri mobocrats were flocking to the standard of General Clark from almost every quarter.

Clark, although not the ranking officer, was selected by Governor Boggs as the most fit instrument to carry out his murderous designs; for bad as they were in Missouri, very few commanding officers were yet sufficiently hardened to go all lengths with Boggs in this contemplated inhuman butchery, and expulsion from one of the should-be free and independent states of the Republic of North America, where the Constitution declares that "every man shall have the privilege of worshiping God according to the dictates of his own conscience;" and this was all the offense the Saints had been guilty of.

And here I would state, that while the evil spirits were raging up and down in the state to raise mobs against the "Mormons," Satan himself was no less busy in striving to stir up mischief in the camp of the Saints: and among the most conspicuous of his willing devotees was one Doctor Sampson Avard, who had been in the Church but a short time, and who, although he had generally behaved with a tolerable degree of external decorum, was secretly aspiring to be the greatest of the great, and become the leader of the people. This was his pride and his folly, but as he had no hopes of accomplishing it by gaining the hearts of the people openly he watched his opportunity with the brethren—at a time when mobs oppressed, robbed, whipped, burned, plundered and slew, till forbearance seemed no longer a virtue, and nothing but the grace of God without measure could support men under such trials—to form a secret combination by which he might rise a mighty conqueror, at the expense and the overthrow of the Church. This he tried to accomplish by his smooth, flattering, and winning speeches, which he frequently made to his associates, while his room was well guarded by some of his followers, ready to give him the signal on the approach of anyone who would not approve of his measures.

In these proceedings he stated that he had the sanction of the heads of the Church for what he was about to do; and by his smiles and flattery, persuaded them to believe it, and proceeded to administer to the few under his control, an oath, binding them to everlasting secrecy to everything which should be communicated to them by himself. Thus Avard initiated members into his band, firmly binding them, by all that was sacred, in the protecting of each other in all things that were lawful; and was careful to picture out a great glory that was then hovering over the Church, and would soon burst upon the Saints as a cloud by day, and a pillar of fire by night, and would soon unveil the slumbering mysteries of heaven, which would gladden the hearts and arouse the stupid spirits of the Saints of the latter-day, and fill their hearts with that love which is unspeakable and full of glory, and arm them with power, that the gates of hell could not prevail against them; and would often affirm to his company that the principal men of the Church had put him forward as a spokesman, and a leader of this band, which he named Danites.

Thus he duped many, which gave him the opportunity of figuring as a person of importance. He held his meetings daily, and carried on his crafty work in great haste, to prevent mature reflection upon the matter by his followers, until he had them bound under the penalties of death to keep the secrets and certain signs of the organization by which they were to know each other by day or night.

After those performances, he held meetings to organize his men into companies of tens and fifties, appointing a captain over each company. After completing this organization, he went on to teach the members of it their duty under the orders of their captains; he then called his captains together and taught them in a secluded place.

At this lecture all of the officers revolted, and said it would not do, they would not go into any such measures, and it would not do to name any such thing; "such proceedings would be in open violation of the laws of our country, would be robbing our fellow citizens of their rights, and are not according to the language and doctrine of Christ, or of the Church of Latter-day Saints."

Avard replied, and said there was no laws that were executed in justice, and he cared not for them, this being a different dispensation, a dispensation of the fullness of times; in this dispensation he learned from the scriptures that the kingdom of God was to put down all other kingdoms, and the Lord Himself was to reign, and His laws alone were the laws that would exist.

Avard's teachings were still manfully rejected by all. Avard then said that they had better drop the subject, although he had received his authority from Sidney Rigdon the evening before. The meeting then broke up; the eyes of those present were opened, Avard's craft was no longer in the dark, and but very little confidence was placed in him, even by the warmest of the members of his Danite scheme.

When a knowledge of Avard's rascality came to the Presidency of the Church, he was cut off from the Church, and every means proper used to destroy his influence, at which he was highly incensed, and went about whispering his evil insinuations, but finding every effort unavailing, he again turned conspirator, and sought to make friends with the mob.

And here let it be distinctly understood, that these companies of tens and fifties got up by Avard, were altogether separate and distinct from those companies of tens and fifties organized by the brethren for self-defense, in case of an attack from the mob. This latter organization was called into existence more particularly that in this time of alarm no family or person might be neglected; therefore, one company would be engaged in drawing wood, another in cutting it, another in gathering corn, another in grinding, another in butchering, another in distributing meat, etc., etc., so that all should be employed in turn, and no one lack the necessaries of life. Therefore, let no one hereafter, by mistake or design, confound this organization of the Church for good and righteous purposes, with the organization of the "Danites," of the apostate Avard, which died almost before it had existed.

The mob began to encamp at Richmond on the twenty-sixth, and by this time amounted to about two thousand men, all ready to fulfill the exterminating order, and join the standard of the governor. They took up a line of march for Far West, traveling but part way, where they encamped for the night.

Tuesday, October 30—The advance guard of the mob were patrolling the country and taking many prisoners, among whom were Brother Stephen Winchester, and Brother Carey, whose skull they laid open by a blow from a rifle barrel. In this mangled condition, the mob laid him in their wagon and went on their way, denying him every comfort, and thus he remained that afternoon and night.

General Clark was in camp at Chariton under a forced march to Richmond, with about a thousand men, and the governor's exterminating order.

For the history of this day at Haun's Mills, on Shoal creek, I quote the following affidavit of Elder Joseph Young, First President of the Seventies:

See History of the Church, Vol. 3, 183.

General Atchison withdrew from the army at Richmond as soon as the governor's extermination order was received. Up to this time we were ignorant at Far West of the movements of the mob at Richmond, and the governor's order of extermination.

On the 30th of October a large company of armed soldiers were seen approaching Far West. They came up near to the town, and then drew back about a mile, and encamped for the night. We were informed that they were militia, ordered out by the governor for the purpose of stopping our proceedings, it having been represented to his excellency, by wicked and designing men from Daviess that we were the aggressors, and had committed outrages in Daviess county. They had not yet got the governor's order of extermination, which I believe did not arrive till the next day.

Wednesday, October 31—The militia of Far West guarded the city the past night, and arranged a temporary fortification of wagons, timber, etc., on the south. The sisters, many of them, were engaged in gathering up their most valuable effects, fearing a terrible battle in the morning, and that the houses might be fired and they obliged to flee. The enemy was five to one against us.

About eight o'clock a flag of truce was sent from the enemy, which was met by several of our people, and it was hoped that matters would be satisfactorily arranged after the officers had heard a true statement of all the circumstances. Colonel Hinkle went to meet the flag, and secretly made the following engagement: first, to give up their (the Church's) leaders to be tried and punished; second, to make an appropriation of the property of all who had taken up arms, for the payment of their debts, and indemnify for the damage done by them; third, that the remainder of the Saints should leave the state, and be protected while doing so by the militia; but they were to be permitted to remain under protection until further orders were received from the commander-in-chief; fourth, to give up their arms of every description, which would be receipted for.

The enemy was reinforced by about one thousand five hundred men today, and news of the destruction of property by the mob reached us from every quarter.

Towards evening I was waited upon by Colonel Hinkle, who stated that the officers of the militia desired to have an interview with me and some others, hoping that the difficulties might be settled without having occasion to carry into effect the exterminating orders which they had received from the governor. I immediately complied with the request, and in company with Elders Sidney Rigdon and Parley P. Pratt, Colonel Wight and George W. Robinson, went into the camp of the militia. But judge of my surprise, when, instead of being treated with that respect which is due from one citizen to another, we were taken as prisoners of war, and treated with the utmost contempt. The officers would not converse with us, and the soldiers, almost to a man, insulted us as much as they felt disposed, breathing out threats against me and my companions. I cannot begin to tell the scene which I there witnessed. The loud cries and yells of more than one thousand voices, which rent the air and could be heard for miles, and the horrid and blasphemous threats and curses which were poured upon us in torrents, were enough to appall the stoutest heart. In the evening we had to lie down on the cold ground, surrounded by a strong guard, who were only kept back by the power of God from depriving us of life. We petitioned the officers to know why we were thus treated, but they utterly refused to give us any answer, or to converse with us. After we arrived in the camp, Brother Stephen Winchester and eleven other brethren who were prisoners, volunteered, with permission of the officers, to carry Brother Carey into the city to his family, he having lain exposed to the weather for a show to the inhuman wretches, without having his wound dressed or being nourished in any manner. He died soon after he reached home.

Thursday, November 1—Brothers Hyrum Smith and Amasa Lyman were brought prisoners into camp. The officers of the militia held a court martial, and sentenced us to be shot, on Friday morning, on the public square of Far West as a warning to the "Mormons." However, notwithstanding their sentence and determination, they were not permitted to carry their murderous sentence into execution. Having an opportunity of speaking to General Wilson, I inquired of him why I was thus treated. I told him I was not aware of having done anything worthy of such treatment; that I had always been a supporter of the Constitution and of democracy. His answer was, "I know it, and that is the reason why I want to kill you, or have you killed."

The militia went into the town, and without any restraint whatever, plundered the houses, and abused the innocent and unoffending inhabitants and left many destitute. They went to my house, drove my family out of doors, carried away most of my property. General Doniphan declared he would have nothing to do with such cold-blooded murder, and that he would withdraw his brigade in the morning.

This morning General Lucas ordered the Caldwell militia to give up their arms.

Hinkle, having made a treaty with the mob on his own responsibility, to carry out his treachery, marched the troops out of the city, and the brethren gave up their arms, their own property, which no government on earth had a right to require.

The mob (called Governor's troops) then marched into town, and under pretense of searching for arms, tore up floors, upset haystacks, plundered the most valuable effects they could lay their hands on, wantonly wasted and destroyed a great amount of property, compelled the brethren at the point of the bayonet to sign deeds of trust to pay the expenses of the mob, even while the place was desecrated by the chastity of women being violated. About eighty men were taken prisoners, the remainder were ordered to leave the state, and were forbidden, under threat of being shot by the mob to assemble more than three in a place.

Friday, November 2—About this time Sampson Avard was found by the mob secreted in the hazel brush some miles from Far West, and brought into camp, where he and they were "hail fellows well met;" for Avard told them that Daniteism was an order of the Church, and by his lying tried to make the Church a scape-goat for his sins.

Myself and fellow prisoners were taken to the town, into the public square, and before our departure we, after much entreaty, were suffered to see our families, being attended all the while by a strong guard. I found my wife and children in tears, who feared we had been shot by those who had sworn to take our lives, and that they would see me no more. When I entered my house, they clung to my garments, their eyes streaming with tears, while mingled emotions of joy and sorrow were manifested in their countenances. I requested to have a private interview with them a few minutes, but this privilege was denied me by the guard. I was then obliged to take my departure. Who can realize the feelings which I experienced at that time, to be thus torn from my companion, and leave her surrounded with monsters in the shape of men, and my children, too, not knowing how their wants would be supplied; while I was to be taken far from them in order that my enemies might destroy me when they thought proper to do so. My partner wept, my children clung to me, until they were thrust from me by the swords of the guards. I felt overwhelmed while I witnessed the scene, and could only recommend them to the care of that God whose kindness had followed me to the present time, and who alone could protect them, and deliver me from the hands of my enemies, and restore me to my family.

After this painful scene I was taken back to the camp, and with the rest of my brethren, namely, Sidney Rigdon, Hyrum Smith, Parley P. Pratt, Lyman Wight, Amasa Lyman, and George W. Robinson, started off for Independence, Jackson county, and encamped at night on Crooked river, under a strong guard commanded by Generals Lucas and Wilson.

Saturday, November 3—We continued our march and arrived at the Missouri river, which separated us from Jackson county, where we were hurried across the ferry when but few troops had passed. The truth was, General Clark had sent an express from Richmond to General Lucas, to have the prisoners sent to him, and thus prevent our going to Jackson county, both armies being competitors for the honor of possessing "the royal prisoners." Clark wanted the privilege of putting us to death himself, and Lucas and his troops were desirous of exhibiting us in the streets of Independence.

Sunday, November 4—We were visited by some ladies and gentlemen. One of the women came up, and very candidly inquired of the troops which of the prisoners was the Lord whom the "Mormons" worshipped? One of the guards pointed to me with a significant smile, and said, "This is he." The woman then turning to me inquired whether I professed to be the Lord and Savior? I replied, that I professed to be nothing but a man, and a minister of salvation, sent by Jesus Christ to preach the gospel.

This answer so surprised the woman that she began to inquire into our doctrine, and I preached a discourse, both to her and her companions, and to the wondering soldiers, who listened with almost breathless attention while I set forth the doctrine of faith in Jesus Christ, and repentance, and baptism for remission of sins, with the promise of the Holy Ghost, as recorded in the second chapter of the Acts of the Apostles.

The woman was satisfied, and praised God in the hearing of the soldiers, and went away, praying that God would protect and deliver us. Thus was fulfilled a prophecy which had been spoken publicly by me a few months previous—that a sermon should be preached in Jackson county by one of our elders, before the close of 1838.

The troops having crossed the river about ten o'clock, we proceeded on and arrived at Independence, past noon, in the midst of a great rain, and a multitude of spectators who had assembled to see us, and hear the bugles sound a blast of triumphant joy, which echoed through the camp. We were ushered into a vacant house prepared for our reception, with a floor for our beds and blocks of wood for our pillows.

General Clark arrived at Far West with one thousand six hundred men, and five hundred more were within eight miles of the city.

Thus, Far West has been visited by six thousand men in one week, when the militia of the city (before any were taken prisoners) amounted only to about five hundred. After depriving these of their arms the mob continued to hunt the brethren like wild beasts, and shot several, ravished the women, and killed one near the city. No Saint was permitted to go in or out of the city; and meantime the Saints lived on parched corn.

General Clark ordered General Lucas, who had previously gone to Adam-ondi-Ahman with his troops, "to take the whole of the men of the 'Mormons' prisoners, and place such a guard around them and the town as will protect the prisoners and secure them until they can be dealt with properly," and secure all their property, till the best means could be adopted for paying the damages the citizens had sustained.

Monday, November 5—We were kept under a small guard, and were treated with some degree of hospitality and politeness, while many flocked to see us. We spent most of our time in preaching and conversation, explanatory of our doctrines and practice, which removed mountains of prejudice, and enlisted the populace in our favor, notwithstanding their old hatred and wickedness towards our society.

The brethren at Far West were ordered by General Clark to form a line, when the names of fifty-six present were called and made prisoners to await their trial for something they knew not what. They were kept under a close guard.

Thursday, November 8—There was a severe snowstorm yesterday and today.

General Wilson arrived at Adam-ondi-Ahman; he placed guards around the town so that no persons might pass out or in without permission. All the men in town were then taken and put under guard, and a court of inquiry was instituted, with Adam Black on the bench; the said Adam Black belonged to the mob, and was one of the leaders of it from the time mobbing first commenced in Daviess county. The attorney belonged to General Clark's army.

Shortly after our arrival in Jackson county, Colonel Sterling Price, from the army of General Clark, came with orders from

General Clark, who was commander-in-chief of the expedition, to have us forwarded forthwith to Richmond.

Accordingly, on Thursday morning, we started with three guards only, and they had been obtained with great difficulty, after laboring all the previous day to get them. Between Independence and Roy's ferry, on the Missouri river, they all got drunk, and we got possession of their arms and horses.

It was late in the afternoon, near the setting of the sun. We traveled about half a mile after we crossed the river, and put up for the night.

Friday, November 9—This morning there came a number of men, some of them armed. Their threatenings and savage appearance were such as to make us afraid to proceed without more guards. A messenger was therefore dispatched to Richmond to obtain them. We started before their arrival, but had not gone far before we met Colonel Price with a guard of about seventy-four men, and were conducted by them to Richmond, and put into an old vacant house, and a guard set.

Some time through the course of that day General Clark came in, and we were introduced to him. We inquired of him the reason why we had been thus carried from our homes, and what were the charges against us. He said that he was not then able to determine, but would be in a short time; and with very little more conversation withdrew.

Some short time after he had withdrawn, Colonel Price came in with two chains in his hands, and a number of padlocks. The two chains he fastened together. He had with him ten men, armed, who stood at the time of these operations with a thumb upon the cock of their guns. They first nailed down the windows, then came and ordered a man by the name of John Fulkerson, whom he had with him, to chain us together with chains and padlocks, being seven in number. After that he searched us, examining our pockets to see if we had any arms. He found nothing but pocket knives, but these he took away with him.

Saturday, November 10—General Clark had spent his time since our arrival at Richmond in searching the laws to find authority for trying us by court martial. Had he not been a lawyer of eminence, I should have supposed it no very difficult task to decide that quiet, peaceful unoffending, and private citizens too, except as ministers of the gospel, were not amenable to a military tribunal, in a country governed by civil laws.

The three days' investigation having closed at Adam-ondi-Ahman, every man was honorably acquitted, Adam Black being judge.

General Wilson then ordered every family to be out of Diahman in ten days, with permission to go to Caldwell, and there tarry until spring, and then leave the state under pain of extermination. The weather is very cold, more so than usual for this season of the year.

In keeping the order of General Wilson the Saints had to leave their crops and houses, and to live in tents and wagons, in this inclement season of the year. As for their flocks and herds, the mob had relieved them from the trouble of taking care of them, or from the pain of seeing them starve to death—by stealing them.

An arrangement was made in which it was stipulated that a committee of twelve, which had been previously appointed, should have the privilege of going from Far West to Daviess county, for the term of four weeks, for the purpose of conveying their crops from Daviess to Caldwell. The committee were to wear white badges on their hats for protection.

About thirty of the brethren have been killed, many wounded, about a hundred are missing, and about sixty at Richmond awaiting their trial—for what they know not.

Sunday, November 11—While in Richmond we were under the charge of Colonel Price from Chariton county, who allowed all manner of abuses to be heaped upon us. During this time my afflictions were great, and our situation was truly painful.

General Clark informed us that he would turn us over to the civil authorities for trial. Joseph Smith, Jun., Hyrum Smith, Sidney Rigdon, Parley P. Pratt, Lyman Wight, Amasa Lyman, George W. Robinson, Caleb Baldwin, Alanson Ripley, Washington Voorhees, Sidney Turner, John Buchanan, Jacob Gates, Chandler Holbrook, George W. Harris, Jesse D. Hunter, Andrew Whitlock, Martin C. Allred, William Allred, George D. Grant, Darwin Chase, Elijah Newman, Alvin G. Tippets, Zedekiah Owens, Isaac Morley, Thomas Beck, Moses Clawson, John J. Tanner, Daniel Shearer, Daniel S. Thomas, Alexander McRae, Elisha Edwards, John S. Higbee, Ebenezer Page, Benjamin Covey, Ebenezer Robinson, Luman Gibbs, James M. Henderson, David Pettegrew, Edward Partridge, Francis Higbee, David Frampton, George Kimball, Joseph W. Younger, Henry Zobriskie, Allen J. Stout, Sheffield Daniels, Silas Maynard, Anthony Head, Benjamin Jones, Daniel Garn, John T. Earl, and Norman Shearer, were brought before Austin A. King, at Richmond, for trial, charged with the several crimes of high treason against the state, murder, burglary, arson, robbery, and larceny.

Monday, November 12—The first act of the court was to send out a body of armed men, without a civil process, to obtain witnesses.

Tuesday, November 13—We were placed at the bar, Austin A. King presiding, and Thomas C. Burch, the state's attorney. Witnesses were called and sworn at the point of the bayonet.

Dr. Sampson Avard was the first brought before the court. He had previously told Mr. Oliver Olney that if he (Olney) wished to save himself, he must swear hard against the heads of the Church, as they were the ones the court wanted to criminate; and if he could swear hard against them, they would not (that is, neither court nor mob) disturb him. "I intend to do it," said he, "in order to escape, for if I do not, they will take my life."

This introduction is sufficient to show the character of his testimony, and he swore just according to the statement he had made, doubtless thinking it a wise course to ingratiate himself into the good graces of the mob.

The following witnesses were examined in behalf of the state, many of whom, if we may judge from their testimony, swore upon the same principle as Avard, they were: Wyatt Cravens, Nehemiah Odle, Captain Samuel Bogart, Morris Phelps, John Corrill, Robert Snodgrass, George Walton, George M. Hinkle, James C. Owens, Nathaniel Carr, Abner Scovil, John Cleminson, Reed Peck, James C. Owens (reexamined), William Splawn, Thomas M. Odle, John Raglin, Allen Rathbun, Jeremiah Myers, Andrew J. Job, Freeburn H. Gardner, Burr Riggs, Elisha Camron, Charles Bleckley, James Cobb, Jesse Kelly, Addison Price, Samuel Kimball, William W. Phelps, John Whitmer, James B. Turner, George W. Worthington, Joseph H. McGee, John Lockhart, Porter Yale, Benjamin Slade, Ezra Williams, Addison Green, John Taylor, Timothy Lewis, and Patrich Lynch.

We were called upon for our witnesses, and we gave the names of some forty or fifty. Captain Bogart was despatched with a company of militia to procure them. He arrested all he could find, thrust them into prison, and we were not allowed to see them.

During the week we were again called upon most tauntingly for witnesses; we gave the names of some others, and they were thrust into prison, so many as were to be found.

In the meantime Malinda Porter, Delia F. Pine, Nancy Rigdon, Jonathan W. Barlow, Thoret Parsons, Ezra Chipman, and Arza Judd, Jun., volunteered, and were sworn, on the defense, but were prevented as much as possible by threats from telling the truth. We saw a man at the window by the name of Allen, and beckoned him to come in, and had him sworn, but when he did not testify to please the court, several rushed upon him with their bayonets, and he fled the place; three men took after him with loaded guns, and he barely escaped with his life. It was of no use to get any more witnesses, even if we could have done so.

Thus this mock investigation continued from day to day, till Saturday, when several of the brethren were discharged by Judge King.

Our Church organization was converted, by the testimony of the apostates, into a temporal kingdom, which was to fill the whole earth, and subdue all other kingdoms.

The judge, who by the way was a Methodist, asked much concerning our views of the prophecy of Daniel: "In the days of these kings shall the God of heaven set up a kingdom which shall break in pieces all other kingdoms, and stand for ever" &c "And the kingdom and the greatness of the kingdom, under the whole heaven, shall be given to the Saints of the Most High." As if it were treason to believe the Bible.

Wednesday, November 28—Daniel Ashby, a member of the state senate, wrote General Clark that he was in the battle (massacre) at Haun's Mills, that thirty-one "Mormons" were killed, and seven of his party wounded.

The remaining prisoners were all released or admitted to bail, except Lyman Wight, Caleb Baldwin, Hyrum Smith, Alexander McRae, Sidney Rigdon, and myself, who were sent to Liberty, Clay county, to jail, to stand our trial for treason and murder. Our treason consisted of having whipped the mob out of Daviess county, and taking their cannon from them; the murder, of killing the man in the Bogart battle; also Parley P. Pratt, Morris Phelps, Luman Gibbs, Darwin Chase, and Norman Shearer, who were put into Richmond jail to stand their trial for the same "crimes."

During the investigation we were confined in chains and received much abuse.

The matter of driving away witnesses or casting them into prison, or chasing them out of the county, was carried to such length that our lawyers, General Doniphan and Amos Rees, told us not to bring our witnesses there at all; for if we did, there would not be one of them left for final trial; for no sooner would Bogart and his men know who they were, than they would put them out of the country.

As to making any impression on King, Doniphan said, if a cohort of angels were to come down, and declare we were innocent, it would all be the same; for he (King) had determined from the beginning to cast us into prison. We never got the privilege of introducting our witnesses at all; if we had, we could have disproved all the evidence of our enemies.

Friday, November 30—About this time those of us who had been sentenced thereto, were conveyed to Liberty jail, put in close confinement, and all communication with our friends cut off.

During our trial William E. McLellin, accompanied by Burr Riggs and others, at times were busy in plundering and robbing the houses of Sidney Rigdon, George Morey, the widow Phebe Ann Patten, and others, under pretense or color of law, on an order from General Clark, as testified to by the members of the different families robbed.

This day (16th December) Elder David H. Redfield arrived in Jefferson City, and on Monday, 17th, presented the petition of the brethren to General David R. Atchison and others, who were very anxious to hear from Caldwell, as there were many reports in circulation, such as "the Mormons kept up the Danite system," "were going to build the Lord's house," and "more blood would be spilled before they left the state," which created a hardness in the minds of the people.

In the afternoon Brother Redfield had an interview with Governor Boggs, who inquired about our people and property with as much apparent interest as though his whole soul was engaged for our welfare; and said that he had heard that "the citizens were committing depredations on the 'Mormons,' and driving off their stock."

Brother Redfield informed him that armed forces came in the place and abused men, women and children, stole horses, drove off cattle, and plundered houses of everything that pleased their fancy.

Governor Boggs said that he would write Judge King and Colonel Price, to go to Far West, and put down every hostile appearance. He also stated that "the stipulations entered into by the 'Mormons' to leave the state, and to sign the deed of trust, were unconstitutional, and not valid."

Brother Redfield replied, "We want the legislature to pass a law to that effect, showing that the stipulations and deeds of trust are not valid and are unconstitutional; and unless you do pass such a law, we shall not consider ourselves safe in the state. You say there has been a stain upon the character of the state, and now is the time to pass some law to that effect; and unless you do, farewell to the virtue of the state; farewell to her honor and good name; farewell to her Christian virtue, until she shall be peopled by a different race of men; farewell to every name that binds man to man; farewell to a fine soil and a glorious home; they are gone, they are rent from us by a lawless banditti."

Tuesday, December 25—My brother, Don Carlos, and my cousin George A. Smith returned (from missions through Kentucky and Tennessee), having traveled fifteen hundred miles—nine hundred on foot, and the remainder by steamboat and otherwise. They visited several branches, and would have accomplished the object of their mission, had it not been for the troubles at Far West.

When nearly home they were known and pursued by the mob, which compelled them to travel one hundred miles in two days and nights. The ground at the time was slippery, and a severe northwest wind was blowing in their faces; they had but little to eat, and narrowly escaped freezing both nights.

Thursday, December 27—Anson Call went to Ray county, near Elk Horn, to sell some property, and was taken by ten of the mob and one old negro. Some of the mob were two of Judge Dickey's sons, a Mr. Adams, and a constable. They ordered him to disarm himself. He told them he had no arms about his person. They ordered him to turn his pockets wrong side out. They then said they would peel off his naked back before morning, with a hickory gad. They beat him with their naked hands times without number; they struck him in the face with a bowie knife, and severely hurt him a number of times.

After abusing him about four hours, saying he was a —— "Mormon," and they would serve him as they had others, tie him with a hickory withe and gad him, and keep him till morning, they then started off and came to a hazel grove; while consulting together what course to pursue with him, he leaped into the bush, when they pursued him, but he made his escape and returned to Far West.

After much controversy and angry disputation, as the papers of Missouri, published at the time, abundantly testify, our petition and memorial was laid on the table until the 4th of July following; thus utterly refusing to grant the request of the memorialists to investigate the subject.

After we were cast into prison, we heard nothing but threatenings, that, if any judge or jury, or court of any kind, should clear any of us, we should never get out of the state alive.

The state appropriated two thousand dollars to be distributed among the people of Daviess and Caldwell counties, the "Mormons" of Caldwell not excepted. The people of Daviess thought they could live on "Mormon" property, and did not want their thousand, consequently it was pretended to be given to those of Caldwell. Judge Cameron, Mr. McHenry, and others attended to the distribution. Judge Cameron would drive in the brethren's hogs (many of which were identified) and shoot them down in the streets; and without further bleeding, and half dressing, they were cut up and distributed by McHenry to the poor, at a charge of four and five cents per pound; which, together with a few pieces of refuse goods, such as calicoes at double and treble prices soon consumed the two thousand dollars; doing the brethren very little good, or in reality none, as the property destroyed by them, (i.e. the distributing commission) was equal to what they gave the Saints.

The proceedings of the legislature were warmly opposed by a minority of the house—among whom were David R. Atchison, of Clay county, and all the members from St. Louis, and Messrs. Rollins and Gordon, from Boone county, and by various other members from other counties; but the mob majority carried the day, for the guilty wretches feared an investigation—knowing that it would endanger their lives and liberties. Sometime during this session the legislature appropriated two hundred thousand dollars to pay the troops for driving the Saints out of the state.

Many of the state journals tried to hide the iniquity of the state by throwing a covering of lies over her atrocious deeds. But can they hide the governor's cruel order for banishment or extermination? Can they conceal the facts of the disgraceful treaty of the generals with their own officers and men at the city of Far West? Can they conceal the fact that twelve or fifteen thousand men, women and children, have been banished from the state without trial or condemnation? And this at an expense of two hundred thousand dollars—and this sum appropriated by the state legislature, in order to pay the troops for this act of lawless outrage? Can they conceal the fact that we have been imprisoned for many months, while our families, friends and witnesses have been driven away? Can they conceal the blood of the murdered husbands and fathers, or stifle the cries of the widows and the fatherless? Nay! The rocks and mountains may cover them in unknown depths, the awful abyss of the fathomless deep may swallow them up, and still their horrid deeds will stand forth in the broad light of day, for the wondering gaze of angels and of men! They cannot be hid.

Some time in December Heber C. Kimball and Alanson Ripley were appointed, by the brethren in Far West, to visit us at Liberty jail as often as circumstances would permit, or occasion required, which duty they faithfully performed. We were sometimes visited by our friends, whose kindness and attention I shall ever remember with feelings of lively gratitude; but frequently we were not suffered to have that privilege. Our food was of the coarsest kind, and served up in a manner which was disgusting.

Thus, in a land of liberty, in the town of Liberty, Clay county, Missouri, my fellow prisoners and I in chains, and dungeons, saw the close of 1838.

Chapter Eleven

1839

Tuesday, January 1, 1839—The day dawned upon us as prisoners of hope, but not as sons of liberty. O Columbia, Columbia! How thou art fallen! "The land of the free, the home of the brave!" "The asylum of the oppressed"—oppressing thy noblest sons, in a loathsome dungeon, without any provocation, only that they have claimed to worship the God of their fathers according to His own word, and the dictates of their own consciences. Elder Parley P. Pratt and his companions in tribulation were still held in bondage in their doleful prison in Richmond.

Monday, January 7—Anson Call returned to his farm on the three forks of Grand river, to see if he could secure any of the property he had left in his flight to Adam-ondi-Ahman, and was there met by the mob, and beaten with a hoop pole about his limbs, body and head; the man that used the pole about his person was George W. O'Neal. With much difficulty Brother Call returned to Far West, with his person much bruised, and from that time gave up all hopes of securing any of his property.

Tuesday, January 29—The committee who had been appointed for removing the poor from the state of Missouri, viz., William Huntington, Charles Bird, Alanson Ripley, Theodore Turley,

Daniel Shearer, Shadrach Roundy, and Jonathan H. Hale, met in the evening of that day (January 29, 1839) at the house of Theodore Turley, and organized by appointing William Huntington chairman, Daniel Shearer treasurer, and Alanson Ripley clerk, and made some arrangements for carrying into operation the business of removing the poor. President Brigham Young got eighty subscribers to the covenant the first day, and three hundred the second day.

Monday, February 4—Mr. Turner's bill of 16th January came up for the first reading, "when Mr. Wright moved that the bill be laid on the table until the 4th day of July next; and upon this question Mr. Primm desired the yeas and nays, which were ordered, and the decision was in the affirmative" by eleven majority, which by many was considered an approval of all the wrongs the Saints had sustained in the state.

February 6th and 7th—The committee on the removal of the Saints from Missouri were in session. Stephen Markham started for Illinois, with my wife and children, and Jonathan Holmes and wife.

Tuesday, February 12—The committee (on removal) sent a delegation to Sister Murie to ascertain her necessities. Daniel Shearer and Erastus Bingham went. Applications for assistance were made from Sister Morgan L. Gardner, Jeremiah Mackley's family, Brother Forbush, Echoed Cheney, T.D. Tyler, D. McArthur and others.

Wednesday, February 13—Voted that Theodore Turley be appointed to superintend the management of the teams provided for removing the poor, and see that they are furnished for the journey.

Thursday, February 14—The persecution was so bitter against Elder Brigham Young (on whom devolved the presidency of the Twelve by age, Thomas B. Marsh having apostatized) and his life was so diligently sought for, that he was compelled to flee; and he left Far West on this day for Illinois.

My brother Don Carlos Smith had carried a petition to the

mob, to get assistance to help our father's family out of Missouri. I know not how much he obtained, but my father and mother started this day for Quincy, with an ox team.

The committee on removal discussed the propriety of paying the debts of the Saints in Clay county. Alanson Ripley was requested to call on lawyer Barnet, who was in town, and make arrangements concerning the matter. A letter of attorney was drawn up for the brethren to sign, who felt willing to dispose of their real estate to discharge their debts, appointing Alanson Ripley their attorney for that purpose. This was not exactly according to the minds of the committee, for they only directed Brother Ripley to confer with the person above named for the purpose of obtaining information without reference to his being appointed an attorney for that purpose, independent of any other person or persons.

Friday, February 15—My family arrived at the Mississippi, opposite Quincy, after a journey of almost insupportable hardships, and Elder Markham returned immediately to Far West.

Tuesday, February 19—The committee on removal appointed Charles Bird to visit the several parts of Caldwell county, and William Huntington the town of Far West, to ascertain the number of families that would have to be assisted in removing, and solicit means from those who are able to give for the assistance of the needy, and make report as soon as possible.

Saturday, February 25—At a meeting of the Democratic Association, held this evening at Quincy, Adams county, Illinois, Mr. Lindsay introduced a resolution setting forth that the people called "Latter-day Saints" were many of them in a situation requiring the aid of the citizens of Quincy, and recommending that measures be adopted for their relief, which resolution was adopted, and a committee consisting of eight persons appointed by the chair; of which committee J.W. Whitney was chairman. The association then adjourned to meet on Wednesday evening next after instructing the committee to procure the Congregational church as a place of meeting, and to invite as many of our people to attend as should choose to do so; for it was in their behalf that the meeting was to be held. Also all other citizens of the town who felt to do so were invited to attend. The committee not being able to obtain the meeting house, procured the Court House for that purpose.

After we were cast into prison, we heard nothing but threatenings, that if any judge or jury, or court of any kind, should clear any of us, we should never get out of the state alive.

This soon determined our course, and that was to escape out of their hands as soon as we could, and by any means we could. After we had been some length of time in prison, we demanded a habeas corpus of Judge Turnham, one of the county judges, which with some considerable reluctance, was granted. Great threatenings were made at this time, by the mob, that if any of us were liberated, we should never get out of the county alive.

After the investigation, Sidney Rigdon was released from prison by the decision of the judge; the remainder were committed to jail; he, however, returned with us until a favorable opportunity offered for his departure. Through the friendship of the sheriff, Mr. Samuel Hadley, and the jailor, Mr. Samuel Tillery, he was let out of the jail secretly in the night, after having declared in prison, that the sufferings of Jesus Christ were a fool to his; and being solemnly warned by them to be out of the state with as little delay as possible, he made his escape. Being pursued by a body of armed men, it was through the direction of a kind Providence that he escaped out of their hands, and safely arrived in Quincy, Illinois.

About this time, Elders Heber C. Kimball and Alanson Ripley were at Liberty, where they had been almost weekly importuning at the feet of the judges; and while performing this duty on a certain occasion, Judge Hughes stared them full in the face, and observed to one of his associates, that "by the look of these men's eyes, they are whipped, but not conquered; and let us beware how we treat these men; for their looks bespeak innocence;" and at that time he entreated his associates to admit of bail for all the prisoners; but the hardness of their hearts would not admit of so charitable a

"TEMPTATION FOLLOWED TEMPTATION, AND BEING YOUNG IN THE CAUSE, THE SAINTS SUFFERED THEMSELVES TO BE BUFFETED BY THEIR ADVERSARY."

deed. But the brethren continued to importune at the feet of the judges, and also to visit the prisoners. No one of the ruling part of the community disputed the innocence of the prisoners, but said, in consequence of the fury of the mob, that even-handed justice could not be administered; Elders Kimball and Ripley were therefore compelled to abandon the idea of importuning at the feet of the judges, and leave the prisoners in the hands of God.

When Elder Israel Barlow left Missouri in the fall of 1838, either by missing his way, or some other cause, he struck the Des Moines river some distance above its mouth. He was in a destitute situation; and making his wants known, found friends who assisted him, and gave him introductions to several gentlemen, among whom was Dr. Isaac Galland, to whom he communicated the situation of the Saints; the relation of which enlisted Mr. Galland's sympathies, or interest, or both united, and hence a providential introduction of the Church to Commerce (the place of residence of Mr. Galland) and its vicinity; for Brother Barlow went direct to Quincy, the place of his destination, and made known his interview with Dr. Galland to the Church.

While the persecutions were progressing against us in Missouri, the enemy of all righteousness was no less busy with the Saints in England, according to the length of time the gospel had been preached in that kingdom. Temptation followed temptation, and being young in the cause, the Saints suffered themselves to be buffeted by their adversary. From the time that Elder Willard Richards was called to the apostleship, in July, 1838, the devil seemed to take a great dislike to him, and strove to stir up the minds of many against him. Elder Richards was afflicted with sickness, and several times was brought to the borders of the grave, and many were tempted to believe that he was under transgression, or he would not be thus afflicted. Some were tried and tempted because Elder Richards took to himself a wife; they thought he should have given himself wholly to the ministry, and followed Paul's advice to the letter. Some were tried because his wife wore a veil, and others because she carried a muff to keep herself warm when she walked out in cold weather; and even the president of the Church (Joseph Fielding) there, thought "she had better done without it;" she had nothing ever purchased by the Church; and to gratify their feelings, wore the poorest clothes she had, and they were too good, so hard was it to buffet the storm of feeling that arose from such foolish causes. Sister Richards was very sick for some time, and some were dissatisfied because her husband did not neglect her entirely and go out preaching; and others, that she did not go to meeting when she was not able to go so far.

From such little things arose a spirit of jealousy, tattling, evil speaking, surmising, covetousness, and rebellion, until the Church but too generally harbored more or less of those unpleasant feelings; and this evening (March 9th) Elder Halsal came out openly in council against Elder Richards, and preferred some heavy charges, none of which he was able to substantiate. Most of the elders in Preston were against Elder Richards for a season, except James Whitehead, who proved himself true in the hours of trial.

Sunday, March 10—When Elder Richards made proclamation from the pulpit, that if anyone had aught against him, or his wife, Jennetta, he wished they would come to him and state their grievances, and if he had erred in anything, he would acknowledge his fault, one only of the brethren came to him, and that to acknowledge his own fault to Elder Richards in harboring unpleasant feelings without a cause.

Sister Richards bore all these trials and persecutions with patience. Elder Richards knew the cause of these unpleasantries, his call (to the apostolate) having been made known to him by revelation; but he told no one of it. The work continued to spread in Manchester and vicinity, among the Staffordshire potteries, and other places in England.

This day, 17th of March, Parley P. Pratt's wife left the prison house, where she had voluntarily been with her husband most of the winter, and returned to Far West, to get passage with some of the brethren for Illinois.

Monday, March 25—About this time, Elders Kimball and Turley started on their mission to see the governor. They called on the sheriff of Ray county and the jailer for a copy of the mittimus, by which the prisoners were held in custody, but they confessed they had none. They went to Judge King, and he made out a kind of mittimus. At this time we had been in prison several months without even a mittimus; and that too for crimes said to have been committed in another county.

Elders Kimball and Turley took all the papers by which we were held, or which were then made out for them, with our petition to the supreme judges, and went to Jefferson City.

The governor was absent. The secretary of state treated them very kindly; and when he saw the papers, could hardly believe those were all the documents by which the prisoners were held in custody, for they were illegal.

Lawyer Doniphan had also deceived them in his papers and sent them off with such documents, that a change of venue could not be effected in time. The secretary was astonished at Judge King acting as he did, but said he could do nothing in the premises, and if the governor were present, he could do nothing. But the secretary wrote a letter to Judge King.

The brethren then started to find the supreme judges, and get writs of habeas corpus; and after riding hundreds of miles to effect this object, returned to Liberty on the 30th of March, having seen Matthias McGirk, George Thompkins and John C. Edwards, the supreme judges, but did not obtain the writ of habeas corpus in consequence of a lack in the order of commitment, although the judges seemed to be friendly.

We were informed that Judge King said, that there was nothing against my brother Hyrum, only that he was a friend to the Prophet. He also said there was nothing against Caleb Baldwin, and Alexander McRae.

Brother Horace Cowan was put into Liberty jail today for debt, in consequence of the persecution of the mob.

Thursday, April 4—Brothers Kimball and Turley called on Judge King, who was angry at their having reported the case to the governor, and, said he, "I could have done all the business for you properly, if you had come to me; and I would have signed the petition for all except Joe, and he is not fit to live." I bid Brothers Kimball and Turley to be of good cheer, "for we shall be delivered; but no arm but God's can deliver us now. Tell the brethren to be of good cheer and get the Saints away as fast as possible."

Brothers Kimball and Turley were not permitted to enter the prison, and all the communication we had with them was through the grate of the dungeon. The brethren left Liberty on their return to Far West.

Friday, April 5—Brothers Kimball and Turley arrived at Far West.

This day a company of about fifty men in Daviess county swore that they would never eat or drink, until they had murdered "Joe Smith." Their captain, William Bowman, swore, in the presence of Theodore Turley, that he would "never eat or drink, after he had seen Joe Smith, until he had murdered him."

Also eight men—Captain Bogart, who was the county judge, Dr. Laffity, John Whitmer, and five others—came into the committee's room (i.e. the room or office of the committee on removal) and presented to Theodore Turley the paper containing the revelation of July 8, 1838, to Joseph Smith, directing the Twelve to take their leave of the Saints in Far West on the building site of the Lord's house on the 26th of April, to go to the isles of the sea, and then asked him to read it. Turley said, "Gentlemen, I am well acquainted with it." They said, "Then you, as a rational man, will give up Joseph Smith's being a prophet and an inspired man? He and the Twelve are now scattered all over creation; let them come here if they dare; if they do, they will be murdered. As that revelation cannot be fulfilled, you will now give up your faith."

Turley jumped up and said, "In the name of God that revelation will be fulfilled." They laughed him to scorn. John Whitmer hung down his head. They said, "If they (the Twelve) come, they will get murdered; they dare not come to take their leave here; that is like all the rest of Joe Smith's d——n prophecies." They commenced on Turley and said, he had better do as John Corrill had done; "he is going to publish a book called 'Mormonism Fairly Delineated;' he is a sensible man, and you had better assist him."

Turley said, "Gentlemen, I presume there are men here who have heard Corrill say, that 'Mormonism' was true, that Joseph Smith was a prophet, and inspired of God. I now call upon you, John Whitmer; you say Corrill is a moral and a good man; do you believe him when he says the Book of Mormon is true, or when he says it is not true? There are many things published that they say are true, and again turn around and say they are false?" Whitmer asked, "Do you hint at me?" Turley replied, "If the cap fits you, wear it; all I know is that you have published to the world that an angel did present those plates to Joseph Smith." Whitmer replied: "I now say, I handled those plates; there were fine engravings on both sides. I handled them;" and he described how they were hung, and "they were shown to me by a supernatural power;" he acknowledged all.

Turley asked him, "Why is not the translation now true?" He said, "I could not read it (in the original) and I do not know whether it (i.e., the translation) is true or not." Whitmer testified all this in the presence of eight men.

The committee (on removal of the Saints from Missouri) met, and Brother William Huntington made report of his journey to Liberty on business of the committee.

The subject of providing some clothing for the prisoners at Richmond was discussed, and the propriety of sending two brethren to Liberty, to make sales of some lands, was taken up, and Elders H.G. Sherwood and Theodore Turley were appointed.

A bill of clothing for the Richmond prisoners having been made up, was presented and given to those appointed to go to Liberty, that they might procure the goods on the sales of land.

Saturday, April 6—Judge King evidently fearing a change of venue, or some movement on our part to escape his unhallowed persecution (and most probably expecting that we would be murdered on the way) hurried myself and fellow prisoners off to Daviess county, under a guard of about ten men, commanded by Samuel Tillery, deputy jailer of Clay county. We were promised that we should go through Far West, which was directly on our route, which our friends at that place knew, and expected us; but instead of fulfilling their promise, they took us around the city, and out of the direct course some eighteen miles; far from habitations, where every opportunity presented for a general massacre.

Sunday, April 7—The committee met in council at Brother Turley's. Brother Erastus Snow made a report of his visit to the judges at Jefferson city. A letter from the prisoners at Liberty was read and Daniel Shearer and Heber C. Kimball were appointed to see Mr. Hughes and get him to go to Daviess county and attend the sitting of the court there.

We continued our travels across the prairie, while the brethren at Far West, anxious for our welfare, gave a man thirty dollars to convey a letter to us in Daviess county, and return an answer.

Monday, April 8—After a tedious journey—for our long confinement had enfeebled our bodily powers—we arrived in Daviess county, about a mile from Gallatin, where we were delivered into the hands of William Morgan, sheriff of Daviess county, with his guard, William Bowman, John Brassfield and John Pogue. The Liberty guard returned immediately, but became divided, or got lost on their way; a part of them arrived in Far West after dark, and got caught in the fence; and calling for help, Elder Markham went to their assistance and took them to the tavern. From them he got a letter I had written to the committee, informing them of our arrival in Daviess county.

Tuesday, April 9—Our trial commenced before a drunken grand jury, Austin A. King, presiding judge, as drunk as the jury; for they were all drunk together. Elder Stephen Markham had been dispatched by the committee to visit us, and bring a hundred dollars that was sent by Elder Kimball, as we were destitute of means at that time. He left Far West this morning, and swimming several streams he arrived among us in the afternoon, and spent the evening in our company. Brother Markham brought us a written copy of a statute which had passed the legislature, giving us the privilege of a change of venue on our own affadavit.

Judge Morin arrived from Mill Port, and was favorable to our escape from the persecution we were enduring, and spent the evening with us in prison, and we had as pleasant a time as such circumstances would permit, for we were as happy as the happiest; the Spirit buoyed us above our trials, and we rejoiced in each other's society.

Wednesday, April 10—The day was spent in the examination of witnesses before the grand jury. Dr. Sampson Avard was one of the witnesses. Brother Markham was not permitted to give his testimony.

Our guard went home, and Colonel William P. Peniston, Blakely, and others took their place.

Thursday, April 11—The examination of witnesses was continued, and Elder Markham was permitted to give his testimony. After he had closed, Blakely, one of the guard, came in and said to Markham, that he wanted to speak to him. Brother Markham walked out with him, and around the end of the house when Blakely called out, "—— you —— old Mormon; I'll kill you;" and struck at Markham with his fist and then with a club. Markham took the club from him and threw it over the fence.

There were ten of the mob who immediately rushed upon Markham to kill him, Colonel William P. Peniston, captain of the guard, being one of the number. But Markham told them he could kill the whole of them at one blow apiece, and drove them off. The court and grand jury stood and saw the affray, and heard the mob threaten Markham's life, by all the oaths they could invent, but they took no cognizance of it.

The ten mobbers went home after their guns to shoot Markham, and the grand jury brought in a bill for "murder, treason, burglary, arson, larceny, theft, and stealing," against Lyman Wight, Alexander McRae, Caleb Baldwin, Hyrum Smith and myself.

This evening the committee (on removal) assembled at Daniel Shearer's. After prayer by Brother James Newberry, he was ordained an elder on the recommendation of Elder Heber C. Kimball, under the hands of Hiram Clark and William Huntington.

Elder Kimball reported that Jessie P. Maupin, the thirty-dollar messenger they had sent to us, had returned; that the prisoners were well and in good spirits.

Brother Rogers, who had returned from Jackson county, reported that he had sold all the lands in Jackson. Elder Kimball was requested to attend a meeting of the Daviess county officials tomorrow, and as an individual, mention the case of the committee (on removal) and the brethren generally, and learn their feelings, whether they would protect the brethren from the abuse of the mob, in case they came immediately to drive them out, as they had recently threatened.

During this night the visions of the future were opened to my understanding; when I saw the ways and means and near approach of my escape from imprisonment, and the danger that my beloved Brother Markham was in. I awoke Brother Markham, and told him if he would rise very early and not wait for the judge and lawyers, as he had contemplated doing, but rise briskly, he would get safe home, almost before he was aware of it; and if he did not the mob would shoot him on the way; and I told him to tell the brethren to be of good cheer, but lose no time in removing from the country [county].

Friday, April 12—This morning Brother Markham arose at dawn of day, and rode rapidly towards Far West, where he arrived before nine a.m. The mobbers pursued to shoot him, but did not overtake him.

Saturday, April 13—Elder Markham went to Independence to close the business of the Church in that region.

Sunday, April 14—The committee (on removal) in council resolved to send Sisters Fosdick and Meeks, and Brother William Monjar and another family, with Brothers Jones, Burton, and Barlow's teams, which had recently arrived at Quincy.

The committee moved thirty-six families into Tenney's Grove, about twenty-five miles from Far West; and a few men were appointed to chop wood for them, while Brother Turley was to furnish them with meal and meat, until they could be removed to Quincy. The corn was ground at the committee's horse mill, in Far West. Elder Kimball was obliged to secret himself in the cornfields during the day, and was in at night counseling the committee and brethren.

Monday, April 15—Having procured a change of venue we started for Boone county, and were conducted to that place by a strong guard.

This evening the committee (on removal) met to make arrangements concerning teams and the moving of the few families who yet remained at Far West.

This evening our guard got intoxicated. We thought it a favorable opportunity to make our escape; knowing that the only object of our enemies was our destruction; and likewise knowing that a number of our brethren had been massacred by them on Shoal creek, amongst whom were two children; and that they sought every opportunity to abuse others who were left in that state; and that they were never brought to an account for their barbarous proceedings, which were winked at and encouraged by those in authority. We thought that it was necessary for us, inasmuch as we loved our lives, and did not wish to die by the hand of murderers and assassins; and inasmuch as we loved our families and friends, to deliver ourselves from our enemies, and from that land of tyranny and oppression, and again take our stand among a people in whose bosoms dwell those feelings of republicanism and liberty which gave rise to our nation: feelings which the inhabitants of the state of Missouri were strangers to. Accordingly, we took advantage of the situation of our guard and departed, and that night we traveled a considerable distance.

Wednesday, April 17—We [continued] our jouney towards Illinois, keeping off from the main road as much as possible, which impeded our progress.

Thursday, April 18—This morning Elder Kimball went into the committee room and told the committee (on removal) to wind up their affairs and be off, or their lives would be taken. Stephen Markham had gone over the Missouri river on business. Elders Turley and Shearer were at Far West.

Twelve men went to Elder Turley's with loaded rifles to shoot him. They broke seventeen clocks into matchwood. They broke tables, smashed in the windows; while Bogart (the county judge) looked on and laughed. One Whitaker threw iron pots at Turley, one of which hit him on the shoulder, at which Whitaker jumped and laughed like a madman. The mob shot down cows while the girls were milking them. The mob threatened to send the committee "to hell jumping," and "put daylight through them."

The same day, previous to the breaking of the clocks, some of the same company met Elder Kimball on the public square in Far West, and asked him if he was a "—— Mormon;" he replied, "I am a Mormon." "Well, —— you, we'll blow your brains out, you —— Mormon," and tried to ride over him with their horses. This was in the presence of Elias Smith, Theodore Turley, and others of the committee.

The brethren gathered up what they could and left Far West in one hour; and the mob staid [stayed] until they left, then plundered thousands of dollars' worth of property which had been left by the exiled brethren and sisters to help the poor to remove.

One mobber rode up, and finding no convenient place to

fasten his horse, shot a cow that was standing near, and while the poor animal was yet struggling in death, he cut a strip of her hide from her nose to the tip of her tail, this he tied round a stump, to which he fastened his halter.

During the commotion this day, a great portion of the records of the committee, accounts, history, etc., were destroyed or lost, so that but few definite items can be registered in their place.

When the Saints commenced removing from Far West they shipped as many families and goods as possible at Richmond to go down the Missouri river to Quincy, Illinois. This mission was in charge of Elder Levi Richards and Reuben Hedlock, who were appointed by the committee.

I continued on my journey with my brethren towards Quincy.

Friday, April 19—Elders Turley and Clark had traveled but a few miles from Far West when an axle-tree broke, and Brother Clark had to go to Richmond after some boxes, which delayed them some days.

Saturday, April 20—The last of the Saints left Far West.

Sunday, April 21—I had still continued my journey.

Monday, April 22—We continued on our journey, both by night and by day; and after suffering much fatigue and hunger, I arrived in Quincy, Illinois, amidst the congratulations of my friends, and the embraces of my family, whom I found as well as could be expected, considering what they had been called to endure. Before leaving Missouri I had paid the lawyers at Richmond thirty-four thousand dollars in cash, lands, etc.; one lot which I let them have, in Jackson county, for seven thousand dollars, they were soon offered ten thousand dollars for it, but would not accept it. For other vexatious suits which I had to contend against the few months I was in this state, I paid lawyers' fees to the amount of about sixteen thousand dollars, making in all about fifty thousand dollars, for which I received very little in return; for sometimes they were afraid to act on account of the mob, and sometimes they were so drunk as to incapacitate them for business. But there were a few honorable exceptions.

Among those who have been the chief instruments and leading characters in the cruel persecutions against the Church of Latter-day Saints, the following stand conspicuous, viz., Generals Clark, Wilson and Lucas, Colonel Price, and Cornelius Gillium; Captain Bogart also, whose zeal in the cause of oppression and injustice was unequalled, and whose delight has been to rob, murder, and spread devastation among the Saints. He stole a valuable horse, saddle, and bridle from me, which cost two hundred dollars, and then sold the same to General Wilson. On understanding this, I applied to General Wilson for the horse, who assured me, upon the honor of a gentleman and an officer, that I should have the horse returned to me; but this promise has not been fulfilled.

All the threats, murders, and robberies, which these officers have been guilty of, are entirely overlooked by the executive of the state; who, to hide his own iniquity, must of course shield and protect those whom he employed to carry into effect his murderous purposes.

I was in their hands, as a prisoner, about six months; but notwithstanding their determination to destroy me, with the rest of my brethren who were with me, and although at three different times (as I was informed) we were sentenced to be shot, without the least shadow of law (as we were not military men), and had the time and place appointed for that purpose, yet through the mercy of God, in answer to the prayers of the Saints, I have been preserved and delivered out of their hands, and can again enjoy the society of my friends and brethren, whom I love, and to whom I feel united in bonds that are stronger than death; and in a state where I believe the laws are respected, and whose citizens are humane and charitable.

During the time I was in the hands of my enemies, I must say, that although I felt great anxiety respecting my family and friends, who were so inhumanly treated and abused, and who had to mourn the loss of their husbands and children who had been slain, and, after having been robbed of nearly all that they possessed, were driven from their homes, and forced to wander as strangers in a strange country, in order that they might save themselves and their little ones from the destruction they were threatened with in Missouri, yet as far as I was concerned, I felt perfectly calm, and resigned to the will of my Heavenly Father. I knew my innocence as well as that of the Saints, and that we had done nothing to deserve such treatment from the hands of our oppressors. Consequently, I could look to that God who has the lives of all men in His hands, and who had saved me frequently from the gates of death, for deliverance; and notwithstanding that every avenue of escape seemed to be entirely closed, and death stared me in the face, and that my destruction was determined upon, as far as man was concerned, yet, from my first entrance into the camp, I felt an assurance that I, with my brethren and our families, should be delivered. Yes, that still small voice, which has so often whispered consolation to my soul, in the depths of sorrow and distress, bade me be of good cheer, and promised deliverance, which gave me great comfort. And although the heathen raged, and the people imagined vain things, yet the Lord of Hosts, the God of Jacob was my refuge; and when I cried unto Him in the day of trouble, He delivered me; for which I call upon my soul, and all that is within me, to bless and praise His holy name. For although I was "troubled on every side, yet not distressed; perplexed, but not in despair; persecuted, but not forsaken; cast down, but not destroyed."

The conduct of the Saints, under their accumulated wrongs and sufferings, has been praiseworthy; their courage in defending their brethren from the ravages of the mobs; their attachment to the cause of truth, under circumstances the most trying and distressing which humanity can possibly endure; their love to each other; their readiness to afford assistance to me and my brethren who were confined in a dungeon; their sacrifice in leaving Missouri, and assisting the poor widows and orphans, and securing them houses in a more hospitable land; all conspire to raise them in the estimation of all good and virtuous men, and has secured them the favor

"THAT STILL SMALL VOICE . . . BADE ME BE OF GOOD CHEER, AND PROMISED DELIVERANCE, WHICH GAVE ME GREAT COMFORT."

and approbation of Jehovah, and a name as imperishable as eternity. And their virtuous deeds and heroic actions, while in defense of truth and their brethren, will be fresh and blooming when the names of their oppressors shall be either entirely forgotten, or only remembered for their barbarity and cruelty.

Their attention and affection to me, while in prison, will ever be remembered by me; and when I have seen them thrust away and abused by the jailer and guard, when they came to do any kind offices, and to cheer our minds while we were in the gloomy prison-house, gave me feelings which I cannot describe; while those who wished to insult and abuse us by their threats and blasphemous language, were applauded, and had every encouragement given them.

However, thank God, we have been delivered. And although some of our beloved brethren have had to seal their testimony with their blood, and have died martyrs to the cause of truth—

> Short though bitter was their pain,
> Everlasting is their joy.

Let us not sorrow as "those without hope;" the time is fast approaching when we shall see them again and rejoice together, without being afraid of wicked men. Yes, those who have slept in Christ, shall He bring with Him, when He shall come to be glorified in His Saints, and admired by all those who believe, but to take vengeance upon His enemies and all those who obey not the gospel.

At that time the hearts of the widows and fatherless shall be comforted, and every tear shall be wiped from their faces. The trials they have had to pass through shall work together for their good, and prepare them for the society of those who have come up out of great tribulation, and have washed their robes and made them white in the blood of the Lamb.

Marvel not, then, if you are persecuted; but remember the words of the Savior: "The servant is not above his Lord; if they have persecuted me, they will persecute you also;" and that all the afflictions through which the Saints have to pass, are the fulfillment of the words of the prophets which have spoken since the world began.

We shall therefore do well to discern the signs of the times as we pass along, that the day of the Lord may not "overtake us as a thief in the night." Afflictions, persecutions, imprisonments, and death, we must expect, according to the scriptures, which tell us that the blood of those whose souls were under the altar could not be avenged on them that dwell on the earth, until their brethren should be slain as they were.

If these transactions had taken place among barbarians, under the authority of a despot, or in a nation where a certain religion is established according to law, and all others proscribed, then there might have been some shadow of defense offered. But can we realize that in a land which is the cradle of liberty and equal rights, and where the voice of the conquerors who had vanquished our foes had scarcely died away upon our ears, where we frequently mingled with those who had stood amidst "the battle and the breeze," and whose arms have been nerved in the defense of their country and liberty, whose institutions are the theme of philosophers and poets, and held up to the admiration of the whole civilized world—in the midst of all these scenes, with which we were surrounded, a persecution the most unwarrantable was commenced, and a tragedy the most dreadful was enacted, by a large portion of the inhabitants of one of those free and sovereign states which comprise this vast Republic; and a deadly blow was struck at the institutions for which our fathers had fought many a hard battle, and for which many a patriot had shed his blood. Suddenly was heard, amidst the voice of joy and gratitude for our national liberty, the voice of mourning, lamentation and woe. Yes! in this land, a mob, regardless of those laws for which so much blood had been spilled, dead to every feeling of virtue and patriotism which animated the bosom of free men, fell upon a people whose religious faith was different from their own, and not only destroyed their homes, drove them away, and carried off their property, but murdered many a free-born son of America—a tragedy which has no parallel in modern, and hardly in ancient, times; even the face of the red man would be ready to turn pale at the recital of it. It would have been some consolation, if the authorities of the state had been innocent in this affair; but they are involved in the guilt thereof, and the blood of innocence, even of children, cries for vengeance upon them.

I ask the citizens of this Republic whether such a state of things is to be sufferd to pass unnoticed, and the hearts of widows, orphans, and patriots to be broken, and their wrongs left without redress? No! I invoke the genius of our Constitution. I appeal to the patriotism of Americans to stop this unlawful and unholy procedure; and pray that God may defend this nation from the dreadful effects of such outrages.

Is there no virtue in the body politic? Will not the people rise up in their majesty, and with that promptitude and zeal which are so characteristic of them, discountenance such proceedings, by bringing the offenders to that punishment which they so richly deserve, and save the nation from that disgrace and ultimate ruin, which otherwise must inevitably fall upon it?

Elder Markham had closed his business in Jackson county and returned to Far West, having been chased as far as the river by the mob on horses at full speed, for the purpose of shooting him. Brother Markham tarried in and near Far West until the 24th of April.

All this day I spent in greeting and receiving visits from my brethren and friends, and truly it was a joyful time.

Wednesday, April 24—Elder Parley P. Pratt and his fellow prisoners were brought before the grand jury of Ray county at Richmond, and Darwin Chase and Norman Shearer were dismissed, after being imprisoned about six months. Mrs. Morris Phelps, who had been with her husband in prison some days, hoping he would be released, now parted from him, and, with her little infant, started for Illinois. The number of prisoners at Richmond was now reduced to four. King Follett having been added about the middle of April: he was dragged from his distressed family just as they were leaving the state. Thus of all the prisoners which were taken at an expense of two hundred thousand dollars, only two of the original ones who belonged to the Church, now remained (Luman Gibbs having denied the faith to try to save his life); these were Morris Phelps and Parley P. Pratt. All who were let to bail were banished from the state, together with those who bailed them.

Thus none are like to have a trial by law but Brothers Pratt and Phelps, and they are without friends or witnesses in the state.

Elders Clark and Turley met Alpheus Cutler, Brigham Young, Orson Pratt, George A. Smith, John Taylor, Wilford Woodruff, John E. Page, Daniel Shearer, and others, going up from Quincy to Far West, to fulfill the revelation on the 26th of April, and Clark and Turley turned and went back with them.

Elder Markham visited at Tenney's Grove. This evening I met the Church in council.

Thursday, April 25—I accompanied the committee to Iowa to select a location for the Saints. Elder Markham returned from Tenney's Grove to Far West, waiting the arrival of the brethren from Quincy.

Thus was fulfilled a revelation of July 8, 1838, which our enemies had said could not be fulfilled, as no "Mormon" would be permitted to be in the state.

As the Saints were passing away from the meeting, Brother Turley said to Elders Page and Woodruff, "Stop a bit, while I bid Isaac Russell good bye;" and knocking at the door, called Brother Russell. His wife answered, "Come in, it is Brother Turley." Russell replied, "It is not; he left here two weeks ago;" and appeared quite alarmed; but on finding it was Brother Turley, asked him to sit down; but the latter replied, "I cannot, I shall lose my company." "Who is your company?" enquired Russell. "The Twelve." "The Twelve!" "Yes, don't you know that this is the twenty-sixth, and the day the Twelve were to take leave of their friends on the foundation of the Lord's house, to go to the islands of the sea? The revelation is now fulfilled, and I am going with them." Russell was speechless, and Turley bid him farewell.

The brethren immediately returned to Quincy, taking with them the families from Tenney's Grove.

Wednesday, May 1—I this day purchased, in connection with others of the committee, a farm of Hugh White, consisting of one hundred and thirty-five acres, for the sum of five thousand dollars; also a farm of Dr. Isaac Galland, lying west of the White purchase, for the sum of nine thousand dollars; both of which were to be deeded to Alanson Ripley, according to the counsel of the committee; but Sidney Rigdon declared that "no committee should control any property which he had anything to do with;" consequently the Galland purchase was deeded to George W. Robinson, Rigdon's son-in-law, with the express understanding that he should deed it to the Church, when the Church had paid for it according to their obligation in the contract.

Thursday, May 9—I started with my family for Commerce, Hancock county, and stayed this night at Uncle John Smith's, at Green Plains, where we were most cordially received.

Friday, May 10—I arrived with my family at the White purchase and took up my residence in a small log house on the bank of the river, about one mile south of Commerce City, hoping that I and my friends may here find a resting place for a little season at least.

A bill of indictment having been found by a grand jury of the mob in Ray county, against Parley P. Pratt, Morris Phelps and Luman Gibbs, for murder, and against King Follet for robbery, and having obtained a change of venue to Boone county, they were handcuffed together two by two on the morning of the twenty-second, (of May) with irons around the wrists of each, and in this condition they were taken from prison and placed in a carriage. The people of Richmond gathered around them to see them depart, but none seemed to feel for them except two persons. One of these (General Park's lady) bowed to them through the window, and looked as if touched with pity. The other was a Mr. Hugins, merchant of Richmond, who bowed with some feeling as they passed.

They then took leave of Richmond, accompanied by Sheriff Brown, and four guards with drawn pistols, and moved towards Columbia. It had been thundering and raining for some days, and the thunder storm lasted with but short cessations from the time they started till they arrived at the place of destination, which took five days. The small streams were swollen, making it very difficult to cross them.

Thursday, May 23—The prisoners came to a creek which was several rods across, with a strong current and very deep. It was towards evening, and far from any house, and they had received no refreshments through the day. Here the company halted, and knew not what to do; they waited awhile for the water to fall, but it fell slowly. All hands were hungry and impatient, and a lowery night seemed to threaten that the creek would rise before morning by the falling of additional rains.

In this dilemma some counseled one thing and some another. At last Mr. Pratt proposed to the sheriff, that if he would take off his irons, he would go into the water to bathe, and by that means ascertain the depths and bottom. This the sheriff consented to after some hesitation. Brother Pratt then plunged into the stream and swam across, and attempted to wade back; he found it to be a hard bottom, and the water about up to his chin, but a very stiff current.

After this, Mr. Brown, the sheriff, undertook to cross on his horse, but was thrown off and buried in the stream. This accident decided the fate of the day. Being now completely wet, the sheriff resolved to effect the crossing of the whole company bag and baggage. Accordingly several stripped off their clothes and mounted on the bare backs of the horses, and taking their clothing, saddles and arms, together with one trunk, and bedding, upon their shoulders, they bore them across in safety, without wetting. This was done by riding backwards and forwards across the stream several times. In this sport and labor prisoners, guards and all mingled in mutual exertion. All was now safe but the carriage. Brother Phelps then proposed to swim that across, by hitching two horses before it; and he mounted on one of their backs, while Brother Pratt and one of the guards swam by the side of the carriage to keep it from upsetting by the force of the current; and thus they all got safe to land. Everything was soon replaced; prisoners in the carriage and suite on horseback, moving swiftly on, and at dark arrived at a house of entertainment, amid a terrible thunder shower.

I was busy in counseling, writing letters and attending to general business of the Church this week.

Friday, May 24—The Twelve made a report of the proceeding of the Seventies, which I sanctioned. I also approved of the Twelve going to England.

This day the Missouri prisoners crossed the Missouri river at "Arrow Rock," so called from the Lamanites coming from all quarters to get a hard rock from the bluff out of which to make arrow points. During this journey the prisoners had slept each night on their backs on the floor; being all four of them ironed together with hand and ankle irons made for the purpose. This being done the windows and doors were all fastened, and then five guards with their loaded pistols staid in the room, and one at a time sat up and watched during the night. This cruelty was inflicted on them more to gratify a wicked disposition than anything else; for it was vain for them to have tried to escape, without any irons being put on them; and had they wished to escape, they had a tolerably good opportunity at the creek.

Tuesday, May 28—I was at home.

When the Missouri prisoners arrived at Columbia they applied to Judge Reynolds for a special term of court to be holden for their trials. The petition was granted and July 1st was appointed for the sitting of the court.

Wednesday, May 29—I was about home until the latter part of the week, when I went to Quincy in company with my counselors. I continued to assist in making preparations to lay our grievances before the general government, and many of the brethren were making their reports of damages sustained in Missouri.

Wednesday, June 5—I returned to Commerce and spent the remainder of the week at home.

Sunday, June 9—I attended meeting with my wife and family at Brother Bosier's. Elder John E. Page preached.

Monday, June 10—Elder Page baptized one woman. I was engaged in study preparatory to writing my history.

Tuesday, June 11—I commenced dictating my history for my clerk, James Mulholland, to write. About this time Elder Theodore Turley raised the first house built by the Saints in this place (Commerce); it was built of logs, about twenty-five or thirty rods north north-east of my dwelling, on the north-east corner of lot 4, block 147, of the White purchase.

When I made the purchase of White and Galland, there were one stone house, three frame houses, and two block houses, which constituted the whole city of Commerce. Between Commerce and Mr. Davidson Hibbard's, there was one stone house and three log houses, including the one that I live in, and these were all the houses in this vicinity, and the place was literally a wilderness. The land was mostly covered with trees and bushes, and much of it so wet that it was with the utmost difficulty a footman could get through, and totally impossible for teams. Commerce was so unhealthful, very few could live there; but believing that it might become a healthful place by the blessing of heaven to the Saints, and no more eligible place presenting itself, I considered it wisdom to make an attempt to build up a city.

Friday, June 28—I was transacting business of various kinds; counseling, consulting the brethren, etc., etc.

Saturday, June 29—I was mostly at home.

Sunday, June 30—I attended meeting at Brother Bosier's. There was a crowded audience, and I bore testimony concerning the truth of the work, and also of the truth of the Book of Mormon.

This day Sister Morris Phelps, who had traveled one hundred and fifty miles, in company with her brother, John W. Clark, to see her husband, arrived at Columbia jail.

Monday, July 1—I spent the day principally in counseling the brethren.

This day also the court was called for the trial of Parley P. Pratt, and brethren in prison in Boone county; but as they were not ready for trial (all their witnesses had been banished [by] the state), the court was adjourned to the 23rd of September.

Tuesday, July 2—Spent the forenoon of this day on the Iowa side of the river.

Went, in company with Elders Sidney Rigdon, Hyrum Smith, and Bishops Whitney and Knight, and others, to visit a purchase lately made by Bishop Knight as a location for a town, and advised that a town be built there, and called Zarahemla.

In the afternoon met with the Twelve and some of the Seventies who are about to proceed on their mission to Europe, and the nations of the earth, and islands of the sea.

The meeting was opened by singing and prayer, after which the Presidency proceeded to bless two of the Twelve who had lately been ordained into the quorum, namely, Wilford Woodruff and George A. Smith; and one of the Seventies, namely, Theodore Turley; after which, blessings were also pronounced by them (the Presidency) on the heads of the wives of some of those about to go abroad.

The meeting was then addressed by President Hyrum Smith, by way of advice to the Twelve, chiefly concerning the nature of their mission; their practicing prudence and humility in their plans or subjects for preaching; necessity of their not trifling with their office, and of holding on strictly to the importance of their mission, and the authority of the priesthood.

I then addressed them and gave much instruction calculated to guard them against self-sufficiency, self-righteousness, and self-importance; touching upon many subjects of importance and value to all who wish to walk humbly before the Lord, and especially teaching them to observe charity, wisdom and fellow-feeling, with love one towards another in all things, and under all circumstances, in substance as follows:

See The Prophet's Address to the Twelve.

Ever keep in exercise the principle of mercy, and be ready to forgive our brother on the first intimations of repentance, and asking forgiveness; and should we even forgive our brother, or even our enemy, before he repent or ask forgiveness, our heavenly Father would be equally as merciful unto us.

Again, let the Twelve and all Saints be willing to confess all their sins, and not keep back a part; and let the Twelve be humble, and not be exalted, and beware of pride, and not seek to excel one above another, but act for each other's good, and pray for one another, and honor our brother or make honorable mention of his name, and not backbite and devour our brother. Why will not man learn wisdom by precept at this late age of the world, when we have such a cloud of witnesses and examples before us, and not be obliged to learn by sad experience everything we know? Must the new ones that are chosen to fill the places of those that are fallen, of the quorum of the Twelve, begin to exalt themselves, until they exalt themselves so high that they will soon tumble over and have a great fall, and go wallowing through the mud and mire and darkness, Judas like, to the buffetings of Satan, as several of the quorum have done, or will they learn wisdom and be wise? O God! give them wisdom, and keep them humble, I pray.

When the Twelve or any other witnesses stand before the congregations of the earth, and they preach in the power and demonstration of the Spirit of God, and the people are astonished and confounded at the doctrine, and say, "That man has preached a powerful discourse, a great sermon," then let that man or those men take care that they do not ascribe the glory unto themselves, but be careful that they are humble, and ascribe the praise and glory to God and the Lamb; for it is by the power of the Holy Priesthood and the Holy Ghost that they have power thus to speak. What art thou, O man, but dust? And from whom receivest thou thy power and blessings, but from God?

Then, O ye Twelve! notice this key, and be wise for Christ's sake, and your own soul's sake. Ye are not sent out to be taught, but to teach. Let every word be seasoned with grace. Be vigilant; be sober. It is a day of warning, and not of many words. Act honestly before God and man. Beware of Gentile sophistry; such as bowing and scraping unto men in whom you have no confidence. Be honest, open, and frank in all your intercourse with mankind.

O ye Twelve! and all Saints! profit by this important key—that in all your trials, troubles, temptations, afflictions, bonds, imprisonments and death, see to it, that you do not betray heaven; that you do not betray Jesus Christ; that you do not betray the brethren; that you do not betray the revelations of God, whether in the Bible, Book of Mormon, or Doctrine and Covenants, or any other that ever was or ever will be given and revealed unto man in this world or that which is to come. Yea, in all your kicking and flounderings, see to it that you do not this thing, lest innocent blood be found upon your skirts, and you go down to hell. All other sins are not to be compared to sinning against the Holy Ghost and proving a traitor to the brethren.

I will give you one of the keys of the mysteries of the kingdom. It is an eternal principle, that has existed with God from all eternity: That man who rises up to condemn others, finding fault with the Church, saying that they are out of the way, while he himself is righteous, then know assuredly, that that man is in the high road to apostasy; and if he does not repent, will apostatize, as God lives. The principle is as correct as the one that Jesus put forth in saying that he who seeketh a sign is an adulterous person; and that principle is eternal, undeviating, and firm as the pillars of heaven; for whenever you see a man seeking after a sign, you may set it down that he is an adulterous man.

About this time, in reply to many inquiries, I also gave an explanation of the Priesthood, and many principles connected therewith, of which the following is a brief synopsis:

See The Prophet on Priesthood.

The Priesthood was first given to Adam; he obtained the First Presidency, and held the keys of it from generation to generation. He obtained it in the Creation, before the world was formed, as in Gen. 1:26, 27, 28. He had dominion given him over every living creature. He is Michael the Archangel, spoken of in the scriptures. Then to Noah, who is Gabriel; he stands next in authority to Adam in the Priesthood; he was called of God to this office, and was the father of all living in his day, and to him was given the dominion. These men held keys first on earth, and then in heaven.

The Priesthood is an everlasting principle, and existed with God from eternity, and will to eternity, without beginning of days or end of years. The keys have to be brought from heaven whenever the gospel is sent. When they are revealed from heaven, it is by Adam's authority.

Daniel in his seventh chapter speaks of the Ancient of Days; he means the oldest man, our Father Adam, Michael, he will call his children together and hold a council with them to prepare them for the coming of the Son of Man. He (Adam) is the father of the human family, and presides over the spirits of all men, and all that have had the keys must stand before him in this grand council. This may take place before some of us leave this stage of action. The Son of Man stands before him, and there is given him glory and dominion. Adam delivers up his stewardship to Christ, that which was delivered to him as holding the keys of the universe, but retains his standing as head of the human family.

The spirit of man is not a created being; it existed from eternity, and will exist to eternity. Anything created cannot be eternal; and earth, water, etc., had their existence in an elementary state, from eternity. Our Savior speaks of children and says, Their angels always stand before my Father. The Father called all spirits before Him at the creation of man, and organized them. He (Adam) is the head, and was told to multiply. The keys were first given to him, and by him to others. He will have to give an account of his stewardship, and they to him.

The Priesthood is everlasting. The Savior, Moses, and Elias, gave the keys to Peter, James, and John, on the mount, when they were transfigured before him. The Priesthood is everlasting—without beginning of days or end of years; without father, mother, etc. If there is no change of ordinances, there is no change of Priesthood. Wherever the ordinances of the gospel are administered, there is the Priesthood.

How have we come at the Priesthood in the last days? It came down, down, in regular succession. Peter, James, and John had it given to them and they gave it to others. Christ is the Great High Priest; Adam next. Paul speaks of the Church coming to an innumerable company of angels—to God the Judge of all—the spirits of just men made perfect; to Jesus the Mediator of the new covenant. —Heb. 12:23.

I saw Adam in the valley of Adam-ondi-Ahman. He called together his children and blessed them with a patriarchal blessing. The Lord appeared in their midst, and he (Adam) blessed them all, and foretold what should befall them to the latest generation.

This is why Adam blessed his posterity; he wanted to bring them into the presence of God. They looked for a city, etc., ("whose builder and maker is God." Heb. 11:10). Moses sought to bring the children of Israel into the presence of God, through the power of the Priesthood, but he could not. In the first ages of the world they tried to establish the same thing; and there were Eliases raised up who tried to restore these very glories, but did not obtain them; but they prophesied of a day when this glory would be revealed. Paul spoke of the dispensation of the fullness of times, when God would gather together all things in one, etc.; and those men to whom these keys have been given, will have to be there; and they without us cannot be made perfect.

Those men are in heaven, but their children are on the earth. Their bowels yearn over us. God sends down men for this reason. "And the Son of Man shall send forth His angels, and they shall gather out of His kingdom all things that give offense and them that do iniquity." —(Matt. 13:41). All these authoritative characters will come down and join hand in hand in bringing about this work.

The kingdom of heaven is like a grain of mustard seed. The mustard seed is small, but brings forth a large tree, and the fowls lodge in the branches. The fowls are the angels. Thus angels come down, combine together to gather their children, and gather them. We cannot be made perfect without them, nor they without us; when these things are done, the Son of Man will descend, the Ancient of Days sit; we may come to an innumerable company of angels, have communion with and receive instructions from them. Paul told about Moses' proceedings; spoke of the children of Israel being baptized. —(1 Cor. 10:1–4). He knew this, and that all the ordinances and blessings were in the Church. Paul had these things, and we may have the fowls of heaven lodge in the branches, etc.

The "Horn" made war with the Saints and overcame them, until the Ancient of Days came; judgment was given to the Saints of the Most High from the Ancient of Days; the time came that the Saints possessed the kingdom. This not only makes us ministers here, but in eternity.

Salvation cannot come without revelation; it is in vain for anyone to minister without it. No man is a minister of Jesus Christ without being a prophet. No man can be a minister of Jesus Christ except he has the testimony of Jesus; and this is the spirit of prophecy. Whenever salvation has been administered, it has been by testimony. Men of the present time testify of heaven and hell, and have never seen either; and I will say that no man knows these things without this.

Men profess to prophesy. I will prophesy that the signs of the coming of the Son of Man are already commenced. One pestilence will desolate after another. We shall soon have war and bloodshed. The moon will be turned into blood. I testify of these things, and that the coming of the Son of Man is nigh, even at your doors. If our souls and our bodies are not looking forth for the coming of the Son of Man; and after we are dead, if we are not looking forth, we shall be among those who are calling for the rocks to fall upon them.

The hearts of the children of men will have to be turned to the fathers, and the fathers to the children, living or dead, to prepare them for the coming of the Son of Man. If Elijah did not come, the whole earth would be smitten.

There will be here and there a stake (of Zion) for the gathering of the Saints.

Some may have cried peace, but the Saints and the world will have little peace from henceforth. Let this not hinder us from going to the stakes; for God has told us to flee, not dallying, or we shall be scattered, one here, and another there. There your children shall be blessed, and you in the midst of friends where you may be blessed. The gospel net gathers of every kind.

I prophesy, that that man who tarries after he has an opportunity of going, will be afflicted by the devil. Wars are at hand; we must not delay; but are not required to sacrifice. We ought to have the building up of Zion as our greatest object. When wars come, we shall have to flee to Zion. The cry is to make haste. The last revelation says, Ye shall not have time to have gone over the earth, until these things come. It will come as did the cholera, war, fires, and earthquakes; one pestilence after another, until the Ancient of Days comes, then judgment will be given to the Saints.

"SOME MAY HAVE CRIED PEACE, BUT THE SAINTS AND THE WORLD WILL HAVE LITTLE PEACE FROM HENCEFORTH."

Whatever you may hear about me or Kirtland, take no notice of it; for if it be a place of refuge, the devil will use his greatest efforts to trap the Saints. You must make yourselves acquainted with those men who like Daniel pray three times a day toward the house of the Lord. Look to the Presidency and receive instruction. Every man who is afraid, covetous, will be taken in a snare. The time is soon coming, when no man will have any peace but in Zion and her stakes.

I saw men hunting the lives of their own sons, and brother murdering brother, women killing their own daughters, and daughters seeking the lives of their mothers. I saw armies arrayed against armies. I saw blood, desolation, fires. The Son of Man has said that the mother shall be against the daughter, and the daughter against the mother. These things are at our doors. They will follow the Saints of God from city to city. Satan will rage, and the spirit of the devil is now enraged. I know not how soon these things will take place; but with a view of them, shall I cry peace? No! I will lift up my voice and testify of them. How long you will have good crops, and the famine be kept off, I do not know; when the fig tree leaves, know then that the summer is nigh at hand.

We may look for angels and receive their ministrations, but we are to try the spirits and prove them, for it is often the case that men make a mistake in regard to these things. God has so ordained that when He has communicated, no vision is to be taken but what you see by the seeing of the eye, or what you hear by the hearing of the ear. When you see a vision, pray for the interpretation; if you get not this, shut it up, there must be certainty in this matter. An open vision will manifest that which is more important. Lying spirits are going forth in the earth. There will be great manifestations of spirits, both false and true.

Being born again, comes by the Spirit of God through ordinances. An angel of God never has wings. Some will say that they have seen a spirit; that he offered them his hand, but they did not touch it. This is a lie. First, it is contrary to the plan of God: a spirit cannot come but in glory; an angel has flesh and bones; we see not their glory. The devil may appear as an angel of light. Ask God to reveal it; if it be of the devil, he will flee from you; if of God, he will manifest himself, or make it manifest. We may come to Jesus and ask Him; He will know all about it; if He comes to a little child, He will adapt himself to the language and capacity of a little child.

Every spirit, or vision, or singing, is not of God. The devil is an orator; he is powerful; he took our Savior on to a pinnacle of the temple, and kept Him in the wilderness for forty days. The gift of discerning spirits will be given to the Presiding Elder. Pray for him that he may have this gift. Speak not in the gift of tongues without understanding it, or without interpretation. The devil can speak in tongues; the adversary will come with his work; he can tempt all classes; can speak in English or Dutch. Let no one speak in tongues unless he interpret, except by the consent of the one who is placed to preside; then he may discern or interpret, or another may. Let us seek for the glory of Abraham, Noah, Adam, the apostles, who have communion with (knowledge of) these things, and then we shall be among that number when Christ comes.

Wednesday, July 3—I baptized Dr. Isaac Galland, and confirmed him at the water's edge; and about two hours afterwards I ordained him to the office of an elder.

Afternoon. I was engaged in dictating my history.

Friday, July 5—I was dictating history, I say dictating, for I seldom use the pen myself. I always dictate all my communications, but employ a scribe to write them.

Saturday, July 6—I was at home reviewing the Church records.

Sunday, July 7—I was at the meeting held in the open air, at which a large assemblage was expected to listen to the farewell addresses of the Twelve, who were then about to take their departure on a most important mission, namely to the nations of the earth and the islands of the sea.

Monday, Tuesday, and Wednesday, July 8th, 9th, and 10th—I was with the Twelve selecting hymns, for the purpose of compiling a hymn book.

About this time much sickness began to manifest itself among the brethren, as well as among the inhabitants of the place, so that this week and the following were generally spent in visiting the sick and administering to them; some had faith enough and were healed; others had not.

Sunday, July 21—There was no meeting on account of much rain and much sickness; however many of the sick were this day raised up by the power of God, through the instrumentality of the elders of Israel ministering unto them in the name of Jesus Christ.

Monday and Tuesday, July 22nd and 23rd—The sick were administered unto with great success, but many remain sick, and new cases are occurring daily.

Sunday, August 4—The Church came together for prayer meeting and sacrament. I exhorted the Church at length, concerning the necessity of being righteous, and clean at heart before the Lord. Many others also spoke; especially some of the Twelve, who were present, professed their willingness to proceed on their mission to Europe, without either purse or scrip. The sacrament was administered; a spirit of humility and harmony prevailed, and the Church passed a resolution that the Twelve proceed on their mission as soon as possible, and that the Saints provide for their families during their absence.

Sunday, September 1—I attended meeting, and spoke concerning some errors in Parley P. Pratt's writings. This week sickness much decreased.

Monday, September 9, and the greater part of the week—I spent in visiting the sick, and attending to the settlement of our new town.

Saturday, September 14—President Brigham Young started from his home at Montrose, for England. His health was very poor; he was unable to go thirty rods to the river without assistance. After he had crossed the ferry he got Brother Israel Barlow to carry him on his horse behind him to Heber C. Kimball's where he remained sick until the 18th. He left his wife sick with a babe only ten days old, and all his children sick, unable to wait upon each other. I returned home this evening.

Sunday, September 15—I was visiting the sick.

Monday and Tuesday, September 16 and 17—Was engaged in arranging the town lots.

Wednesday, September 18—Went to Burlington, Iowa Territory. Elders Young and Kimball left Sister Kimball and all her children sick, except little Heber; went thirteen miles on their journey towards England, and were left at Brother Osmon M. Duel's, who lived in a small cabin near the railway between Commerce and Warsaw. They were so feeble as to be unable to carry their trunks into the house without the assistance of Sister Duel, who received them kindly, prepared a bed for them to lie on, and made them a cup of tea.

Thursday, September 19—I returned this evening from Burlington.

Brother Duel carried Elders Young and Kimball in his wagon to Lima, sixteen miles, where another brother received them and carried them to Father Mikesell's near Quincy, about twenty miles; the fatigue of this day was too much for their feeble health; they were prostrated, and obliged to tarry a few days to recruit.

Friday and Saturday, September 20 and 21—At home attending to domestic and Church business.

Elders George A. Smith, Reuben Hedlock, and Theodore Turley started for England, and upset their wagon on the bank of the river, before they got out of sight of Commerce. Elders Smith and Turley were so weak they could not get up, and Brother Hedlock had to lift them in again. Soon after, some gentlemen met them and asked who had been robbing the burying ground—so miserable was their appearance through sickness.

Sunday, September 22—I presided at the meeting, and spoke concerning the "other Comforter," as I had previously taught the Twelve.

This week I spent in transacting various business at home, except when visiting the sick, who are in general recovering, though some of them but slowly.

Sunday, September 29—Held meeting at my own house. After others had spoken I spoke and explained concerning the uselessness of preaching to the world about great judgments, but rather to preach the simple gospel. Explained concerning the coming of the Son of Man; also that it is a false idea that the Saints will escape all the judgments, whilst the wicked suffer; for all flesh is subject to suffer, and "the righteous shall hardly escape;" still many of the Saints will escape, for the just shall live by faith; yet many of the righteous shall fall a prey to disease, to pestilence, etc., by reason of the weakness of the flesh, and yet be saved in the kingdom of God. So that it is an unhallowed principle to say that such and such have transgressed because they have been preyed upon by disease or death, for all flesh is subject to death; and the Savior has said, "Judge not, lest ye be judged."

Tuesday, October 29—I left Nauvoo accompanied by Sidney Rigdon, Elias Higbee, and Orrin P. Rockwell, in a two-horse carriage for the city of Washington, to lay before the Congress of the United States, the grievances of the Saints while in Missouri. We passed through Carthage, and stayed at Judge Higbee's over night, and the next day we arrived at Quincy.

Wednesday, November 27—While on the mountains some distance from Washington, our coachman stepped into a public house to take his grog, when the horses took fright and ran down the hill at full speed. I persuaded my fellow travelers to be quiet and retain their seats, but had to hold one woman to prevent her throwing her infant out of the coach. The passengers were exceedingly agitated, but I used every persuasion to calm their feelings; and opening the door, I secured my hold on the side of the coach the best way I could, and succeeded in placing myself in the coachman's seat, and reining up the horses, after they had run some two or three miles, and neither coach, horses, or passengers received any injury. My course was spoken of in the highest terms of commendation, as being one of the most daring and heroic deeds, and no language could express the gratitude of the passengers, when they found themselves safe, and the horses quiet. There were some members of Congress with us, who proposed naming the incident to that body, believing they would reward such conduct by some public act; but on inquiring my name, to mention as the author of their safety, and finding it to be Joseph Smith the "Mormon Prophet," as they called me, I heard no more of their praise, gratitude, or reward.

Thursday, November 28—I arrived in Washington City this morning, and put up at the corner of Missouri and Third streets.

The following is a copy of our petition to Congress for redress of our Missouri grievances:

See History of the Church Vol. 4, 24.

Saturday, December 21—I arrived in Philadelphia, direct from Washington City, by the railroad, where I spent several days preaching and visiting from house to house, among the brethren and others.

Chapter Twelve

1840

Wednesday, January 8—The High Council at Nauvoo voted to loan all the moneys possible for the relief of the poor Saints.

This evening President Young preached at a school house in the south west part of Richmond, when the people present commenced making a noise and disturbing the meeting, and when President Young was reproving them for their disgraceful conduct, some of those present fired lucifer matches. President Young rebuked them severely, and taught them better manners, and proposed to send them some Indians from the West to civilize them.

During my stay I had an interview with Martin Van Buren, the President, who treated me very insolently, and it was with great reluctance he listened to our message, which, when he had heard, he said: "Gentlemen, your cause is just, but I can do nothing for you;" and "If I take up for you I shall lose the vote of Missouri." His whole course went to show that he was an office-seeker, that self-aggrandizement was his ruling passion, and that justice and righteousness were no part of his composition. I found him such a man as I could not conscientiously support at the head of our noble Republic. I also had an interview with Mr. John C. Calhoun, whose conduct towards me very ill became his station. I became satisfied there was little use for me to tarry, to press the just claims of the Saints on the consideration of the President or Congress, and stayed but a few days, taking passage in company with Porter Rockwell and Dr. Foster on the railroad and stages back to Dayton, Ohio.

Friday, February 7—High Council at Montrose voted to disfellowship all brethren who should persist in keeping tippling shops in that branch of the Church.

Wednesday, March 4—I arrived safely at Nauvoo, after a wearisome journey, through alternate snow and mud, having witnessed many vexatious movements in government officers, whose sole object should be the peace and prosperity and happiness of the whole people; but instead of this, I discovered that popular clamor and personal aggrandizement were the ruling principles of those in authority; and my heart faints within me when I see, by the visions of the Almighty, the end of this nation, if she continues to disregard the cries and petitions of her virtuous citizens, as she has done, and is now doing.

I have also enjoyed many precious moments with the Saints during my journey.

On my way home I did not fail to proclaim the iniquity and insolence of Martin Van Buren, toward myself and an injured people, which will have its effect upon the public mind; and may he never be elected again to any office of trust or power, by which he may abuse the innocent and let the guilty go free.

I depended on Dr. Foster to keep my daily journal during this journey, but he has failed me.

At this time the work of the Lord is spreading rapidly in the United States and England—elders are traveling in almost every direction, and multitudes are being baptized.

Monday, June 1—The Saints have already erected about two hundred and fifty houses at Nauvoo, mostly block houses, a few framed, and many more are in course of construction.

The gospel is spreading through the States, Canada, England, Scotland, and other places, with great rapidity.

Monday, June 8—Since Congress has decided against us, the Lord has begun to vex this nation, and He will continue to do so except they repent; for they now stand guilty of murder, robbery and plunder, as a nation, because they have refused to protect their citizens, and to execute justice according to their own Constitution. A hailstorm has visited South Carolina; some of the stones are said to have measured nine inches in circumference, which swept the crops, killing some cattle. Insects are devouring crops on the high lands, where the floods of the country have not reached, and great commercial distress prevails everywhere.

Monday, August 17—Met with the high council of Nauvoo at my office, also the high council of Iowa. John Batten preferred many charges against Elijah Fordham. After the testimony, and the councilors had spoken, I addressed the council at some length, showing the situation of the contending parties, that there was in reality no cause of difference; that they had better be reconciled without an action, or vote of the council, and henceforth live as brethren, and never more mention their former difficulties. They settled accordingly.

Friday, September 11—There was a terrible earthquake at Mount Ararat, which destroyed the town of Makitchevan, damaged all the buildings at Erivan, and devastated the two districts of Sharour and Sourmate in Armenia. A considerable mass was loosened from Mount Ararat and destroyed everything in its way for nearly five miles. The village of Akhouli was buried, with one thousand inhabitants.

Sunday, September 13—Elder Kimball baptized four in London.

Monday, September 14—My father, Joseph Smith, Sen., patriarch of the whole Church of Jesus Christ of Latter-day Saints, died at Nauvoo.

Wednesday, December 16—This day the act chartering the "City of Nauvoo," the "Nauvoo Legion," and the "University of the City of Nauvoo," was signed by the governor, having previously passed the House and Senate.

The City Charter of Nauvoo is of my own plan and device. I concocted it for the salvation of the Church, and on principles so broad, that every honest man might dwell secure under its protective influence without distinction of sect or party.

Chapter Thirteen

1841

Monday, February 8—City Council met according to adjournment and opened by prayer, which was made a standing rule of the council. I reported a bill for the survey of a canal through the city, which was accepted; and I was appointed to contract for its survey. I also reported a bill for an ordinance on temperance, which was read and laid over.

In the discussion of the foregoing bill, I spoke at great length on the use of liquors, and showed that they were unnecessary, and operate as a poison in the stomach, and that roots and herbs can be found to effect all necessary purposes.

April 6—The first day of the twelfth year of the Church of Jesus Christ of Latter-day Saints! At an early hour the several companies comprising the "Nauvoo Legion," with two volunteer companies from Iowa Territory, making sixteen companies in all, assembled at their several places of rendezvous, and were conducted in due order to the ground assigned for general review. The appearance, order and movements of the legion, were chaste, grand and imposing, and reflected great credit upon the taste, skill and tact of the men comprising said legion. We doubt whether the like can be presented in any other city in the western country. At half-past seven o'clock a.m., the fire of artillery announced the arrival of Brigadier-Generals Law and Don Carlos Smith, at the front of their respective cohorts; and at 8 o'clock Major-General Bennett was conducted to his post, under the discharge of cannon, and took command of the legion.

At half-past nine o'clock a.m., Lieutenant-General Smith, with his guard, staff, and field officers, arrived at the ground, and were presented with a beautiful silk national flag by the ladies of Nauvoo, which was respectfully received and hailed by the firing of cannon, and borne off by Colonel Robinson, the cornet, to the appropriate position in the line; after which the lieutenant-general with his suite passed the lines in review.

At twelve a.m., the procession arrived upon the temple ground, enclosing the same in a hollow square, with Lieutenant-General Smith, Major-General Bennett, Brigadier-Generals Wilson Law and Don Carlos Smith, their respective staffs, guard, field officers, distinguished visitors, choir, band, &c., in the centre, and the ladies and gentlemen, citizens, surrounding in the interior. The superior officers, together with the banner, architects, principal speaker, &c., were duly conducted to the stand at the principal corner stone, and the religious services were commenced by singing from page 65 of the new hymn book.

President Sidney Rigdon then addressed the assembly, and remarked the circumstances under which he addressed the people were of no ordinary character, but of peculiar and indescribable interest, that it was the third occasion of a similar nature, wherein he had been called upon to address the people, and to assist in laying the corner stones of houses to be erected in honor of the God of the Saints.

The architects then, by the direction of the First Presidency, lowered the first (the south-east corner) stone to its place, and President Joseph Smith pronounced the benediction.

The services were then declared closed, and the military retired to the parade-ground and were dismissed with the approbation and thanks of the commanding officer. The military band, under the command of Captain Duzette, made a conspicuous and dignified appearance, and performed their part honorably. Their soul-stirring strains met harmoniously the rising emotions that swelled each bosom, and stimulated us onward to the arduous but pleasing and honorable duties of the day. The choir also, under the direction of B.S. Wilber, deserve commendation.

What added greatly to the happiness we experienced on this interesting occasion, is the fact that we heard no obscene or profane language; neither saw we anyone intoxicated. Can the same be said of a similar assemblage in any other city in the Union? Thank God that the intoxicating beverage, the bane of humanity in these last days, is becoming a stranger in Nauvoo.

In conclusion, we will say we never witnessed a more imposing spectacle than was presented on this occasion, and during the sessions of the conference. Such a multitude of people moving in harmony, in friendship, in dignity, told in a voice not easily misunderstood, that they were a people of intelligence, and virtue and order; in short, that they were Saints; and that the God of love, purity and light, was their God, their Examplar, and Director; and that they were blessed and happy.

Saturday, May 15—Good news has recently reached us from Tennessee, New York, Upper Canada, and New Orleans. The elders are baptizing in all directions.

Friday, June 4—I called on Governor Carlin, at his residence in Quincy. During my visit with the governor, I was treated with the greatest kindness and respect; nothing was said about any requisition having come from the governor of Missouri for my arrest. In a very few hours after I had left the governor's residence he sent Thomas King, sheriff of Adams county, Thomas Jasper, a constable of Quincy, and some others as a posse, with an officer from Missouri, to arrest me and deliver me up to the authorities of Missouri.

Saturday, June 5—While I was staying at Heberlin's Hotel, Bear creek, about twenty-eight miles south of Nauvoo, Sheriff King and posse arrested me. Some of the posse, on learning the spirit of the officer from Missouri, left the company in disgust and returned to their own homes. I accordingly returned to Quincy and obtained a writ of habeas corpus from Charles A. Warren, Esq., Master in Chancery; and Judge Stephen A. Douglas happening to come to Quincy that evening, he appointed to give a hearing on the writ on the Tuesday following, in Monmouth, Warren county, where the court would then commence a regular term.

Sunday, June 6—News of my arrest having arrived in Nauvoo last night, and being circulated through the city, Hosea Stout, Tarleton Lewis, William A. Hickman, John S. Higbee, Elijah Able, Uriel C. Nickerson, and George W. Clyde started from the Nauvoo landing, in a skiff in order to overtake me and rescue me, if necessary. They had a heavy head wind, but arrived in Quincy at dusk; went up to Benjamin Jones's house, and found that I had gone to Nauvoo in charge of two officers.

I returned to Nauvoo in charge of the officers (Sheriff King had been suddenly seized with sickness; I nursed and waited upon him in my own house, so that he might be able to go to Monmouth), and notified several of my friends to get ready and accompany me the next morning.

Monday, June 7—I started very early for Monmouth, seventy-five miles distant (taking Mr. King along with me and attending him during his sickness), accompanied by Charles C. Rich, Amasa Lyman, Shadrack Roundy, Reynolds Cahoon, Charles Hopkins, Alfred Randall, Elias Higbee, Morris Phelps, John P. Greene, Henry G. Sherwood, Joseph Younger, Darwin Chase, Ira Miles, Joel S. Miles, Lucien Woodworth, Vinson Knight, Robert B. Thompson, George Miller and others. We traveled very late, camping about midnight in the road.

Tuesday, June 8—Arrived at Monmouth and procured breakfast at the tavern; found great excitement prevailing in the public mind, and great curiosity was manifested by the citizens who were extremely anxious to obtain a sight of the Prophet, expecting to see me in chains. Mr. King, (whose health was now partly restored) had considerable difficulty in protecting me from the mob that had gathered there. Mr. Sidney A. Little, for the defense, moved "That the case of Mr. Smith should be taken up," but was objected to by the States' Attorney, pro tern., on account of his not being prepared, not having had sufficient notice of the trial. By mutual consent it was accordingly postponed until Wednesday morning.

In the evening, great excitement prevailed, and the citizens employed several attorneys to plead against me.

I was requested to preach to the citizens of Monmouth; but as I was a prisoner, I kept closeted in my room, for I could not even come down stairs to my meals, but the people would be crowding the windows to get a peep at me, and therefore appointed Elder Amasa Lyman to preach in the court house on Wednesday evening.

Wednesday, June 9—At an early hour the court house was filled with spectators desirous to hear the proceedings.

Mr. Morrison, on behalf of the people, wished for time to send to Springfield for the indictment, it not being found with the rest of the papers. This course would have delayed the proceedings, and, as it was not important to the issue, the attorneys for the defense admitted that there was an indictment, so that the investigation might proceed.

Mr. Warren, for the defense, then read the petition, which stated that I was unlawfully held in custody, and that the indictment, in Missouri, was obtained by fraud, bribery and duress, all of which I was prepared to prove.

Mr. Little then called upon the following witnesses, viz., Morris Phelps, Elias Higbee, Reynolds Cahoon and George W. Robinson, who were sworn. The counsel on the opposite side objected to hearing evidence on the merits of the case, as they could not go beyond the indictment. Upon this a warm and long discussion occurred, which occupied the attention of the court during the entire day.

All the lawyers on the opposite side, excepting two, viz.,

Messrs. Knowlton and Jennings, confined themselves to the merits of the case, and conducted themselves as gentlemen; but it was plainly evident that the design of Messrs. Knowlton and Jennings was to excite the public mind still more on the subject and inflame the passions of the people against me and my religion.

The counsel on behalf of the defense, Messrs. Charles A. Warren, Sidney H. Little, O. H. Browning, James H. Ralston, Cyrus Walker, and Archibald Williams, acted nobly and honorably, and stood up in the defense of the persecuted, in a manner worthy of high-minded and honorable gentlemen.

Some had even been told that if they engaged on the side of the defense, they need never look to the citizens of that county for any political favors. But they were not to be overawed by the popular clamor or deterred from an act of public duty by any insinuations or threats whatever, and stated, that if they had not before determined to take a part in the defense, they, after hearing the threats of the community, were now fully determined to discharge their duty. The counsel for the defense spoke well without exception; and strongly urged the legality of the court examining the testimony to prove that the whole proceedings on the part of Missouri, were base and illegal, and that the indictment was obtained through fraud, bribery and corruption.

The court, after hearing the counsel, adjourned about half past six p.m. When I was at dinner, a man rushed in and said, "Which is Jo Smith? I have got a five dollar Kirtland bill, and I'll be damned if he don't take it back I'll sue him, for his name is to it." I replied, "I am the man;" took the bill and paid him the specie, which he took very reluctantly, being anxious to kick up a fuss.

The crowd in the court was so intense that Judge Douglas ordered the sheriff of Warren county to keep the spectators back; but he neglected doing so, when the judge fined him ten dollars. In a few minutes he again ordered the sheriff to keep the men back from crowding the prisoner and witnesses. He replied, "I have told a constable to do it," when the judge immediately said, "Clerk, add ten dollars more to that fine." The sheriff, finding neglect rather expensive, then attended to his duty.

A young lawyer from Missouri volunteered to plead against me; he tried his utmost to convict me, but was so high with liquor, and chewed so much tobacco, that he often called for cold water. Before he had spoken many minutes, he turned sick, requested to be excused by the court and went out of the court house, puking all the way down stairs. As the Illinoians call the Missouri people "pukes," this circumstance caused considerable amusement to the members of the bar. During his plea, his language was so outrageous that the judge was twice under the necessity of ordering him to be silent.

Mr. O. H. Browning then commenced his plea, and in a short time the puking lawyer returned, and requested the privilege of finishing his plea, which was allowed.

Afterwards Mr. Browning resumed his pleadings which were powerful; and when he gave a recitation of what he himself had seen at Quincy, and on the banks of the Mississippi river when the Saints were "exterminated from Missouri," where he tracked the persecuted women and children by their bloody footmarks in the snow, they were so affecting that the spectators were often dissolved in tears. Judge Douglas himself and most of the officers also wept.

Elder Amasa Lyman during the evening, preached a brilliant discourse in the court house, on the first principles of the gospel, which changed the feelings of the people very materially.

Thursday, June 10—The court was opened about 8 o'clock a.m. when Judge Douglas delivered his opinion on the case.

This decision was received with satisfaction by myself and the brethren, and all those whose minds were free from prejudice. It is now decided that before another writ can issue, a new demand must be made by the governor of Missouri. Thus have I been once more delivered from the fangs of my cruel persecutors, for which I thank God, my Heavenly Father.

I was discharged about 11 a.m., when I ordered dinner for

my company now increased to about sixty men; and when I called for the bill, the unconscionable fellow replied, "Only one hundred and sixty dollars."

About 2 p.m., the company commenced their return, traveled about twenty miles, and camped by the wayside.

Friday, June 11—Started very early, arrived at La Harpe for dinner and returned safely to Nauvoo by 4 p.m., where I was met by the acclamation of the Saints.

Sunday, July 25—Attended meeting in the grove. Elders Orson Pratt and George A. Smith preached in the forenoon. In the afternoon Elder Sidney Rigdon preached a general funeral sermon, designed to comfort and instruct the Saints, especially those who had been called to mourn the loss of relatives and friends. I followed him, illustrating the subject of the resurrection by some familiar figures.

Elder George A. Smith married Bathsheba W. Bigler. Don Carlos Smith performed the ceremony, which was the last official act of his life, he being very feeble at the time.

Brother William Yokum had his leg amputated by Dr. John F. Weld, who operated free of charge; he was wounded in the massacre at Haun's Mill, October 30th, 1838, and had lain on his back ever since; and now it was found the only chance to save his life was to have his leg cut off. He was also shot through the head at the same massacre.

Saturday, August 7—My youngest brother, Don Carlos Smith, died at his residence in Nauvoo this morning, at twenty minutes past two o'clock, in the 26th year of his age. He was born 25th March, 1816, was one of the first to receive my testimony, and was ordained to the Priesthood when only 14 years of age. The evening after the plates of the Book of Mormon were shown to the eight witnesses, a meeting was held, when all the witnesses, as also Don Carlos bore testimony to the truth of the latter-day dispensation. He accompanied father to visit grandfather, Asael Smith, and relatives in St. Lawrence county, New York, in August, 1830.

Don Carlos visited us several times while we were in Liberty jail, and brought our wives to see us, and some money and articles to relieve our necessities. He took charge of father's family in his flight from Missouri, and saw them removed to Quincy, Illinois.

In June, 1839, he commenced making preparations for printing the *Times and Seasons.* The press and type had been resurrected by Elias Smith, Hyrum Clark, and others, from its grave in Dawson's yard, Far West, where it was buried for safety the night that General Lucas surrounded the city with the mob militia. The form for a number of the *Elders' Journal* was buried with the ink on it. The types were considerably injured by the damp; it was therefore necessary to get them into use as soon as possible, and in order to do this, Don Carlos was under the necessity of cleaning out a cellar through which a spring was constantly flowing, as the only place where he could put up the press. Ebenezer Robinson and wife being sick, threw the entire burden on him.

As a great number of brethren lay sick in the town, on Tuesday, 23rd July, 1839, I told Don Carlos and George A. Smith to go and visit all the sick, exercise mighty faith, and administer to them in the name of Jesus Christ, commanding the destroyer to depart, and the people to arise and walk; and not leave a single person on the bed between my house and Ebenezer Robinson's, two miles distant; they administered to over sixty persons, many of whom thought they would never sit up again; but they were healed, arose from their beds, and gave glory to God; some of them assisted in visiting and administering to others who were sick.

Working in the damp cellar, and administering to the sick impaired his health so that the first number of the *Times and Seasons* was not issued until November. He edited thirty-one numbers.

He was elected major in the Hancock county militia, and on the death of Seymour Brunson, was made lieutenant-colonel.

He was elected on 1st February, 1841, a member of the city council of Nauvoo, and took the necessary oath on 3rd February, and on the fourth he was elected brigadier-general of the second cohort of the Nauvoo Legion.

He was six feet four inches high, was very straight and well made, had light hair, and was very strong and active. His usual weight when in health was 200 pounds. He was universally beloved by the Saints.

He left three daughters, namely, Agnes C., Sophronia C., and Josephine D.

Thursday, August 12—A considerable number of the Sac and Fox Indians have been for several days encamped in the neighborhood of Montrose. The ferryman brought over a great number on the ferryboat and two flat boats for the purpose of visiting me. The military band and a detachment of Invincibles (part of the legion) were on shore ready to receive and escort them to the grove, but they refused to come on shore until I went down. I accordingly went down, and met Keokuk, Kis-kikosh, Appenoose, and about one hundred chiefs and braves of those tribes, with their families. At the landing, I was introduced by Brother Hyrum to them; and after salutations, I conducted them to the meeting grounds in the grove, and instructed them in many things which the Lord had revealed unto me concerning their fathers, and the promises that were made concerning them in the Book of Mormon. I advised them to cease killing each other and warring with other tribes; also to keep peace with the whites; all of which was interpreted to them.

Keokuk replied that he had a Book of Mormon at his wigwam which I had given him some years before. "I believe," said he, "you are a great and good man; I look rough, but I also am a son of the Great Spirit. I have heard your advice—we intend to quit fighting, and follow the good talk you have given us."

After the conversation they were feasted on the green with good food, dainties, and melons by the brethren; and they entertained the spectators with a specimen of their dancing.

Sunday, August 15—My infant son, Don Carlos, died, aged 14 months, 2 days. Conference met in Zarahemla, and was addressed by Elders Brigham Young and George Miller on building the temple in Nauvoo.

Sunday, September 5—I preached to a large congregation at the stand, on the science and practice of medicine, desiring to persuade the Saints to trust in God when sick, and not in an arm of flesh, and live by faith and not by medicine, or poison; and when they were sick, and had called for the elders to pray for them, and they were not healed, to use herbs and mild food.

Wednesday, September 22—A company of the brethren started for the pinery, some five or six hundred miles north, on the river, for the purpose of procuring lumber for the temple and Nauvoo house.

Monday, October 10—The Twelve met for the purpose of counsel, and spent most of the day in visiting the sick.

Elder Erastus Snow writes from Northbridge, Massachusetts. He had been laboring in Salem and vicinity four weeks, organized a branch of thirty members, and the prospects are flattering.

Friday, October 29—Those of the Twelve Apostles who were in Nauvoo, met in council.

In obedience to an order from the mayor, I called out two companies of the Nauvoo Legion, and removed a grog shop kept by Pulaski S. Cahoon, which had been declared a nuisance by the city council.

Sunday, November 7—Elder William O. Clark preached about two hours, reproving the Saints for a lack of sanctity, and a want of holy living, enjoining sanctity, solemnity, and temperance in the extreme, in the rigid sectarian style.

I reproved him as pharisaical and hypocritical and not edifying the people; and showed the Saints what temperance, faith, virtue, charity, and truth were. I charged the Saints not to follow the example of the adversary in accusing the brethren, and said, "If you do not accuse each other, God will not accuse you. If you have no accuser you will enter heaven, and if you will follow the revelations and instructions which God gives you through me, I will take you into heaven as my back load. If you will not accuse me, I will not accuse you. If you will throw a cloak of charity over my sins, I will over yours—for charity covereth a multitude of sins. What many people call sin is not sin; I do many things to break down superstition, and I will break it down;" I referred to the curse of Ham for laughing at Noah, while in his wine, but doing no harm. Noah was a righteous man, and yet he drank wine and became intoxicated; the Lord did not forsake him in consequence thereof, for he retained all the power of his priesthood, and when he was accused by Canaan, he cursed him by the priesthood which he held, and the Lord had respect to his word, and the priesthood which he held, notwithstanding he was drunk, and the curse remains upon the posterity of Canaan until the present day.

Monday, November 8—At five o'clock p.m., I attended the dedication of the baptismal font in the Lord's house. President Brigham Young was spokesman.

The baptismal font is situated in the center of the basement room, under the main hall of the temple; it is constructed of pine timber, and put together of staves tongued and grooved, oval shaped, sixteen feet long east and west, and twelve feet wide, seven feet high from the foundation, the basin four feet deep, the moulding of the cap and base are formed of beautiful carved work in antique style. The sides are finished with panel work. A flight of stairs in the north and south sides lead up and down into the basin, guarded by side railing.

The font stands upon twelve oxen, four on each side, and two at each end, their heads, shoulders, and fore legs projecting out from under the font; they are carved out of pine plank, glued together, and copied after the most beautiful five-year-old steer that could be found in the country, and they are an excellent striking likeness of the original; the horns were formed after the most perfect horn that could be procured.

The oxen and ornamental mouldings of the font were carved by Elder Elijah Fordham, from the city of New York, which occupied eight months of time. The font was enclosed by a temporary frame building sided up with split oak clapboards, with a roof of the same material, and was so low that the timbers of the first story were laid above it. The water was supplied from a well thirty feet deep in the east end of the basement.

This font was built for the baptisms for the dead until the temple shall be finished, when a more durable one will supply its place.

Friday, November 26—I attended city council and presented a bill for "an Ordinance in relation to Hawkers, Pedlars, Public Shows, and Exhibitions, in order to prevent any immoral or obscene exhibition," which passed the council by unanimous vote.

Sunday, November 28—I spent the day in the council with the Twelve Apostles at the house of President Young, conversing with them upon a variety of subjects. Brother Joseph Fielding was present, having been absent four years on a mission to England. I told the brethren that the Book of Mormon was the most correct of any book on earth, and the keystone of our religion, and a man would get nearer to God by abiding by its precepts, than by any other book.

Saturday, December 11—Late this evening, while sitting in council with the Twelve in my new store on Water street, I directed Brigham Young, president of the Twelve Apostles, to go immediately and instruct the building committee in their duty, and forbid them receiving any more property for the building of the temple, until they received it from the Trustee in Trust, and if the committee did not give heed to the instruction, and attend to their duty, to put them in the way so to do.

Elder Willard Richards has left Warsaw for Nauvoo, it being considered unnecessary for him to tarry there any longer.

Since I have been engaged in laying the foundation of the Church of Jesus Christ of Latter-day Saints, I have been prevented in various ways from continuing my journal and history in a manner satisfactory to myself or in justice to the cause. Long imprisonments, vexatious and long-continued law-suits, the treachery of some of my clerks, the death of others, and the poverty of myself and brethren from continued plunder and driving, have prevented my handing down to posterity a connected memorandum of events desirable to all lovers of truth; yet I have continued to keep up a journal in the best manner my circumstances would allow, and dictate for my history from time to time, as I have had opportunity so that the labors and suffering of the first elders and Saints of this last kingdom might not wholly be lost to the world.

Sunday, December 12—I preached in the morning at Snyder's Hotel.

In the evening, the Twelve met in council at Brother Heber C. Kimball's.

Monday, December 13—I appointed Willard Richards recorder for the temple, and my private secretary and general clerk, and he commenced his labors in my new office in the brick store.

Tuesday, December 14—I commenced opening, unpacking, and assorting a lot of dry goods in the second story of my new store, situate on the northwest corner of block 155. The joiners and masons are yet at work in the lower part of the building.

Sunday, December 26—The public meeting of the Saints was at my house this evening, and after Patriarch Hyrum Smith and Elder Brigham Young had spoken on the principles of faith, and the gifts of the Spirit, I read the 13th chapter of First Corinthians, also a part of the 14th chapter, and remarked that the gift of tongues was necessary in the Church; but that if Satan could not speak in tongues, he could not tempt a Dutchman, or any other nation, but the English, for he can tempt the Englishman, for he has tempted me, and I am an Englishman; but the gift of tongues by the power of the Holy Ghost in the Church, is for the benefit of the servants of God to preach to unbelievers, as on the day of Pentecost. When devout men from every nation shall assemble to hear the things of God, let the Elders preach to them in their own mother tongue, whether it is German, French, Spanish or "Irish," or any other, and let those interpret who understand the language spoken, in their own mother tongue, and this is what the apostle meant in First Corinthians 14:27.

Chapter Fourteen

1842

Wednesday, January 5—William Wightman signed over and delivered the town plat of Ramus to me, as sole Trustee in Trust for the Church of Jesus Christ of Latter-day Saints.

My new store was opened for business this day for the first time, it was filled with customers, and I was almost continually behind the counter, as clerk, waiting on my friends.

Thursday, January 6—The new year has been ushered in and continued thus far under the most favorable auspices, and the Saints seem to be influenced by a kind and indulgent Providence in their dispositions and (blessed with) means to rear the temple of the Most High God, anxiously looking forth to the completion thereof as an event of the greatest importance to the Church and the world, making the Saints in Zion to rejoice, and the hypocrite and sinner to tremble. Truly this is a day long to be remembered by the Saints of the last days; a day in which the God of heaven has begun to restore the ancient order of His kingdom unto His servants and His people; a day in which all things are concurring to bring about the completion of the fullness of the gospel, a fullness of the dispensation of dispensations, even the fullness of times; a day in which God has begun to make manifest and set in order in His Church those things which have been, and those things which the ancient prophets and wise men desired to see but died without beholding them; a day in which those things begin to be made manifest, which have been hid from before the foundation of the world, and which Jehovah has promised should be made known in His own due time unto His servants, to prepare the earth for the return of His glory, even a celestial glory, and a kingdom of priests and kings to God and the Lamb, forever, on Mount Zion, and with Him the hundred and forty and four thousand whom John the Revelator saw, all of which is to come to pass in the restitution of all things.

Conference held at Zarahemla, at which that stake was discontinued; a branch was organized in place thereof, and John Smith appointed president.

Wednesday, January 12—I rode south about seven miles to my wood land, accompanied by Brother John Sanders and Peter Maughan, and found a vein of coal about eighteen inches thick, apparently of good quality for the western country.

Elder Benjamin Winchester was suspended by the quorum of the Twelve until he made satisfaction for disobedience to the First Presidency.

Tuesday, January 18—This day revoked my power of attorney given to Dr. Isaac Galland to transact business for the Church.

After transacting a variety of business, sleeping an hour from bodily infirmities, I read for correction in the Book of Mormon, and debated in the evening with the mayor (John C. Bennett) concerning the Lamanites and Negroes.

Wednesday, January 26—The Church is in a prosperous condition, and the Saints are exerting themselves to build the temple. The health of the city is good.

Friday, January 28—While I was at my office, Emma and Sister Whitney came in and spent an hour.

I also decided that Elder John Snyder should go out on a mission, and if necessary some one go with him and raise up a church, and get means to go to England, and carry the epistle required in the revelation of December 22nd; and instructed the Twelve, Brigham Young, Heber C. Kimball, Wilford Woodruff and Willard Richards being present, to call Elder Snyder into their council and instruct him in these things, and if he will not do these things he shall be cut off from the Church, and be damned.

Elias Higbee, of the temple committee, came into my office, and I said unto him:

> The Lord is not well pleased with you; and you must straighten up your loins and do better, and your family also; for you have not been as diligent as you ought to have been, and as spring is approaching, you must arise and shake yourself, and be active, and make your children industrious, and help build the temple.

Tuesday, March 1—During the forenoon I was at my office and the printing office, correcting the first plate or cut of the records of Father Abraham, prepared by Reuben Hedlock, for the *Times and Seasons*, and in council in my office, in the afternoon; and in the evening with the Twelve and their wives at Elder Woodruff's, at which time I explained many important principles in relation to progressive improvement in the scale of intelligent existence.

Tuesday, March 15—I officiated as grand chaplain at the installation of the Nauvoo Lodge of Free Masons, at the grove near the temple. Grand Master Jonas, of Columbus, being present, a large number of people assembled on the occasion. The day was exceedingly fine; all things were done in order, and universal satisfaction was manifested. In the evening I received the first degree in Free Masonry in the Nauvoo Lodge, assembled in my general business office.

Thursday, March 17—The high council withdrew the hand of fellowship from Elder Oliver Olney for setting himself up as a prophet, and took his license.

I assisted in commencing the organization of "The Female Relief Society of Nauvoo" in the Lodge Room. Sister Emma Smith, president, and Sister Elizabeth Ann Whitney and Sarah M. Cleveland, counselors. I gave much instruction, read in the New Testament, and Book of Doctrine and Covenants, concerning the elect lady, and showed that the elect meant to be elected to a certain work, &c., and that the revelation was then fulfilled by Sister Emma's election to the Presidency of the Society, she having previously been ordained to expound the scriptures. Emma was blessed, and her counselors were ordained by Elder John Taylor.

Sunday, March 20—I preached to a large assembly in the grove, near the temple on the west. The body of a deceased child of Mr. Windsor P. Lyon being before the assembly, changed my design in the order of my remarks.

Thursday, March 24—I attended by request, the Female Relief Society, whose object is the relief of the poor, the destitute, the widow and the orphan, and for the exercise of all benevolent purposes. Its organization was completed this day. Mrs. Emma Smith takes the presidential chair; Mrs. Elizabeth Ann Whitney and Sarah M. Cleveland are her counselors; Miss Elvira Cole is treasurer, and our well-known and talented poetess, Miss Eliza R. Snow, secretary. There was a very numerous attendance at the organization of the society, and also at the subsequent meetings, of some of our most intelligent, humane, philanthropic and respectable ladies; and we are well assured from a knowledge of those pure principles of benevolence that flow spontaneously from their humane and philanthropic bosoms, that with the resources they will have at command, they will fly to the relief of the stranger; they will pour in oil and wine to the wounded heart of the distressed; they will dry up the tears of the orphan and make the widow's heart to rejoice.

Our women have always been signalized for their acts of benevolence and kindness; but the cruel usage that they received from the barbarians of Missouri, has hitherto prevented their extending the hand of charity in a conspicuous manner; yet in the midst of their persecution, when the bread has been torn from their helpless offspring by their cruel oppressors, they have always been ready to open their doors to the weary traveler, to divide their scant pittance with the hungry, and from their robbed and impoverished wardrobes, to divide with the more needy and destitute; and now that they are living upon a more genial soil, and among a less barbarous people, and possess facilities that they have not heretofore enjoyed, we feel convinced that with their concentrated efforts, the condition of the suffering poor, of the stranger and the fatherless will be ameliorated.

We had the privilege of being present at their organization, and were much pleased with their *modus operandi*, and the good order that prevailed. They are strictly parliamentary in their proceedings.

An earthquake at Falmouth this morning.

Friday, March 25—Attending to a variety of business; counseling, &c.

Saturday, March 26—Elder John Snyder received his final instructions from the president, and received his blessing from Elder Brigham Young, with the laying on of the hands of President Joseph Smith, John E. Page and Willard Richards, and started for England this day.

Sunday, March 27—After speaking to the Saints for some time on the subject of baptism for the dead, I baptized one hundred and seven individuals.

I also witnessed the landing of 170 English brethren from the steamer *Ariel*, under the presidency of Elder Lyman Wight; also about $3,000 worth of goods for the temple and Nauvoo house.

Monday, March 28—I was at the office. Received Parley P. Pratt's donations from England, and attended to a variety of business; as also on the 29th and 30th.

Sunday, April 10—I preached in the grove, and pronounced a curse upon all adulterers, and fornicators, and unvirtuous persons, and those who have made use of my name to carry on their iniquitous designs.

Saturday evening, April 16—On this day the first number of *The Wasp*, a miscellaneous weekly newspaper was first published at my office, William Smith, editor, devoted to the arts, sciences, literature, agriculture, manufacture, trade, commerce, and the general news of the day, on a small sheet, at $1.50 per annum.

Sunday, April 17—Spent the day with my family at home.

Monday, April 18—In consequence of the utter annihilation of our property by mob violence in the state of Missouri, and the immense expenses which we were compelled to incur, to defend ourselves from the cruel persecutions of that state, we were reduced to the necessity of availing ourselves of the privileges of the general bankrupt law; therefore I went to Carthage with my brothers Hyrum and Samuel H. Smith, and severally testified to our list of insolvency before the clerk of the county commissioner's court. Sidney Rigdon and many more brethren were at Carthage the same day on business. My clerk, Dr. Richards, went with us.

Sunday, April 24—Preached on the hill near the temple, concerning the building of the temple, and reproved the merchants and the rich who would not assist in building it.

Monday, April 25, Tuesday, April 26, and Wednesday, April 27—I was engaged in reading, meditation, &c., mostly with my family.

Thursday, April 28—At two o'clock I met the members of the "Female Relief Society," and after presiding at the admission of many new members, gave a lecture on the priesthood, showing how the sisters would come in possession of the privileges, blessings and gifts of the priesthood, and that the signs should follow them, such as healing the sick, casting out devils, &c., and that they might attain unto these blessings by a virtuous life, and conversation, and diligence in keeping all the commandments; a synopsis of which was reported by Miss Eliza R. Snow.

Friday, April 29—A conspiracy against the peace of my household was made manifest, and it gave me some trouble to counteract the design of certain base individuals, and restore peace. The

Lord makes manifest to me many things, which it is not wisdom for me to make public, until others can witness the proof of them.

Saturday, April 30—I received a visit from Judge James Adams, of Springfield, and spent most of the day with him and my family. Signed deeds to James and Charles Ivins, and many others.

Sunday, May 1—I preached in the grove, on the keys of the kingdom, charity, &c. The keys are certain signs and words by which false spirits and personages may be detected from true, which cannot be revealed to the elders till the temple is completed. The rich can only get them in the temple; the poor may get them on the mountain top as did Moses. The rich cannot be saved without charity, giving to feed the poor when and how God requires, as well as building. There are signs in heaven, earth and hell; the elders must know them all, to be endowed with power, to finish their work and prevent imposition. The devil knows many signs, but does not know the sign of the Son of Man, or Jesus. No one can truly say he knows God until he has handled something, and this can only be in the holiest of holies.

Tuesday, May 3—Passed the day mostly with my family.

Wednesday, May 4—I spent the day in the upper part of the store, that is in my private office (so called because in that room I keep my sacred writings, translate ancient records, and receive revelations) and in my general business office, or lodge room (that is where the Masonic fraternity meet occasionally, for want of a better place) in council with General James Adams, of Springfield, Patriarch Hyrum Smith, Bishops Newel K. Whitney and George Miller, and President Brigham Young, and Elders Heber C. Kimball and Willard Richards, instructing them in the principles and order of the priesthood, attending to washings, anointings, endowments and the communication of keys pertaining to the Aaronic Priesthood, and so on to the highest order of the Melchisedek Priesthood, setting forth the order pertaining to the Ancient of Days, and all those plans and principles by which anyone is enabled to secure the fullness of those blessings which have been prepared for the Church of the First Born, and come up and abide in the presence of the Eloheim in the eternal worlds. In this council was instituted the ancient order of things for the first time in these last days. And the communications I made to this council were of things spiritual, and to be received only by the spiritual minded: and there was nothing made known to these men but what will be made known to all the Saints of the last days, so soon as they are prepared to receive, and a proper place is prepared to communicate them, even to the weakest of the Saints; therefore let the Saints be diligent in building the temple, and all houses which they have been, or shall hereafter be, commanded of God to build; and wait their time with patience in all meekness, faith, perseverance unto the end, knowing assuredly that all these things referred to in this council are always governed by the principle of revelation.

Saturday, May 7—Nauvoo Legion on parade—I would remark that the day passed very harmoniously, without drunkenness, noise or confusion. There was an immense congregation of spectators, and many distinguished strangers expressed much satisfaction. But one thing I will notice: I was solicited by General Bennett to take command of the first cohort during the sham battle; this I declined. General Bennett next requested me to take my station in the rear of the cavalry, without my staff, during the engagement; but this was counteracted by Captain A. P. Rockwood, commander of my life guards, who kept close to my side, and I chose my own position. And if General Bennett's true feelings toward me are not made manifest to the world in a very short time, then it may be possible that the gentle breathings of that Spirit, which whispered me on parade, that there was mischief concealed in that sham battle, were false; a short time will determine the point. Let John C. Bennett answer at the day of judgment, "Why did you request me to command one of the cohorts, and also to take my position without my staff, during the sham battle, on the 7th of May, 1842, where my life might have been the forfeit, and no man have known who did the deed?"

Saturday, May 14—I attended city council in the morning, and advocated strongly the necessity of some active measures being taken to suppress houses and acts of infamy in the city; for the protection of the innocent and virtuous, and the good of public morals; showing clearly that there were certain characters in the place, who were disposed to corrupt the morals and chastity of our citizens, and that houses of infamy did exist, upon which a city ordinance concerning brothels and disorderly characters was passed, to prohibit such things. It was published in this day's *Wasp*.

I also spoke at length for the repeal of the ordinance of the city licensing merchants, hawkers, taverns, and ordinaries, desiring that this might be a free people, and enjoy equal rights and privileges, and the ordinances were repealed.

After council, I worked in my garden, walked out in the city, and borrowed two sovereigns to make a payment.

Brother Amos Fielding arrived from Liverpool.

It was reported in Nauvoo, that ex-Governor Boggs of Missouri had been shot.

Tuesday, May 17—John C. Bennett resigned the office of mayor of Nauvoo.

Thursday, May 19—It rained, and I was at home until one o'clock; when I attended a special session of the city council. John C. Bennett having discovered that his whoredoms and abominations were fast coming to light, and that the indignation of an insulted and abused people were rising rapidly against him, thought best to make a virtue of necessity, and try to make it appear that he was innocent, by resigning his office of mayor, which the council most gladly accepted; and Joseph Smith was elected mayor of the city of Nauvoo by the council, and Hyrum Smith vice-mayor.

While the election was going forward, I received and wrote the following revelation:

> Verily thus saith the Lord unto you, my servant Joseph, by the voice of my Spirit, Hiram Kimball has been insinuating evil, and forming

> evil opinions against you, with others; and if he continue in them, he and they shall be accursed, for I am the Lord thy God, and will stand by thee and bless thee. Amen.

This I threw across the room to Hiram Kimball, one of the councillors.

Friday, May 20—Charges having been preferred against Robert D. Foster, by Samuel H. Smith before a special council, for abusive language towards Samuel H. Smith; also for abusing the marshal of the city, I spent the day in council, and such was the proof against Foster, I had considerable labor to get him clear, even after his confession, which I desired to do, hoping he would amend.

Tuesday, May 24—Chauncey L. Higbee was cut off from the Church by the high council, for unchaste and unvirtuous conduct towards certain females, and for teaching it was right, if kept secret, &c. He was also put under $200 bonds to keep the peace, on my complaint against him for slander, before Ebenezer Robinson, justice of the peace.

Wednesday, May 25—I spent the day in counseling the bishops, and assisting them to expose iniquity.

Notice was this day given to John C. Bennett, that the First Presidency, Twelve, and bishops had withdrawn fellowship from him, and were about to publish him in the paper, but on his humbling himself, and begging we would spare him from the paper, for his mother's sake, the notice was withdrawn from the paper.

Thursday, May 26—This forenoon I attended a meeting of nearly a hundred of the brethren in the lodge room, to whom John C. Bennett acknowledged his wicked and licentious conduct toward certain females in Nauvoo, and that he was worthy of the severest chastisements, and cried like a child, and begged that he might be spared, in any possible way; so deep was his apparent sense of his guilt and unfitness for respectable society; so deeply did he feign, or really feel contrition for the moment, that he was forgiven still. I plead for mercy for him.

"IT WAS A TRICK OF THE DEVIL TO KILL MY CLERK."

Saturday, May 28—The high council were in session, as they had been from day to day through the week, investigating charges against various individuals for unvirtuous conduct, committed through the teachings and influence of John C. Bennett; several were cut off, and some were forgiven on confession.

Wednesday, June 8—I was about home. Sent Dr. Richards to Carthage on business. On his return, old Charley, while on a gallop, struck his knees and breast instead of his feet, fell in the street, and rolled over in an instant, and the doctor narrowly escaped with his life. It was a trick of the devil to kill my clerk. Similar attacks have been made on myself of late, and Satan is seeking our destruction on every hand.

Saturday, June 11—Riots and mobs are multiplying in the land.

Saturday, June 25—Transacted business with Brother Hunter, and Mr. Babbitt, and sat for a drawing of my profile to be placed on a lithograph of the map of the city of Nauvoo.

Messrs. Stephens and Catherwood have succeeded in collecting in the interior of America a large amount of relics of the Nephites, or the ancient inhabitants of America treated of in the Book of Mormon, which relics have recently been landed in New York.

Sunday, July 3—This morning I preached at the grove to about 8,000 people.

The subject matter of my discourse was from the Prophet Daniel's saying, that in the last days the God of heaven would set up a kingdom, &c.

Wednesday, July 6—Transacted business in the city, and rode to La Harpe with Emma.

Two keel boats, sloop-rigged, and laden with provisions and apparatus necessary for the occasion, and manned with fifty of the brethren, started this morning on an expedition to the upper Mississippi, among the pineries, where they can join those already there, and erect mills, saw boards and plank, make shingles, hew timber, and return next spring with rafts, for the temple of God,

Nauvoo house, &c., to beautify the city of Nauvoo, according to the prophets.

Thursday, July 7—Weather very cool at Nauvoo, thermometer at six degrees.

Saturday, July 9—I rode on the prairie with Brothers Clayton and Gheen to look at some land. Dined on my farm; hoed potatoes, &c., and in the afternoon returned to the city and transacted a variety of business.

Monday, July 11—In the morning, transacting business with Mr. Hunter. In the afternoon, at the printing office reading the papers, and bought a horse of Harmon T. Wilson, which I named Joe Duncan.

Saturday, August 6—Passed over the river to Montrose, Iowa, in company with General Adams, Colonel Brewer, and others, and witnessed the installation of the officers of the Rising Sun Lodge Ancient York Masons, at Montrose, by General James Adams, deputy grand-master of Illinois. While the deputy grand-master was engaged in giving the requisite instructions to the master-elect, I had a conversation with a number of brethren in the shade of the building on the subject of our persecutions in Missouri and the constant annoyance which has followed us since we were driven from that state. I prophesied that the Saints would continue to suffer much affliction and would be driven to the Rocky Mountains, many would apostatize, others would be put to death by our persecutors or lose their lives in consequence of exposure or disease, and some of you will live to go and assist in making settlements and build cities and see the Saints become a mighty people in the midst of the Rocky Mountains.

Tuesday, August 16—Brother Derby has taken the greatest interest in my welfare, and I feel to bless him.

Blessed is Brother Erastus H. Derby, and he shall be blessed of the Lord. He possesses a sober mind, and a faithful heart. The snares therefore that will subsequently befall other men, who are treacherous and rotten hearted, shall not come nigh unto his doors, but shall be far from the path of his feet. He loveth wisdom and shall be found possessed of her. Let there be a crown of glory and a diadem upon his head. Let the light of eternal truth shine forth upon his understanding; let his name be had in everlasting remembrance; let the blessings of Jehovah be crowned upon his posterity after him, for he rendered me consolation in the lonely places of my retreat. How good and glorious it has seemed unto me, to find pure and holy friends, who are faithful, just, and true, and whose hearts fail not; and whose knees are confirmed and do not falter, while they wait upon the Lord, in administering to my necessities, in the day when the wrath of mine enemies was poured out upon me.

In the name of the Lord, I feel in my heart to bless them, and to say in the name of Jesus Christ of Nazareth, that these are the ones that shall inherit eternal life. I say it by virtue of the Holy Priesthood, and by the ministering of holy angels, and by the gift and power of the Holy Ghost.

How glorious were my feelings when I met that faithful and friendly band, on the night of the eleventh, on Thursday, on the island at the mouth of the slough, between Zarahemla and Nauvoo: with what unspeakable delight, and what transports of joy swelled my bosom, when I took by the hand, on that night, my beloved Emma—she that was my wife, even the wife of my youth, and the choice of my heart. Many were the reverberations of my mind when I contemplated for a moment the many scenes we had been called to pass through, the fatigues and the toils, the sorrows and sufferings, and the joys and consolations, from time to time, which had strewed our paths and crowned our board. Oh what a commingling of thought filled my mind for the moment, again she is here, even in the seventh trouble—undaunted, firm, and unwavering—unchangeable, affectionate Emma!

There was Brother Hyrum who next took me by the hand—a natural brother.

Thought I to myself, Brother Hyrum, what a faithful heart

you have got! Oh may the Eternal Jehovah crown eternal blessings upon your head, as a reward for the care you have had for my soul! O how many are the sorrows we have shared together; and again we find ourselves shackled with the unrelenting hand of oppression. Hyrum, thy name shall be written in the book of the law of the Lord, for those who come after thee to look upon, that they may pattern after thy works.

Said I to myself, Here is Brother Newel K. Whitney also. How many scenes of sorrows have strewed our paths together; and yet we meet once more to share again. Thou art a faithful friend in whom the afflicted sons of men can confide, with the most perfect safety. Let the blessings of the Eternal also be crowned upon his head. How warm that heart! How anxious that soul! For the welfare of one who has been cast out, and hated of almost all men. Brother Whitney, thou knowest not how strong those ties are that bind my soul and heart to thee.

My heart was overjoyed as I took the faithful band by the hand, that stood upon the shore, one by one. William Law, William Clayton, Dimick B. Huntington, George Miller, were there. The above names constituted the little group.

I do not think to mention the particulars of the history of that sacred night, which shall forever be remembered by me; but the names of the faithful are what I wish to record in this place. These I have met in prosperity, and they were my friends; and I now meet them in adversity, and they are still my warmer friends. These love the God that I serve; they love the truths that I promulgate; they love those virtuous, and those holy doctrines that I cherish in my bosom with the warmest feelings of my heart, and with that zeal which cannot be denied. I love friendship and truth; I love virtue and law; I love the God of Abraham, of Isaac, and of Jacob; and they are my brethren, and I shall live; and because I live they shall live also. These are not the only ones who have administered to my necessity and whom the Lord will bless. There is Brother John D. Parker and Brother Amasa Lyman, and Brother Wilson Law, and Brother Henry G. Sherwood. My heart feels to reciprocate the unwearied kindnesses that have been bestowed upon me by these men. They are men of noble stature, of noble hands, and of noble deeds; possessing noble, and daring, and giant hearts and souls. There is Brother Joseph B. Noble also, I would call up in remembrance before the Lord. There is Brother Samuel H. Smith, a natural brother—he is even as Hyrum. There is Brother Arthur Millikin also, who married my youngest sister, Lucy: he is a faithful, an honest, and an upright man.

While I call up in remembrance before the Lord these men, I would be doing injustice to those who rowed me in the skiff up the river that night, after I parted with the lovely group—who brought me to this my safe, and lonely, and private retreat—Brother Jonathan Dunham, and the other, whose name I do not know. Many were the thoughts that swelled my aching heart, while they were toiling faithfully with their oars. They complained not of hardship and fatigue to secure my safety. My heart would have been harder than an adamantine stone, if I had not prayed for them with anxious and fervent desire. I did so, and the still small voice whispered to my soul: These, that share your toils with such faithful hearts, shall reign with you in the kingdom of their God; but I parted with them in silence, and came to my retreat. I hope I shall see them again, that I may toil for them, and administer to their comfort also. They shall not want a friend while I live; my heart shall love those, and my hands shall toil for those, who love and toil for me, and shall ever be found faithful to my friends. Shall I be ungrateful? Verily no! God forbid!

I design to continue this subject at a future time.

Tuesday, August 23—There are many souls whom I have loved stronger than death. To them I have proved faithful—to them I am determined to prove faithful, until God calls me to resign up my breath. O Thou, who seest and knowest the hearts of all men—Thou eternal, omnipotent, omniscient, and omnipresent Jehovah—God—Thou Eloheim, that sittest, as saith the psalmist, "enthroned in heaven," look down upon Thy servant Joseph at this time; and let faith on the name of Thy Son Jesus Christ, to a greater degree than Thy servant ever yet has enjoyed, be conferred upon him, even the faith of Elijah; and let the lamp of eternal life be lit up in his heart, never to be taken away; and let the words of eternal life be poured upon the soul of Thy servant, that he may know Thy will, Thy statutes, and Thy commandments, and Thy judgments, to do them.

As the dews upon Mount Hermon, may the distillations of Thy divine grace, glory, and honor, in the plenitude of Thy mercy, and power, and goodness, be poured down upon the head of Thy servant. O Lord, God, my Heavenly Father, shall it be in vain, that Thy servant must needs be exiled from the midst of his friends, or be dragged from their bosoms, to clank in cold and iron chains; to be thrust within the dreary prison walls; to spend days of sorrow, and of grief, and misery there, by the hand of an infuriated, incensed, and infatuated foe; to glut their infernal and insatiable desire upon innocent blood; and for no other cause, on the part of Thy servant, than for the defense of innocence; and Thou a just God will not hear his cry? Oh, no; Thou wilt hear me—a child of woe, pertaining to this mortal life, because of sufferings here, but not for condemnation that shall come upon him in eternity; for Thou knowest, O God, the integrity of his heart. Thou hearest me, and I knew that Thou wouldst hear me, and mine enemies shall not prevail; they all shall melt like wax before Thy face, and, as the mighty floods and waters roar, or as the bellowing earthquake's devouring gulf, or rolling thunder's loudest peal, or vivid forked lightning's flash, or sound of the archangel's trump, or voice of the Eternal God—so shall the souls of my enemies be made to feel in an instant, suddenly, and shall be taken, and ensnared, and fall backwards, and stumble in the ditch they have dug for my feet, and the feet of my friends, and perish in their own infamy and shame, be thrust down to an eternal hell, for their murderous and hellish deeds!

Friday, September 2—Spent the day at home. A report reached the city this afternoon that the sheriff was on his way to Nauvoo with an armed force.

Saturday, September 3—In the morning at home, in company with John F. Boynton.

Sunday, October 2—About ten o'clock in the forenoon, a messenger arrived from Quincy, stating that the governor had offered a reward of $200 for Joseph Smith, Jun., and also $200 for Orrin P. Rockwell. This report was fully established on receipt of the mail papers. The *Quincy Whig* also stated that Governor Reynolds has offered a reward, and published the governor's proclamation offering a reward of $300 for Joseph Smith, Jun., and $300 for Orrin P. Rockwell. It is not expected that much will be effected by the rewards.

Emma continued very sick. I was with her all day.

Monday, October 3—Emma was a little better. I was with her all day.

Tuesday, October 4—Emma is very sick again. I attended with her all the day, being somewhat poorly myself.

Wednesday, October 5—My dear Emma was worse. Many fears were entertained that she would not recover. She was baptized twice in the river, which evidently did her much good. She grew worse again at night, and continued very sick indeed. I was unwell, and much troubled on account of Emma's sickness.

Thursday, October 13—The brethren arrived from Wisconsin with a raft of about 90,000 feet of boards and 24,000 cubic feet of timber for the temple and Nauvoo house.

Saturday, October 15—Brother John D. Parker returned to Nauvoo and informed my friends that I was well.

Sunday, October 23—This day the temple committee laid before the Saints the propriety and advantages of laying a temporary floor in the temple, that the brethren might henceforth meet in the temple to worship, instead of meeting in the grove. This was my instructions, and the Saints seemed to rejoice at this privilege very much.

Friday, October 28—Soon after daylight this morning, I returned home again to visit my family. I found Emma worse; the remainder of the family well. In the afternoon I rode out into the city and took a little exercise. From the appearance of things abroad, we are encouraged to believe that my enemies will not trouble me much more at present.

This day the brethren finished laying the temporary floor, and seats in the temple, and its appearance is truly pleasant and cheering. The exertions of the brethren during the past week to accomplish this thing are truly praiseworthy.

Saturday, October 29—About ten in the forenoon I rode up and viewed the temple. I expressed my satisfaction at the arrangements, and was pleased with the progress made in the sacred edifice. After conversing with several of the brethren, and shaking hands with numbers who were very much rejoiced to see their prophet again, I returned home; but soon afterwards went over to the store, where a number of brethren and sisters were assembled, who had arrived this morning from the neighborhood of New York, Long Island, &c. After Elders Taylor, Woodruff, and Samuel Bennett had addressed the brethren and sisters, I spoke to them at considerable length, showing them the proper course to pursue, and how to act in regard to making purchases of land, &c.

I showed them that it was generally in consequence of the brethren disregarding or disobeying counsel that they became dissatisfied and murmured; and many when they arrived here, were dissatisfied with the conduct of some of the Saints, because everything was not done perfectly right, and they get angry, and thus the devil gets advantage over them to destroy them. I told them I was but a man, and they must not expect me to be perfect; if they expected perfection from me, I should expect it from them; but if they would bear with my infirmities and the infirmities of the brethren, I would likewise bear with their infirmities.

I told them it was likely I would have again to hide up in the woods, but they must not be discouraged, but build up the city, the temple, &c. When my enemies take away my rights, I will bear it and keep out of the way; but if they take away your rights, I will fight for you. I blessed them and departed.

Sunday, October 30—The Saints met to worship on a temporary floor, in the temple, the walls of which were about four feet high above the basement; and notwithstanding its size, it was well filled. It had been expected that I would address them, but I sent word that I was so sick that I could not meet with them; consequently Elder John Taylor delivered a discourse. In the evening I went to visit the sick, &c.

Monday, October 31—I rode out to my farm with my children, and did not return until after dark.

Tuesday, November 1—I rode with Emma to the temple for the benefit of her health. She is rapidly gaining. In the afternoon went to see Dr. Willard Richards, who was very sick at Elder Woodruff's; afterwards, accompanied by my children and William Clayton, rode out towards the farm. When going down the hill, near Casper's the carriage got over-balanced and upset. I was thrown some distance from the carriage, and all three of the children almost under it. I arose and enquired if any of the children were killed; but upon examination, there was no one seriously hurt. Frederick G. Williams had his cheek bruised, which was the worst injury received.

It seemed miraculous how we escaped serious injury from this accident; and our escape could not be attributed to any other power than that of Divine Providence. I feel thankful to God for this instance of His kind and watchful care over His servant and family.

The carriage was so much broken, we left it, and putting the children in Brother Stoddard's buggy, returned. In the evening I rode to the temple with two of my children.

Saturday, November 5—I tarried at home on account of the rain. I received a visit from some Indians, who were accompanied by a

Negro interpreter. They expressed great friendship for the Mormon people, and said they were their friends. After considerable conversation and partaking of victuals, they departed, evidently highly gratified with their visit.

I told Dr. Richards the Mississippi would be frozen over in less than a month, although the weather was then warm and pleasant.

Monday, November 7—Spent the forenoon in council with Brother Hyrum Smith and some of the Twelve, and in giving instructions concerning the contemplated journey to Springfield on the 15th December next, and what course ought to be pursued in reference to the case of bankruptcy. In the afternoon Calvin A. Warren, Esq., arrived, and I called upon some of the Twelve and others to testify before Squire Warren what they knew in reference to the appointment of trustee-in-trust, &c., showing also from the records that I was authorized by the Church to purchase and hold property in the name of the Church, and that I had acted in all things according to the counsel given to me.

Thursday, November 17—There was a severe snow storm, and Elder Alpheus Harmon (who was just returning from a mission), and another man, were frozen to death on the prairie between Nauvoo and Carthage. The Mississippi was frozen over, which fulfilled my prophecy of the 5th instant.

Saturday, November 26—In the evening went to see Brigham Young, in company with Dr. Richards. He was suddenly and severely attacked by disease, with strong symptoms of apoplexy. We immediately administered to him by laying on of hands and prayer, accompanied with the use of herbs. Profuse vomiting and purging followed, which were favorable indications. Although few so violently attacked ever survive long, yet the brethren were united in faith, and we had firm hopes of his recovery.

Sunday, November 27—At home, except visiting President Young, who remained extremely sick.

Wednesday, December 7—Dined with Elder Orson Hyde and family. Elder Hyde has this day returned home from his mission to Jerusalem. His presence was truly gratifying. Spent the day with Elder Hyde and drawing wood.

Thursday, December 8—Spent the day at home. Received a visit from Elder Hyde and wife.

This day, Thomas Ford, governor of Illinois, in his inaugural address to the Senate and House of Representatives, remarked that a great deal has been said about certain charters granted to the people of Nauvoo. These charters are objectionable on many accounts, but particularly on account of the powers granted. The people of the state have become aroused to the subject, and anxiously desire that these charters should be modified so as to give the inhabitants of Nauvoo no greater privileges than those enjoyed by others of our fellow citizens.

Friday, December 9—I chopped wood all day. My Brother Hyrum started for Springfield to attend to his case of bankruptcy, with Benjamin Covey as witness.

Tuesday, December 20—Chopping and drawing wood with my own hands and team, as I had done mostly since the 9th. President Young continued very sick.

Monday, December 26—In the morning, held court, and I was afterwards arrested by General Wilson Law, on the proclamation of Governor Carlin, and Elders Henry G. Sherwood, and William Clayton went to Carthage to obtain a writ of habeas corpus to take me before the court at Springfield. General Law gave me into the custody of Dr. Richards, with whom I visited Sister Morey, who was severely afflicted. We prescribed lobelia for her, among other things, which is excellent in its place. I have learned the value of it by my own experience. It is one of the works of God, but, like the power of God, or any other good, it becomes an evil when improperly used. Brother Morey gave me a walking stick, the body of which was from the tooth of the sperm whale, and the top of whale ivory, with an interstice of mahogany. On my return home, I found my wife Emma sick. She was delivered of a son, which did not survive its birth.

Tuesday, December 27—At nine in the morning, started in custody of Wilson Law for Springfield, in company with Hyrum Smith, Willard Richards, John Taylor, William Marks, Levi Moffit, Peter Haws, Lorin Walker and Orson Hyde. On our way to Carthage, we met William Clayton and Henry G. Sherwood, who had obtained an order for a writ of habeas corpus from the master in chancery, as no writ could issue, the clerk of court having been elected to the State Senate.

There was considerable snow, and the traveling heavy; but we arrived at my Brother Samuel's, in Plymouth, a little after sunset, and we were soon joined by Edward Hunter, Theodore Turley, Dr. Tate, and Shadrach Roundy. I supped with Brother William Smith's family, who lived under the same roof, slept with Dr. Willard Richards on a buffalo skin spread upon the floor, and dreamed that I was by a beautiful stream of water and saw a noble handsome fish, which I threw out. Soon after, I saw a number more, and threw them out. I afterwards saw a multitude of fish, and threw out a great abundance, and sent for salt and salted them.

Wednesday, December 28—The morning was wet. We started about eight o'clock, and arrived at Mr. Stevenson's tavern, in Rushville, at three in the afternoon, about twenty miles. Brother William's wife, who was sick, went with us, accompanied by Sister Durphy, who went with us from Nauvoo to take care of her. I spent a part of the evening with Mr. Uriah Brown and family and a part of my company. In conversation respecting the repeal of charters, I told them that to touch the Nauvoo Charter was no better than highway robbery; and that I never would consent to lowering our charter, but they might bring other charters up to it. On my return to the tavern, the brethren took my height, which was six feet, and my Brother Hyrum's the same.

Thursday, December 29—Started early; crossed the Illinois river at eleven, and arrived at Captain Dutche's before five in the evening, about thirty-two miles: the weather extremely cold. General Law asked why the sun was called by a masculine name and the moon by a feminine one. I replied that the root of masculine is stronger, and of feminine weaker. The sun is a governing planet to certain planets, while the moon borrows her light from the sun, and is less or weaker.

Let the government of Missouri redress the wrongs she has done to the Saints, or let the curse follow them from generation to generation until they do.

When I was going up to Missouri, in company with Elder Rigdon and our families, on an extreme cold day, to go forward was fourteen miles to a house, and backward nearly as far. We applied to all the taverns for admission in vain; we were "Mormons," and could not be received. Such was the extreme cold that in one hour we must have perished. We pleaded for our women and children in vain. We counseled together, and the brethren agreed to stand by me, and we concluded that we might as well die fighting as to freeze to death.

I went into a tavern and pleaded our cause to get admission. The landlord said he could not keep us for love or money. I told him we must and would stay, let the consequence be what it might; for we must stay or perish. The landlord replied, "We have heard the Mormons are very bad people; and the inhabitants of Paris have combined not to have anything to do with them, or you might stay." I said to him, "We will stay; but no thanks to you. I have men enough to take the town; and if we must freeze, we will freeze by the burning of these houses." The taverns were then opened, and we were accommodated, and received many apologies in the morning from the inhabitants for their abusive treatment.

Friday, December 30—Started at eight this morning, and arrived at Judge Adams', in Springfield, at half past two o'clock in the afternoon.

Saturday, December 31—The writ was granted, returned, and served in one minute, and I walked up to the bar. Mr. Butterfield read the habeas corpus, and moved the court to take bail till I could have a hearing, which was granted; and although it was only a case of misdemeanor, Generals James Adams and Wilson Law were bailed for me in the sum of $2,000 each, and Monday was set for trial.

The court-room was crowded; and, on our returning, as General Law came to the top of the stairs, one of the crowd observed, "There goes Smith the Prophet, and a good looking man he is;" "And (said another) as damned a rascal as ever lived." Hyrum replied, "And a good many ditto." "Yes, (said the man,) ditto, ditto, G——d—— you; and everyone that takes his part is as damned a rascal as he is."

When at the foot of the stairs, General Law said, "I am the man, and I'll take his part." Said the man, "You are a damned rascal too." "You are a lying scoundrel," replied Law; and the man began to strip off his clothes and ran out in the street, cursing and swearing, and raising a tumult, when Mr. Prentice, the marshal, interfered, and with great exertions quelled the mob. Much credit is due Mr. Prentice for his zeal to keep the peace.

When the rowdies had dispersed, I went with Mr. Butterfield and Dr. Richards to see Governor Ford, who was sick. He told me he had a requisition from the governor for a renewal of persecution in the old case of treason against Missouri; but he happened to know that it was all dead. We dined with Mr. Butterfield at the American House, where the governor quartered, after which we returned to the general's room. In course of conversation he remarked he was no religionist. I told him I had no creed to circumscribe my mind; therefore the people did not like me. "Well, (said the general) from reports, we had reason to think the Mormons were a peculiar people, different from other people, having horns or something of the kind; but I find they look like other people; indeed, I think Mr. Smith a very good-looking man."

At two in the afternoon, I returned to Judge Adams', and appointed Elders Hyde and Taylor to preach in the Representatives' Hall on the morrow.

This afternoon, a team ran away, and went past the State

House, when the hue-and-cry was raised, "Joe Smith is running away!" which produced great excitement and a sudden adjournment of the House of Representatives.

Chapter Fifteen

1843

Sunday morning, January 1, 1843—The speaker of the House of Representatives called on me to say we might have the hall for preaching this day. Had a pleasant interview with Mr. Butterfield, Judge Douglas, Senator Gillespie, and others. In reply to Mr. Butterfield, I stated that the most prominent difference in sentiment between the Latter-day Saints and sectarians was, that the latter were all circumscribed by some peculiar creed, which deprived its members the privilege of believing anything not contained therein, whereas the Latter-day Saints have no creed, but are ready to believe all true principles that exist, as they are made manifest from time to time.

At the suggestion of the company, I explained the nature of a prophet.

If any person should ask me if I were a prophet, I should not deny it, as that would give me the lie; for, according to John, the testimony of Jesus is the spirit of prophecy; therefore, if I profess to be a witness or teacher, and have not the spirit of prophecy, which is the testimony of Jesus, I must be a false witness; but if I be a true teacher and witness, I must possess the spirit of prophecy, and that constitutes a prophet; and any man who says he is a teacher or preacher of righteousness, and denies the spirit of prophecy, is a liar, and the truth is not in him; and by this key false teachers and imposters may be detected.

At half-past eleven a.m., we repaired to the Representatives' Hall, where Elder Orson Hyde read the hymn "Rejoice ye Saints of Latter Days." Elder Taylor followed in prayer. The Saints then sang "The Spirit of God like a fire is burning." Elder Hyde then preached from the 3rd chapter of Malachi. Most of the members of the Legislature and the various departments of the state were in attendance.

I dined with Judge Adams at one p.m., and at half-past two returned to the hall, and heard Elder Taylor preach from Revelation 14th chapter, 6th and 7th verses, on the first principles of the gospel. There was a respectable congregation, who listened with good attention, notwithstanding the great anxiety to "see the Prophet."

I supped at Brother Bowman's, where I saw Sister Lucy Stringham (who was one of the first fruits of the Church at Colesville, New York) and many more of the Saints. At seven I returned to Judge Adams'.

Monday, January 2—After breakfasting with Judge Adams, I prophesied, in the name of the Lord, that I should not go to Missouri dead or alive. At half-past nine a.m., repaired to the court-room; and at ten, Judge Pope took his seat on the bench, accompanied by several ladies.

My case was called up, when Mr. Lamborn, the attorney-general of Illinois, requested the case to be continued till the next day, and Wednesday morning was set for my trial. My attorney, Mr. Butterfield, filed some objections to points referred to in the habeas corpus, and, half-past ten, I repaired to the Senate lobby, and had conversation with several gentlemen. Dined at the American House. As we rose from table, Judge Brown invited me to his room, and informed me he was about publishing a history of Illinois, and wished me to furnish a history of the rise and progress of the Church of Latter-day Saints to add to it.

At half-past one p.m. returned to General Adams. A gentleman from St. Louis told General Law that the general impression was that Smith was innocent, and it would be a kind of murder to give him up—that "he ought to be whipped a little and let go." It was evident that prejudice was giving way in the public mind.

At four, Mr. Lamborn, Mr. Prentice, the marshal, and some half dozen others called to see me. The marshal said it was the first time during his administration that the ladies had attended court on a trial. A peculiarly pleasant and conciliatory feeling prevailed in the company, and the marshal invited me to a family dinner, when I should be freed.

At five went to Mr. Sollars' with Elders Hyde and Richards. Elder Hyde inquired the situation of the Negro. I replied, they came into the world slaves, mentally and physically. Change their situation with the whites, and they would be like them. They have souls, and are subjects of salvation. Go into Cincinnati or any city, and find an educated Negro, who rides in his carriage, and you will see a man who has risen by the powers of his own mind to his exalted state of respectability. The slaves in Washington are more refined than many in high places, and the black boys will take the shine off many of those they brush and wait on.

Elder Hyde remarked, "Put them on the level, and they will rise above me." I replied, if I raised you to be my equal, and then attempted to oppress you, would you not be indignant and try to rise above me, as did Oliver Cowdery, Peter Whitmer, and many others, who said I was a fallen prophet, and they were capable of leading the people, although I never attempted to oppress them, but had always been lifting them up? Had I anything to do with the Negro, I would confine them by strict law to their own species, and put them on a national equalization.

Because faith is wanting, the fruits are. No man since the world was had faith without having something along with it. The ancients quenched the violence of fire, escaped the edge of the sword, women received their dead, &c. By faith the worlds were made. A man who has none of the gifts has no faith; and he deceives himself, if he supposes he has. Faith has been wanting, not only among the heathen, but in professed Christendom also, so that tongues, healings, prophecy, and prophets and apostles, and all the gifts and blessings have been wanting.

Some of the company thought I was not a very meek prophet; so I told them: "I am meek and lowly in heart," and will personify Jesus for a moment, to illustrate the principle, and cried out with a loud voice, "Woe unto you, ye doctors; woe unto you, ye lawyers; woe unto you, ye scribes, Pharisees, and hypocrites!" &c. But you cannot find the place where I ever went that I found fault with their food, their drink, their house, their lodgings; no, never; and this is what is meant by the meekness and lowliness of Jesus.

Mr. Sollars stated that James Mullone, of Springfield, told him as follows:"I have been to Nauvoo, and seen Joe Smith, the Prophet: he had a gray horse, and I asked him where he got it; and Joe said, 'You see that white cloud.' 'Yes.' 'Well, as it came along, I got the horse from that cloud.'" This is a fair specimen of the ten thousand foolish lies circulated by this generation to bring the truth and its advocates into disrepute.

What is it that inspires professors of Christianity generally with a hope of salvation? It is that smooth, sophisticated influence of the devil, by which he deceives the whole world. But, said Mr. Sollars, "May I not repent and be baptized, and not pay any attention to dreams, visions, and other gifts of the Spirit?" I replied, "Suppose I am traveling and am hungry, and meet with a man and tell I am hungry, and he tells me to go yonder, there is a house of entertainment, go and knock, and you must conform to all the rules of the house, or you cannot satisfy your hunger; knock, call for food, sit down and eat; and I go and knock, and ask for food, and sit down to the table, but do not eat, shall I satisfy my hunger? No. I must eat. The gifts are the food; and the graces of the Spirit are the gifts of the Spirit. When I first commenced this work, and had got two or three individuals to believe, I went about thirty miles with

Oliver Cowdery, to see them. We had only one horse between us. When we arrived, a mob of about one hundred men came upon us before we had time to eat, and chased us all night; and we arrived back again a little after daylight, having traveled about sixty miles in all, and without food. I have often traveled all night to see the brethren; and, when traveling to preach the gospel among strangers, have frequently been turned away without food."

Thus the evening was spent in conversation and teaching, and closed by singing and prayer, when we parted, and Elders Hyde, Richards and myself lay down upon a bed on the floor, and enjoyed refreshing rest till morning.

Tuesday, January 3—After breakfast, called on Sister Crane, and blessed her little baby, Joseph Smith Crane, and returned to Judge Adams', where we conversed with Messrs. Trobridge, Jonas, Browning, and others, on my old Missouri case of treason. At half-past nine, went to the court-room, and had conversation with Messrs. Butterfield, Owen, Pope, Prentice, and others.

At twelve, returned and spent the afternoon at Judge Adams'. At dusk, the marshal called with subpoenas for my witnesses. Spent the evening with the brethren at Judge Adams' in a very social manner, and prophesied in the name of the Lord that no very formidable opposition would be raised at my trial on the morrow. Slept on a sofa as usual while at Springfield.

Wednesday, January 4—At nine o'clock a. m., repaired to the court-room, Judge Pope on the bench, and ten ladies by his side, when Josiah Lamborn, attorney-general of the state of Illinois, appeared and moved to dismiss the proceedings.

My counsel then offered to read, in evidence, affidavits of several persons, showing conclusively that I was at Nauvoo, in the county of Hancock, and state of Illinois, on the whole of the 6th and 7th days of May, in the year 1842, and on the evenings of those days more than three hundred miles distant from Jackson county, in the state of Missouri, where it is alleged that the said Boggs was shot; and that I had not been in the state of Missouri at any time between the 10th day of February and the 1st day of July 1842, the said persons having been with me during the whole of that period. That on the 6th day of May aforesaid, I attended an officer's drill at Nauvoo aforesaid, in the presence of a large number of people; and on the 7th day of May aforesaid I reviewed the Nauvoo Legion in presence of many thousand people.

The reading of these affidavits was objected to by the attorney-general of the state of Illinois, on the ground that it was not competent for Smith to impeach or contradict the return of the habeas corpus. It was contended by my counsel: 1st, that I had a right to prove that the return was untrue; 2nd, that the said affidavits did not contradict the said return, as there was no averment under the oath in said return that I was in Missouri at the time of the commission of the alleged crime, or had fled from the justice of that state. The court decided that the said affidavits should be read in evidence, subject to all objections; and they were read accordingly, all of which will appear on my discharge.

In the course of his plea, Mr. Butterfield showed that Governor Reynolds had subscribed to a lie in his demand for me, as will appear in the papers; and said that Governor Carlin would not have given up his dog on such a requisition. That an attempt should be made to deliver up a man who has never been out of the state, strikes at all the liberty of our institutions. His fate today may be yours tomorrow. I do not think the defendant ought, under any circumstances, to be given up to Missouri. It is a matter of history that he and his people have been murdered or driven from the state. If he goes there, it is only to be murdered, and he had better be sent to the gallows. He is an innocent and unoffending man. If there is a difference between him and other men, it is that this people believe in prophecy, and others do not; the old prophets prophesied in poetry and the modern in prose.

Esquire Butterfield managed the case very judiciously. The court-room was crowded during the whole trial; the utmost decorum and good feeling prevailed, and much prejudice was allayed.

Esquire Lamborn was not severe, apparently saying little more than his relation to the case demanded.

Court adjourned till tomorrow nine a. m., for the making up of opinion. After an introduction to several persons, I retired to Judge Adams', and after dinner spent some time in conversation with Brother Hyrum and Theodore Turley. At half-past five o'clock I rode in Mr. Prentice's carriage to his house, accompanied by General Law and Elder Orson Hyde, where I had a very interesting visit with Mr. Prentice and family, Judge Douglas, Esquires Butterfield, Lamborn and Edwards, Judge Pope's son, and many others; partook of a splendid supper; there were many interesting anecdotes, and everything to render the repast and visit agreeable; and returned to Judge Adams' about eleven o'clock.

Thursday, January 5—At nine a. m., repaired to the courtroom, which was crowded with spectators anxious to "behold the Prophet," and hear the decision of Judge Pope, who soon took his seat, accompanied by half-a-dozen ladies, and gave the following:

See History of the Church, Vol 5, 223–31.

At the close I arose, and bowed to the court, which adjourned to ten o'clock tomorrow. I accepted an invitation to see Judge Pope in his room, and spent an hour in conversation with his honor, in which I explained to him that I did not profess to be a prophet any more than every man ought to who professes to be a preacher of righteousness; and that the testimony of Jesus is the spirit of prophecy; and gave the judge a brief but general view of my principles. Esquire Butterfield asked me "to prophesy how many inhabitants would come to Nauvoo." I said, "I will not tell how many inhabitants will come to Nauvoo; but when I went to Commerce, I told the people I would build up a city, and the old inhabitants replied 'We will be damned if you can.' So I prophesied that I would build up a city, and the inhabitants prophesied that I could not; and we have now about 12,000 inhabitants. I will prophesy that we will build up a great city; for we have the stakes and have only to fill up the interstices."

The judge was very attentive and agreeable, and requested of me that my secretary, Dr. Richards, would furnish him a copy of his decision for the press. Dined at General Adams', and in the afternoon visited Mr. Butterfield with Brother Clayton. In the evening visited Mr. Groves, and lodged at General Adams' with Dr. Richards.

Friday, January 6—In the morning went to see Judge Pope with Dr. Richards, who presented the judge with a report of his decision; called on Mr. Butterfield, and gave him two notes of two hundred and thirty dollars each, having paid him forty dollars as fee for his service in my suit. I took certified copies of the doings of the court, and waited on Governor Ford for his certificate thereto, after which he offered me a little advice, which was, that I "should refrain from all political electioneering." I told him that I had always acted upon that principle, and proved it by General Law and Dr. Richards: and that the "Mormons" were driven to union in their elections by persecution, and not by my influence; and that the "Mormons" acted on the most perfect principle of liberty in all their movements.

During the day I had considerable conversation in the courtroom with the lawyers and others, on various topics and particularly on religion. Judge Pope's son wished me well, and hoped I would not be persecuted any more, and I blessed him. Mr. Butterfield said I must deposit my discharge and all my papers in the archives of the temple when it is completed. My discharge, here referred to, commenced with my petition for habeas corpus and closed with the certificate of Thomas Ford, governor of Illinois, including all the documents relating to my trial on separate sheets of paper, attached by a blue ribbon and secured by the seal of the court.

In the judge's opinion on the bench, he remarked like this: "Were it my prerogative to impeach Congress for any one thing, it would be for granting power for the transportation of fugitives

"IT WAS A REMARKABLE INTERPOSITION OF PROVIDENCE THAT NEITHER OF THE BRETHREN WERE INJURED IN THE LEAST."

on affidavit, and not on indictment alone." He also passed several severe strictures on the actions of different governors and officers concerned in my case, but which I suppose he thought proper to omit in his printed copy.

I received many invitations to visit distinguished gentlemen in Springfield, which time would not permit me to comply with; also a ticket from the manager to attend the theatre this evening; but the play was prevented by the rain.

Saturday, January 7—At half-past eight in the morning, we left Judge Adams' to return to Nauvoo, and arrived at Captain Dutch's at four in the evening. Traveling very bad, with snow and mud, and yet so cold as to whiten the horses with frost.

Monday, January 9—At half-past eight in the morning, started for Plymouth: roads very hard, smooth and icy. When about two miles west of Brooklyn, at half-past twelve p.m., the horses of the large carriage slipped and became unmanageable; and horses and carriage, with Lorin Walker and Dr. Richards in it, went off the embankment some six or eight feet perpendicular, doing no damage except breaking the fore-axletree and top of the carriage. It was a remarkable interposition of Providence that neither of the brethren were injured in the least. The company agreed that Lilburn W. Boggs should pay the damage; cut down a small tree, spliced the axle, drove on, and arrived at Brother Samuel Smith's in Plymouth, about four p.m. After supper, I visited my sister, Catherine Salisbury, accompanied by Dr. Richards and Sister Durphy. This was the first time I had visited my sister in the state of Illinois, and the circumstance brought vividly to my mind many things pertaining to my father's house, of which I spake freely, and particularly of my brother Alvin. He was a very handsome man, surpassed by none but Adam and Seth, and of great strength. When two Irishmen were fighting, and one was about to gouge the other's eyes, Alvin took him by his collar and breeches, and threw him over the ring, which was composed of men standing around to witness the fight.

We returned to Brother Samuel's just before the close of the meeting at the schoolhouse, where Elder John Taylor preached. After passing the usual salutations with several who had called to see me, singing the Jubilee Song, etc., retired to rest.

Tuesday, January 10—At half-past eight in the morning, we started for Nauvoo, and, stopping only to water at the public well at Carthage, arrived at my house at half-past two p. m.; found my family well, who, with many friends, assembled to greet us on our safe return and my freedom. My aged mother came in and got hold of my arm before I saw her, which produced a very agreeable surprise, and she was overjoyed to behold her son free once more.

Wednesday, January 11—I rode out with Emma this morning, designing to go to Brother Daniel Russel's, and apologize for breaking his carriage on our return from Springfield: but broke a sleigh-shoe, and returned home, where I received a visit from a company of gentlemen and ladies from Farmington, on the Des Moines river, who left at half-past two p. m.

I directed letters of invitation to be written from myself and lady for a dinner party at my house on Wednesday next, at ten a.m., to be directed to Brothers Wilson Law, William Law, Hyrum Smith, Samuel Bennett, John Taylor, William Marks, Peter Haws, Orson Hyde, Henry G. Sherwood, William Clayton, Jabez Durphy, H. Tate, Edward Hunter, Theodore Turley, Shadrach Roundy, Willard Richards, Arthur Millikin, Brigham Young, Heber C. Kimball, Wilford Woodruff, George A. Smith, Alpheus Cutler, Reyholds Cahoon, and ladies; also Mr. Levi Moffat, and Carlos Granger, and ladies; my mother, Lucy Smith, and Sisters Eliza R. Snow and Hannah Ells.

Thursday, January 12—At home all day.

Friday, January 13—At home till near sunset; then went to Brother William Marks' with Dr. Richards, to see Sophia Marks, who was sick; heard her relate her vision or dream of a visit from her two brothers who were dead, touching the associations and relations of another world.

Saturday, January 14—Rode out with Emma in the morning. At ten attended city council, and in the evening called the quorum of the Twelve together in my chamber, to pray for Sophia Marks, who was very sick.

Sunday, January 15—I spent at home with my family.

Tuesday, January 17—This being the time appointed by the Twelve as a day of humiliation, fasting, praise, prayer, and thanksgiving before the great Eloheim, I attended a public meeting in my own house, which was crowded to overflowing. Many other meetings were held in various parts of the city, which were well attended, and there was great joy among the people, that I had once more been delivered from the grasp of my enemies. In the evening I attended a referee case, with six others, on a land case of Dr. Robert D. Foster's.

Wednesday, January 18—At ten o'clock in the morning, the party invited began to assemble at my house, and before twelve they were all present, except Levi Moffatt and wife, and Brother Hyrum's wife, who was sick. I distributed cards among them, printed for the occasion, containing the Jubilee Song of Brothers Law and Richards; also one by Sister Eliza R. Snow, as printed on the 96th page, 4th volume of *Times and Seasons*, which were sung by the company with warmest feelings.

I then read John C. Bennett's letter to Messrs. Sidney Rigdon and Orson Pratt, of the 10th instant, and told them that Mr. Pratt showed me the letter. Mr. Rigdon did not want to have it known that he had any hand in showing the letter, but wanted to keep it a secret, as though he were holding a private correspondence with Bennett; but as soon as Mr. Pratt got the letter, he brought it to me, which proves that Mr. Pratt had no correspondence with Bennett, and had no fellowship for his works of darkness. I told them I had sent word to Governor Ford, by Mr. Backenstos, that, before I would be troubled any more by Missouri, I would fight.

Conversation continued on various topics until two o'clock,

when twenty-one sat down to the dinner-table, and Emma and myself waited on them, with other assistants. My room was small, so that but few could be accommodated at a time.

Twenty sat down to the second table, which was served as the first, and eighteen at the third, among whom were myself and Emma; and fifteen at the fourth table, including children and my household.

Many interesting anecdotes were related by the company, who were very cheerful, and the day passed off very pleasantly. President Brigham Young was present, although very feeble. This was the first time that he had been out of his house since he was taken sick. His fever had been so severe, that he had lain in a log-house, rather open, without fire most of the time, when it was so cold that his attendants, with great coat and mittens on, would freeze their toes and fingers while fanning him. One thing more, which tended to give a zest to the occasion, was, that it was fifteen years this day since I was married to Emma Hale.

Friday, January 20—In the afternoon I attended a council of the Twelve, at President Young's. There were present, Brigham Young, Heber C. Kimball, Orson Hyde, Orson Pratt, John Taylor, Wilford Woodruff, George A. Smith, Willard Richards, and Brother Hyrum Smith. We had conversation on a great variety of subjects. I related my dream: "I dreamed this morning that I was in the lobby of the Representatives' Hall, at Springfield, when some of the members, who did not like my being there, began to mar, and cut, and pound my shins with pieces of iron. I bore it as long as I could, then jumped over the rail into the hall, caught a rod of iron, and went at them, cursing and swearing at them in the most awful manner, and drove them all out of the house. I went to the door, and told them to send me a clerk, and I would make some laws that would do good. There was quite a collection around the State House, trying to raise an army to take me, and there were many horses tied round the square. I thought they would not have the privilege of getting me; so I took a rod of iron, and mowed my way through their ranks, looking after their best race-horse, thinking they might catch me where they could find me. Then I awoke." To dream of flying signifies prosperity and deliverance from enemies. To dream of swimming in deep water signifies success among many people, and that the word will be accompanied with power.

I told Elder Hyde that when he spoke in the name of the Lord, it should prove true; but he must not curse the people—rather bless them.

I prophesy, in the name of the Lord God, as soon as we get the temple built, so that we shall not be obliged to exhaust our means thereon, we will have means to gather the Saints by thousands and tens of thousands.

Wednesday, February 8—This morning, I read German, and visited with a brother and sister from Michigan, who thought that "a prophet is always a prophet;" but I told them that a prophet was a prophet only when he was acting as such. After dinner Brother Parley P. Pratt came in; we had conversation on various subjects. At four in the afternoon, I went out with my little Frederick, to exercise myself by sliding on the ice.

Thursday, February 9—A man came to me in Kirtland, and told me he had seen an angel, and described his dress. I told him he had seen no angel, and that there was no such dress in heaven. He grew mad, and went into the street and commanded fire to come down out of heaven to consume me. I laughed at him, and said, "You are one of Baal's prophets; your God does not hear you; jump up and cut yourself;" and he commanded fire from heaven to consume my house.

When I was preaching in Philadelphia, a Quaker called out for a sign. I told him to be still. After the sermon, he again asked for a sign. I told the congregation the man was an adulterer; that a wicked and adulterous generation seeketh after a sign; and that the Lord had said to me in a revelation, that any man who wanted a sign was an adulterous person. "It is true," cried one, "for I caught him in the very act," which the man afterwards confessed, when he was baptized.

Saturday, February 11—This day had an interview with Elder Rigdon and his family. They expressed a willingness to be saved. Good feelings prevailed, and we again shook hands together.

At ten o'clock attended the city council. I prophesied to James Sloan, city recorder, that it would be better for him ten years hence, not to say anything more about fees; and addressed the new council, urging the necessity of their acting upon the principle of liberality, and of relieving the city from all unnecessary expenses and burdens, and not attempt to improve the city, but enact such ordinances as would promote peace and good order; and the people would improve the city; capitalists would come in from all quarters and build mills, factories, and machinery of all kinds; new buildings would arise on every hand, and Nauvoo would become a great city. I prophesied that if the council would be liberal in their proceedings, they would become rich, and spoke against the principle of pay for every little service rendered, and especially of committees having extra pay for their services; reproved the judges of the late election for not holding the polls open after six o'clock, when there were many wishing to vote.

Thursday, February 16—After breakfast, we [the prophet, Mr. Cowan and their party] proceeded towards Shokoquon. After traveling five miles, Brothers Hyde and Pratt's sleigh upset. Brother Hyde hurt his hand; the horse ran away, and we brought it back. After dinner, at McQueen's Mills, we went to Shokoquon, viewed the place and found it a very desirable location for a city, when we returned to the place where we dined. Elder Hyde prayed and I preached to a large and attentive audience two hours (from Rev. 19:10), and proved to the people that any man that denied himself as being a prophet was not a preacher of righteousness. They opened their eyes, and appeared well pleased. When we had returned as far as McQueen's Mills, Mr. Cowan halted and proposed to call. While waiting a moment, Mr. Crane's horse, (Mr. Crane came with our company) which was behind us, ran and jumped into our sleigh as we jumped out, and thence over our horse and the fence, sleigh and all, the sleigh being still attached to the horse, and the fence eight rails high; and both horses ran over lots and through the woods, clearing themselves from the sleighs, and had their frolic out without hurting themselves or drivers. It was a truly wonderful feat, and as wonderful a deliverance for the parties. We took supper at Mr. Crane's, and I stayed at Mr. Rose's that night.

Dr. Richards invited the brethren to come to my house on Monday next to chop and pile up my wood.

Saturday, February 18—Mostly about home and at the office. Several called for counsel on points of law. Esquire Warren, of Quincy, called on me. He had hurt his horse, and said it was not the first time he had missed it by not following my advice. While at dinner, I remarked to my family and friends present, that when the earth was sanctified and became like a sea of glass, it would be one great Urim and Thummim, and the Saints could look in it and see as they are seen.

Monday, February 20—About seventy of the brethren came together, according to previous notice, and drawed, sawed, chopped, split, moved, and piled up a large lot of wood in my yard. The day was spent by them with much pleasantry, good humor and feeling. A white oak log, measuring five feet four inches in diameter was cut through with a cross-cut saw, in four-and-a-half minutes, by Hyrum Dayton and Brother John Tidwell. This tree had been previously cut and hauled by my own hands and team.

While the court was in session, I saw two boys fighting in the street, near Mills' Tavern. I left the business of the court, ran over immediately, caught one of the boys (who had begun the fight with clubs,) and then the other; and, after giving them proper instruction, I gave the bystanders a lecture for not interfering in such cases, and told them to quell all disturbances in the street at the first onset. I returned to the court, and told them that nobody was allowed to fight in Nauvoo but myself.

In the evening, called at Brother Heber C. Kimball's.

John Quincy Adams presented to the House of Representatives of the United States a petition signed by 51,863 citizens of Massachusetts, praying congress to pass such acts and propose such amendments to the Constitution as would separate the petitioners from all connection with the institution of slavery.

Sunday, February 26—At home all day. My mother was sick with inflammation of the lungs, and I nursed her with my own hands.

Monday, February 27—I nursed my mother most of the day, who continued very sick. I issued a search warrant for Brother Dixon to search —— Fidler's and John Eagle's houses for a box of stolen shoes.

Tuesday, February 28—Mostly with my mother and family. Mr. John Brassfield, with whom I became acquainted in Missouri, called on me and spent the day and night. In the afternoon, mother was somewhat easier; and at four o'clock I went to Elder Orson Hyde's to dinner.

Wednesday, March 1—This morning I read and recited in German, went to my office, and reviewed my valedictory letter in the *Times and Seasons*, No. 7, Vol. 4; after which, I went with Marshal Henry G. Sherwood to procure some provisions for Thomas Morgan and Robert Taylor, who, on petition of the inhabitants of the city, I had directed should work out their punishment on the highways of Nauvoo.

Elder Orson Hyde called on me this afternoon to borrow a horse. I instructed my ostler to put the lieutenant-general's saddle on my horse, "Joe Duncan," and let Elder Hyde ride the "governor" on the lieutenant-general's saddle.

Signed a power of attorney, dated February 28th, to Amasa Lyman, to sell all the lands in Henderson county, Illinois, deeded to me by Mr. McQueen.

The Mississippi froze up on the 19th of November last, and still continues so.

Wagons and teams constantly pass over on the ice to Montrose.

I am constantly receiving applications from abroad for elders, which were replied to in the *Times and Seasons* of this day—that the conference on the 6th of April next, will attend to as many of the applications as possible.

Friday, March 3—Bishop Newel K. Whitney returned from Ramus this evening, with five teams loaded with provisions and grain, as a present to me, which afforded me very seasonable relief. I pray the Lord to bless those who gave it abundantly; and may it be returned upon their heads an hundred fold!

Saturday, March 4—On returning to my office after dinner, I spoke the following proverb: For a man to be great, he must not dwell on small things, though he may enjoy them; this shows that a prophet cannot well be his own scribe, but must have someone to write for him.

The battle of Gog and Magog will be after the millennium. The remnant of all the nations that fight against Jerusalem were commanded to go up to Jerusalem to worship in the millennium.

I told Dr. Richards that there was one thing he failed in as a historian, and that was noting surrounding objects, weather, etc.

This day, Mr. Warren, in the State Senate, moved to take from the table the bill to repeal the charter of the city of Nauvoo; but the senate refused to repeal it. Nays, 17; ayes, 16.

Orrin Porter Rockwell was taken prisoner in St. Louis by the Missourians, on an advertisement accusing him of shooting ex-Governor Boggs on the 6th day of May, 1842.

Sunday, March 5—I stayed at home all day to take care of my mother, who was still sick.

A severe shock of an earthquake felt at Memphis, Tenn.

Monday, March 6—I read, in the *Boston Bee*, a letter from Elder George J. Adams, and also another communication showing the progress of the truth in Boston and vicinity. At nine o'clock, called in my office, and requested Dr. Richards to write to the *Bee*; after which, I recited in German until dinner, and in the evening rode out to visit the sick.

Saturday, March 11—Very cold last night. The water froze in the warmest rooms in the city.

At nine a.m., I started in company with Brother Brigham Young, to Ramus, and had a delightful drive. Arrived at Brother McClary's at a quarter to four. Lodged with Brother Benjamin F. Johnson. In the evening, when pulling sticks, I pulled up Justus A. Morse, the strongest man in Ramus, with one hand.

Sunday, March 12—I preached to the Saints at Ramus, in the morning, taking for a text 14th chapter of John, 2nd verse: "In my Father's house are many mansions."

I found the brethren well, and in good spirits. In the afternoon, Brother Brigham preached. Stayed at Brother Benjamin F. Johnson's all night.

Elder George J. Adams having been called to Nauvoo, twelve hundred inhabitants of Boston petitioned for Elders Heber C. Kimball and Orson Hyde to come and labor in that place. A similar petition was also sent from Salem, Massachusetts, by Elder Erastus Snow.

Monday, March 13—I wrestled with William Wall, the most expert wrestler in Ramus, and threw him.

In the afternoon, held a Church meeting. Almon W. Babbitt was appointed, by the vote of the people, the presiding elder of that place.

In the evening meeting twenty-seven children were blessed, nineteen of whom I blessed myself, with great fervency. Virtue went out of me, and my strength left me, when I gave up the meeting to the brethren.

Mercury was three degrees below zero, at sunrise in Nauvoo.

Mr. Ivins arrived at Nauvoo, and stated that Orrin Porter Rockwell came with him from New Jersey to St. Louis, when Rockwell was arrested by advertisement on the 4th of March, and put in St. Louis jail.

Elder Hyde went to Quincy to preach.

Newspapers report that iron filings and sulphur have fallen in the form of a snow storm in five counties in Missouri.

Tuesday, March 14—Elder Jedediah M. Grant enquired of me the cause of my turning pale and losing strength last night while blessing children. I told him that I saw that Lucifer would exert his influence to destroy the children that I was blessing, and I strove with all the faith and spirit that I had to seal upon them a blessing that would secure their lives upon the earth; and so much virtue went out of me into the children, that I became weak, from which I have not yet recovered; and I referred to the case of the woman touching the hem of the garment of Jesus. (Luke, 8th chapter). The virtue here referred to is the spirit of life; and a man who exercises great faith in administering to the sick, blessing little children, or confirming, is liable to become weakened.

Elder Brigham Young and myself returned from Ramus, and after a severely cold ride in a heavy snowstorm, arrived in Nauvoo about four p.m.

Wednesday, March 15—I prophesied, in the name of the Lord Jesus Christ, that Orrin Porter Rockwell would get away honorably from the Missourians. I cautioned Peter Hawes to correct his boys: for if he did not curtail them in their wickedness, they would eventually go to prison.

I dreamed last night that I was swimming in a river of pure water, clear as crystal, over a shoal of fish of the largest size I ever saw. They were directly under my belly. I was astonished, and felt afraid that they might drown me or do me injury.

A great fire at Valparaiso, unequalled heretofore in Chili. Damage $2,000,000.

Thursday, March 16—In the office, reading papers, and gave counsel to Brother Hyrum, Dr. Foster, and many others.

Friday, March 17—Part of the day in my office; the remainder at home. Settled with Father Perry; gave him a deed for eighty acres of land and city lot, and prophesied that it would not be six months before he could sell it for cash.

At four p.m., Newel K. Whitney brought in a letter from R.S. Blennarhassett, Esq., St. Louis, dated 7th instant, concerning Orrin Porter Rockwell; which I immediately answered.

Reports reached us that new indictments had been found against myself, Brother Hyrum, and some hundred others, on the old Missouri troubles, and that John C. Bennett was making desperate threats.

The Island of Hong-Kong was ceded to Great Britain by the Emperor of China, who opened five ports to the English trade by treaty.

Saturday, March 18—I was most of the forenoon in the office, in cheerful conversation with Dr. Willard Richards and others. Finishing writing a letter to Arlington Bennett.

About noon, I lay down on the writing table, with my head on a pile of law books, saying, "Write and tell the world I acknowledge myself a very great lawyer; I am going to study law, and this is the way I study it;" and then fell asleep.

Rode out in the afternoon with William Clayton, looking at lots for Bishop Newel K. Whitney, and afterwards played ball with the boys.

The French seized upon the Society group of Pacific Isles.

Sunday, March 19—Rode out with Emma and visited my farm; returned about eleven, a.m., and spent the remainder of the day at home.

Monday, March 27—Opened court to try Field for drunkenness and abusing his wife. I fined him $10 and costs, and required him to find bail of $50 to keep the peace for six months.

A conference held at Hartland, Niagara county, New York. Three elders and one priest were ordained, and five added to the Church.

It is estimated that the Chinese loss, in their recent war with England, was 15,000 men, 1,500 pieces of cannon, and a great portion of their navy.

Tuesday, March 28—I removed my office from the smoke house (which I have been obliged to occupy for some months) to the small upper room in the new brick store.

Josiah Butterfield came to my house and insulted me so outrageously that I kicked him out of the house, across the yard, and into the street.

Elder Brigham Young visited George A. Smith, who was very sick.

Friday, March 31—At ten, a.m., I opened court for trial of Amos Lower, for assaulting John H. Burghard. After hearing testimony, fined lower $10.

Spent the afternoon at Mr. Lucian Woodworth's in company with Brother Hyrum, Heber C. Kimball, Orson Hyde, Wilford Woodruff, and Brother Chase, with our wives; had a good time, and feasted on a fat turkey.

Sunday, April 2—Wind N.E. Snow fell several inches, but melted more or less. At ten a.m. went to meeting. Heard Elder Orson Hyde preach, comparing the sectarian preachers to crows living on carrion, as they were more fond of lies about the Saints than the truth. Alluding to the coming of the Savior, he said, "When He shall appear, we shall be like Him, &c. He will appear on a white horse as a warrior, and maybe we shall have some of the same spirit. Our God is a warrior. (John 24:23.) It is our privilege to have the Father and Son dwelling in our hearts, &c."

We dined with my sister Sophronia McCleary, when I told Elder Hyde that I was going to offer some corrections to his sermon this morning. He replied, "They shall be thankfully received."

At one p,m., attended meeting, I read the 5th chapter of Revelation, referring particularly to the 6th verse, showing from that the actual existence of beasts in heaven. Probably those were beasts which had lived on another planet, and not ours. God never made use of the figure of a beast to represent the kingdom of heaven. When it is made use of, it is to represent an apostate church. This is the first time I have ever taken a text in Revelation; and if the young elders would let such things alone it would be far better.

Then corrected Elder Hyde's remarks, the same as I had done to him privately. At the close of the meeting we expected to start for Carthage, but the bad weather prevented; so I called another meeting in the evening.

Between meetings I read in Revelation with Elder Hyde, and expounded the same, during which time several persons came in and expressed their fears that I had come in contact with the old scriptures.

At seven o'clock meeting, I resumed the subject of the beast, and showed very plainly that John's vision was very different from Daniel's prophecy—one referring to things actually existing in heaven; the other being a figure of things which are on earth.

"What is the meaning of the scripture, 'He that is faithful over a few things shall be made ruler over many; and he that is faithful over many, shall be made ruler over many more'? What is the meaning of the parable of the Ten Talents? Also the conversation with Nicodemus, 'Except a man be born of water and of the Spirit'?" were questions put to me which I shall not answer at present.

I closed by flagellating the audience for their fears, and called upon Elder Hyde to get up and fulfill his covenant to preach three-quarters of an hour, otherwise I would give him a good whipping.

Elder Hyde arose and said "Brothers and sisters, I feel as though all had been said that can be said. I can say nothing, but bless you."

At the close of the meeting, we returned to Benjamin F. Johnson's, where we slept; and I remarked that the hundred and forty-four thousand sealed are the priests who should be anointed to administer in the daily sacrifice.

Dimick B. Huntington returned from Chicago, having had a very cold and severe journey. The ice in Chicago harbor was three feet thick. Brought me a letter from Mr. Justin Butterfield.

Thursday, April 6—I was detained from conference to hear a case of assumpsit, Widow Thompson, versus Dixon, until eleven a.m.

The first day of the fourteenth year of the Church of Jesus Christ of Latter-day Saints. Sun shone clear, warm and pleasant. The snow has nearly all disappeared, except a little on the north side of the hill above Zarahemla, Iowa. The ice is about two feet thick on the Mississippi, west of the temple. A considerable number of the brethren crossed from the Iowa side of the river to the conference, on the ice. The walls of the temple are from four to twelve feet above the floor.

Wednesday, April 12—Before the elders' conference closed, the steamer *Amaranth* appeared in sight of the temple, coming up the river, and about noon landed her passengers at the wharf opposite the old post office building, consisting of about two hundred and forty Saints from England, under the charge of Elder Lorenzo Snow, who left Liverpool last January, after a mission of nearly three years. With a large company of the brethren and sisters I was present to greet the arrival of our friends, and gave notice to the new-comers to meet at the temple tomorrow morning at ten o'clock, to hear instructions.

After unloading the Saints, the *Amaranth* proceeded up the river, being the first boat up this season.

About five p.m. the steamer *Maid of Iowa* hauled up at the Nauvoo House landing, and disembarked about two hundred Saints, in charge of Elders Parley P. Pratt and Levi Richards. These had been detained at St. Louis, Alton, Chester, etc. through the winter, having left Liverpool last fall. Dan Jones, captain of the *Maid of Iowa*, was baptized a few weeks since: he has been eleven days coming from St. Louis, being detained by ice. I was present at the landing and the first on board the steamer, when I met Sister Mary Ann Pratt (who had been to England with Brother Parley) and her little daughter, only three or four days old. I could not refrain from shedding tears.

So many of my friends and acquaintances arriving in one day kept me very busy receiving their congratulations and answering their questions. I was rejoiced to meet them in such good health and fine spirits; for they were equal to any that had ever come to Nauvoo.

Monday, April 17—Elder E.M. Webb writes that he has been laboring with success in several counties in Michigan, when he came to Comstock, in Kalamazoo county, Dr. John C. Bennett was lecturing in Kalamazoo, the shire town, and was told that there was a Mormon elder in the neighborhood. Bennett said, "That is one of Joe Smith's destroying angels, who is come to kill me;" and he left in such haste that he forgot to pay his tavern bill, also the poor Presbyterians for lighting and warming the house for him. Elder Webb commenced preaching there, baptized twenty-four and organized a branch.

Tuesday, April 18—In the evening had a talk with three Indian chiefs, who had come as a delegation from the Pottawatamie tribe, who complained of having their cattle, horses, &c., stolen. They were much troubled, and wanted to know what they should do. They had borne their grievances patiently.

Monday, May 1—I rode out with Lucien Woodworth, and paid him £20 for the Nauvoo House, which I borrowed of William Allen.

I insert fac-similes of the six brass plates found near Kinderhook, in Pike county, Illinois, on April 23, by Mr. Robert Wiley and others, while excavating a large mound. They found a skeleton about six feet from the surface of the earth, which must have stood nine feet high. The plates were found on the breast of the skeleton and were covered on both sides with ancient characters.

I have translated a portion of them, and find they contain the history of the person with whom they were found. He was a descendant of Ham, through the loins of Pharaoh; king of Egypt, and that he received his kingdom from the Ruler of heaven and earth.

Saturday, May 6—In the morning, had an interview with a lecturer on mesmerism and phrenology. Objected to his performing in the city. Also had an interview with a Methodist preacher, and conversed about his God without body or parts.

At half-past nine a.m., I mounted with my staff, and with the band, and about a dozen ladies, led by Emma, and proceeded to the general parade-ground of the Nauvoo Legion, east of my farm on the prairie. The Legion looked well—better than on any former occasion, and they performed their evolutions in admirable style.

The officers did honor to the legion. Many of them were equipped and armed *cap-a-pie*. The men were in good spirits. They had made great improvements both in uniform and discipline, and we felt proud to be associated with a body of men, which, in point of discipline, uniform, appearance, and a knowledge of military tactics, are the pride of Illinois, one of its strongest defenses, and a great bulwark of the western country.

In the course of my remarks on the prairie, I told the legion that when we have petitioned those in power for assistance, they have always told us they had no power to help us. Damn such traitors! When they give me the power to protect the innocent, I will never say I can do nothing for their good; I will exercise that power, so help me God. At the close of the address, the legion marched to the city and disbanded in Main Street, about two p.m., the day being windy and very cold.

There were two United States officers and General Swazey, of Iowa, present, who expressed great satisfaction at our appearance and evolutions.

In the evening, attended Mr. Vicker's performance of wire dancing, legerdemain, magic, etc.

Tuesday, May 9—In company with my wife, mother, and my adult family, also Sidney Rigdon, Parley P. Pratt, John Taylor, Wilford Woodruff, and about one hundred gentlemen and ladies, went aboard the *Maid of Iowa*, started at ten minutes before eight a.m., from the Nauvoo dock, under a salute of cannon, having on board a fine band of music.

We had an excellent address from our esteemed friend, Parley P. Pratt. The band performed its part well. Much good humor and hilarity prevailed. The captain and officers on board did all they could to make us comfortable, and we had a very agreeable and pleasant trip.

We started with the intention of visiting Augusta; but, in

consequence of the lowness of Shunk river, it was impracticable. We therefore altered our course to Burlington, touching at Fort Madison on our way up, and at Shokoquon on our return.

In consequence of the governor of Iowa having refused to withdraw a writ reported to have been issued on a demand from the executive of Missouri, on the same charge as that for which I had been discharged by Judge Pope, I dispensed with the pleasure of calling upon my friends in Burlington and Fort Madison. During our stay at those places, I kept myself concealed on the boat.

The *Maid of Iowa* did well. Her accomodations are good for the size of the boat, and she performed her trip in less time than we anticipated, and we returned home about eight p.m.

Friday, May 12—Purchased half of the steamer, *Maid of Iowa*, from Moffatt; and Captain Dan Jones commenced running her between Nauvoo and Montrose as a ferry-boat.

At sunrise, Bishop George Miller arrived with a raft of 50,000 feet of pine lumber for the temple and Nauvoo House from the pinery on Black River, Wisconsin, where the snow was about 2 ½ feet deep in the winter.

Monday, May 15—Emma having arrived at Yelrome, last night from Quincy, with the carriage, we rode home together. On our way, we stopped a short time at Brother Perry's. Brothers George A. Smith and Wilford Woodruff rode in my buggy. I was asked if the horse would stand without tying. I answered, "Yes; but never trust property to the mercy or judgment of a horse."

Sunday, May 21—At half-past ten a.m. I arrived at the temple, and had to press my way through the crowd in the aisles to get to the stand, when I remarked that there were some people who thought it a terrible thing that anybody should exercise a little power. I thought it a pity that anybody should give occasion to have power exercised, and requested the people to keep out of the aisles; for if they did not, I might some time run up and down and hit some of them; and called on two constables to keep the aisles clear.

After singing and prayer, I read 1st chapter of 2nd Epistle of Peter, and preached thereon.

Monday, May 22—Called at the office at nine, a. m., having received letters from Sisters Armstrong and Nicholson, of Philadelphia, complaining of the slanderous conduct of Benjamin Winchester; and I directed the Twelve Apostles to act upon the matter.

This morning received a large hickory walking stick having a silver head, with the motto "BEWARE."

Wednesday, May 24—Elder Addison Pratt presented the tooth of a whale, coral, bones of an Albatross' wing and skin of a foot, jaw-bone of a porpoise, and tooth of a South Sea seal as the beginning for a museum in Nauvoo.

Sunday, May 28—Cold, rainy day.

At five p. m. I met with brother Hyrum, Brigham Young, Heber C. Kimball, Willard Richards, Newel K. Whitney, and James Adams, in the upper room to attend to ordinances and counseling. Prayed that James Adams might be delivered from his enemies, and that Orrin P. Rockwell might be delivered from prison, and that the Twelve be prospered in collecting means to build the Nauvoo House.

Of the Twelve Apostles chosen in Kirtland, and ordained under the hands of Oliver Cowdery, David Whitmer and myself, there have been but two but what have lifted their heel against me—namely Brigham Young and Heber C. Kimball.

Friday, June 2—Closed the contract whereby I gave two notes for $1,375, and became half owner of the steamboat *Maid of Iowa*. Continued in the office with Captain Dan Jones most of the morning, which was very rainy.

In the afternoon rode out in the city to invite several friends to take an excursion on *Maid of Iowa* tomorrow, and had a long conversation with a Presbyterian minister.

Saturday, June 3—This morning, I, with my family and a large company of brethren and sisters, started for Quincy, on a pleasure voyage on the steamboat *Maid of Iowa*, had a fine band of music in attendance, and arrived there at about one p.m.

At five p.m. started on our return, but tied up at Keokuk, at one a.m. on account of a severe storm until daylight, when we started home and were glad to arrive in Nauvoo at seven a. m. of the 4th.

Sunday, June 11—At half-past two p.m., I introduced to the congregation Mr. De Wolf, a clergyman of the Episcopal church, and requested the attention of the congregation in his behalf. He read the 6th chapter of Hebrews, and then kneeled and prayed, dressed in his black clerical gown, which excited some curiosity among some of the Saints. After the choir sang a hymn, he preached from Hebrews, 6th chapter, 1st and 2nd verses, touching on such principles only that are acknowledged and received by the Church. In his closing remarks he observed—"I may never meet you all again this side of the eternal world; but I will appoint a meeting—i.e. when the Lord Jesus shall descend with his angels to call the dead from their graves and sit in judgment on all the world."

During the appointing of the high council, Elder Kimball made some general remarks upon the Word of Wisdom.

He commenced by saying that he always despised a penurious principle in any man, and that God despised it also; for he was liberal and did not look at every little thing as we do. He looked at the integrity of the heart of man. He said some would strain, nip and tuck at the Word of Wisdom, and at the same time they would turn away a poor brother from their door when he would ask for a little meal for his breakfast. He compared it to a man that was stretched upon the iron bedstead; if he was too long, they would cut him off; if he was too short, they would stretch him out. And again, he said, it made him think of the old Indian's tree, which stood so straight that it leaned a little the other way, and the best way was to stand erect.

In the after part of the day he renewed the subject by saying that he did not wish to have anyone take any advantage of what he had said, for he spoke in general terms; but said he had always obeyed the Word of Wisdom, and wanted every Saint to observe the same. He said that, when he was in England, he only taught it once or twice in public, and the Saints saw his example and followed it. So likewise when the elders go to preach, if they will observe the Word of Wisdom, all of those will whom they bring into the kingdom; but if they do not, they cannot expect their children will, but they will be just like themselves; for every spirit begets its own. Neither will such elders be able to do much good; for the Holy Ghost will not dwell in them, neither will the Father nor the Son; for they will not dwell where the Holy Ghost will not, and neither of them will dwell in unholy temples.

Tuesday, June 13—I started north with Emma and the children to see her sister, Mrs. Wasson and family, living near Dixon, Lee county, Illinois.

Elder Wilford Woodruff, when going to the prairie with several brethren to fence his five-acre lot broke the reach of his wagon and it fell into a pile together. The wheel fell on his arm and bruised him considerably; but he was able to mend his wagon and continue his journey. After working hard all day he went to Brother Cheney's house to obtain a drink of water, when an ugly dog bit him through the calf of the leg, which made him very lame.

Wednesday, June 14—Business is progressing. Buildings are going up in every direction, and the citizens manifest a determination that Nauvoo shall be built up. The stones of the temple begin to rise tier upon tier, and it already presents a stately and noble appearance.

The Mississippi has been rising three or four days, and is now three or four inches above high water mark.

Friday, June 16—Judge James Adams wrote by express from Springfield, at ten p. m., that Governor Thomas Ford had told him that he was going to issue a writ for me on the requisition of the governor of Missouri, and that it would start tomorrow.

Thursday, June 22—Another meeting of the laborers in the grove near the temple concerning wages.

I had previously given out an appointment to preach this day at Dixon, but on account of the change in circumstances, I wrote to Dixon, telling the people there was a writ out for me, and therefore declined preaching; and I kept myself quiet all day, telling my friends that if I started for home I might be arrested where I had no friends and be kidnapped into Missouri, and thought it best to tarry at Inlet and see the result. Many (at Dixon) were desirous to hear me preach, but were disappointed.

Lawyer Edward Southwick, of Dixon, having heard of the writ being out against me, rode twelve miles to inform me. I thanked him for his kindness, paid him twenty-five dollars and introduced him to my friends, Markham and Clayton, showing that I had received previous information.

Friday, June 23—Judge Adams arrived at Nauvoo from Springfield.

At eight a.m. a company of the brethren gathered to remove the timbers from the temple to the grove.

I sent William Clayton to Dixon at ten a.m., to try and find out what was going on there. He met Mr. Joseph H. Reynolds, the sheriff of Jackson county, Missouri, and Constable Harmon T. Wilson, of Carthage, Illinois, about half way, but they being disguised, they were not known by him; and when at Dixon they represented themselves as Mormon elders who wanted to see the Prophet. They hired a man and team to carry them, for they had run their horses almost to death.

They arrived at Mr. Wasson's while the family were at dinner, about two p. m.

They came to the door and said they were Mormon elders, and wanted to see Brother Joseph. I was in the yard going to the barn when Wilson stepped to the end of the house and saw me. He accosted me in a very uncouth, ungentlemanly manner, when Reynolds stepped up to me, collared me, then both of them presented cocked pistols to my breast, without showing any writ or serving any process. Reynolds cried out, "G——d—— you, if you stir I'll shoot; G——d—— if you stir one inch, I shoot you, be still, or I'll shoot you, by G——." I enquired "What is the meaning of all this?" "I'll show you the meaning, by G——; and if you stir one inch, I'll shoot you, G——d—— you." I answered, "I am not afraid of your shooting; I am not afraid to die." I then bared my breast and told them to shoot away. "I have endured so much oppression, I am weary of life; and kill me, if you please. I am a strong man, however, and with my own natural weapons could soon level both of you; but if you have any legal process to serve, I am at all times subject to law, and shall not offer resistance." Reynolds replied, "G——d—— you, if you say another word I will shoot you, by G——." I answered, "Shoot away; I am not afraid of your pistols."

By this time Stephen Markham walked deliberately towards us. When they saw him coming, they turned their pistols from me to him, and threatened his life if he came any nearer; but he paid no attention to their threats, and continued to advance nearer. They then turned their pistols on me again, jamming them against my side, with their fingers on the triggers, and ordered Markham to stand still or they would shoot me through, As Markham was advancing rapidly towards me, I said, "You are not going to resist the officers, are you, Brother Markham?" He replied, "No, not if they are officers: I know the law too well for that."

They then hurried me off, put me in a wagon without serving any process, and were for hurrying me off without letting me see or bid farewell to my family or friends, or even allowing me time to get my hat or clothes, or even suffer my wife or children to bring them to me. I then said, "Gentlemen, if you have any legal process, I wish to obtain a writ of habeas corpus," and was answered, "G——d—— you, you shan't have one." They still continued their punching me on both sides with their pistols.

Markham then sprung and seized the horses by the bits, and held them until my wife could bring my hat and coat. Reynolds and Wilson again threatening to shoot Markham, who said, "There is no law on earth that requires a sheriff to take a prisoner without his clothes." Fortunately at this moment I saw a man passing, and said to him, "These men are kidnapping me, and I wish a writ of habeas corpus to deliver myself out of their hands." But as he did not appear to go, I told Markham to go, and he immediately proceeded to Dixon on horseback, where the sheriff also proceeded with me at full speed, without even allowing me to speak to my family or bid them goodbye. The officers held their pistols with the muzzles jamming into my side for more than eight miles, and they only desisted on being reproached by Markham for their cowardice in so brutally ill-treating an unarmed, defenseless prisoner. On arriving at the house of Mr. McKennie, the tavern-keeper, I was thrust into a room and guarded there, without being allowed to see anybody; and fresh horses were ordered to be ready in five minutes.

I again stated to Reynolds, "I wish to get counsel," when he answered, "G——d—— you, you shan't have counsel: one word more, G——d—— you, and I'll shoot you." "What is the use of this so often?" said I. "I have repeatedly told you to shoot; and I now tell you again to shoot away!" I saw a person passing and shouted to him through the window, "I am falsely imprisoned here, and I want a lawyer." Lawyer Edward Southwick came, and had the door banged in his face, with the old threat of shooting him if he came any nearer.

Another lawyer (Mr. Shepherd G. Patrick) afterwards came and received the same treatment, which began to cause considerable excitement in Dixon.

A Mr. Lucien P. Sanger asked Markham what was the matter, when he told him all, and stated that the sheriff intended to drag me away immediately to Missouri, and prevent my taking out a writ of habeas corpus.

Sanger soon made this known to Mr. Dixon, the owner of the house, and his friends, who gathered around the hotel door, and gave Reynolds to understand that if that was their mode of doing business in Missouri, they had another way of doing it in

Dixon. They were a law-abiding people and Republicans, and gave Reynolds to understand that he should not take me away without giving me the opportunity of a fair trial, and that I should have justice done me; but that if he persisted in his course, they had a very summary way of dealing with such people.

Mr. Reynolds finding further resistance to be useless, allowed Mr. Patrick and Mr. Southwick to come into the room to me, (but Wilson was inside guarding the door, and Reynolds guarded the outside of the door) when I told them I had been taken prisoner by these men without process; I had been insulted and abused by them. I showed them my flesh, which was black for about eighteen inches in circumference on each side, from their punching me with their pistols; and I wanted them to sue out a writ of habeas corpus, whereupon Reynolds swore he should only wait half-an-hour to give me a chance. A messenger was immediately sent by Mr. Dixon to Mr. Chamberlain, the master-in-chancery, who lived six miles distant, and, another message to Cyrus H. Walker, who happened to be near, to have them come down and get out the writ of habeas corpus.

A writ was sued out by Markham before a justice of the peace against Reynolds and Wilson for threatening his life. They were taken into custody by the constable. He sued out another writ for assault and threatening my life, whereupon they were again arrested.

At this time Markham rushed into the room and put a pistol (unobserved) into my pocket, although Reynolds and Wilson had their pistols cocked at the same time and were threatening to shoot him.

About midnight he sued out a writ for a violation of the law in relation to writs of habeas corpus, Wilson having transferred me to the custody of Reynolds, for the purpose of dragging me to Missouri, and thereby avoiding the effect and operation of said writ, contrary to law, which was put over to be heard at ten o'clock tomorrow morning; and I was conducted back to the room and guarded through the night.

Saturday, June 24—As my favorite horse, Joe Duncan, was somewhat jaded, with being ridden so hastily by Brother Clayton, I hired a man with his horse and buggy to carry Brother Clayton to Rock Island, where the steamer *Amaranth* fortunately came in about fifteen minutes, on which he took passage to Nauvoo, to inform my brother Hyrum of what was being done, and request him to send me some assistance forthwith.

About eight, the master-in-chancery arrived and issued a writ of habeas corpus returnable before the Hon. John D. Caton, Judge of the 9th Judicial Circuit at Ottawa, which was duly served on Reynolds and Wilson.

Mr. Cyrus Walker, who was out electioneering to become the representative for Congress, told me that he could not find time to be my lawyer unless I could promise him my vote. He being considered the greatest criminal lawyer in that part of Illinois, I determined to secure his aid, and promised him my vote. He afterwards went to Markham and joyfully said, "I am now sure of my election, as Joseph Smith has promised me his vote, and I am going to defend him."

At ten a.m. another writ was issued—this time from the Circuit Court of Lee county, against Reynolds and Wilson for private damage and for false imprisonment, claiming ten thousand dollars damages upon the ground that the writ issued by the governor of Illinois was a void writ in law; upon which said writ they were held to bail in ten thousand dollars each, and they had to send to Missouri for bondsmen and were placed in the custody of the sheriff of Lee county.

Reynolds and Wilson felt bad when these last writs were served on them, and began to cool in their conduct a little; after which they also obtained a writ of habeas corpus, for the purpose of being discharged before Judge Caton.

I was conveyed by Reynolds and Wilson, upon the first writ of habeas corpus, towards Ottawa, as far as Pawpaw Grove, thirty-two miles, where I was again abused by Reynolds and Wilson, which was observed by the landlord.

Esquire Walker sent Mr. Campbell, sheriff of Lee county, to my assistance, and he came and slept by me. In the morning certain men wished to see me, but I was not allowed to see them.

The news of my arrival had hastily circulated about the neighborhood; and very early in the morning the largest room in the hotel was filled with citizens, who were anxious to hear me preach and requested me to address them.

Sheriff Reynolds entered the room and said, pointing to me, "I wish you to understand this man is my prisoner, and I want you to disperse: you must not gather around here in this way." Upon which Mr. David Town, an aged gentleman, who was lame and carried a large hickory walking-stick, advanced towards Reynolds, bringing his hickory upon the floor, and said:

"You damned infernal puke, we'll learn you to come here and interrupt gentlemen. Sit down there, (pointing to a very low chair) and sit still. Don't open your head till General Smith gets through talking. If you never learned manners in Missouri, we'll teach you that gentlemen are not to be imposed upon by a niggerdriver. You cannot kidnap men here, if you do in Missouri; and if you attempt it here, there's a committee in this grove that will sit on your case; and, sir, it is the highest tribunal in the United States, as from its decision there is no appeal."

Reynolds, no doubt aware that the person addressing him was the head of a committee who had prevented the settlers on the public domain from being imposed upon by land speculators, sat down in silence while I addressed the assembly for an hour-and-a-half on the subject of marriage, my visitors having requested me to give them my views of the laws of God respecting marriage. My freedom commenced from that hour.

Immediately after I left Dixon, my wife and children started with my carriage from Inlet Grove for Nauvoo being driven by her nephew, Lorenzo D. Wasson.

Sunday, June 25—At Pawpaw Grove it was ascertained that Judge Caton was on a visit to New York, whereupon Reynolds, Wilson, Walker, Southwick, Patrick, Dixon, Stephen Markham and myself, with others, started about eight a.m., and returned to the town of Dixon, arriving about four p.m., when I was again locked in a room and guarded through the night.

The water has fallen in the Mississippi more than a foot since last Sunday. At ten a.m., meeting at the temple. Elder Lyman Wight preached on charity; and in the afternoon, Elder Maginn was preaching, when my brother Hyrum went to the stand and requested the brethren to meet him at the Masonic Hall in thirty minutes.

The brethren immediately went there in such numbers that one fourth of them could not get into the room; so they adjourned to the green and formed a hollow square, when my brother Hyrum informed them that Elder William Clayton had arrived about two, and told him that Joseph H. Reynolds, sheriff of Jackson county, Missouri, and Harmon T. Wilson, of Carthage, had come upon me by surprise and arrested me, and related the occurrence as far as known, up to my arrival in Dixon. He wanted a company to go up to my assistance and see that I had my rights. He called for volunteers, when upwards of three hundred volunteered, from whom they selected such as were wanted.

Generals Law and Charles C. Rich started the same evening, with a company of about one hundred and seventy-five men on horseback. Previous to starting, Elder Wilford Woodruff went to the company and donated a barrel of rifle powder, when every man filled his horn or flask.

Wilson Law declared he would not go a step unless he could have money to bear his expenses, upon which Elder Brigham Young said the money should be forthcoming, although he did not know at the time where he could raise a dollar. In about thirty minutes he got on the track, and in the course of two hours he had borrowed seven hundred dollars, and put it in the hands of Hyrum Smith and Wilson Law, to defray the expenses of the expedition. About seventy-five on board the *Maid of Iowa*, with Captain Dan Jones, went up the Illinois river for Peoria, and to examine the steamboats, suspecting I might be a prisoner on board one of them, as they supposed me on the road to Ottawa.

Several of the Pottawatamie Indians called to see the Nauvoo House and temple. They wanted to talk, but their interpreter could not speak much.

The writ of habeas corpus (the one first issued and made returnable before Judge Caton at Ottawa) was returned endorsed thereon, "Judge absent," when another writ of habeas corpus was issued at seven a.m. by the master-in-chancery, and was worded at Colonel Markham's request, "Returnable before the nearest tribunal in the Fifth Judicial District authorized to hear and determine writs of habeas corpus;" and the sheriff of Lee county served it on them (Reynolds and Wilson) in a few minutes afterwards. I, my lawyers, Markham, Dixon and other friends held a council and arranged to start before nine a.m., to go before Judge Stephen A. Douglas, at Quincy, a distance of about two hundred and sixty miles. I employed Mr. Lucien P. Sanger with the stage coach to convey us on our journey towards Quincy.

After these arrangements were made, I sent Markham with a letter to General Wilson Law, directing him to meet me at Monmouth on Wednesday evening, with sufficient force to prevent my being kidnapped into Missouri, as I well knew that the whole country was swarming with men anxious to carry me there and kill me, without any shadow of law or justice, although they well knew that I had not committed any crime worthy of death or bonds.

Monday, June 26—It was reported that there were state writs in Nauvoo to take Lyman Wight, Parley P. Pratt, and Alexander McRae to Missouri, who armed themselves to prevent being kidnapped.

Tuesday, June 27—I started with the company, and took dinner at Genesseo. At about two p.m., we resumed our journey. While crossing Fox River, I requested Reynolds to give me the privilege of riding on horseback, which he refused; but, by the intercession of Sheriff Campbell and Mr. Cyrus Walker, Walker took my seat in the stage-coach, and I his in the buggy with Mr. Montgomery, son-in-law and law student of Cyrus Walker. In about two miles we met Peter W. Conover and William L. Cutler, and shook hands with both of them at the same time, and could not refrain from tears at seeing the first of my friends to come to meet me, and then said to Mr. Montgomery, "I am not going to Missouri this time. These are my boys."

I next enquired how many were with them, and was answered, There were ten started, but they had sent one with my letter to Wilson Law, and two to Monmouth.

While we were talking, Markham, with Captain Thomas Grover, and the other five brethren, rode up. At the same time, the company who started with me from Dixon rode up. I then said to Reynolds, "Now, Reynolds, I can have the privilege of riding old Joe Duncan," and mounted my favorite horse; and the entire company then rode towards a farm house, where we made a halt.

Reynolds and Wilson, who trembled much, then rode up to Conover, who was an old acquaintance of Wilson's; when Conover asked Wilson, "What is the matter with you? Have you got the ague?" Wilson replied, "No."

Reynolds asked, "Is Jem Flack in the crowd?" and was answered, "He is not now, but you will see him tomorrow about this time." "Then," said Reynolds, "I am a dead man; for I know him of old." Conover told him not to be frightened, for he would not be hurt.

Reynolds stood trembling like an aspen-leaf, when Markham walked up to him and shook hands with him, Reynolds said, "Do I meet you as a friend? I expected to be a dead man when I met you again." Markham replied, "We are friends, except in law: That must have its course."

The company moved on to Andover, where the sheriff of Lee

county requested lodgings for the night for all the company. I was put up into a room and locked up with Captain Grover. It was reported to me that some of the brethren had been drinking whisky that day in violation of the Word of Wisdom.

I called the brethren in and investigated the case, and was satisfied that no evil had been done.

Here Conover exchanged with me one of Allen's four-inch barrel six-shooter revolvers for the single shooter which Markham had slipped into my pocket at Dixon.

About eight p.m., Reynolds, Wilson, and the landlord consulted about sending out to raise a company to take me by force, and run with me to the mouth of Rock River on the Mississippi, as there was a company of men ready to kidnap me over the river. Markham overheard the conversation, and notified the sheriff of Lee county, who immediately ordered a guard placed, so that no one might pass in or out of the house during the night.

Markham started at daybreak, and went about twenty miles, passing through Andover at eight a.m.; and about nine he met Captain Thomas Grover and a company of ten men, to whom he delivered my message. Held a council and forwarded it on to General Law by Philander Colton. Markham turned back with the company.

My wife and children arrived in Nauvoo this evening, having burned off one arm of the carriage going home.

Many strangers reported in the city; the watch was doubled in the night.

Wednesday, June 28—We left Andover about eight o'clock; went to a little grove at the head of Elleston creek, where we stayed an hour to feed our animals. Reynolds said, "Now, we will go from here to the mouth of Rock River and take steamboat to Quincy." Markham said, "No; for we are prepared to travel, and will go by land."

Wilson and Reynolds both spoke and said, "No, by G——, we won't; we will never go by Nauvoo alive;" and both drew their pistols on Markham, who turned round to Sheriff Campbell, of Lee county, saying, "When these men took Joseph a prisoner, they took his arms from him, even to his pocket-knife. They are now prisoners of yours, and I demand of you to take their arms from them, that is according to law."

They refused to give them up, when the sheriff was told, "If you cannot take the arms from them, there are men enough here, and you can summon a posse to do it; for it is plain to be seen that they are dangerous men."

Reynolds and Wilson then reluctantly gave up their arms to the sheriff. The company then started, taking the middle road towards Nauvoo to within six miles of Monmouth, and stopped at a farmhouse, having traveled about forty miles; got there about sundown, and called for supper and lodging.

Peter W. Conover laid down at the S.W. corner of the building outside the house. In about ten minutes, Reynolds and Wilson came out of the house with the son of the landlord. They talked for some time, and came to the conclusion to take the carriage horses, go to Monmouth, raise a mob, and come to the farmhouse in the night, seize Joseph, and convey him to the Mississippi river, and take him to Missouri, as they had a steamboat in readiness at the mouth of Rock River for that purpose.

After completing their plan of operations, Reynolds, Wilson and the boy separated and went towards the stable. Conover, who had heard the plot unobserved, immediately rose and came to me, and told me what he had just heard.

I consulted with Cyrus Walker, the landlord, and Sheriff Campbell, who took Reynolds and Wilson into his custody, and put them in the upper room, placing a guard of two men at the door, with orders not to allow any man to pass in or out of the house, except the landlord, who, as soon as he was told of the attempt to get his son into difficulty, put a stop to his proceedings at once.

Some anxiety at Nauvoo about so many strangers and suspicous characters being in the city.

Thursday, June 29—Continued our journey this morning, leaving Monmouth on our left, and Oquaka five miles on our right; and after passing Monmouth about three miles, William Empy, Gilbert Rolfe, James Flack, and three others met us.

I called Flack to my side and told him not to injure Reynolds, whatever provocation he had previously received from him, as I had pledged myself to protect him, and requested Flack to bury his feelings against Reynolds.

Reynolds then got out of the stage, exchanged seats with one of the horsemen, and Flack and Reynolds rode by themselves about a quarter-of-a-mile, when they again joined the company and rode together. The company continued to Henderson River, and took dinner at a farmhouse owned by Mr. Alanson Hagerman.

While staying at this farmhouse, General Wilson Law, and William Law, and about sixty men came up in several little squads. I walked out several rods to meet the company. William and Wilson Law jumped from their horses, and unitedly hugged and kissed me, when many tears of joy were shed.

I consulted with my lawyers, and told them that Nauvoo was the nearest place where writs of habeas corpus could be heard and determined. They examined the subject and decided I was correct, when we turned our steps towards Nauvoo, which gladdened my heart at the prospect of soon being in the midst of my friends again. I sent a messenger to inform the citizens of Nauvoo of the glad change; and I requested Conover to ride ahead to Mr. Michael Crane's, on Honey creek, and call for supper for one hundred men.

After dinner we traveled about fifteen miles. On arriving at Crane's, I jumped out of the buggy, and instead of going through the gate or climbing the fence, walked up and jumped over the fence without touching it. Mr. Crane ran out and embraced me, and bade me welcome.

A flock of turkeys and chickens were killed, and a substantial supper was provided for all; and the company feasted, sang, and had a happy time that night. I showed my sides to Mr. Crane and the company, which still continued black and blue from the bruises I had received from the pistols of Reynolds and Wilson, while riding from Inlet Grove to Dixon eight days ago.

Friday, June 30—A messenger started from my company in the night, and arrived in Nauvoo early in the morning, saying that I and the company would be in the city about noon. Dr. Willard Richards and Wilford Woodruff arranged the seats in the court-room, preparatory to my arrival.

At half-past ten o'clock, the Nauvoo Brass Band and Martial Band started with Emma and my brother Hyrum to meet me; also a train of carriages, containing a number of the principal inhabitants.

At eight a.m., the company with me again started; arrived at the Big Mound about half-past ten, where the brethren decorated the bridles of their horses with the flowers of the prairie, and were met by a number of the citizens. Continued our journey; and at 11:25 a.m., I was gladdened, when opposite my brother Hyrum's farm, about one-and-a-half miles east of the temple, with seeing the train approaching towards us; and I directed Colonel Rockwood to place my life guards in their appropriate position in the procession. I was in a buggy with Mr. Montgomery. Sheriff Reynolds and Wilson, with my three lawyers, Cyrus Walker, Shepherd G. Patrick, and Edward Southwick, were in the stage coach with Lucien P. Sanger, the stage proprietor. Mr. Campbell, the sheriff of Lee county, and a company of about 140 were with me on horseback.

I was a prisoner in the hands of Reynolds, the agent of Missouri, and Wilson, his assistant. They were prisoners in the hands of Sheriff Campbell, who had delivered the whole of us into the hands of Colonel Markham, guarded by my friends, so that none of us could escape.

When the company from the city came up, I said I thought I would now ride a little easier; got out of the buggy; and, after embracing Emma and my brother Hyrum, who wept tears of joy at my return, as did also most of the great company who surrounded us, (it was a solemn, silent meeting) I mounted my favorite horse, "Old Charley," when the band struck up "Hail Columbia," and proceeded to march slowly towards the city, Emma riding by my side into town.

The carriages having formed in line, the company with me followed next, and the citizens fell in the rear. As we approached the city, the scene continued to grow more interesting; the streets were generally lined on both sides with the brethren and sisters, whose countenances were joyous and full of satisfaction to see me once more safe.

I was greeted with the cheers of the people and firing of guns and cannon. We were obliged to appoint a number of men to keep the streets open for the procession to pass, and arrived at my house about one o'clock, where my aged mother was at the door to embrace me, with tears of joy rolling down her cheeks, and my children clung around me with feelings of enthusiastic and enraptured pleasure. Little Fred exclaimed, "Pa, the Missourians won't take you away again; will they?" The friends from Dixon gazed with astonishment and rapture to see the enthusiastic attachment of my family and the Saints towards me.

The multitude seemed unwilling to disperse until after I had arisen on the fence and told them, "I am out of the hands of the Missourians again, thank God. I thank you all for your kindness and love to me. I bless you all in the name of Jesus Christ. Amen. I shall address you at the grove, near the temple, at four o'clock this afternoon."

When I went to dinner with my family, Reynolds and Wilson were placed at the head of the table, with about 50 of my friends, and were served with the best that the table afforded, by my wife, whom they refused to allow me to see, when they so cruelly arrested and ill-treated me, which contrasted strongly with their treatment to me when I was first arrested by them, and until my friends met me.

As soon as we arrived in the city, the Municipal Court came together, when I told them, "The writ of habeas corpus granted by the master in chancery at Dixon was made returnable to the nearest court having jurisdiction; and you are that court."

Mr. Reynolds refused to submit to the writ, but submitted to the attachment, and I was delivered into the hands of the marshal of the city. I told the court I had an appointment to preach to the people, and requested the privilege from the court, which they granted, and adjourned until eight o'clock tomorrow morning.

At five p.m., I went to the grove and delivered an address to the public. While I was speaking, Reynolds and Wilson started for Carthage, in company with Lawyer Davis, of Carthage, threatening to raise the militia and come again and take me out of Nauvoo.

Sunday, July 2—A large congregation met at the grove, near the temple, and heard an interesting address from Elder Orson Hyde. After he closed, Messrs. Walker, Southwick, Patrick, and Wasson spoke on the stand, stating that I had subjected myself to the law in every particular, and had treated my persecutors and kidnappers with courtesy and kindness. They also spoke on the unlawful conduct of my enemies.

Judge Adams came from Carthage and stated that Wilson and Reynolds were inciting the people to mobocracy, and sending a petition to Governor Ford for a posse to retake me.

A petition to the governor, praying him not to issue any more writs, was immediately made out, and signed by about 150 citizens of Nauvoo; and also a remonstrance against the Carthage proceedings was gotten up. Signed and forwarded the same to Carthage by Messrs. Southwick and Patrick.

Colonel Markham returned from Carthage in the evening, and reported that on his arriving at Carthage, he found that Reynolds and Wilson had filed their affidavits, that he (Markham) had with armed force taken Joseph Smith out of their hands at the head of Elleston Grove, and that they had also got up a petition, which was signed by the inhabitants of Carthage, and sent it to Governor Ford by the hands of Reynolds and Wilson, requesting him to raise a posse comitatus, and they would come to Nauvoo and take me.

They were to start by the mail early this morning; and Markham requested Jacob Backenstos to go with the mail to Governor Ford and request him to suspend all proceedings until documents would be got to show the true state of the case.

Monday, July 10—I rode out with Emma to the farm.

Tuesday, July 11—I rode out with my family in the carriage.

Wednesday, July 12—I received the following revelation in the presence of my brother Hyrum and Elder William Clayton:

See Doctrine and Covenants 132.

Hyrum took the revelation and read it to Emma.

I directed Clayton to make out deeds of certain lots of land to Emma and the children.

Elders Brigham Young, Wilford Woodruff, and George A. Smith arrived in Louisville, and visited Mr. Porter, the "Kentucky baby!" 7 feet 7 inches high, and weighing 250 pounds.

Thursday, July 13—I was in conversation with Emma most of the day, and approved of the revised laws of the legion.

Elders Ezra T. Benson, Q. S. Sparks, and Noah Rogers preached at Cabbotville, Mass. While Elder Rogers was preaching, some person threw stones through the windows, and one hit Elder Benson on the thigh. The mob threw stones at them which flew like hail, when they left the room, but did not injure the brethren.

Friday, July 14—Spent the day at home. I was visited by a number of gentlemen and ladies who had arrived from Quincy on a steamboat. They manifested kind feelings.

Saturday, July 15—Spent the day at home. Weather very hot. A shower this morning wet the ground one inch.

At six p.m. went with my family and about one hundred others on a pleasure excursion on the *Maid of Iowa*, from the Nauvoo House landing to the north part of the city, and returned at dusk.

A theatrical performance in the evening by Mr. Chapman.

Sunday, July 16—Preached in the morning and evening at the stand in the grove, near the west of the temple, concerning a man's foes being those of his own household.

"The same spirit that crucified Jesus is in the breast of some who profess to be Saints in Nauvoo. I have secret enemies in the city intermingling with the Saints," etc. Said I would not prophesy any more, and proposed Hyrum to hold the office of prophet to the Church, as it was his birthright.

"I am going to have a reformation, and the Saints must regard Hyrum, for he has the authority, that I might be a priest of the Most High God; and slightly touched upon the subject of the everlasting covenant, showing that a man and his wife must enter into that covenant in the world, or he will have no claim on her in the next world. But on account of the unbelief of the people, I cannot reveal the fullness of these things at present."

Tuesday, July 18—I was making hay on my farm.

Monday, July 24—This morning I had a long conversation with Mr. Hoge, the Democratic candidate for Congress. I showed him the corruption and folly of the governor's sending an armed force to take me, &c., and told him this made the 38th vexatious lawsuit against me for my religion.

Exhibition of Divine, the Fire King, in the court room.

Settled with William and Wilson Law. They were $167 in my debt, for which William Law gave his note.

Tuesday, July 25—Being sick, I lay on my bed in the middle of the room; visited by Dr. Willard Richards.

Elder Noah Rogers administered to Sister Webster at Farmington, Connecticut, who had been unable to walk for several years past.

Wednesday, July 26—Sister Webster arose from her bed this morning and walked.

Tuesday, August 1—The temple is progressing steadily. The walls of the noble edifice continue to rise, and its completion is looked forward to with great interest and anxiety by many.

All kinds of improvements are going on rapidly in Nauvoo and vicinity. Houses are going up in every direction in the city and farms are being inclosed without. "The wilderness" will soon "blossom as the rose."

Elder Luman A. Shurtliff writes that he has traveled in the New England states, and recently baptized twenty persons.

Wednesday, August 2—I was a little easier today and rode out to Jacob Baum's to borrow money. In the evening conversing with Dr. J. M. Bernhisel.

A subscription has been got up to build a house for Elder Willard Richards, to which I subscribed a city lot. The brethren subscribed $25 cash, 10 cords of stone, 30 bushels of lime, 105 days of work, $59 in work, 15,900 bricks, glass, lumber and other materials, together with a quantity of produce. I hope the day is not far distant when my clerk will have a comfortable house for his family.

Friday, August 4—My health improving, I rode out to the farm. In the evening went with Emma to visit Elder Cahoon, where I met my brother Hyrum and his wife.

Sunday, August 6—Meeting at the stand. Elder Parley P. Pratt preached on testimony.

When he closed, I told the people I would preach my sermon next Sunday, I was not able today; but I would now speak on another subject, viz., the election.

Emma started to St. Louis to transact some business for me, it not being prudent for me to go to Missouri.

Monday, August 7—Election of Representatives to Congress and state and county officers, the Democratic ticket prevailing in Nauvoo by an overwhelming majority.

Saturday, August 12—Emma returned from St. Louis. I was sick at home.

Robert D. Foster having on Monday last been elected school commissioner, and George W. Thatcher, clerk of county commissioner's court, they went to Carthage to give bonds and take oath of office. When before the court, Harmon T. Wilson, John Wilson,

Franklin J. Morrill and Prentice, and twelve or fifteen others, came in armed with hickory clubs, knives, dirks and pistols, and told the court they must not approve the bonds (of the above officers elect) or swear them into office; if they did blood would be spilt; and pledged their word, honor and reputation, to keep them out of office and put down the Mormons. The bonds, however, were accepted, and the mob gave notice of a meeting of the anti-Mormons of Hancock county for Saturday next, to consider about the Mormons retaining their offices.

Elder Willard Richards was sworn into office as recorder of the city of Nauvoo.

Tuesday, August 22—Held mayor's court, and fined Stephen Wilkinson for selling spirits without a license.

We constantly hear rumors that the people of Carthage are determined to raise a mob to drive the Mormons out of the state.

Friday, August 25—My brother Hyrum in the office, conversing with me about the new revelation upon celestial marriage.

Rain in gentle showers through the day, being the first of any amount that has fallen in Nauvoo since the 1st of June. The earth has been exceedingly dry, and the early potatoes nearly destroyed. Corn has been stunted in its growth and even vines much injured by the drouth.

Saturday, August 26—Six hundred houses destroyed by fire in Kingston, Jamaica: estimated damage, $1,500,000.

The U.S. steam frigate *Missouri* destroyed by fire.

Elder Jonathan Dunham returned from his exploring excursion west.

Sunday, September 10—Cold, and considerable rain. Kindled a fire in the office for the first time this fall. This is the first rain of any consequence since the first of June. There have been occasional—say three or four slight showers, but not enough to wet the potatoe hills, and the vegetables in the gardens have generally stopped growing, on account of the drougth. Even corn is seriously injured—much of it by a worm in the ear. Early potatoes are scarcely worth digging.

Monday, September 11—Six, p.m., I met with my Brother Hyrum, William Law, Newel K. Whitney, and Willard Richards in my private room, where we had a season of prayer for Brother Law's little daughter, who was sick, and Emma, who was somewhat better.

Tuesday, September 12—Rainy day.

Wednesday, September 13—I attended a lecture at the grove, by Mr. John Finch, a Socialist, from England, and said a few words in reply.

Thursday, September 14—I attended a second lecture on socialism, by Mr. Finch; and after he got through, I made a few remarks, alluding to Sidney Rigdon and Alexander Campbell getting up a community at Kirtland, and of the big fish there eating up all the little fish. I said I did not believe the doctrine.

Mr. Finch replied in a few minutes, and said—"I am the voice of one crying in the wilderness. I am the spiritual prophet—Mr. Smith the temporal."

Elder John Taylor replied to the lecture at some length.

Friday, September 15—I put up a sign. "NAUVOO MANSION."

In consequence of my house being constantly crowded with strangers and other persons wishing to see me, or who had business in the city, I found myself unable to support so much company free of charge, which I have done from the foundation of the Church. My house has been a home and resting-place for thousands, and my family many times obliged to do without food, after having fed all they had to visitors; and I could have continued the same liberal course, had it not been for the cruel and untiring persecution of my relentless enemies. I have been reduced to the necessity of opening "The Mansion" as a hotel. I have provided the best table accommodations in the city; and the Mansion, being large and convenient, renders travelers more comfortable than any other place on the Upper Mississippi. I have erected a large and commodious brick stable, and it is capable of accommodating seventy-five horses at one time, and storing the requisite amount of forage, and is unsurpassed by any similar establishment in the State.

There was an officers' drill in Nauvoo.

Rhoda Ann, daughter of Willard and Jenetta Richards, was born at fifteen minutes to three, p.m., in Nauvoo.

Saturday, September 16—General parade of the Nauvoo Legion near my farm.

Went in company with my staff to the muster, was met by an escort, and arrived before the legion about noon. I was received and saluted with military honors. The legion was dismissed at about one, p.m., for two hours, and I rode home to dinner. I returned about twenty minutes after three, attended the review, and with my staff inspected the legion; after which, I took my post and gave orders.

After the inspection, I made a speech to the legion on their increasing prosperity, and requested the officers to increase the legion in numbers.

I was highly gratified with the officers and soldiers, and I felt extremely well myself.

About sundown the legion was dismissed. I rode home with my staff, highly delighted with the day's performance, and well paid for my services.

Sunday, September 17—I was at meeting; and while Elder Almon W. Babbitt was preaching, I took my post as mayor outside the assembly to keep order and set an example to the other officers.

After preaching, I gave some instructions about order in the congregation, men among women, and women among men, horses in the assembly, and men and boys on the stand who do not belong there, &c.

In the evening Mr. Blodgett, a Unitarian minister, preached. I was gratified with his sermon in general, but differed in opinion on some points, on which I freely expressed myself to his great satisfaction, viz., on persecution making the work spread, like rooting up a flower-garden or kicking back the sun!

Saturday, September 23—Elder Stephen Markham returned from Dixon, the trial of Reynolds and Wilson being postponed till May next.

Bishop George Miller returned from the pinery. He reports the water in Black River so low that they could not get their raft into the Mississippi.

I had an interview with Elder Orson Spencer, from whom I borrowed $75 for the temple.

Thursday, October 5—This morning I rode out with Esquire Butterfield to the farm.

In the afternoon, rode to the prairie to show some of the brethren some land.

Evening, at home, and walked up and down the streets with my scribe. Gave instructions to try those persons who were preaching, teaching, or practicing the doctrine of plurality of wives; for, according to the law, I hold the keys of this power in the last days; for there is never but one on earth at a time on whom the power and its keys are conferred; and I have constantly said no man shall have but one wife at a time, unless the Lord directs otherwise.

Thursday, November 2—We agreed to write a letter to the five candidates for the presidency of the United States, to inquire what their feelings were towards us as a people, and what their course of action would be in relation to the cruelty and oppression that we have suffered from the state of Missouri, if they were elected.

Sunday, November 5—Rode out with mother and others for her health.

At dinner I was taken suddenly sick; went to the door and vomited all my dinner, dislocated my jaw, and raised fresh blood, and had many symptoms of being poisoned.

In the evening a prayer-meeting in the hall over the store.

Mr. Cole having kept a school in the hall for some time, the noise proved a nuisance for the clerks in the history office, and I gave Dr. W. Richards orders to tell Mr. Cole he must find some other room in which to teach school, as the room is needed for councils.

Meeting at the stand. Elder Rigdon preached.

Received a letter from Reuben Hedlock, dated Liverpool,

October 16. He informs me there is a great call for preaching, and many Elders are wanted throughout the British Isles. Much opposition. The Saints are anxious to have the *Star* continue its publication, as 1,600 copies are circulated.

Also received a letter from Hyrum Clark, giving a partial account of the business affairs of the emigration and publishing offices.

Monday, November 6—Domestic affairs kept me busy in the morning, and in the afternoon listened to William W. Phelps giving a relation of his visit to the governor, which amused me.

Tuesday, November 7—Mr. Cole moved the tables back into the hall, when Richards and Phelps called to report that the noise in the school disturbed them in the progress of writing the History. I gave them orders that Cole must look out for another place, as the history must continue and not be disturbed, as there are but few subjects that I have felt a greater anxiety about than my history, which has been a very difficult task, on account of the death of my best clerks and the apostasy of others, and the stealing of records by John Whitmer, Cyrus Smalling and others.

Wednesday, November 8—From nine to eleven, a.m., had an interview with Richards and Phelps, read and heard read part of my history, then attended to settling some accounts with several individuals. In the afternoon, I examined a sample of fringe designed for the pulpits of the temple; and from two to three, conversed with Phelps, Lewis, John Butler and others.

Monday, November 20—Two gentlemen from Vermont put up at the Mansion.

I rode around with them in the afternoon to show them the improvements in the city. In the evening, several of the Twelve and others called to visit me. My family sang hymns, and Elder John Taylor prayed and gave an address, to which they paid great attention, and seemed very much interested.

Tuesday, November 21—Council of the Twelve and others at my old house all day. Dictated to my clerk an appeal to the Green Mountain boys of Vermont, my native State.

Also instructed Elders Richards, Hyde, Taylor and Phelps to write a "Proclamation to the Kings of the Earth."

Wednesday, November 22—Rode out to the prairie with W. Clayton and Lorenzo D. Wasson, and found Arthur Smith cutting timber on my land without my consent, which I objected to.

Prayer-meeting in the evening at the old house. Five deaths in the city during the past week.

Thursday, November 23—Met in council in the old house; then walked down to the river to look at the stream, rocks, &c., about half-past eleven, a.m. Suggested the idea of petitioning Congress for a grant to make a canal over the falls, or a dam to turn the water to the city, so that we might erect mills and other machinery.

Saturday, November 25—In the evening the high council sat on the case of Harrison Sagers, charged with seduction, and having stated that I had taught it was right. Charge not sustained. I was present with several of the Twelve, and gave an address tending to do away with every evil, and exhorting them to practice virtue and holiness before the Lord; told them that the Church had not received any permission from me to commit fornication, adultery, or any corrupt action; but my every word and action has been to the contrary. If a man commit adultery, he cannot receive the celestial kingdom of God. Even if he is saved in any kingdom, it cannot be the celestial kingdom. I did think that the many examples that have been made manifest, such as John C. Bennett's and others, were sufficient to show the fallacy of such a course of conduct.

I condemned such actions *in toto*, and warned the people present against committing such evils; for it will surely bring a curse upon any person who commits such deeds.

Saturday, December 2—Prayer-meeting from one to six p.m., in the assembly room over the store. Orson Hyde, Parley P. Pratt, Wilford Woodruff, George A. Smith, and Orson Spencer received their endowments and further instructions in the priesthood. About thirty-five persons present.

Sunday, December 3—I arrived at the assembly room about noon: found all present, except Hyrum and his wife. He had slipped and turned his knee-joint backward, and sprained the large muscle of his leg, and I had been ministering unto him. Emma had been unwell during the night. After the meeting was organized, William W. Phelps read my "Appeal to the Green Mountain Boys," which was dedicated by prayer after all had spoken upon it. We also prayed for Nathan Pratt, who was very sick, Hyrum, and others. I afterwards instructed them in the things of the priesthood.

Monday, December 4—At six in the evening, I attended the adjourned meeting of citizens in the assembly room, which was crowded with a select congregation. Many could not get admission. There were two Missourians present. I made some observations at the opening of the meeting, requested them to be calm and cool, but let the spirit of '76 burn in their bosoms, and when occasion requires, say little, but act; and when the mob comes, mow a hole through them.

My "Appeal to the Green Mountain Boys" was read by W. W. Phelps. Elder Parley P. Pratt read his "Appeal to the State of New York."

My clerk, Willard Richards, read the memorial to Congress, when the assembly unanimously voted their approbation of the memorial, when I spoke two-and-a-half hours, relating many circumstances which transpired in Missouri, not mentioned in the memorial. I have already had thirty-eight vexatious lawsuits, and have paid Missouri $150,000 for land. I borrowed $500 of Judge Young in Washington, to pay the expenses of the party that accompanied me, and had to borrow of others.

Daniel Avery and his son were kidnapped from the neighborhood of Warsaw by a company of Missourians, assisted by some anti-Mormons of the county, and carried into Missouri.

Thursday, December 7—The German brethren met at the

assembly room at six p.m., and chose Bishop Daniel Garn as their Presiding Elder, and organized to have preaching in their native language.

Sunday, December 10—Rainy day. I stayed at home.

A prayer-meeting held this evening in the assembly room. I was not present.

Brigham Young presided. Several sick persons were prayed for.

By letter from J. White, deputy sheriff of Clark county, Missouri, I learn that Mr. Daniel Avery is in Marion county prison, without trial. The sheriff requests several men to go there as witnesses. It is evidently a trap to get some more of our people into their power. When I was in prison in Missouri, my witnesses were arrested before they got into court to testify, except one, who was kicked out of the court by an officer, Lieutenant Cook, who damned him, and ordered some of his company to shoot him. After which, the state's attorney, Birch, turned to me tauntingly, saying, "Why the hell don't you bring on your witnesses?" and Judge King laughed at my discomfiture. The Saints have had enough of Missouri mob justice.

Thursday, December 14—At home.

Philander Avery arrived in Nauvoo, having made his escape from his kidnappers in Missouri.

Friday, December 15—I awoke this morning in good health, but was soon suddenly seized with a great dryness of the mouth and throat, sickness of the stomach, and vomited freely. My wife waited on me, assisted by my scribe, Dr. Willard Richards, and his brother Levi, who administered to me herbs and mild drinks. I was never prostrated so low, in so short a time, before; but by evening was considerably revived.

Very warm for the season.

Saturday, December 16—This morning I felt considerably better; arose at 10, and sat all day in the city council, which was held in my house for my accommodation.

Sunday, December 17—Mr. King Follet, one of the constables of Hancock county, started with ten men this afternoon to arrest

John Elliott for kidnapping Daniel Avery, upon a warrant granted by Aaron Johnson, Esq., J.P.

Monday, December 18—After dinner, Constable Follet returned with John Elliott, a schoolmaster, when an examination was had before Esq. Johnson, in the assembly room. Elliott was found guilty of kidnapping Avery, and bound over in the sum of $3,000 to the circuit court of Carthage for trial.

About 10 p.m., two young men arrived as express, stating that a mob was collecting at Warsaw, also at Colonel Levi Williams' house; and messengers had gone to the mob in Missouri to reinforce their number there.

Tuesday, December 19—At home. About 9 a.m., a part of the company who went with Hosea Stout returned, and stated that they went within two miles of Colonel Williams', when they were informed that a body of men, armed with rifles, &c., were collected at his house, and he judged it prudent to return for weapons and help; also that Brother Chester Loveland told them that he had seen thirty armed men following Constable King Follett some miles on his way, when he had Elliott in custody.

Esq. Johnson immediately wrote to Loveland to have him come to Nauvoo and make affidavit of the warlike movements of the mob, that he might send to the governor.

I directed my clerks to make copies of the affidavits respecting the kidnapping of the Averys to send to Governor Ford, that he might be left without excuse, although he may probably not read them.

At one p.m. I was present when the legion paraded near the temple, were inspected by the officers, and instructed to prepare themselves with arms and ammunition and to hold themselves in readiness, for a moment's notice. Brother Henry Boley was shot severely under the arm by the accidental discharge of his gun.

Thursday, December 21—About one o'clock in the morning I was alarmed by the firing of a gun, got up, and went down to the river bank to see the guard, and inquire the cause of it. To my surprise, they had not heard it, although I felt sure it was fired in Montrose.

The morning proved it to be correct, some rowdies in Montrose had been firing in the night.

At noon met with the city council which voted that Councilor Orson Pratt present the Memorial and Ordinance to Congress.

Passed "An ordinance to prevent unlawful search or seizure of person or property by foreign (i.e. outside) process in the city of Nauvoo."

I gave instructions to the marshal and policemen to see that all carrion is removed out of the city, and all houses kept in order, to stop the boys when fighting in the streets, and prevent children from floating off on the ice, and correct anything out of order, like fathers; and I offered to build the city jail, if it was left to my dictation, which the council authorized me to do.

Friday, December 22—At home at nine o'clock, a.m., reading a magazine to my children.

A little after twelve went into the store-room occupied by Butler and Lewis, and commenced a conversation with Dr. John F. Charles, to convince him that mobocracy is not justifiable, and that I did not deal in politics.

David Holman, living about two miles from Ramus, went out in the evening with his family visiting. About ten o'clock he discovered his house on fire. The neighbors had inquired how long he would be gone. A man rode to Carthage. A company went up, secured the provisions to themselves, and fired the house.

Warm and pleasant weather.

Monday, December 25—This morning, about one o'clock, I was aroused by an English sister, Lettice Rushton, widow of Richard Rushton, Senior, (who, ten years ago, lost her sight) accompanied by three of her sons, with their wives, and her two daughters, with their husbands, and several of her neighbors, singing, "Mortals, awake! with angels join," &c., which caused a thrill of pleasure to run through my soul. All of my family and boarders arose to hear the serenade, and I felt to thank my Heavenly Father for their visit, and blessed them in the name of the Lord. They also visited my brother

Hyrum, who was awakened from his sleep. He arose and went out of doors. He shook hands with and blessed each one of them in the name of the Lord, and said that he thought at first that a cohort of angels had come to visit him, it was such heavenly music to him.

At home all day. About noon, gave counsel to some brethren who called on me from Morley Settlement, and told them to keep law on their side, and they would come out well enough.

At two o'clock, about fifty couples sat down at my table to dine. While I was eating, my scribe called, requesting me to solemnize the marriage of his brother, Dr. Levi Richards, and Sara Griffiths; but as I could not leave, I referred him to President Brigham Young, who married them.

A large party supped at my house, and spent the evening in music, dancing, &c., in a most cheerful and friendly manner. During the festivities, a man with his hair long and falling over his shoulders, and apparently drunk, came in and acted like a Missourian. I requested the captain of the police to put him out of doors. A scuffle ensued, and I had an opportunity to look him full in the face, when, to my great surprise and joy untold, I discovered it was my long-tried, warm, but cruelly persecuted friend, Orrin Porter Rockwell, just arrived from nearly a year's imprisonment, without conviction, in Missouri.

Daniel Avery was liberated from his imprisonment in Missouri by habeas corpus.

This was, no doubt, on account of our vigilance in communicating with the governor, and endeavoring to prosecute the kidnappers, and continually making public the conduct of Missouri.

Warm day; rain in the evening.

Tuesday, December 26—At home. I rejoiced that Rockwell had returned from the clutches of Missouri, and that God had delivered him out of their hands. Brother Daniel Avery also arrived about dusk this evening; and the Missourians have no longer the pleasure of exulting over any Mormon victims for the present; but their blood-thirstiness will not long be satisfied unless they seek out another victim on whom to glut their malice and vengeance.

Saturday, December 30—At nine a.m., held Mayor's court. Two boys, Roswell and Evander White, were brought up for stealing six hens and a rooster. They were sentenced to pay for the fowls, and to ten days' hard labor each on the streets.

In the afternoon, met in the assembly room with the quorum. William Law and wife were not present. Warm and rainy.

Sunday, December 31st—At home.

In the afternoon, called with Elder Parley P. Pratt to see his wife.

At early candle-light, went to prayer-meeting; administered the sacrament; after which I retired. At midnight, about fifty musicians and singers sang Phelps' New Year's Hymn under my window.

Chapter Sixteen

1844

Monday, January 1, 1844—A cold, blustering rainstorm ushered in the new year.

At sunrise, Thomas Miller, James Leach, James Bridges, and John Frodsham were brought before me by the police, charged with disorderly conduct. Fined Miller $5: the others were discharged.

A large party took a New Year's supper at my house, and had music and dancing till morning. I was in my private room with my family, Elder John Taylor and other friends.

Thursday, January 4—At home.

I took dinner in the north room, and was remarking to Brother Phelps what a kind, provident wife I had—that when I wanted a little bread and milk, she would load the table with so many good things, it would destroy my appetite. At this moment Emma came in, while Phelps, in continuation of the conversation said, "You must do as Bonaparte did—have a little table, just large enough for the victuals you want yourself." Mrs. Smith replied, "Mr. Smith is a bigger man than Bonaparte: he can never eat without his friends." I remarked, "That is the wisest thing I ever heard you say."

Friday, January 5—Can it be possible that the traitor whom Porter Rockwell reports to me as being in correspondence with my Missouri enemies, is one of my quorum? The people in the town were astonished, almost every man saying to his neighbor, "Is it possible that Brother Law or Brother Marks is a traitor, and would deliver Brother Joseph into the hands of his enemies in Missouri?" If not, what can be the meaning of all this? "The righteous are as bold as a lion."

Saturday, January 6—Snow about four inches deep. I rode out with Emma in a sleigh.

The bishops and lesser priesthood met at Henry W. Miller's hall.

Sunday, January 7—At home in the morning. In the afternoon, rode out to my farm, and preached in Brother Cornelius P. Lott's house.

The Twelve Apostles attended meetings and preached in different parts of the city.

At six p.m. attended prayer-meeting with the quorum in the assembly room.

Law and Marks absent.

Monday, January 8—At home in the morning.

At eleven went to my office to investigate a difficulty between John D. Parker and his wife. After laboring with them about two hours, brought about a reconciliation.

Thursday, January 11—The Twelve Apostles gave an invitation to the Saints in Nauvoo to cut and draw for me seventy-five or one hundred cords of wood on the 15th and 16th instant.

Monday, January 29—At ten, a.m., the Twelve Apostles, together with Brother Hyrum and John P. Greene, met at the mayor's office, to take into consideration the proper course for this people to pursue in relation to the coming Presidential election.

The candidates for the office of President of the United States at present before the people are Martin Van Buren and Henry Clay. It is morally impossible for this people, in justice to themselves, to vote for the re-election of President Van Buren—a man who criminally neglected his duties as chief magistrate in the cold and unblushing manner which he did, when appealed to for aid in the Missouri difficulties. His heartless reply burns like a firebrand in the breast of every true friend of liberty—"Your cause is just, but I can do nothing for you."

As to Mr. Clay, his sentiments and cool contempt of the people's rights are manifested in his reply—"You had better go to Oregon for redress," which would prohibit any true lover of our constitutional privileges from supporting him at the ballot-box.

It was therefore moved by Willard Richards, and voted unanimously—that we will have an independent electoral ticket, and that Joseph Smith be a candidate for the next Presidency; and that we use all honorable means in our power to secure his election.

Tuesday, January 30—At eleven, a.m., I went into the office with Colonel Jackson.

One, p.m., held mayor's court at my office, on the case "City versus Thomas Coates." Fined the defendant $25 and costs for beating John Ellison.

A Millerite preached again in the assembly room, and Elder Rigdon replied to him. There was a full house.

Prayer-meeting at Elder Brigham Young's.

Wednesday, January 31—Eleven, a.m., I called at the office, and told Benjamin Winchester to go to Warsaw and preach the first principles of the gospel, get some lexicons, and return home.

Prayer-meeting at Elder Brigham Young's in the evening. There seems to be quite a revival throughout Nauvoo, and an inquiry after the things of God, by all the quorums and the Church in general.

Sunday, February 4—I attended prayer-meeting with the quorum in the assembly room, and made some remarks respecting the hundred and forty-four thousand mentioned by John the Revelator, showing that the selection of persons to form that number had already commenced.

Monday, February 5—In the afternoon, Elder William Weeks

(whom I had employed as architect of the temple) came in for instruction. I instructed him in relation to the circular windows designed to light the offices in the dead work of the arch between stories. He said that round windows in the broad side of a building were a violation of all the known rules of architecture, and contended that they should be semicircular—that the building was too low for round windows. I told him I would have the circles, if he had to make the temple ten feet higher than it was originally calculated; that one light at the centre of each circular window would be sufficient to light the whole room; that when the whole building was thus illuminated, the effect would be remarkably grand. "I wish you to carry out my designs. I have seen in vision the splendid appearance of that building illuminated, and will have it built according to the pattern shown me."

Wednesday, February 7—A piece of doggerel appears in the *Warsaw Message* of this date, entitled "Buckeye's Lamentations for the Want of More Wives," evidently the production of Wilson Law, and breathing a very foul and malicious spirit.

Thursday, February 8—Held mayor's court, and tried two Negroes for attempting to marry white women: fined one $25, and the other $5.

Saturday, February 17—The high council met and settled several cases of difficulty betwixt brethren.

The anti-Mormons held a convention at Carthage, the object being to devise ways and means of expelling the Saints from the State. Among other resolutions was one appointing the 9th of March next as the day of fasting and prayer, wherein the pious of all orders are requested to pray to Almighty God that He would speedily bring the false Prophet Joseph Smith to deep repentance, or that He will make a public example of him and his leading accomplices.

The ice broke up in the river.

Sunday, February 18—Beautiful day. Southwest wind.

A very large assembly of the Saints met at the stand, near the temple, when I preached a lengthy discourse.

Four p.m., went to my office with Hyrum and two gentlemen from St. Louis.

Heard Dr. Richards read my correspondence with Senator Calhoun, and Phelps read my "Views of the Power and Policy of the General Government."

At seven, attended prayer-meeting in the assembly room.

Tuesday, February 20—At ten a.m. went to my office, where the Twelve Apostles and some others met in council with Brothers Mitchell Curtis and Stephen Curtis, who left the pinery on Black river, 1st January. They were sent by Lyman Wight and Bishop Miller to know whether Lyman should preach to the Indians, the Menominees and Chippeways having requested it.

The Chippeways had given Brother Wight some wampum as a token of peace, and the brethren had given them half a barrel of flour and an ox to keep the Indians from starving, and Wight had gone through to Green Bay with them to make a road.

I told them to tell Brother Wight I had no counsel to give him on the subject. He is there on his own ground and must act on his own responsibility, and do what he thinks best in relation to the Indians, understanding the laws and nature of the subject as well as I can here, and he shall never be brought into difficulty about it by us.

I instructed the Twelve Apostles to send out a delegation and investigate the locations of California and Oregon, and hunt out a good location, where we can remove to after the temple is completed, and where we can build a city in a day, and have a government of our own, get up into the mountains, where the devil cannot dig us out, and live in a healthful climate, where we can live as old as we have a mind to.

Warm. The ice floating down the river.

A meeting of the citizens of Hancock county was held at

the court-house in Carthage. Passed a resolution that the second Saturday of March be appointed for a general wolf-hunt, being the same day selected by the convention of the 17th instant for a day of fasting and prayer for my destruction.

Friday, February 23—W. W. Phelps received a letter from John Whitmer in relation to certain records, and a book containing some of the early history of the Church which had been written by my clerks, and was Church property, and which had been fraudulently detained from my possession by John Whitmer; to which Dr. Richards replied.

Met with the Twelve in the assembly room concerning the Oregon and California Exploring Expedition; Hyrum and Sidney present. I told them I wanted an exploration of all that mountain country. Perhaps it would be best to go direct to Santa Fe. "Send twenty-five men: let them preach the gospel wherever they go. Let that man go that can raise $500, a good horse and mule, a double barrel gun, one barrel rifle, and the other smooth bore, a saddle and bridle, a pair of revolving pistols, bowie-knife, and a good sabre. Appoint a leader, and let them beat up for volunteers. I want every man that goes to be a king and a priest. When he gets on the mountains he may want to talk with his God; when with the savage nations have power to govern, &c. If we don't get volunteers, wait till after the election."

George D. Watt said, "Gentlemen, I shall go." Samuel Bent, Joseph A. Kelting, David Fullmer, James Emmett, Daniel Spencer, Samuel Rolfe, Daniel Avery, and Samuel W. Richards, volunteered to go.

Sunday, February 25—I preached at the temple block. Hyrum also preached. Evening I attended prayer-meeting in the assembly room. We prayed that "General Joseph Smith's Views of the Powers and Policy of the United States," might be spread far and wide, and be the means of opening the hearts of the people. I gave some important instructions, and prophesied that within five years we should be out of the power of our old enemies, whether they were apostates or of the world; and told the brethren to record it, that when it comes to pass they need not say they had forgotten the saying.

Some rain in the evening; cloudy and foggy.

Saturday, March 9—Met in the city council, and gave my reasons in favor of the repeal of the hog law. (The subject was discussed at some length.)

Council adjourned for one hour. In the afternoon city council rejected the petition to repeal the hog law.

I proposed to license Hiram Kimball and Mr. Morrison, who own the land opposite to the wharf, to make wharves and collect wharfage; then the city can dispense with a wharf-master; that Kimball and Morrison pay a tax for the landing of every boat; and they could tax the boat, or not, as they liked.

The Female Relief Society met twice in the assembly room, and sanctioned "The Voice of Innocence From Nauvoo," and then adjourned for one week to accommodate others who could not get into the room at either of the meetings.

Our worthy brother, King Follett, died this morning, occasioned by the accidental breaking of a rope, and the falling of a bucket of rock upon him while engaged in walling up a well, and the men above were in the act of lowering the rock to him.

Sunday, March 10—Frost in the night; beautiful day. South wind.

Brother King Follett was buried this day with Masonic honors.

I attended meeting at the stand, and preached on the subject of Elias, Elijah, and Messiah.

Friday, May 10—The court-martial was held in the mayor's office on the charge against Robert D. Foster, surgeon-general, for unbecoming and unofficer-like conduct, &c; Brigadier-General George Miller presiding. The charges were sustained.

A prospectus of the *Nauvoo Expositor* was distributed among the people by the apostates.

The jury of Lee county, Illinois, awarded $40 damages and the costs against Joseph H. Reynolds and Harmon T. Wilson for illegal imprisonment and abuse, which I suffered from them last June in that county.

Tuesday, May 21—A very pleasant morning. I rode out on horseback to the prairie, with Porter Rockwell and Mr. Reid. At 7 a.m., Elders Brigham Young, Heber C. Kimball, Lyman Wight, and about a hundred elders, left this city on the steamer *Osprey* (Captain Anderson) for St. Louis.

I was at home towards night with Emma, who is somewhat better. I shoveled dirt out of the ditch, while Wasson stood on the corner of the fence to watch. An officer arrived having a summons and an attachment to take me to Carthage, but he could not find me. I rode out in the evening to see David Yearsley's child, who was sick, and returned home at 9 p.m.

Wednesday, May 22—At home, watching, as the officers from Carthage were after me.

At 10 a.m., about 40 Indians of the Sacs and Foxes came up in front of the Mansion, four or five of them being mounted, among whom was Black Hawk's brother, Kis-kish-kee, &c. I was obliged to send word I could not see them at present. They encamped in the council chamber afternoon and night. I was with the police on duty, and saw several individuals lurking around.

Very pleasant day.

Thursday, May 23—Emma rather better.

At one p.m., had a talk with the Sac and Fox Indians in my back kitchen. They said—"When our fathers first came here, this land was inhabited by the Spanish; when the Spaniards were driven off, the French came, and then the English and Americans; and our fathers talked a great deal with the Big Spirit." They complained that they had been robbed of their lands by the whites, and cruelly treated.

I told them I knew they had been wronged, but that we had bought this land and paid our money for it. I advised them not to sell any more land, but to cultivate peace with the different tribes and with all men, as the Great Spirit wanted them to be united and to live in peace. "The Great Spirit has enabled me to find a book (showing them the Book of Mormon), which told me about your fathers, and Great Spirit told me, 'You must send to all the tribes that you can, and tell them to live in peace;' and when any of our people come to see you, I want you to treat them as we treat you."

At 3 p.m., the Indians commenced a war dance in front of my old house. Our people commenced with music and firing cannon. After the dance, which lasted about two hours, the firing of cannon closed the exercise, and with our music marched back to the office. Before they commenced dancing, the Saints took up a collection to get the Indians food.

Saturday, May 25—At home, keeping out of the way of the expected writs from Carthage. Towards evening, Edward Hunter and William Marks, of the grand jury returned from Carthage; also Marshal John P. Greene and Almon W. Babbitt, who informed me there were two indictments found against me, one charging me with false swearing on the testimony of Joseph H. Jackson and Robert D. Foster, and one charging me with polygamy, or something else, on the testimony of William Law, that I had told him so! The particulars of which I shall learn hereafter.

Friday, June 7—Robert D. Foster called professedly to make some concessions in order to return to the Church. He wanted a private interview, which I declined. I had some conversation with him in the hall, in the presence of several gentlemen. I told him I would meet with him in the presence of friends. I would choose three or four, and he might choose an equal number, and that I was willing to settle everything on righteous principles. In the evening a report was circulated that Foster had said that I would receive him back on any terms, and give him a hatful of dollars into the bargain.

I went to the printing office about 2 p.m., and instructed Elder John Taylor to answer a certain bill or receipt of George W. Harris.

The first and only number of the *Nauvoo Expositor* was published; edited by Sylvester Emmons.

In the evening I received an extremely saucy and insulting letter from Robert D. Foster. Pleasant evening.

Saturday, June 8—From 10 a.m. to 1 p.m. in city council; also from 3 to 6:30 p.m. The subject the *Nauvoo Expositor* was taken under consideration. An ordinance was passed concerning the city attorney and his duties.

Elder Jedediah M. Grant preached in the Mansion this evening. Thunder and rain this evening and during the night.

Monday, June 10—I was in the city council from 10 a.m., to 1:20 p.m., and from 2:20 p.m. to 6:30 p.m. investigating the merits of the *Nauvoo Expositor*, and also the conduct of the Laws, Higbees, Fosters, and others, who have formed a conspiracy for the purpose of destroying my life, and scattering the Saints or driving them from the state.

An ordinance was passed concerning libels. The council passed an ordinance declaring the *Nauvoo Expositor* a nuisance, and also issued an order to me to abate the said nuisance. I immediately ordered the marshal to destroy it without delay, and at the same time issued an order to Jonathan Dunham, acting Major-General of the Nauvoo Legion, to assist the marshal with the legion, if called upon so to do.

About 8 p.m., the marshal returned and reported that he had removed the press, type, printed paper, and fixtures into the street, and destroyed them. This was done because of the libelous and slanderous character of the paper, its avowed intention being to destroy the municipality and drive the Saints from the city. The posse accompanied by some hundreds of the citizens, returned with the marshal to the front of the Mansion, when I gave them a short address, and told them they had done right and that not a hair of their heads should be hurt for it; that they had executed the orders which were given me by the city council; that I would never submit to have another libelous publication established in the city; that I did not care how many papers were printed in the city, if they would print the truth: but would submit to no libels or slanders from them. I then blessed them in the name of the Lord. This speech was loudly greeted by the assembly with three-times-three cheers. The posse and assembly then dispersed all in good order. Francis M. Higbee and others made some threats.

East wind. Very cold and cloudy.

Tuesday, June 11—I had an interview with Elder G. J. Adams out of doors and then returned home to dinner.

At 2 p.m. I went into court. Many people were present. I talked an hour or two on passing events, the mob party, &c., and told the people I was ready to fight, if the mob compelled me to, for I would not be in bondage. I asked the assembly if they would stand by me, and they cried "Yes" from all quarters. I returned home.

Our communications by mail appear to be cut off, as no part of our extensive correspondence has come to hand by the U.S. mail for the last three weeks, and Dr. Hickok seems to be aware of it. Instructed Dr. Richards to answer Dr. Hickok's letter, and then rode out with O. P. Rockwell.

Elders Jedediah M. Grant and George J. Adams preached at my house in the evening. Cloudy and cool day.

The captain of the steamer *Osprey* called this forenoon at the printing office to see me. I rode with him to his boat, which was at the upper landing. When I came up, Charles A. Foster called the passengers to see the meanest man in the world. Mr. Eaton stopped him, and told the passengers that it was Foster who was the meanest man in the world. Rollison attempted to draw a pistol, but Eaton silenced him, and kept them all down.

David Harvey Redfield reported that last evening, while on the hill, just before the police arrived, Francis M. Higbee said while speaking of the printing press of the *Nauvoo Expositor*, if they lay their hands upon it or break it, they may date their downfall from that very hour, and in ten days there will not be a Mormon left in Nauvoo. What they do, they may expect the same in return. Addison Everett also heard him.

Jason R. Luse reported that Ianthus Rolf said, while the press was burning that before three weeks the Mansion House would be strung to the ground, and he would help to do it; and Tallman Rolf said the city would be strung to the ground within ten days. Moses Leonard also heard him, Joshua Miller being also present.

Bryant (merchant of Nauvoo) said before he would see such things, he would wade to his knees in blood.

It is reported that runners have gone out in all directions to try to get up a mob; and the mobbers are selling their houses in Nauvoo and disposing of their property.

Wednesday, June 12—At 10 a.m. in my office.

At half-past one I was arrested by David Bettisworth.

After the officer got through reading the writ, I referred him to the clause in the writ—"Before me or some other justice of the peace of said county," saying, "We are ready to go to trial before Esquire Johnson or any justice in Nauvoo, according to the requirements of the writ;" but Bettisworth swore he would be damned but he would carry them to Carthage before Morrison, who issued the writ and seemed very wrathy. I asked him if he intended to break the law, for he knew the privilege of the prisoners, and they should have it. I called upon all present to witness that I then offered myself (Hyrum did the same) to go forthwith before the nearest justice of the peace, and also called upon them to witness whether the officer broke the law or not.

I felt so indignant at his abuse in depriving me of the privilege of the statute of Illinois in going before "some other justice," that I determined to take out a writ of habeas corpus.

Tuesday, June 13—In the evening I attended meeting in the Seventies' Hall.

George J. Adams preached and I made some observations afterwards, and related a dream which I had a short time since. I thought I was riding out in my carriage, and my guardian angel was along with me. We went past the temple, and had not gone much further before we espied two large snakes so fast locked together that neither of them had any power. I inquired of my guide what I was to understand by that. He answered, "Those snakes represent

Dr. Foster and Chauncey L. Higbee. They are your enemies and desire to destroy you; but you see they are so fast locked together that they have no power of themselves to hurt you." I then thought I was riding up Mulholland street, but my guardian angel was not along with me. On arriving at the prairie, I was overtaken and seized by William and Wilson Law and others, saying "Ah! ah! we have got you at last! We will secure you and put you in a safe place!" and, without any ceremony dragged me out of my carriage, tied my hands behind me, and threw me into a deep, dry pit, where I remained in a perfectly helpless condition, and they went away. While struggling to get out, I heard Wilson Law screaming for help hard by. I managed to unloose myself so as to make a spring, when I caught hold of some grass which grew at the edge of the pit.

I looked out of the pit and saw Wilson Law at a little distance attacked by ferocious wild beasts, and heard him cry out, "Oh! Brother Joseph, come and save me!" I replied, "I cannot, for you have put me into this deep pit." On looking out another way, I saw William Law with outstretched tongue, blue in the face, and the green poison forced out of his mouth, caused by the coiling of a large snake around his body. It had also grabbed him by the arm, a little above the elbow, ready to devour him. He cried out in the intensity of his agony, "Oh, Brother Joseph, Brother Joseph, come and save me, or I die!" I also replied to him, "I cannot, William; I would willingly, but you have tied me and put me in this pit, and I am powerless to help you or liberate myself." In a short time after my guide came and said aloud, "Joseph, Joseph, what are you doing there?" I replied, "My enemies fell upon me, bound me and threw me in." He then took me by the hand, drew me out of the pit, set me free, and we went away rejoicing.

Two of the brethren arrived this evening from Carthage, and said that about three hundred mobbers were assembled there, with the avowed intention of coming against Nauvoo; also that Hamilton was paying a dollar per bushel for corn to feed their animals.

Saturday, June 15—At home. Two brethren came from Lima,

and said that Colonel Levi Williams had demanded the arms belonging to the Mormons in that neighborhood. They wished my advice on the subject. I told them that when they gave up their arms, to give up their lives with them as dearly as possible.

It is reported that a company of men were constantly training at Carthage. Mr. John M. Crane, from Warsaw, said that several boxes of arms had arrived at Warsaw from Quincy. There was some considerable excitement, but expected they were going to wait the meeting at Carthage, which was fixed for the middle of next week.

The *Maid of Iowa* arrived at half-past two p.m., while I was examining the painting, "Death on the Pale Horse," by Benjamin West, which has been exhibiting in my reading room for the last three days. The *Maid* had lost her lighter, which was loaded at the time with corn and lumber, it having broken in two on a snag in the Iowa river.

This morning Samuel James started for Springfield to carry letters and papers to Governor Ford concerning the destruction of the *Expositor* press.

Sunday, June 16—Judge Jesse B. Thomas came to Nauvoo, and advised me to go before some justice of the peace of the county, and have an examination of the charges specified in the writ from Justice Morrison of Carthage; and if acquitted or bound over, it would allay all excitement, answer the law and cut off all legal pretext for a mob, and he would be bound to order them to keep the peace.

Some forty gentlemen from Madison came down on a steamer to inquire into our difficulties. I met them at the Masonic Hall at 2 p.m., and gave them the desired information. Dr. Richards, the city recorder, read the minutes of the council declaring the *Nauvoo Expositor* a nuisance. They expressed themselves satisfied. I then went to the temple stand and met some thousands of the brethren. I instructed them to keep cool, and prepare their arms for defense of the city, as it was reported that a mob was collecting in

Carthage and other places. I exhorted them to be quiet and make no disturbance, and instructed the brethren to organize into the capacity of a public meeting and send delegates to all the surrounding towns and villages, to explain the cause of the disturbance, and show them that all was peace at Nauvoo, and that there was no cause for any mobs.

A messenger arrived stating that the clerk of the county court expected to be driven out of Carthage tomorrow, and the only way to prevent the shedding of blood was to get the governor in person to come down with his staff.

Brother Butler, from Bear creek, came in and made affidavit before the recorder that fifteen hundred Missourians were to cross the Mississippi to Warsaw the next morning, on their way to Carthage.

Monday, June 17—This morning I was arrested, together with Samuel Bennett, John Taylor, William W. Phelps, Hyrum Smith, John P. Greene, Dimick B. Huntington, Jonathan Dunham, Stephen Markham, Jonathan H. Holmes, Jesse P. Harmon, John Lytle, Joseph W. Coolidge, H. David Redfield, O. P. Rockwell, and Levi Richards, by Constable Joel S. Miles, on a writ issued by Daniel H. Wells, on complaint of W. G. Ware, for a riot on the 10th inst. in destroying the *Nauvoo Expositor* press. At 2 p.m. we went before Justice Wells at his house; and after a long and close examination we were discharged.

Edward Hunter, Philip B. Lewis and Major John Bills started with the affidavit of Thomas G. Wilson and my letter, &c., to take to Governor Ford. I charged Edward Hunter, under oath, to tell Governor Ford all he knew concerning me, good or bad, as he has known me for several years; and I said to him, "Brother Hunter, you have always wished you had been with us from the commencement. If you will go to Springfield and do this business for me now in this time of danger, it shall be as though you had been in Missouri and had always been with us."

I also issued an order to Col. A. P. Rockwood to call out my guard and staff immediately to my headquarters; and I also ordered the legion to parade tomorrow at 10 a.m.

The mob is still increasing in numbers at Carthage and other places.

It is reported that William and Wilson Law have laid a plan to burn the printing office of the *Nauvoo Neighbor* this night. I therefore stationed a strong police round the premises and throughout the city.

The captain of the steamer *Osprey* called upon me.

About 11 p.m. a Negro came into my office with an open letter, without any date or name, and said that Dr. Foster gave it to him at Madison to give Henry O. Norton. In that letter Foster said that Dunham and Richards swore in my presence that they would kill him (Foster) in two days, and that there was a man in Madison would swear he had heard them say so at my house.

I closed the issuing of orders about 12 at night, ready to retire to rest. Pleasant weather.

Tuesday, June 18—At 8 a.m. the legion assembled according to orders, and organized at 9 a.m., under Acting Major-General Jonathan Dunham. The first cohort under the command of Colonel Stephen Markham, acting brigadier-general, and the second cohort under Colonel Hosea Stout, acting brigadier-general.

Just before, I was informed that there were several boxes of arms landed at the upper stone house, which were secured by the marshal. Soon after it was discovered that the arms (40 stand) had been sent by Henry G. Sherwood, and the marshal bought them for the city.

About 1:45 p.m. I proclaimed the city under martial law.

About 2 p.m. the legion was drawn up in the street close by the Mansion. I stood in full uniform on the top of the frame of a building.

Judge Phelps read the *Warsaw Signal* extra of the 17th, wherein all the "old citizens" were called upon to assist the mob in exterminating the leaders of the Saints and driving away the people.

About 3:15 p.m., I took the command, and with my staff rode

in front of the legion, marched up Main Street, and returned to our former parade-ground. The number on parade was very large, considering the number of elders who had been sent on missions. After dismissing the legion to their several commands, I returned home and gave orders to the several commanders only to receive official communications through my aides-de-camp, the proper official channel.

Nine messengers arrived from Carthage, and reported that the mob had received intelligence from the governor, who would take no notice of them; and they damned the governor as being as bad as Joe Smith. They did not care for him, and they were just as willing he would not help them as if he would.

There was a body of armed men in Carthage, and a mob meeting at Fountain Green, which attracted considerable attention.

Shadrach Roundy, a policeman, reported at 10 p.m., after I had retired, that a man by the name of Norton had threatened to shoot me. An examination was immediately had, but no proof was found.

This evening I appointed Theodore Turley armorer-general of the legion.

Wednesday, June 19 The legion assembled on the parade ground. A company of the legion came in from Green Plains about 11 a.m. I met them at the front of the Mansion, and an escort came down from the parade-ground below the temple and escorted them to the ground.

At 1 p.m. a company of volunteers arrived from Iowa and were also escorted to the parade-ground.

On Sunday, the 16th, a committee of the mob, headed by James Charles, a constable of Hancock county, went to the house of Captain Chester Loveland, who lives four miles southeast of Warsaw, and required him to call out his company to join the posse of David Bettisworth to go to Nauvoo and arrest me and the city council. He peremptorily refused to comply with their request. The same posse returned on the 17th with an order, as they stated, from the governor, which Loveland believed (and no doubt correctly) to be a forgery, and therefore still refused to go on any terms. The posse then reported his refusal to Colonel Williams, who appointed a committee of twelve to lynch, tar and feather Captain Loveland on the 18th; which committee went that evening and arrived about midnight.

Loveland, who had been informed of Williams' order, prepared himself for defense and kept watch. As soon as they came and he saw their number, and that they were provided with tar bucket, bag of feathers and a bundle of withes, in addition to their fire-arms, he blew out his light and placed himself in a suitable position to defend the door (which he had fastened) and the window. They went around his house several times, tried his door, rapped, called him by name, and consulted together. Some were for breaking the door; others thought it too dangerous. They knew he must be in there, for they were near his door when the light was blown out. Finally their courage failed; and notifying him to leave the country immediately, they took their departure. During this trying time Loveland did not speak.

In the afternoon I gave orders to General Dunham to have a picket-guard under Col. Markham, posted on all the roads leading out of the city; also an inner guard, under Major Jesse P. Harmon, posted in all the streets and alleys in the city, and also on the river bank. I also gave orders to have all the powder and lead in the city secured, and to see that all the arms were in use, and that all unclaimed arms be put in the hands of those who could use them.

From the best information they could learn, there were two hundred armed men at Rocky Run precinct, two hundred at Warsaw, two hundred in Missouri, and the whole receiving constant additions.

At 9 p.m. I was at home. The city all quiet.

Thursday, June 20—At daybreak I went with my staff and Major-General Dunham to the prairie, to view the situation of the ground, and to devise plans for the defense of the city, and select the proper locations to meet the mob, and made arrangements for provisions for the city, instructing my agent to pledge my farms for the purpose.

At 10 a.m. Dr. Southwick from Louisiana arrived, and reported that there was not much excitement in St. Louis; that a cannon had arrived at Warsaw from Quincy, and that it had been reported to him that there was great excitement in Upper Missouri.

At 11, I reviewed the legion facing the Mansion, and went to parade on the banks of the river.

I had sent orders to Captain Almon W. Babbitt, commander of the company at Ramus, to come immediately with his company to Nauvoo, and help to defend the place; and this morning my brother-in-law, William McLeary, informs me that when the letter was read to the company, Babbitt refused to come, and said it was a foolish move, and objected to any of the company coming. The company was marshaled into line, when Babbitt said, "If any of you go, not one will ever get to Nauvoo alive," when immediately my Uncle John Smith stepped in front of the line and said; "Every man that goes at the call of the Prophet shall go and return safe, and not a hair of his head shall be lost, and I bless you in the name of the Lord."

The company immediately threw the command upon Uriah H. Yager, who accepted of it, and started for Nauvoo, although many of them were destitute of boots or shoes. The company had not traveled five miles before they suddenly came upon double their number of the mob, who had two red flags flying, and who had paraded their company and taken a position in a wood that commanded the road. The company from Macedonia opened file about ten feet apart and marched past them within rifle shot, while the mob fired several guns at them, the balls whizzing past their heads. They came here at daybreak this morning, and I directed the quartermaster to furnish those who needed with shoes.

I wrote to those of the Twelve Apostles who are absent on missions to come home immediately, namely Brigham Young, Boston;

Heber C. Kimball, Washington; Orson Hyde, Philadelphia; Parley P. Pratt, New York; Orson Pratt, Washington; Wilfrod Woodruff, Portage, New York; William Smith, Philadelphia; George A. Smith, Peterboro; John E. Page, Pittsburg; and Lyman Wight, Baltimore. Also to Amasa Lyman, Cincinnati, Ohio, and George Miller, Richmond, Madison county, Kentucky. I sent the letters by express by Aaron M. York to the Illinois river, on account of the stoppage of the mails.

At 8 p.m. Thomas Bullock came and read to me the affidavits of Isaac Morley, Gardner Snow, John Edmiston, Edmund Durfee, Solomon Hancock, Allen T. Waite, James Guyman, Obadiah Bowen, Alvah Tippetts, Hiram B. Mount, and John Cunningham, with the affiants; and afterward the affidavits were all sworn to before Aaron Johnson, Esquire.

Ten p.m. John Pike and Henry Gates went to the quarters of the major-general, and informed him they had seen a number of men driving about three hundred head of cattle in the direction of the mob camp. The drovers reported themselves as having come from Missouri, and were about nine miles from Nauvoo.

I gave directions to Theodore Turley to commence the manufacture of artillery.

He asked me if he should not rent a building, and set some men to repairing the small arms which were out of order. I told him in confidence that there would not be a gun fired on our part during this fuss.

I advised my brother Hyrum to take his family on the next steamboat and go to Cincinnati. Hyrum replied, "Joseph, I can't leave you." Whereupon I said to the company present, "I wish I could get Hyrum out of the way, so that he may live to avenge my blood, and I will stay with you and see it out."

Friday, June 21—About 10 a.m. I rode out with my guard up Main Street past the major-general's quarters, and reviewed the legion.

After the news had reached the city of the governor's arrival at

Carthage, an express was sent to Keokuk to stop an express which I had sent to the governor at Springfield before I had learned of his arrival at Carthage.

An officer of the United States army, having arrested a deserter, came to Nauvoo, and stayed at my house all night.

Col. Brewer and lady arrived at the Mansion about 9 p.m. Also James W. Woods, Esq., my attorney from Burlington.

At 10 p.m., Private —— Minor gave information that as he was passing, an hour since, about two miles out of the city to his home, he was fired upon by some unknown person. General Stephen Markham ordered out a detachment to proceed to the designated place, scour that part of the country, and see that all was right.

Saturday, June 22—Legion met as usual; and after receiving instructions, were dismissed until 6 p.m., when they met again.

At 7 p.m. I instructed General Dunham to cause the regiment of the 2nd cohort to turn out tomorrow, and work by turns three or four hours each, with entrenching tools, and to take the best measures in case of attack. I also gave orders that a standard be prepared for the nations.

Almon W. Babbitt arrived from Carthage this morning, having come at the request of the governor, who thought it not wisdom to have Richards and Phelps and others of the city council go to Carthage.

It appears that the governor, on arriving at Carthage, ordered the entire mob into service, adopted the lies and misrepresentations circulated against us by our enemies as truth, turned Supreme Court, and decided on the legality of our municipal ordinances and proceedings, which is the business of the judiciary alone. He charges us in his letter, based upon most cursed falsehoods, with violations of law and order, which have never been thought of by us. He treated our delegates very rudely. My communications that were read to him were read in the presence of a large number of our worst enemies, who interrupted the reader at almost every line with, "That's a damned lie!" and "That's a G——d——d lie!" He

"JUST AS SURE
AS WE FALL
INTO THEIR
HANDS
WE ARE
DEAD MEN."

never accorded to them the privilege of saying one word to him only in the midst of such interruptions as, "You lie like hell!" from a crowd of persons present. These facts show conclusively that he is under the influence of the mob spirit, and is designedly intending to place us in the hands of murderous assassins, and is conniving at our destruction, or else that he is so ignorant and stupid that he does not understand the corrupt and diabolical spirits that are around him.

I had a consultation for a little while with my brother Hyrum, Dr. Richards, John Taylor and John M. Bernhisel, and determined to go to Washington and lay the matter before President Tyler.

About 7 p.m. I requested Reynolds Cahoon and Alpheus Cutler to stand guard at the Mansion, and not to admit any stranger inside the house.

At sundown I asked O. P. Rockwell if he would go with me a short journey, and he replied he would.

[Abraham C. Hodge says that soon after dusk, Joseph called Hyrum, Willard Richards, John Taylor, William W. Phelps, A. C. Hodge, John L. Butler, Alpheus Cutler, William Marks and some others, into his upper room and said, "Brethren, here is a letter from the governor which I wish to have read." After it was read through Joseph remarked, "There is no mercy—no mercy here." Hyrum said, "No; just as sure as we fall into their hands we are dead men." Joseph replied, "Yes; what shall we do, Brother Hyrum?" He replied, "I don't know." All at once Joseph's countenance brightened up and he said, "The way is open. It is clear to my mind what to do. All they want is Hyrum and myself; then tell everybody to go about their business, and not to collect in groups, but to scatter about. There is no doubt they will come here and search for us. Let them search; they will not harm you in person or property, and not even a hair of your head. We will cross the river tonight, and go away to the West." He made a move to go out of the house to cross the river. When out of doors he told Butler and Hodge to take the *Maid of Iowa*, (in charge of Repsher) get it to the upper landing, and put his and Hyrum's families and effects upon her; then go down the Mississippi and up the Ohio river to Portsmouth, where they should hear from them. He then took Hodge by the hand and said, "Now, Brother Hodge, let what will come, don't deny the faith, and all will be well."]

I told Stephen Markham that if I and Hyrum were ever taken again we should be massacred, or I was not a prophet of God. I want Hyrum to live to avenge my blood, but he is determined not to leave me.

[Five days later, Joseph and Hyrum were killed in Carthage Jail]

0 26575 15136 7